ON THIS DAY
IN
GOLF HISTORY

ON THIS DAY
IN
GOLF HISTORY

by Randy Walker

New Chapter Press

"On This Day In Golf History" is published by New Chapter Press (www.NewChapterMedia.com) and is distributed by the Independent Publishers Group (www.IPGBook.com).

Also get the "On This Day In Golf History" mobile app and look for our ebook and audio book!

For more information on this title or New Chapter Press contact:
Randy Walker
Managing Partner
New Chapter Press
1175 York Ave
Suite #3s
New York, NY 10065
Rwalker@NewChapterMedia.com

Dedicated to my father, Ewing Walker, who stoked my love of golf with trips to many golf events, starting with the 1982 Westchester Classic and the 1983 U.S. Open at Oakmont

Contents

JANUARY 1

FEBRUARY 38

MARCH 68

APRIL... 102

MAY 150

JUNE 185

JULY 237

AUGUST.. 285

SEPTEMBER 330

OCTOBER 364

NOVEMBER 390

DECEMBER 414

From The Author

Tennis is my first love but golf was a close second. Golf actually inspired me to write my first book "On This Day In Tennis History" when I was working for the U.S. Tennis Association. While watching the Masters, I remember CBS frequently showcasing historic moments at Augusta in a "On This Day In Masters History" feature. I thought this should be something that needed to be implemented at the U.S. Open tennis championships, which I promptly researched and created. Through the years, my "On This Day In U.S. Open History" was added onto my "On This Day In U.S. Davis Cup Team History" and then into a "On This Day In Tennis History" compilation that I published as a book in 2008 and then as an annually updated mobile app (www.TennisHistoryApp.com) and an audio book. Now, in the spirit of my creation in tennis, I have done the same in golf with "On This Day In Golf History." I hope you enjoy my work!

–Randy Walker
 New York, N.Y., 2017

JANUARY

January 1

1969 – Paul Stewart Lawrie, the winner of the 1999 Open Championship, is born in Aberdeen, Scotland. Lawrie wins a dramatic Open Championship at Carnoustie in a playoff with Jean van de Velde and Justin Leonard, overcoming the largest third-round deficit ever faced by a major championship winner, trailing van de Velde by 10 shots entering the final round. Lawrie, curiously, was never the leader or co-leader in the tournament until van de Velde blows a three-shot lead on the final hole of the championship, forcing the playoff.

1932 – The United States Golf Association standardizes the golf ball, stating that the ball could weigh no more than 1.62 ounces and measure no less than 1.68 inches in diameter.

January 2

1974 – Defending champion Jack Nicklaus is a late arrival to the first PGA tournament of the year, the Bing Crosby National Pro-Am at Pebble Beach, Calif., and declares he hasn't picked up a golf club in exactly a month. "I haven't touched a club since the last round of the Disney," says Nicklaus the afternoon before the start of the new season of his victory that closed out his seven-win 1973 season. "I just haven't played any at all since then – not seriously, not in fun. I haven't touched a club. Now I've got to get in a month's practice in two hours." Nicklaus goes on to finish in a tie for 24th at the event, 10 shots behind winner Johnny Miller, who wins by four shots over runner-up Grier Jones.

2002 – Sergio Garcia meets with the media prior to competing in the Mercedes Championships in Maui, Hawaii for the first time and answers more questions about Tiger Woods than his own game. Garcia is asked, "Are players less intimidated by Tiger now? Do you see any similarities between yourself now at 22 and when Tiger was at 22? Tiger seems to motivate you. Is that a correct read?" Answers Garcia of Woods, "I'll say he's capable of doing some things that some of us can't do, like hitting a two-iron 270 yards straight up in the air and things like that. But I also think that we're able to do some things that maybe he can't do. I think that we can be as good as him. I mean, me, as I see myself almost 22 years old, you know, he's 26, I think that I can be as good as he is at 26 when I'm 26, or hopefully sooner." Five days later, Garcia wins the event, his third career PGA Tour title, beating David Toms in a playoff.

January 3

2014 – Derek Ernst hits the first tee shot of 2014 on the PGA Tour at the Hyundai Tournament of Championship in Maui, Hawaii, which, for the first time is not the opening event of the PGA Tour season. The event is the seventh tournament of the season, as, for the first time, the PGA Tour kicks off its season in October at the Frys.com Open in San Martin, Calif. Ernst qualifies for the Tournament of Champions, a field that only features tournament winners from the previous year, by winning the Wells Fargo Championship in Charlotte in May as the No. 1,207-ranked player in the world.

1982 – Chief Petty Officer Kevin Murray of Chicago, Ill., makes the longest albatross (double eagle) on record when he makes a two on the 647-yard par-5 second hole at the Guam Navy Golf Club. Playing after a typhoon passed through the area, with a

40 mph wind at his back, Murray hits a 387-yard drive, followed with a 260-yard four-iron which rolls into the hole. His effort, however, is eclipsed on the 663-yard 18th hole at the Kapalua Plantation course in Hawaii by professional Andy Bean in 1991 and by amateur Brett Stowkowy in 2010.

January 4

1962 – Jack Nicklaus tees it up in his first round as a professional player in the first round of the Los Angeles Open at the Rancho Park golf course in West Los Angeles. The 21-year-old Nicklaus shoots a three-over par 74 in his first round as a pro.

1974 – One day after rain washed away the opening day of the PGA Tour season, unheralded Gary McCord takes the surprising first-round lead at the Bing Crosby National Pro-Am shooting a seven-under-par 65 at Cypress Point. Writes United Press International, "Gary McCord had to pinch himself twice to believe it. A year ago this time, he was trying to borrow $4,500 as a stake for the mini-tour. Today he's the leader after one round in the $185,000 Bing Crosby National Pro-Am." McCord follows his impressive opening round with a 73 and an 80 to finish in 24th place in the rain-shortened event. McCord, who turned professional in 1971, played 400 PGA Tour events in his career, never winning, but finishing in second place at the Greater Milwaukee Open in 1975 and 1977. However, McCord found greater fame starting in 1986 when he became a charismatic golf commentator for CBS Sports.

January 5

1959 – Ken Venturi shoots an eight-under-par round of 63 to win the $35,000 Los Angeles Open by two shots over Art Wall, Jr., at the Rancho Park municipal golf course. Venturi comes back from eight shots back to win the $5,300 first prize.

2013 – The start of 2013 PGA Tour season is delayed for a second straight day as winds over 40 mph again prevent play at the Tournament of Champions at Plantation Course at Kapalua on Maui, Hawaii. No player hits a shot due to the wind after 24 players tee off the previous day before the wind cancels the round, negating all the scores of all the players who began their round. Says Slugger White, the PGA Tour's vice president of rules and competition, "On the 10th hole, we dropped a ball on the back of the green and it rolled 20 yards off the front."

January 6

1950 – Eleven months after nearly being killed in a head-on car collision with a Greyhound bus, Ben Hogan returns to tournament golf, teeing it up in the first round of the Los Angeles Open. The *Los Angeles Times* reports that a record first-day gallery of 9,000 fans watch Hogan shoot a two-over-par 73 at the Riviera Country Club. After 72 holes, Hogan loses the tournament to Sam Snead in a playoff.

1961 – Arnold Palmer hits four straight balls out of bounds on the ninth hole at Rancho Park Golf Course at the Los Angeles Open and makes a 12. Palmer hits a perfect drive down the middle of the fairway, but slices his next two shots out of bounds into the driving range, then hooks his next two shots on the road to the left. He hits the green with his fifth attempt and two putts for his 12. Club members, subsequently, install a stone plaque to commemorate the event. "I had to make a tough putt just to get my 12," Palmer says to the *Los Angeles Times* in 1990 of his infamous hole. "Instead of being close to the lead, I missed the cut. I think you could say there was no lasting effect. I won the next two tournaments on the tour and then had three winning tournaments at Rancho in future years. I've always enjoyed playing there."

2014 – Zach Johnson makes three straight birdies on the back nine and shoots a final-round 66 to win the Hyundai Tournament of Champions in Maui, Hawaii by one shot over Jordan Spieth. The title is the 11th win of the 2007 Masters champion's career – only Tiger Woods, Phil Mickelson and Vijay Singh winning more titles since Johnson joins the tour in 2004.

January 7

1963 – Arnold Palmer wins the Los Angeles Open at Rancho Park golf course for the first of three times, firing a final-round 66 to charge from three strokes behind to win his 36th PGA tournament title and the $9,000 first prize. After making a double bogey on the 11th hole, Palmer makes birdie on No. 12 and No. 16 and makes birdie from off the green from 50 feet away on No. 17 to beat runners-up Gary Player and Al Balding by three shots. Palmer also wins at Rancho Park in 1966 and 1967.

1974 – One day after shooting a two-under-par 70 at rain-soaked Pebble Beach, reigning U.S. Open champion Johnny Miller is declared the winner of the Bing Crosby National Pro Am after only 54 holes due to the wet conditions. The win is Miller's fourth career PGA tournament title. Miller wins the event two more times in 1987 and in 1994 for his 25th and final PGA tournament title.

1973 – Rod Funseth wins the Glen Campbell Los Angeles Open at the Riviera Country Club, his second of three PGA tournament titles and his first since the 1965 Phoenix Open. Funseth, known for his humble, self-deprecating negative attitudes, shoots a final-round 69 to beat runners-up Don Bies, Tom Weiskopf, David Hill and David Graham. Says Bies of Funseth, "Rod is a lot better golfer than he thinks he is," which prompts Funseth to retort to his friend, "Don and my wife always say I think negatively. In that last round, I wasn't negative. I felt really great."

January 8

1962 – Jack Nicklaus receives his first paycheck as a professional player, earning $33.33 for finishing in a tie for 50th place (tied for last with Billy Maxwell and Don Massengale) at the PGA season-opening Los Angeles Open at the Rancho Park Golf Course. Phil Rodgers wins the title in a Monday finish by nine shots and 21 shots better than Nicklaus.

1978 – Tom Watson scrambles to a final-round 72 and wins the opening event of the 1978 golf season at the Joe Garagiola Tucson Open at the Tucson National Golf Club in Arizona. Watson, the 1977 PGA Player of the Year, shoots an opening round 63 three days earlier to start his year and hangs on to win his ninth PGA tournament title by one shot over Bobby Wadkins and earn $40,000. "I'm very fortunate really very lucky to win," Watson says. "I don't want to downgrade winning but no one win doesn't make a career and it doesn't make a season and if I don't start driving the ball better I won't have the season I did last year. I don't feel the Tom Watson of January 1978 is playing as well as the Tom Watson of 1977. I had one great round and just made it stand up." Like in 1977, Watson goes on to win eight tournament titles in 1978, but unlike his wins at the Masters and Open Championship the year before, he does not capture a major title.

2013 – In a rare Tuesday finish on the PGA Tour, Dustin Johnson wins his seventh career PGA Tour title in the wind-stricken Tournament of Champions at the Kapalua Resort in Maui. Johnson holds a five-shot lead after seven holes, then dropping to a one-shot lead, before winning by four shots over Steve Stricker. The tournament that features only PGA Tour event winners from the previous 12 months doesn't start until the third day because of wind gusts that top 40 mph, forcing tour officials to shorten the event to 54 holes.

2006 – Stuart Appleby birdies two of the last four holes and beats Vijay Singh on the first hole of a playoff to win the Tournament of Champions at Kapalua Resort for the third consecutive year. Appleby becomes the 15th player in PGA Tour history to win the same event three straight years, and the first since Tiger Woods wins the Bay Hill Invitational four straight times starting in 2000. "This one was the hardest," says Appleby. "Obviously, I had to win a playoff against Vijay. He was the hottest player by far."

January 9

2000 – Tiger Woods sinks a 40-foot birdie putt on the second sudden-death playoff hole and beats Ernie Els to win the Mercedes Championship in Hawaii. The victory is the fifth consecutive tournament win for Woods, the most since Ben Hogan wins four consecutive tournaments in 1953. Woods and Els both eagle the 18th hole at the Plantation Course at Kapalua in Maui to force the playoff and, 20 minutes later, Woods makes a six-foot birdie putt on the same hole to continue the playoff. "I think he's a legend in the making," Els says of Woods to the assembled golf media. "You guys have helped, but he's backed it up with his golf game. He's 24. He's probably going to be bigger than Elvis when he gets into his 40s."

1966 – One day after shooting a course-record 62 at Rancho Park golf course, Arnold Palmer hangs on with a final-round 73 to win the Los Angeles Open by three strokes over Miller Barber and Paul Haney. The win in the season-opening event is Palmer's 46th career PGA title, earning him $11,000.

1977 – Dave Stockton, regarded as one of the best putters of all time and one of the golf world's finest putting instructors, three-putts from 35 feet on the first hole of a sudden-death playoff giving Jerry Pate the title at the season-opening Phoenix Open. "I don't usually fold like that," admits Stockton, who won his second PGA Championship title the previous summer. "I really didn't have any business being in the playoff, not the way I was hitting it. If everyone in the field hit the ball the way I did, Pate would've won by 15 strokes." Pate, seven months removed from winning the U.S. Open at the age of 22, wins for the third time on the PGA Tour, earning $40,000 and additional respect. "It's very rewarding very pleasing to start the season like this," says Pate, who also won the Canadian Open in his impressive 1976 debut season. "There's a lot of pressure on me being Rookie of the Year and I didn't want to let it get away."

2012 – Steve Stricker shoots a final-round four-under 69 to post a three-shot victory over Martin Laird of Scotland at the Tournament of Champions at the Kapalua Resort in Maui. The win is the 12th PGA Tour title Sticker wins before his 50th birthday in 2017 and 16 years after his first win at the 1996 Kemper Open at the TPC at Avenel. The unassuming and soft-spoken native of Wisconsin notches his best career tournament wins at the World Golf Championship Match Play Championships in in 2001 in Melbourne, Australia and at FedEx Cup playoff events at the 2007 Barclays Championship at Westchester Country Club in New York and the 2009 Deutsche Bank Championship at the TPC of Boston.

January 10

2014 – Two double-eagles – called an albatross – are registered on different continents on different tours. Joost Luiten holes his second shot on the par-5 tenth hole from 248 yards at the Durban Country Club in South Africa on the European Tour's Volvo Golf Champions. On the PGA Tour at the Sony Open in Hawaii, James Hahn holes his second shot on the par-5 ninth hole at Waialae Country Club from 193 yards.

2010 – Geoff Ogilvy repeats as champion of the season-opening SBS Championship at the Plantation Course at the Kapalua Resort on Maui shooting a final-round six-under 67 for a one-shot victory over Rory Sabbatini. One year after winning the event by six shots, Ogilvy comes back from a two-shot deficit with ten holes to play to join fellow Australian Stuart Appleby as the only repeat winners since the tournament moved to Kapalua in 1999. He becomes only the seventh player in the 58 years of this winners-only tournament to win in consecutive years.

1999 – David Duval wins the inaugural staging of the Tournament of Champions at the Plantation Course at the Kapalua Resort in Maui, shooting a final-round five-under 68 to win by nine shots over Mark O'Meara and Billy Mayfair. "I hope I can do it another 10 or 15 years," says Duval after winning for the eighth time in 15 months. "To think of doing it that doing that at any point is unrealistic but I've done that so I know I can." Duval's margin of victory is the widest on the PGA tour since Tiger Woods wins the Masters by 12 shots in 1997.

January 11

1976 – Johnny Miller wins the Tucson Open in Arizona for a third consecutive year, shooting a final-round 68 to beat runner-up Howard Twitty by three shots. Miller becomes the first player to win a tournament three years in a row since Jack Nicklaus won his third straight title at Disney in Orlando in 1973.

1946 – Frank Conner, one of two men to play in the U.S. Open in golf and tennis, is born in Vienna, Austria. Before joining the PGA Tour in 1975, Conner was a standout American tennis player in the amateur era, competing in the U.S. Nationals in 1965, 1966 and 1967 – before the event officially became known as the U.S. Open in 1968 – reaching the second round in 1967. He went on to become a tennis All-American at Trinity University in Texas, one of the top tennis schools at the time. However, he had picked up and excelled at golf as well and, realizing he could make more money in pro golf than tennis, turned into a golf professional. His best finish at a major in golf came at the 1981 U.S. Open at Merion where he finished tied for sixth. He never won an official PGA Tour title, but lost in a playoff to Tom Watson at the 1982 Heritage Classic on Hilton Head Island, S.C. and to Dave Barr at the 1981 Quad Cities Open. Ellsworth Vines, the 1931 and 1932 winner of the U.S. Championships in tennis, abandoned his tennis career in 1940 to turn his attention to competitive golf. He not only was a competitor at the golf U.S. Open, but in the Masters and the PGA Championship as well. His best finish in the golf majors was a tie for third at the 1951 PGA (he was a losing semifinalist in the match-play format.) In stroke-play majors, his best finish was a tie for 14th at the U.S. Open in 1948 and 1949. His best finish at the Masters was a tie for 24th in 1947.

1981 – Johnny Miller wins the Tucson Open in Arizona for a fourth time, shooting a final-round 65 to beat runner-up Lon Hinkle by two strokes. The win is the 20th career PGA Tour title for Miller and only his second since winning the 1976 Open Championship title. "I don't think I'll ever play enough to be the best again," Miller says. "All I want to do is play a little have some fun and maybe win a tournament here and there."

1998 – Phil Mickelson posts a one-shot victory over Tiger Woods and Mark O'Meara and wins the season-opening Mercedes Championships – his second win in five years at the LaCosta Resort. Woods shoots a final-round 64, but is not able to overtake Mickelson, who wins his 12th PGA Tour title. David Duval fails in his attempt to become the first player since Ben Hogan in 1953 to win four straight PGA Tour events, shooting a final-round 73 to finish six shots behind Mickelson. "This was an important day for me," the 27-year-old Mickelson says.

2009 – Geoff Ogilvy is the wire-to-wire winner at season-opening Mercedes-Benz Championship at Kapalua Resort in Hawaii, beating Anthony Kim and Davis Love, III by six shots. Ogilvy opens the day with a six shot lead that shrinks to one shot on the ninth hole. Ogilvy eagles the ninth hole and finishes with four birdies on the back nine to finish with a five-under 68. "I've never had a six-shot lead before. It's a pretty uncomfortable feeling, to be honest with you," Ogilvy says after his win. "I got to the green and saw I had a one-shot lead – I figured it was mostly gone – and it felt like a normal tournament again. I just told myself, 'It's a great spot to be after 63 holes, get on with it.'"

January 12

2017 – Justin Thomas becomes the seventh player to break 60 on the PGA Tour shooting a 59 in the opening round of the Sony Open at the Waialae Country Club in Honolulu. Thomas sinks a 15-foot putt for eagle on his final hole (the ninth hole at Waialae) to clinch the magical score. "It was the first time I've had a putt for 59," Thomas says, "and I was like, well, who knows if this is gonna happen again, so I might as well try to knock it in." At age 23, Thomas is the youngest player to shoot 59 on the PGA Tour and joins David Duval at the 1999 Bob Hope Chrysler Classic as the only players to finish the round with an eagle. Thomas joins the exclusive list that also includes Al Geiberger from the 1977 Memphis Classic, Chip Beck from the 1991 Las Vegas Invitational, Duval, Paul Goydos at the 2010 John Deere Classic, Stuart Appleby at the 2010 Greenbrier Classic and Jim Furyk at the 2013 BMW Championship. Furyk actually also shoots a 58 the previous summer at the Travelers Championship to be the only player to shoot two rounds under 60. Adam Hadwin joins the 59 club later in the year at the CareerBuilder Challenge to become the eighth player to shoot 59 on the PGA Tour. Thomas goes on to win the title by seven shots over Justin Rose.

1975 – Johnny Miller wins the opening event of the 1975 PGA Tour season in spectacular fashion at the Phoenix Open, winning by a remarkable 14 shots over a field that features U.S. Open champion Hale Irwin, PGA Championship winner Lee Trevino and all of the Top 15 money earners from the previous year except Jack Nicklaus. Miller posts a 24-under score of 260 at the Phoenix Country Club – making 25 birdies and two eagles during his run that United Press International describes as "one of the most powerful performances in PGA history." Miller shoots a final-round 64, following his previous rounds of 67, 61 and 68 with Jerry Heard finishing a distant second place. Writes UPI of Miller, "There are a growing number of pros who think Johnny Miller, the tall, blonde Californian with the big drive and the fine putting touch, is the world's best golfer today and maybe they're right. Certainly this week Miller was, and everyone knows he was the best on the PGA circuit last year when he won eight tournament titles and more than $350,000 in official money." Says Miller of potentially being the best player in golf, "When I'm on my game I feel I'm the best still I'm a streak player and what I have to strive for is more consistency."

1997 – Tiger Woods makes some history and wins the season-opening Mercedes Championships at LaCosta Resort and Spa in Carlsbad, Calif., with a dramatic playoff-hole shot in the rain-shortened event. With heavy rain cancelling the final round, the tournament winner is decided in a playoff between the two 54-hole co-leaders – Woods and Tom Lehman. Using the 186-yard seventh hole for the playoff – the driest hole on the course – Lehman begins the playoff by hitting his tee shot in the water. Woods, with the luxury of likely needing only a par to win, hits his six-iron tee shot to eight inches and the tap-in birdie to win his third career PGA Tour title in only his ninth start as a professional. The $216,000 first prize pushes Woods to over $1 million in career prize money, the fastest any player had achieved the feat. Woods, who turned 21 just 14 days earlier, becomes the third youngest player to win three PGA events, trailing only Gene Sarazen and Horton Smith.

2003 – Ernie Els wins the season-opening Mercedes Championships by eight shots, setting a new PGA Tour scoring record in relation to par with a 31-under score, capped by a final-round 67. The previous 72-hole record in relation to par was 28-under set by John Huston at the 1998 Hawaiian Open and by Mark Calcavecchia from 2001 at the Phoenix Open. Els finishes at 261 breaking by five shots the tournament record set four years earlier by David Duval. "You want to say when you win majors that you played your best then," Els says. "But this is right up there. It's an unbelievable week for me."

2014 – Jimmy Walker fires a final round 63 and wins the Sony Open in Honolulu for his second PGA Tour victory. Walker, a seven-year PGA veteran, goes 187 starts before winning his first event on tour at the Frys.com Open the previous October, but wins his second tour event in his last six starts with his win in Hawaii. "It took me a long time to do it," Walker says. "I felt very calm and controlled. That's what you've got to feel and do when it's time to win. It's easy to say, hard to do. But today was awesome. Really cool golf."

2015 – Patrick Reed wins the Tournament of Champions at Kapalua on the first hole of sudden death with Jimmy Walker. Reed, who trails Walker by four shots with four holes to play, makes an eagle two from 80-yards out in the fairway at the 16th hole to draw even with Walker before closing out with a final-round 67. The 24-year-old Reed makes an 18-foot birdie on the first playoff hole to win his fourth PGA Tour in his last 35 starts to become one of four players in the last 20 years to win as many PGA Tour titles before their 25th birthday, joining Rory McIlroy, Tiger Woods and Sergio Garcia.

2007 – Tadd Fujikawa, at the age of 16 years and four days, becomes the youngest player in 50 years to make a cut on the PGA Tour at the Sony Open in Honolulu, Hawaii. Fujikawa caps his second-round 66 with an eagle on the 18th hole to become the youngest player to make a PGA cut since Bob

Panasik at the age of 15 years, eight months and 20 days at the 1957 Canadian Open. Fujikawa shoots 66 and 72 in his final two rounds and finishes in a tie for 20th. Fujikawa and Panasik's marks are eclipsed in 2013 when 14-year-old Guan Tianlang of China makes the cut at the Masters and, subsequently, the Zurich Classic in New Orleans.

January 13

1991 – Phil Mickelson, a 20-year-old junior at Arizona State University, wins his first PGA Tour event at the Northern Telecom Open in Tucson, Ariz., becoming only the second amateur since Gene Littler at the San Diego Open in 1954 to win on the PGA Tour. Mickelson recovers from making a triple bogey 8 on the 14th hole to win by two shots over runners-up Tom Purtzer and Bob Tway, who split the first and second-place prize money. "I went from having the biggest knot in my stomach to the greatest joy in a half hour," says Mickelson. The last amateur to win on the PGA Tour was Scott Verplank at the 1985 Western Open. Mickelson goes on to win the event as a professional in 1995 and 1996.

1933 – The Augusta National Golf Club formally opens in Augusta, Georgia. Created and designed by Bobby Jones and Alister MacKenzie, the club hosts grand opening ceremonies where many club members ride in chartered Atlantic Coast Line Railroad cars from New York to Augusta in a "private train party" as stated in the invitations. The club was actually opened for use one month earlier in December of 1932. The land for the club had been purchased in 1931 with construction starting shortly thereafter. The first edition of course's signature event, the Masters, is held in 1934.

1974 – One week after winning a rain-shortened Bing Crosby National Pro Am at Pebble Beach, Johnny Miller also wins the second tournament of the year with a one shot victory at the

Phoenix Open. Miller, the U.S. Open winner the previous year, birdies the final two holes, including a five-footer on the final hole, to beat Lanny Wadkins by one stroke. Wadkins sinks a 30-foot eagle putt on the final hole to briefly take the lead by one shot, before Miller finishes with his final two birdies. "Up until the U.S. Open last year, I had been reading, and it was true, that I couldn't get the big shots when I needed them," Miller says. "I was afraid I might get the Tommy Aaron lag of always coming close. That's not bad, but I want to be a winner."

2013 – Only three months after earning his PGA Tour card, Russell Henley wins the Sony Open in Hawaii in his rookie-event as an official pro, making birdie on the last five holes to shot a final-round 63 and shatter the tournament scoring record by four shots. Henley becomes the fifth player to win in their first official PGA Tour event as a pro, joining Garrett Willis (2001 Tucson), Robert Gamez (1990 Tucson), Ben Crenshaw (1973 San Antonio) and Marty Fleckman (1967 Lafayette, La.). Henley's score of 24-under score of 256 is the second-lowest in PGA Tour history for a 72-hole event, two shots behind Tommy Armour III in 2003 at the Texas Open.

1980 – Craig Stadler wins his first of 13 career PGA Tour event at the Bob Hope Desert Classic, posting a 17-under par score of 343 over five rounds to beat runners-up Tom Purtzer and Mike Sullivan by two shots and $50,000. "I'm glad it's finally here," says Stadler, a four-year pro after the Monday finish. "It's got to be easier from here on." Stadler wins again three months later at the Greater Greensboro Open and for a total of 13 times in his PGA Tour career, including his lone major at the 1982 Masters.

January 14

1945 – Byron Nelson wins the Phoenix Open – his first of his record 18 tournament wins during the 1945 season. Nelson enters 30 tournaments during the year and famously wins 11 straight events, beginning with the Miami Four-Ball Championship in March, ending in August at the Memphis Open, where he finished fourth.

1990 – Former University of Arizona standout Robert Gamez, who receives a last-minute tournament sponsor's invitation after former Masters champion Art Wall decides the event is too much of a challenge for him at age 66, wins the Northern Telecom Tucson Open in Arizona in his debut pro event. Gamez shoots a final-round 70 at the TPC Starr Pass – including a double-bogey on the final hole – to beat runners-up Mark Calcavecchia and Jay Haas by four strokes. Gamez becomes the third player to win their first ever event on the PGA Tour joining Marty Fleckman in 1967 and Ben Crenshaw in 1973.

2001 – Jim Furyk makes a 10-foot birdie putt on the final hole, then watches Rory Sabbatini miss a three-foot birdie putt to force a playoff as Furyk wins his sixth career PGA Tour title at the Mercedes Championships at the Plantation Course at the Kapalua Resort in Hawaii. "You'd like to win an event with a more heroic finish," says Furyk, who trails Sabbatini by four shots heading into the final round.

2007 – Winless in 11 years and in his last 256 tournaments, Paul Goydos makes three birdies on the final four holes and wins the Sony Open in Hawaii by one shot over Charles Howell III and Luke Donald. "I never felt like I was going to win," says the 42-year-old Goydos of his play down the stretch. The title is his second of two career PGA Tour titles for Goydos, whose other victory came at the Bay Hill Invitational in Orlando in 1996.

January 15

2004 – Fourteen-year-old Michelle Wie becomes the fourth, and youngest, female to play a PGA Tour event when, given a sponsor's exemption, competes at the Sony Open in Honolulu

Hawaii. She shoots an opening round of two-over-par 72 and, the following day, shoots a two-under-par 68 but misses the cut by one shot. Wie's 68 is the lowest round by a woman on the PGA Tour. She goes on to play at the Sony Open again in 2005, 2006 and 2007 but doesn't make the cut, despite equaling her low round of 68 in the second round in 2006. Wie also plays in the John Deere Classic and 84 Lumber Classic events on the PGA Tour in 2006 and the Reno-Tahoe Open in 2007 but does not make the cut in any event.

2001 – Garrett Willis wins in his debut event on the PGA Tour at the Touchstone Energy Tucson Open, beating runner-up Kevin Sutherland by one stroke. Willis becomes the fourth player to win in his first start as a member of the PGA Tour, joining Marty Fleckman (1967),Ben Crenshaw (1973) and Robert Gamez (1990).

2006 – One day after shooting a course-record 61 at the Wailae Country Club in Honolulu, David Toms cruises to a five-shot victory at the Sony Open in Honolulu, shooting a five-under 65 to win his 12th PGA Tour event and $918,000.

1950 – Sam Snead misses an eight-foot putt on the final hole to finish in a four-way tie for first place at the Bing Crosby Invitational at Pebble Beach. Snead's miss keeps him in a tie with Jackie Burke Jr., Dave Douglas, and Smiley Quick, who are all declared co-champions of the event, no sudden-death playoff being played in the 54-hole event.

January 16

2000 – Paul Azinger wins on the PGA Tour for the first time since his 1993 PGA Championship triumph – and his recovery from cancer – claiming a seven-shot victory over Stuart Appleby at the Sony Open in Hawaii. Azinger, just 10 days after turning 40, shoots a bogey-free five-under 65 in the final round for the wire-to-wire victory, his 12th career PGA Tour win. Azinger was diagnosed with lymphoma in his right shoulder in December 1993 and missed most of the next season.

2011 – Mark Wilson doesn't make a bogey during a 36-hole marathon, shooting rounds of 65-67 and earns a two-shot over victory over Tim Clark at the Sony Open in Hawaii. Wilson wakes up before dawn and holds a one-shot lead after his morning 18 holes, then only has six minutes before he starts his final 18 holes.

1972 – Jack Nicklaus makes an 18-foot birdie on the first hole of a sudden-death playoff with Johnny Miller to win the Bing Crosby National Pro-Am at Pebble Beach. The win is the 39th title of his career and earns Nicklaus $28,000. "Pebble usually is a wet course," says Nicklaus when asked to size up the course that will host the U.S. Open for the first time in June. "It was dry for this year's Crosby and should be even drier in June. I think that will make it a very difficult course to putt on." Nicklaus goes on to win six more titles during the 1972 season, including his fourth Masters title and again at Pebble Beach at the U.S. Open.

1949 – Ben Hogan wins the Bing Crosby Invitational Tournament at Pebble Beach, shooting a final-round 70 to beat runner-up Jim Ferrier by three shots. Hogan's final round is watched by galleries of 10,000 fans, "one of the biggest golf galleries ever assembled" according to United Press International.

1980 – Sam Snead, Bob Goalby, Don January, Julius Boros, Dan Sikes and Gardner Dickinson hold a meeting to lay the groundwork for the creation of the Champions Tour.

1983 – Gil Morgan wins the Los Angeles Open by two strokes to sweep the first two titles of the 1983 PGA Tour season. One week after winning the opening event of the year in Tucson, Ariz., Morgan shoots a final-round 68 to win by two shots over Lanny

Wadkins, Gibby Gilbert and Mark McCumber. Says Morgan simply, "It's nice to win." The title is the fifth career tournament win for Morgan, referred to as "Dr. Gil" since earning a Doctor of Optometry degree from the Southern College of Optometry in Memphis in 1972. Morgan only wins one more title on the PGA Tour at the 1990 Kemper Open, but wins 25 titles after turning 50 on the Champions Tour.

January 17

1937 – Sam Snead wins his first PGA Tour event at the Oakland Open in California beating runner-up Ralph Guldahl by two strokes. Snead, described by the Associated Press as "a 24-year-old mountaineer who learned the game as a caddy and turned professional three years ago," shoots a final-round 67 to earn the first-prize of $1,200. As years go by and record keeping in sports becomes more professional, Snead's victory the previous year at the 1936 West Virginia "Closed" Pro at The Greenbrier is counted as Snead's first pro win, despite it being a two-day, 54-hole event that was an afterthought to officials and media finishing the day after the West Virginia Amateur. Snead wins 82 PGA titles in his career, the final victory coming at the Greater Greensboro Open in 1965 at the age of 52.

1995 – The Golf Channel, the 24-hour television network devoted entirely to golf, makes its debut after a ceremonial flip of the switch by co-founder Arnold Palmer. The idea for the network comes from media entrepreneur Joseph Gibbs of Birmingham, Ala., who thinks of the idea in 1991 and, with help of Palmer, secures $80 million in financing to help launch the channel, the first of its kind devoted exclusively to a singular sport.

January 18

1998 – Fred Couples wins his 13th PGA Tour title beating Bruce Lietzke in a playoff to win the Bob Hope Chrysler Classic in LaQuinta, Calif. Couples birdies the 18th hole to tie Lietzke at 28-under-par to force the playoff, then birdies it again 20 minutes later to win the title. "This is not the greatest win I have ever had, but it was a great time to win a tournament," says Couples, whose father passed away from leukemia two months earlier.

2014 – Rory McIlroy is hit with a two-stroke penalty in the third round of the Abu Dhabi HSBC Championship that ends up costing him the tournament title. When playing the second hole, McIlroy hits his tee shot into the rough into the spectator crosswalk area, which is an automatic relief situation with no penalty. However, after the free drop, McIlroy's foot is still within the "ground under repair" area and he is penalized two shots. Says McIlroy of the rule after the round, "There are a lot of stupid rules in golf and this is one of them." McIlroy ends losing the tournament by one stroke as Pablo Larrazabal shoots a final round 69 the next day to beat McIlroy and Phil Mickelson by one stroke.

2015 – Martin Kaymer loses a six-shot lead on the final day of the Abu Dhabi Golf Championships, allowing world No. 357 Gary Stal of France to win his first European Tour title. Kaymer actually leads by as many as 10 shots after five holes into the final round, but proceeds to make bogey at the sixth hole, followed by a double bogey at No. 10 and a triple bogey on No. 13 to lose the lead to the Frenchman. Stal is eight shots behind Kaymer to start the day and shoots a bogey-free round of 65 for the two-shot win over the German.

2014 – Patrick Reed shoots his third straight round of 63 and breaks the PGA Tour record for lowest 54 hole score in relation to par with a score of 27-under par. He goes on to win the title the next day by two shots, by "ballooning" to a final-round 71.

2004 – Ernie Els wins the Sony Open in Hawaii for the second consecutive year making a 30-foot birdie putt on the third playoff hole to beat out Harrison Frazar. Els becomes the first player to win back-to-back titles at the Sony in 17 years.

January 19

1975 – One week after winning the Phoenix Open by an incredible 14 shots, Johnny Miller blitzes the field once again at the Tucson Open, winning his 13th career title by nine shots. Miller fires a final round 61, a tournament record at the Tucson National Golf Club course, finishing with a 25-under-par score of 263. Miller, the defending champion, calls his final-round 61 in Tucson "the greatest I've ever played in my life, even better than the 63 I got to win the U.S. Open two years ago. I hit the ball so good. It was a joke." John Mahaffey finishes as the runner-up with Tom Watson 10 strokes back in third place. It marks the second straight year that Miller wins wire-to-wire in Tucson and is the second straight year where he wins the opening two events of the year, after winning the first three events in 1974. Miller's game cools off at the Bing Crosby National Pro-Am the following week, finishing nine shots back of winner Gene Littler.

2003 – Ernie Els beats Aaron Baddeley on the second playoff hole at the Sony Open in Hawaii with an incredible 43-foot birdie putt from the fringe of the 10th green at Waialae Country Club. A week after winning the Mercedes Championship in Maui, Els becomes the first golfer in 13 years to win the first two tour events of the season. Says Baddeley of the winning stroke by Els, "I don't think he was supposed to hole that putt."

1992 – John Cook holes out from 30 yards for an eagle on the fourth hole of a sudden-death playoff to beat Gene Sauers and win the Bob Hope Desert Classic in LaQuinta, Calif. Cook and Sauers are part of a record five-man playoff that also includes Mark O'Meara, Tom Kite and Rick Fehr, O'Meara and Kite falling out after the first playoff hole and Fehr after the second hole. The win is the fourth PGA Tour title for Cook, the former Ohio State standout member of the Buckeye's 1979 NCAA Championship team and the U.S. Amateur champion in 1978.

1997 – John Cook wins the Bob Hope Desert Classic for a second time, following up his 11-birdie Saturday round of 62 with a nine-birdie final-round 63 to post a 33-under-par score over five rounds to edge Mark Calcavecchia by one stroke. The win is the ninth of 11 career PGA Tour titles for Cook, who ties a PGA Tour 36-hole record with his 62-63 finish, both at the Indian Wells Country Club course, described by Tommy Bonk of the *Los Angeles Times* as "where Desi Arnaz was one of the original investors and where Fred and Ethel Mertz probably could break par." Says Cook of his birdie barrage, "I don't know what to say. I hope I didn't blow my quota for the rest of the year." Quips Calcavecchia of his runner-up finish, "If I can't win shooting 32 under, what do I have to do?"

January 20

1985 – Calvin Peete shoots a final-round 68 to win his ninth career PGA Tour event at the Phoenix Open, two shots clear of runners-up Doug Tewell and Morris Hatalsky. The win is the eighth in three years for the 41-year-old Peete, who famously doesn't learn to play the game until the age of 22 and doesn't receive his PGA Tour card until he is 33. "I never imagined I'd be where I am today," says Peete, who learns golf while peddling goods to migrant workers in Rochester, N.Y. "When I first came out on the tour, I was happy to win a paycheck, any kind of paycheck. I never dreamed of winning a tournament, but I went along, I made improvements. Now I feel I can win anytime I tee it up."

2002 – Playing in a tournament for the first time in five months, Phil Mickelson wins the Bob Hope Desert Classic for this 20th career PGA Tour victory beating David Berganio, Jr., on the first playoff hole. Mickelson hits an 80-yard wedge next to the hole for a tap-in birdie that clinches the $720,000 first prize. Mickelson becomes the 34th player in PGA Tour history to win 20 or more events, securing a lifetime tour exemption.

1974 – Johnny Miller wins his sixth career PGA Tour title at the Dean Martin Tucson Open, posting a 16-under score of 272, earning $30,000. Miller would also win the next two PGA events at the Bing Crosby National Pro Am and the Phoenix Open and goes on to win eight titles in all for the year.

_____

January 21

_____

1940 – Jack William Nicklaus, regarded by many as the greatest golfer of all time winning 18 pro major titles, is born in Columbus, Ohio.

2017 – Canadian Adam Hadwin shoots the ninth sub-60 round in PGA Tour history firing a 13-under-par 59 in the third round of the CareerBuilder Challenge at the LaQuinta Country Club in California. "I think everybody talks about kind of they were in a zone and I think that's kind of what happened," says Hadwin, a Canadian born in Moose Jaw, Saskatchewan. "I was thinking about it. I knew exactly where I was. I knew exactly what I needed to do. It just didn't seem to matter." Hadwin, however, fails to turn his record score in a tournament victory as he finishes second by one shot the following day to Hudson Swafford. Hadwin's 59 comes nine days after Justin Thomas also shoots 59 in the first round of the Sony Open in Hawaii.

Hadwin makes 13 birdies in his bogey-free round on the par 72 course.

1990 – Patty Sheehan shoots a four-over-par 75 to win the $500,000 Jamaica Classic at Montego Bay and collects $135,000. Sheehan says she will use the prize money to pay for rebuilding her California home badly damaged in the October 17 San Francisco earthquake. Sheehan says the victory is especially gratifying because "I'm broke."

2007 – Hale Irwin wins his record-extending 45th and final PGA Champions Tour event on the MasterCard Championship at Hualalai shooting a final-round 65 to beat runner-up Tom Kite by five strokes.

January 22

1950 – Polly Riley, an amateur, wins the LPGA's first sanctioned event, the Tampa Open at the Palma Ceia Golf & Country Club in Tampa, Fla., beating runner-up Louise Suggs by five strokes. Riley remains an amateur for her career and wins over 100 tournaments. She played on the U.S. Curtis Cup team six times (1948, 1950, 1952, 1954, 1956, 1958) and was runner-up at the 1947 U.S. Women's Open. In 1948, she gave Babe Didrikson Zaharias her most lopsided loss in match-play, winning a 36-hole match-play final at the Texas Women's Open by a 10&9 margin.

1995 – Pat Bradley wins the LPGA HealthSouth Inaugural at Disney in Orlando, Fla., in the first live golf tournament broadcast on the Golf Channel.

2016 – Robert Allenby makes his 10th career hole-in-one in the second round of the CareerBuilder Challenge in LaQuinta, Calif., tying Hal Sutton for the most by a PGA Tour player.

Allenby hits his ace on the Nicklaus Tournament course's 12th hole with a seven-iron from 165 yards.

2006 – Chad Campbell wins the Bob Hope Classic in LaQuinta, Calif., by three shots, despite hitting two balls in the water and firing a one-under-par 71. "It wasn't the prettiest day out there for me but I grinded it out," says Campbell after beating Scott Verplank and Jesper Parnevik.

2006 – Chris DiMarco wins the inaugural Abu Dhabi Golf Championship in the United Arab Emirates by one shot over Henrik Stenson. "This is four years to the month that I have not been in the winner's circle," says DiMarco, who last won the Phoenix Open in 2002. "It feels great to be in the winner's circle. A win anywhere is a win – and this in an unbelievable field. We had four guys in the top 11 here, so we had very good field,"

1989 – Mark Calcavecchia wins his fourth PGA Tour title at the Phoenix Open, shooting a final-round 64 to beat runner-up Chip Beck by nine strokes. Calcavecchia wins again in two weeks at the Los Angeles Open by one stroke over Sandy Lyle and then, later in the summer, at the Open Championship at Troon in playoff with Wayne Grady and Greg Norman to win his first and only major championship.

January 23

1977 – Tom Watson wins for the first time at Pebble Beach, shooting a final-round 71 to win the Bing Crosby National Pro-Am at the storied links, one shot better than runner-up Tony Jacklin. Both Watson and Jacklin battle inner-demons during the final round, but Watson's boldness helps him win his fourth PGA Tour title, including his win at the 1975 Open Championship. "I fought my inner self all day," Watson admits. "But I'm more mature and confident now than I was when I lost those leads in the U.S. Open at Winged Foot and Medinah.

There was no way I wasn't going to use a driver on 18." Jacklin, playing in the group ahead of Watson, makes bogey on the 18th hole with a conservative strategy, giving Watson a two-shot cushion on the final hole. "All I could remember on the 18th tee was that one I whipped into the water five years ago when I took an 8 on the hole and it blew me right out of third-place money," says Jacklin. "So what was second worth today? S29,800? That's better than a sharp stick in the eye, isn't it? When I made that 8, 1 decided never to take a wood off that tee again." Watson wins a Pebble Beach again the following year at the Crosby in a playoff with Ben Crenshaw and then again, famously, in 1982 at the U.S. Open, buoyed by his famous chip-in birdie on the 17th hole in the final round.

2011 – Jhonattan Vegas becomes the first Venezuelan to win a PGA Tour event when he makes a 13-foot par putt on the second playoff hole to win the Bob Hope Classic over Gary Woodland. Vegas becomes the first rookie to win the 52-year-old Hope Classic and wins on only his fifth start on the PGA Tour. "It's a dream come true," says Vegas. "It's something you dream about, but you have to make it happen." Bill Haas is also part of the playoff, but is eliminated on the first hole when Vegas and Woodland each make birdie.

2000 – Despite being distracted and shaken after hitting a spectator on the head with an errant tee-shot on the 15th hole of his final round, Jesper Parnevik of Sweden birdies the final hole for a one-shot win at the Bob Hope Desert Classic in LaQuinta, Calif. "He was down on the ground and it looked like a big golf ball was growing out of his forehead," Parnevik says of the spectator he hit. "It was a terrible sight. I asked if he was O.K., and he said: 'I'm fine. As long as you win the tournament, I'm O.K.'" Parnevik's 18th-hole birdie gives him a final-round 65 to beat out Rory Sabbatini by a shot.

2011 – Martin Kaymer bumps Tiger Woods out as the world No. 2-ranked golfer after winning the Abu Dhabi Championship in the United Arab Emirates for the third time in four years. Kaymer dominates the field that features current major champions Graeme McDowell, Louis Oosthuizen and Phil Mickelson, winning eight shots clear of runner-up Rory McIlroy and 26 shots ahead of world No. 1 Lee Westwood, who finishes in 64th place. The last time Europeans were ranked No. 1 and No. 2 in the world golf rankings was in 1993, when Nick Faldo and Bernhard Langer filled the top two slots.

January 24

1999 – David Duval shoots one of the greatest rounds in the history of golf – a final-round 59 – to come back from seven shots back to win the Bob Hope Chrysler Classic. Duval fires the 13-under-par round at the Arnold Palmer Private Course at PGA West in LaQuinta, Calif., capped by a six-foot eagle putt on the final hole. Duval's historic round gives him a one-shot victory over Steve Pate, his ninth tournament win in 28 starts. ''It's not really something I expected to do in my career,'' says Duval. "In a sense, I feel bad for Steve, because I absolutely stole the golf tournament from him. Tell a guy starting the day that he'll shoot six under and get beat by a 59. He's going to tell you you're crazy. It's a tough situation.'' Duval joins Al Geiberger and Chip Beck as the only players to shoot 59 on the PGA Tour at the time. Geiberger registers his score in 1977 at Colonial Country Club during the second round of the Memphis Classic, while Beck does it in 1991 at Sunrise Country Club, during the third round of the Las Vegas Invitational. Clifton Brown of the New York Times states in his coverage that Duval's score has "even more unusual qualities" writing, "He was the first to shoot 59 on a Sunday, when the pin placements are toughest, and the first to do it under the pressure of being in contention. Duval shot an incredible 28 on the back nine, playing his best when the tension was greatest."

1993 – Larry Mize wins on the PGA Tour for the first time since his incredible chip-in sudden-death playoff win over Greg Norman at the Masters six years earlier, winning the Northern Telecom Open in Tucson, Ariz., Mize shoots a final-round 67 to beat runner-up Jeff Maggert by two strokes. "I think that shot at the Masters hurt me psychologically," Mize admits after winning in Tucson. "After something like that you want to put your expectations pretty high. But you don't want them to be so high that all you get is frustration. I started trying to play perfect golf. You can't do that. I'm trying to stay in the present tense. Be mentally tough. Don't get ahead of yourself. And enjoy playing golf. You're not going to hit every shot perfect, so you need to be in a frame of mind to be able to enjoy playing the trouble shots."

2016 – Jason Dufner performs what NBC TV broadcaster Dan Hicks calls "Escape from Alcatraz" to dramatically hang on a win the CareerBuilder Challenge in LaQuinta, Calif., his first win on the PGA Tour since the 2013 PGA Championship. Tied for the lead on the par-3 17th hole at PGA West's Stadium Course, an island-green hole nick-named "Alcatraz" after the famous San Francisco Bay island prison, Dufner hits his tee shot over the green and into the rocks that guard the green. Dufner is able to get his club on to the ball with his chip, avoiding the rocks, and hits the pin, before tapping in for a par. Dufner then makes par on the final hole and wins a playoff with David Lingmerth on the second extra hole. "It was probably like one in like 50 million that that ball ends up there," Dufner says of his recovery shot from the rocks. "But I'll take it. I'll take it. Some guy won the Powerball a couple weeks ago, he'll take it, right?"

2009 – Following a round of 61on the par-72 PGA West Arnold Palmer course, Steve Stricker shoots a 62 on the PGA West Nicklaus course at the 90-hole Bob Hope Classic in La Quinta, Calif. to set a new PGA Tour record for best 72-hole score and for setting a record low score for consecutive rounds on the PGA Tour. Stricker's 33-under par score beats out the 72-hole record of 31 under set by Ernie Els in his victory at the 2003 Mercedes Classic while his 61-62 was a low for consecutive rounds, besting Mark Calcavecchia who shot 60-64 in the 2001 Phoenix Open, and Pat Perez who carded a 61-63 two days earlier also at the Bob Hope Classic. However, Sticker balloons to a 77 the next day in the final round allowing Perez to come back from three strokes back and win his first PGA Tour title.

January 25

2001 – Andrew Magee makes the first hole-in-one on a Par 4 in PGA Tour history in even remarkable fashion that one can imagine. At the 332-yard No. 17 hole at the TPC Scottsdale at the FBR Open, Magee launches a driver after making double-bogey on the previous hole. The group ahead of Magee – Steve Pate, Gary Nicklaus (the son of Jack Nicklaus) and Tom Byrum – are still on the green putting when Magee's ball bounces on the green. Pate leaps out of the way, but the ball incredibly rolls through the legs of Byrum and, even more incredibly, hits his putter as he is squatting and lining up his putt. The ball then ricochets off the putter and ventures eight feet into the hole.

1997 – Tiger Woods hits one of the most famous shots of golf in the third round of the Phoenix Open, hitting a hole-in-one with a nine-iron at the 155-yard No. 16 hole at the TPC of Scottsdale – the most raucous hole on the PGA Tour. Writes the Associated Press of the shot, "Many in a crowd estimated at 121,500 were seated on the hillside behind the green, adjacent to a hospitality area. A roar audible hundreds of yards away broke out when Woods' nine-iron shot from the tee 155 yards away took one big bounce, one tiny one and dropped in. As Woods left the tee area, fans began to shower it with beer cups. One onlooker ran onto the fairway, then began bowing from the waist in an 'I'm-not-worthy' salute as marshals shooed him away. Woods never saw him."

2010 – Twenty-two years after his father Jay Haas won the Bob Hope Classic, Bill Haas wins the same title in LaQuinta, Calif., for his first PGA Tour victory. Playing in his 140th career PGA Tour event, Haas wins the title with a tap-in birdie putt on the final hole to win by one stroke over Matt Kuchar, Bubba Watson and Tim Clark. The event ends on a Monday, which allows Jay Haas to fly in for the final round after competing on the Champions Tour in Hawaii. "To win the same tournament I won is special, and then for me to get to see it – that's really special," says Jay Haas.

1976 – Ben Crenshaw wins his second career PGA Tour title winning the Bing Crosby National Pro-Am at Pebble Beach, shooting a final-round 69 to beat relative unknown Mike Morley by two strokes. Jack Nicklaus, the 54-hole leader, has a terrible final-round tour around Pebble Beach, ballooning to an 82, with a 45 on the back nine to drop to 18th place. Nicklaus makes triple bogey on the 13th hole and an 8 on the finishing par 5 18th. Writes Dan Jenkins in *Sports Illustrated*, "If Crenshaw's game has been improving steadily, Nicklaus' game disintegrated suddenly Sunday and in various silly ways. It got so absurd that finally even Jack started laughing."

1987 – Paul Azinger wins the first of his 17 career PGA Tour titles at the Phoenix Open, played for the first time at the TPC at Scottsdale. Azinger shoots a final-round 67 to post a one-shot win over defending champion Hal Sutton, who closes with a final-round 64.

1981 – David Graham birdies the final hole to beat runner-up Lon Hinkle by one shot and win his sixth career PGA Tour title at the Phoenix Open at the Phoenix Country Club. Hinkle caps a final-round 63 with an eagle on the final hole that ties Graham. The Australian, however, stripes a one-iron just off the green on the par-5 524-yard 18th hole, chips to four-feet and makes the birdie putt for the win. "I honestly didn't think I had the strength to get it there but I guess the adrenaline was flowing," says Graham of this second shot on the final hole. "I had no choice. I didn't give it a second thought." Four months later, Graham goes on to win the U.S .Open at Merion Golf Club in Pennsylvania, his second major title.

January 26

1997 – Steve Jones wins the Phoenix Open by an incredible 11 shots to register his first tournament victory since the U.S. Open at Oakland Hills the previous summer. Jones fires a final-round 67 for a 26-under par tally – 11-shots better than runner-up Jesper Parnevik but one shot shy of the PGA Tour record of 257 set by Mike Souchak in the 1955 Texas Open. The 11-shot margin of victory is the most on the PGA Tour since Jose Maria Olazabal won the 1990 World Series of Golf by 12 strokes.

1975 – Gene Littler wins the 26th title of his career at the Bing Crosby National Pro Am at Pebble Beach, shooting a final-round 73 to beat runner-up Hubert Green by four shots. "It's a big victory for me," says the 44-year-old Littler, the 1961 U.S. Open champion. "I've been trying to win a Crosby all my life it seems, so in that regard I'm very pleased." Littler goes on to win three more times on the PGA Tour, his 29th and final win coming at the 1977 Houston Open.

1986 – Hal Sutton makes a two-putt birdie on the final hole – after hitting a 246-yard two-iron over the lake at the Phoenix Country Club – and wins his sixth career PGA Tour title at the Phoenix Open by two shots over Calvin Peete and Tony Sills.

January 27

2008 – Tiger Woods sinks a 10-foot birdie on the 18th hole to shoot a one-under 71 to clinch an eight-shot victory at the Buick Invitational at Torrey Pines. It marks his fourth straight title at Torrey Pines, a third straight PGA Tour victory and congratulations from Arnold Palmer, whom Woods ties on the all-time wins list with his 62nd PGA Tour title. "I'm sure that there are many, many more coming in the future," Palmer says. "There isn't any question about that." Woods returns to Torrey Pines five months later and wins the U.S. Open for a third time.

1985 – Lanny Wadkins shatters Johnny Miller's scoring record at the Riviera Country Club by six shots posting a 20-under-par score of 264 to win the Los Angeles Open for his 14th career PGA Tour title. Wadkins shoots a final-round 64 and beats runner-up Hal Sutton by seven shots. Writes Shave Glick in the *Los Angeles Times*, "Wadkins ended up 20-under par (63-70-67-64--264) for four rounds over Hogan's Alley to win his second L.A. Open. By a way of comparison, (Ben) Hogan set a record of nine-under par when he won in 1948, and Miller was 14-under in 1981. When Wadkins won in 1979 he shot 276."

January 28

2013 – Tiger Woods extends to an eight-shot lead with five holes to play but, frustrated with slow play ahead of him, finishes with two bogeys and a double-bogey in his last hour of play and wins the Farmers Insurance Open at Torrey Pines. "I'm excited the way I played all week," Woods says. "I hit the ball well – pretty much did everything well and built myself a nice little cushion. I had some mistakes at the end, but all my good play before that allowed me to afford those mistakes." The win is the 75th of Woods career and his seventh triumph at the tournament and his eighth at Torrey Pines, including the 2008 U.S. Open, setting a PGA Tour record. The event is finished on a Monday for the first time in the event's history, due to fog that cancels play on Saturday. Woods wins five events in all in 2013 before injuries severely hamper his career through 2017.

1979 – Fuzzy Zoeller endures extreme weather conditions to win his first PGA Tour title at the Andy Williams San Diego Open shooting a final-round 72 at Torrey Pines to win by five shots over Tom Watson, Bill Kratzert and Artie McNickle. "Play was hampered all day by the winds that gusted to 50 mph, biting cold and occasional rain and snow squalls," writes the Associated Press of playing conditions. "It was halted for 15 minutes by a hailstorm which covered the greens with ice pellets." Just over three months later, Zoeller wins again on warmer, calmer and much grander stage – the Masters – becoming the first first-time participant to win at Augusta National.

2007 – Tiger Woods wins PGA Tour title No. 55, winning by two-strokes the Buick Invitational at Torrey Pines for a third straight year, stretching his tour winning streak to seven. The streak is the second-longest on the PGA Tour since Byron Nelson wins 11 straight in 1945. "As far as how special seven is, you're in elite company," Woods says. "There's only one person ahead of you. He's one of the greatest legends in the history of the game. To be in company like with Mr. Nelson…it's pretty special."

January 29

1984 – Starting the day six shots out of the lead and in a tie for 18th place, Gary Koch shoots a seven-under-par 65 and sinks a 10-foot-birdie putt on the second playoff hole with Gary Hallberg to win the Isuzu-Andy Williams San Diego Open. Hallberg misses a four-foot par putt to win the title on the 18th hole, 45 minutes after Koch finishes his round. "I didn't really expect that score I shot to be good enough," says Koch, who becomes a popular TV commentator for NBC Sports. "I just thought he was going to make par at 18 and I was going to finish second. But I was just very fortunate that his misfortune was my good fortune and I got the chance to play a few more holes." The win is the fourth of six PGA Tour wins for Koch.

2012 – Brandt Snedeker starts to conduct a post-event press conference about finishing second at the Farmers Insurance Open at Torrey Pines as Kyle Stanley makes a triple-bogey 8 on the final hole to drop into a playoff that Snedeker incredibly wins on the second hole. "It's just crazy," says Snedeker, who trails by nine shots after his first four holes during the final round. "To get my mind around what just happened is tough. I'm excited, and I'm shaking." Stanley was looking for his first PGA Tour victory and leads by as many as seven shots in the final round. "It's tough to take," Stanley says, tearing up in the post-round interview. "I could probably play the 18th 1,000 times without making an 8. I know I'll be back. It's just so hard to swallow right now."

1978 – Jay Haas wins his first PGA Tour title at the Andy Williams San Diego Open, shooting a final-round 70 at Torrey Pines to beat Andy Bean, Gene Littler and John Schroeder by three shots. Haas, the nephew of 1968 Masters champion Bob Goalby, stays a steady force on the PGA Tour for the next 26 years, winning nine titles and achieving a top 20 ranking even as he transitioned onto the 50-and-over Champions Tour in 2004.

2006 – Emerging through an eight-way tie for the lead after making birdie on the 12th hole, Tiger Woods wins his first title in his 30s, winning the Buick Invitational at Torrey Pines in the second-hole of a sudden-death playoff with Jose-Maria Olazabal and Nathan Green. Woods clinches his fourth tournament win at Torrey Pines when Olazabal misses a four-foot putt on the second playoff hole. "You don't ever take pleasure out seeing your friends do that," Woods says of Olazabal's miss. "I would have felt fired up if I made the putt in the playoff for birdie on 18 and ended it right there, but not when a friend of mine misses a short one."

January 30

2011 – With his caddie Jim "Bones" MacKay tending the pin on the 18th hole, Phil Mickelson nearly holes a 72-yard eagle chip shot that would have tied Bubba Watson and forced a playoff at the Farmers Insurance Open at Torrey Pines. Mickelson's chip nearly goes into the hole on the fly, but settles three feet away. He makes the birdie putt but loses by one-shot to Watson. "I don't know how close he hit it. I don't know what he made on the hole. I just know that I won, because that's all I was worried about," says Watson of Mickelson's chip. "If he makes it, I'm getting ready for a playoff. So I'm trying not to get too emotional. I realize it's Phil Mickelson. He can make any shot he wants to."

2015 – Tiger Woods shoots a second-round score of 82 – 11 over par – his worst round as a professional at the time – and he misses the cut at the Waste Management Phoenix Open at the TPC of Scottsdale. His previous worst round – and only other round in his pro career in the 80s – was an 81 from the third round of the 2002 Open Championship during a rainy, windy, cold day at Muirfield. Later in the year, Woods shoots an 85 in the third round of the Memorial Championship, to set a new personal record for worst score as a professional.

1977 – Tom Watson wins for the second consecutive week and for the fifth time on the PGA Tour, shooting a final-round 69 at Torrey Pines to win the Andy Williams San Diego Open by five shots over runners-up Larry Nelson and John Schroeder. The previous week, Watson wins the Bing Crosby National Pro-Am and speaks bullishly of his form. "The way I'm hitting the ball now, especially off the lee where I haven't made a mistake in two weeks, I know I am going to score well," says Watson. "I can't emphasize enough how solidly I'm hitting the ball off the tee. I haven't been under a tree in two weeks and as long as I can keep the ball in the fairway, I'm going to score. The driving takes the pressure off my short game and when I'm in that position I feel confident about my putting." Watson goes on to win three more times in his 1977 season, most notably at the Masters for the first time and for a second time at the Open Championship in an epic duel with Jack Nicklaus at Turnberry.

2016 – Ha Na Jang of South Korea makes the first hole-in-one on a par-4 in the history of the LPGA Tour when she holes out with a three-wood tee shot on the 218-yard, par-4 eighth hole at the Ocean Club Golf Course in the Bahamas in the third round of the Pure Silk LPGA Classic. Says Jang, "I don't see the ball finish, but my dad was, 'Oh, you made it. It's unbelievable. Amazing."

January 31

1982 – Jack Nicklaus shoots a final-round course record 64 on the South Course at Torrey Pines but falls one shot shy of Johnny Miller, who wins his 22nd PGA Tour title at the Andy Williams San Diego Open with his final-round 70. "I figured last night that a 64 would be good enough to win the golf tournament," says Nicklaus, whose prediction comes one shot short. The Nicklaus round features two eagles, five birdies and one bogey. "Nicklaus really put it to me," Miller says. "At first I wasn't worried about him because I didn't think anyone would shoot 64 today."

2013 – Phil Mickelson's 25-foot birdie putt to shoot a 59 cruelly lips out in the first round of the Waste Management Open in Phoenix. "I'm ecstatic to shoot 60. I'm excited and so forth," Mickelson says. "But you don't get chances to shoot 59 very often. To have that putt on-line, I'm kind of mortified that that didn't go in." Mickelson's career-best PGA Tour score of 60 (11 under par) began on the back nine where he shoots a seven under par 29 and followed with four birdies on his final nine holes.

1999 – Rocco Mediate wins his third career PGA Tour title at the Phoenix Open, posting an 11-under-par score of 273 at the TPC of Scottsdale, beating Justin Leonard by two shots. However, Mediate's win is slightly overshadowed in the history of the game by the infamous Tiger Woods "loose impediment" ruling. On the par-five 13th hole, Woods hits his tee shot left into the scruffy desert near a huge boulder that would interfere with his pathway. Woods receives confirmation from the PGA Tour rules official that the boulder is considered a loose impediment – despite weighing a ton – and Woods asks members of his gallery to move the boulder out of his pathway. Woods executes his shot, birdies the hole, but finishes three shots behind Mediate.

2015 – Seventeen-year-old Lydia Ko of New Zealand becomes the youngest golfer to hold the No. 1 spot in the world rankings by tying for second place at the LPGA season-opening Coates Golf Championship in Ocala, Fla. Ko breaks the record set by Tiger Woods, who was the top-ranked man in the world golf rankings at the age of 21 in 1997. Shin Ji-Yai previously holds the women's record when she ranked No. 1 in 2010 aged 22. Ko, born in Korea, leads by as many as four strokes in the final round of the event, but double-bogeys the 17th hole and finishes a shot behind winner Choi Na-Yeon of South Korea. "I didn't really know what I needed to do to get in that position. All I was focused on was trying to play my best out here today," Ko says after the round. "So it's a huge honor to be in that ranking. I'm just going to just focus on my golf, not think about the rankings. The rankings always comes after the results."

1966 – Ken Venturi wins his 14th and final PGA tournament title at the Lucky International Open at Harding Park in San Francisco, the course where he learned to play as a boy. Venturi shoots a final-round 66 to beating runner-up Frank Beard by one stroke.

FEBRUARY

February 1

2009 – Nineteen-year-old Rory McIlroy wins his first professional title at the Dubai Desert Classic in the United Arab Emirates, holding off Justin Rose by one shot with a final-round 70. "This win has definitely moved me up a step and I just want to keep getting better and better," McIlroy says. "Your success only makes you more motivated to do better. I have become a very good player, but I still have a lot of years to progress and I just want to keep improving and hopefully one day I will be able to compete with Tiger [Woods]. I will have to reassess my goals, but I will just go out every week and try and get myself into contention going into the back nine on Sunday and that's my goal every week."

2015 – Rory McIlroy wins the Dubai Desert Classic in the United Arab Emirates for a second time, posting a final-round two-under-par 70 to win by three shots over Sweden's Alexander Noren. "I just wanted to keep my ball in play and not really make any mistakes and try and pick off some birdies when I could on the par 5s," says McIlroy, whose maiden pro victory came on the same event exactly six years to the day. "I did what I needed to do. It wasn't the best round that I've played this year but I got the job done and that's the most important thing."

1981 – John Cook wins a peculiar five-man playoff to win his first PGA Tour title at the 40th Bing Crosby National Pro-Am at Pebble Beach. Cook finishes the weather-shortened 54-hole event at Spyglass Hill, one of the three courses used for the event, and has to drive four miles to Pebble Beach for the playoff. Cook beats out Hale Irwin on the third playoff hole after Ben Crenshaw, Bobby Clampett and Barney Thompson drop out on the first hole after Cook and Irwin both make birdie. Prior to the playoff, after his drive from Spyglass, Cook goes out onto the 18th hole and hits practice balls into Carmel Bay to warm up for the playoff.

1970 – Seven years after becoming the first black player to win a PGA Tour event, Pete Brown wins the second of his two career PGA Tour titles at the Andy Williams San Diego Open Invitational in a playoff with Tony Jacklin.

2016 – Brandt Snedeker wins the Farmers Insurance Open at Torrey Pines in San Diego without having a hit a shot. One day after finishing with a final-round 69 in windy and stormy conditions – nine shots better than the average score in the field – Snedecker only has to wait during the Monday resumption of the weather-delayed round to claim his eighth career PGA Tour title and his second at Torrey Pines. Jimmy Walker, who leads by one to start the day, and K.J. Choi, tied with Snedeker, are unable to tame the wicked winds and cool temperatures on the final eight holes as play of the resumed final day of competition, played without spectators on the course due to continued high winds and multiple trees uprooted around the course. Choi misses a 40-foot birdie putt on the final hole that would have tied Snedecker, while Walker finishes three shots back.

February 2

1949 – Ben Hogan and his wife Valerie survive a serious car accident when they collide with a Greyhound bus on a foggy road east of Van Horn, Texas. Hogan throws himself across the front seat to protect his wife, a move that also saved his own life as the steering column of his car punctured the driver's seat. The 36-year-old Hogan suffers a double-fracture of the pelvis, a fractured collar-bone and left ankle, damaged ribs and near-fatal blood clots. Despite his doctors fearing he would never walk again, let alone play world-class tournament golf, Hogan leaves the hospital 59 days after the accident and returns to tournament golf the following January and wins the 1950 U.S. Open.

1997 – Mark O'Meara shoots a fourth straight round of 67 and wins the AT&T Pebble Beach Pro-Am for a record fifth time, beating runners-up David Duval and Tiger Woods by one shot. "There must be someone floating high above the Monterey Peninsula who's a huge Mark O'Meara fan," says O'Meara of his five wins on the famed golf links. O'Meara, who also won the event in 1992, 1990, 1989 and 1985, chips in for birdie from 15-feet away on the 16th hole, makes a 10-foot birdie on the 17th hole and clinches the win with a par on 18 as Woods, playing in the group in front of him, misses a 35-foot eagle putt on the final hole. Woods, a three-time winner on the PGA Tour, follows his third-round 63 with a final-round 64 to fall just short of beating O'Meara.

1992 – Mark O'Meara wins his record fourth AT&T Pebble Beach National Pro-Am at Pebble Beach with a par on the first hole of a sudden-death playoff with Jeff Sluman. O'Meara makes 35-foot birdie putt on the 18th hole and is followed in the hole by Sluman, who sinks a tying 18-foot birdie to force the playoff. O'Meara makes a 15-foot par putt on the first playoff hole – the 16th hole – to beat Sluman, who lips out for par from 12 feet. "When Jeff made his putt on top of mine on 18, I thought, 'Geez, what's it going to take. I can't take these playoffs anymore,'" says O'Meara, who was 0-4 in his career in playoffs at the time, losing most recently two weeks earlier at the Bob Hope Chrysler Classic. "But to win, you've got to get the right bounce, and today was my day." The win makes O'Meara the only man to win the tournament four times since it was first played on the Monterey Peninsula in 1947.

February 3

2013 – Phil Mickelson closes out a wire-to-wire victory at the Waste Management Phoenix Open – his 41st career PGA Tour win – shooting a final-round 67 to beat Brandt Snedeker by four shots. Mickelson starts the final round with a six-shot lead and needs to shoot a 64 or better to set a new 72-hole PGA Tour record but falls two strokes off the 254 record score set by Tommy Armour III in the 2003 Texas Open. Mickelson opens the event lipping out for a 59 and follows with rounds of 65 and 64. "It's an important one for me, because it's been a while since I won, been a while since I've been in contention," says Mickelson after his first win in 51 weeks. "I was certainly nervous heading into today. I think the thing I'm most excited about was the way I was able to regain control of my thoughts after a few shots early on that I didn't care for."

2008 – Tiger Woods birdies the final two holes, including a 25-foot downhill putt on the final hole, to shoot a seven-under-par 65 to beat Martin Kaymer by one shot and win the Dubai Desert Classic. Woods birdies five of the last seven holes on the day to win his 72nd career global pro tournament and his second tournament of the year in his second start, to go with his win the week before at the Buick Invitational at Torrey Pines. Woods starts the day four-shots off the lead of Ernie Els before posting his largest comeback win since he makes up a five-shot deficit at the AT&T Pebble Beach National Pro-Am in 2000. Writes the Associated Press of the final scene for Woods at the event, "Tiger Woods watched his 25-foot putt race down the slope and bend toward the cup, then he skipped backward and punched the desert air in celebration when it disappeared into the cup for a final birdie."

1990 – Winds are so strong in the third round of the AT&T Pebble Beach National Pro Am tournament that tour professional Ed Dougherty makes a 14 on the par 3 17th hole hitting 11 putts through the 40 mph winds. "He putted the ball toward the hole and it blew back to him three times," says Mike Wiebe, the father of pro Mark Wiebe, to the *San Jose Mercury News.* "On the fourth putt, the ball got five feet past the cup and stopped. He barely tapped it toward the cup and the wind got it and blew it off the green--again." Says Mark O'Meara, who wins the tournament the next day by two shots over Kenny Perry, "Today was like, 'Good morning, welcome to the wind tunnel.' It was hard to stand up out there."

February 4

1968 – Arnold Palmer wins his 53rd career PGA Tour title at the Bob Hope Desert Classic beating former U.S. and British Amateur champion Deane Beman on the second hole of a sudden death playoff. The win is his third career title at the California desert tournament after winning in 1960 and 1962. He would win the title two more times, in 1971 and in 1973, which marked his 62nd and final PGA tournament title. "I like these desert courses," says Palmer after his win. "They are in fine condition. I hit only two drives out of bounds during the whole show. I like the people down here and I enjoy playing all the courses."

2005 – Phil Mickelson shoots a 60 in the second round of the FBR Open at the TPC of Scottsdale in Arizona. Mickelson shoots his lowest round of his career on the PGA Tour by making birdie on the last five holes. "It was a wonderful day," Mickelson says of his round. "No complaints here." Eight years later, Mickelson shoots the same score on the same course in the first round of the tournament, but lips out a birdie putt on his 18th hole in his attempt to shoot 59. Mickelson, a former Scottsdale resident and Arizona State student, wins the event two days later for his first victory since the Masters the previous year.

February 5

1984 – In perhaps the luckiest bounce in the history of professional golf, Hale Irwin's tee shot on the final hole at the Bing Crosby National Pro-Am at Pebble Beach hooks toward the ocean, only to hit a rock and bounce back into play. Irwin, trailing Jim Nelford by one shot, makes birdie on the famed 18th hole to force a sudden-death playoff that he wins on the second hole for his 16th career PGA Tour title. Says Irwin of his near calamitous 18th-hole tee shot, "It was low and it was hooking… It had fifth place written all over it, but…" Writes Dan Jenkins in *Sports Illustrated* of Irwin, "How can you beat somebody at Pebble Beach who's going to bounce a golf ball off an oceanside rock, then carom one off a flagstick to get himself a tie, and then overcome a skied tee shot on the second sudden-death playoff hole with a career two-iron shot out of a fairway bunker? Except for that 213-yard blast, which got him in there for his birdie putt, Irwin looked as if he were winning – or losing – the Bing Crosby National Bumper Pool Championship."

2006 – Tiger Woods beats Ernie Els in a one-hole playoff to win the Dubai Desert Classic, his 57th worldwide win and 10th outside of the PGA Tour. Woods wins the playoff on the 18th hole with a par after Els misses his par putt after hitting his second shot into the water after his tee shot finds a grove of palm trees. The United Arab Emirates is the 10th country different country where Woods wins an official tournament. "Somehow I got lucky," Woods says. "Today it was very fortunate because I didn't really have it, but the other guys didn't run away either."

February 6

1983 – Tom Kite wins his fifth career PGA Tour title at the Bing Crosby National Pro-Am at Pebble Beach by two strokes over runners-up Calvin Peete and Rex Caldwell. Kite's final-round coronation comes a day after he shoots a course and tournament record 62 across the Pebble Beach Golf Links. Kite's record is later equaled by David Duval in 1997. Nine years later, Kite wins his one and only major championship at Pebble Beach at the 1992 U.S. Open.

1994 – Forty-six-year-old mostly-retired Johnny Miller incredibly wins the AT&T Pebble Beach National Pro-Am for his 25th and final PGA Tour title with a one-shot victory over Tom Watson, Jeff Maggert, Corey Pavin and Kirk Triplett. Playing in only his fifth PGA Tour event in the last four years, Miller shoots a final-round 74 and holds on for one of the most improbable victories in golf history. "That didn't really happen," says Miller. "It was a mirage. It was weird, like the whole thing wasn't happening. I had this strange sense of calm." Miller, whose battle with the "yips" kept him from competing, does not three-putt during the final round and benefits from Watson three-putting two of the last three holes. The win was Miller's first since he also won at Pebble Beach on Feb. 1, 1987, his first title in four years, when he beat Payne Stewart by one shot.

February 7

1962 – Sam Snead becomes the first and only man to win an LPGA event, winning the 15-player Royal Poinciana Plaza Invitational in Palm Beach, Fla. The event, a two-day, four-round event at the Palm Beach Par 3 Golf Club, consists of Snead and 14 players from the LPGA, including Mickey Wright, Patty Berg, Kathy Whitworth and Betsy Rawls. Snead wins with a score of five-under par, five shots better than Wright. The previous year, Snead also played in the event and finished third, two shots behind winner Louise Suggs.

1965 – In the first year with Bob Hope's name associated with the tournament, Billy Casper wins the Bob Hope Desert Classic – his 25th career PGA Tour victory – posting a 12-under-par score of 348 over five rounds to earn $15,000.

1960 – Arnold Palmer wins for the first time at the Palm Springs Desert Golf Classic, the tournament that eventually becomes known as the Bob Hope Desert Classic, with a 22-under-par score of 338 over five rounds. Palmer's closing 65 secures the title, the 14th of his PGA Tour career, and earns him the first prize paycheck of $12,000.

1999 – Payne Stewart wins his 10th title on the PGA Tour – without hitting a shot – as the AT&T Pebble Beach National Pro-Am is cancelled due to rain and Stewart, the third-round leader, is declared the winner. The PGA Tour cancels the tournament outright, electing not to wait until Monday, when more rain is expected. Stewart posts a 54-hole total of 10-under par 206, one stroke ahead of runner-up Frank Lickliter. The abbreviated win is the first for Stewart since 1995 and his second since he won the 1991 U.S. Open. ''I'm not going to lie to you, it feels pretty good,'' Stewart says. ''I wanted the opportunity to go out and prove to myself that I could win in 72 holes. That's still a void I have to fill this year. But I'm going to take this and run. It's not a tainted victory. You come here knowing that the weather is liable to be bad. And I was fortunate enough to be ahead after 54 holes.'' Later in the year, Stewart dramatically wins his second U.S. Open title at Pinehurst over Phil Mickelson, but is tragically killed in an airplane crash on October 25.

2016 – Rickie Fowler and Hideki Matsuyama battle down the stretch and in a four-hole playoff at the Waste Management Phoenix Open with Fowler hitting two balls into the water on the par 4 17th hole – once in regulation and once in the decisive playoff hole – as Matsuyama wins his second career PGA Tour title. Fowler leads Matsuyama by two shots on the 17th hole, but hits his driver over the green and into the water on the short par 4. Fowler makes bogey while Matsuyama makes birdie on the hole and both players dramatically make birdies on the final hole to force the playoff. The two players then make pars on the first playoff hole, birdies on the second, and pars on the third before reaching the drivable 17th hole for the fourth playoff hole.

Rather than hitting driver like in regulation, Fowler hits a three-wood, which he hits left into the water. Matsuyama then makes a par to close out the championship.

February 8

1976 – Johnny Miller fires a final-round 63 and successfully defends his title at the Bob Hope Desert Classic by three shots over runner-up Rik Massengale. "I like to have those kind of rounds in my game," says Miller, who shoots the same score in the final round to win the 1973 U.S. Open. Prior to the event, Miller expresses supreme confidence in his game, falling short of predicting he will win the tournament. "Really I'd be surprised if I don't win," he says to reporters before the start of play. "I'm not saying I will win. You can't do that but the way I'm playing, I'll be surprised if I don't win it again. I'm striking the ball awful good and I've had some time off that's important. Most of tournaments I have won have come right after I've had a break. I find playing three in a row is about all I can handle. People want so much of my time when I'm out playing. I just don't have any time for myself and my family. I'm kind of a private person. I like to be by myself – just go hunting or fishing. I need that time off to get my batteries recharged."

2004 – Vijay Singh birdies the first three holes and shoots a final-round 69 to beat runner-up Jeff Maggert by three shots and win AT&T Pebble Beach Pro-Am. Singh posts a 16-under par score of 272, earning $954,000 for his 16th career PGA Tour title. The win is the first of nine tournament victories for Singh on the PGA Tour for the year, which earns him the world No. 1 ranking, a record $10,905,166 in earnings and being named the PGA Tour's Player of the Year.

2015 – Jason Day emerges from a four-man playoff to win the Farmers Insurance Classic at Torrey Pines, his third PGA Tour title. After shooting a final-round two-under par 70, nearly pitching the ball in the water from behind the green on the final hole, Day makes a 15-foot birdie putt on the 16th hole to beat J.B. Holmes on the second playoff hole, after defending champion Scott Stallings and Harris English are eliminated on the first playoff hole.

1942 – Herman Barron becomes the first Jewish golfer to win an official PGA Tour event by winning the Western Open by two strokes over Henry Picard at Phoenix Golf Club in Phoenix, Arizona.

February 9

1986 – Bob Tway wins his first PGA Tour title at the Shearson Lehman Brothers Andy Williams Open beating Bernhard Langer on the second hole of a sudden-death playoff. "It's an indescribable feeling," says Tway. "You play all your life and work endless hours for a moment like this, and sure enough it finally came. I'm just pleased to death." Tway's victory kick-starts a career year for the Oklahoman who goes on to win three more titles during the year – at the Westchester Classic in New York and the Atlanta Classic, both in June, and at the PGA Championship in Toledo, Ohio in August, famously sinking a bunker shot on the final hole to defeat Greg Norman. Tway is later named PGA Player of the Year.

1997 – Mark O'Meara wins for the second consecutive week, winning the Buick Invitational in San Diego at Torrey Pines by two shots over seven golfers – David Ogrin, Donnie Hammond, Jesper Parnevik, Craig Stadler, Lee Janzen, Mike Hulbert and Duffy Waldorf. O'Meara shoots a final-round 71 to claim his 14th career PGA Tour title the week after he wins the AT&T Pebble Beach Pro-Am at Pebble Beach for a record fifth time.

1975 – Despite being up most of the night tending to his sick seven-month-old daughter Casi, Johnny Miller shoots a final-round 68 and wins the Bob Hope Desert Classic. Miller's three-shot win over runner-up Bob Murphy is the 14th of his career and his third of young 1975 season, after also winning in Phoenix and Tucson, also desert courses, the previous month. Despite the harried evening and early morning tending to his daughter, including taking her to be looked at by doctors at the hospital, Miller still has time to attend church before his final round.

1986 – Charlie Owens, a former Army paratrooper, becomes the first player to win an event with an anchored, long-putter when he wins the Treasure Coast Classic in Fort Pierce, Fla., on the PGA Champions Tour. Owens uses the 52-inch putter he created himself that he anchors to his sternum to beat Lee Elder and Don January by three strokes. The anchored putter gains in popularity, helping players win titles all over the world, including the Masters, Open Championship and the U.S. Open and PGA Championship, but is eventually outlawed by the administrators of golf starting at the end of the 2015 season.

February 10

1991 – Corey Pavin sinks a 45-foot chip-shot for birdie on the first hole of a sudden death playoff with Mark O'Meara to win his eighth of 15 career PGA Tour titles at the Bob Hope Chrysler Classic. "I think I stood there for what seemed like an eternity," says Pavin of his incredible winning stroke. "It didn't sink in that I had made it." Both Pavin and O'Meara finish regulation at 29-under-par 331 for the 90-hole tournament, breaking the PGA Tour record at the time of 27-under par.

1974 – Hubert Green wins his fourth PGA Tour title at the Bob Hope Desert Classic, shooting a final-round 65 to beat Bert Yancey by two shots. Green wins three more titles during the year – at the Greater Jacksonville Open, the Philadelphia Golf Classic and the Walt Disney World National Team Championship with

Mac McLendon – marking his most prolific season of his PGA Tour career. Green wins 19 PGA Tour titles in all in his career, including the 1977 U.S. Open and the 1985 PGA Championship.

2017 – Bernd Wiesberger of Austria makes a record nine straight birdies in the second round of the European Tour's Maybank Championship in Kuala Lumpur, Malaysia. "I felt a bit beside myself to be honest, I just kept it going," Wiesberger says to EuropeanTour.com of his birdie run that starts on the seventh hole and ends at the fifteenth hole. "I felt like I was on a good run and I felt comfortable pretty much the whole day after my bogey on four." Wiesberger becomes the first player in European Tour history to record nine straight birdies, but his run does not count as an official record, as the tournament allowed for preferred lies on the afternoon due to the wet conditions.

February 11

1973 – Forty-three-year-old Arnold Palmer wins his 62nd and final PGA Tour title at the Bob Hope Desert Classic, beating out runners-up Jack Nicklaus and Johnny Miller by two strokes. With Palmer leading by one stroke on the final hole, Nicklaus burns the cup with an 18-foot eagle putt, but Palmer clinches his first win in two years by making a seven-foot birdie putt. Palmer calls his win "the sweetest ever" but then tells the media "I hope it's not as long before my next win" which, unfortunately, doesn't come.

1962 – Arnold Palmer wins the Phoenix Open Invitational by 12 strokes – the largest margin of victory for a tournament win in his PGA career – to win his 29th career PGA tour event. Palmer, who starts the day with a five-shot lead, fires a final-round 66 to finish the dozen strokes ahead of runners-up Billy Casper, Don Fairfield, Bob McCallister and PGA Tour rookie Jack Nicklaus, playing in only his sixth official pro event.

1968 – Tom Weiskopf dramatically sinks a 25-foot eagle from just off the green on the 18th hole at Torrey Pines to win his first PGA Tour event at the Andy Williams San Diego Open Invitational. "I never thought the ball would drop in until it was four inches from the cup," says the 25-year-old Weiskopf. "Then I knew I had it." The eagle breaks a three-way tie between Weiskopf, Al Geiberger and Ray Floyd. Geiberger makes a birdie on top of Weiskopf's eagle to finish alone in second place, one shot behind.

February 12

1963 – For the first time – and for one of only three times in the history of golf – the "Big Three" of golf – Arnold Palmer, Gary Player and Jack Nicklaus finish in first, second and third place at a PGA Tour event or major championship at the Phoenix Open Invitational at the Arizona Country Club. Palmer wins the title for the third year in a row beating Player by one shot and by two shots over Nicklaus in third place. The only other times where the "Big Three" finish in the top three of an event comes at the 1964 Whitemarsh Open Invitational in Pennsylvania (Nicklaus winning, Player finishing second and Palmer finishing third) and at the 1965 Masters (Nicklaus winning and Palmer and Player finishing in a tie for second). Player has a chance to tie Palmer on the final hole with a four-foot birdie putt, but misses the putt, in part, due to being rattled when Don January waits for an extended period of time while his putt teeters on the lip of the cup but does not fall in. "I remember that like yesterday," Player says 50 years later to Bob Young of the *Arizona Republic*. "You've got a 4-foot putt to tie, and you're standing around like that. It's quite frustrating, isn't it? I mean, particularly when you've got a putt to tie the tournament, you want to get it over with. And I remember I missed the putt. But I'm not going to make excuses. Too many athletes make excuses today. It's never them. It's the clubs or the balls or something, and it's true in all sports. So, especially 50 years later, I'm not going to use that as an excuse. But it was disconcerting." It is believed that the incident leads to a rule change where a ball hanging on the lip must be addressed within 10 seconds. The final round of the event is delayed two days due to a rare winter thunderstorm that floods the course, uproots trees and causes extension damage to the course and tournament infrastructure.

2012 – Phil Mickelson shoot one of the best final rounds of his career, firing an eight-under 64 at Pebble Beach to win his 40th PGA Tour title at the AT&T Pebble Beach Pro-Am by two-strokes over Charlie Wi. Mickelson starts the day six shots out of the lead in fourth place and draws motivation playing in the same pairing as Tiger Woods, who he beats by 11 shots on the day. "I just feel very inspired when I play with him," says Mickelson. "I love playing with him, and he brings out some of my best golf." It marks the fourth time Mickelson wins at Pebble Beach and puts him elite company of being only the ninth player to win 40 PGA Tour titles in a career.

1995 – One week after winning the AT&T Pebble Beach Pro-Am, Peter Jacobsen wins for the second straight week at the Buick Invitational of California in San Diego. Jacobsen posts a 19-under par score of 269 at Torrey Pines, earning $216,000, and winning by four shots over runners-up Mark Calcavecchia, Hal Sutton, Mike Hulbert and Kirk Triplett. Jacobsen caps his sixth PGA Tour title with a birdie on the final hole, buoyed by a 334-yard drive, a six-iron to 20 feet and two putts on the par 5. "I'm speechless," says the gregarious Jacobsen after the win.

2017 – In his 100th start on the PGA Tour, 23-year-old Jordan Spieth wins his ninth PGA Tour title at the AT&T Pebble Beach Pro-Am, shooting a final-round 70 to win by four shots over Kelly Kraft. Spieth becomes the youngest player to win as many titles since Tiger Woods. "I remember walking up 18 today thinking to myself, 'I don't think that I've enjoyed the wins as much as I've talked to myself about the losses,'" Spieth says. "I don't think I've really enjoyed on the inside how much it takes to win out here and the hard work that goes into winning."

February 13

1945 – Byron Nelson wins the New Orleans Open – and a $1,300 war bond – shooting a course-record 65 at the New Orleans City Park course to beat Harold "Jug" McSpaden by five shots in a playoff. Nelson's score equals the course and tournament record set in 1941 by Henry Picard.

1961 – Arnold Palmer shoots a 67 and beats Doug Sanders by three strokes in an 18-hole playoff to win the Phoenix Open Invitational for his 23rd career PGA Tour victory. After each player make bogey on the first hole, Palmer takes the lead on the second hole and never relinquishes the lead. His only scare comes on the 18th hole when his tee shot gets stuck in a tree, forcing him to take a penalty stroke, but he still manages to make par to close out the victory. Palmer earns $4,300 for the win while Sanders is awarded $3,000 as runner-up. Both men also split one-fourth of the day's gate receipts. The victory marks the first of three straight tournament wins for Palmer in Phoenix. He wins the 1962 title by 12 shots and wins in 1963 by one stroke over Gary Player.

1972 – Bob Rosburg wins his sixth and final PGA Tour title at the Bob Hope Desert Classic, shooting a final-round 67 to beat Lanny Wadkins by one stroke. Rosburg, the 1959 winner of the PGA Championship, goes on to become a roving golf reporter for ABC Sports for more than 30 years.

February 14

1982 – Wayne Levi creates an odd slice of golf history becoming the first player to win on the PGA Tour without the standard white ball as he wins the Hawaiian Open with an optic orange golf ball. "I was with Wilson at the time and they came out with an orange ball. Others also used it, but I was the only one to win with it," Levi tells the *Honolulu Advertiser* 20 years after his trivia question victory. "I got some notoriety from it. Every time the ball came rolling down the fairway, everyone knew it was Wayne Levi."

2016 – Phil Mickelson's final birdie putt that would have forced a playoff with Vaughn Taylor lips out on the 18th hole at Pebble Beach, giving the 39-year-old Taylor the one-stroke win at the AT&T Pebble Beach National Pro-Am. The win is a near fairy tale for Taylor, without a PGA Tour card for three years and 11 years removed from his last PGA Tour win. Vaughn plays Pebble Beach with a light golf bag with a kickstand so he could save money on excess baggage fees while flying. The week before his win at Pebble Beach, Taylor withdraws from a Web.com Tour event in Colombia due to a bad stomach ailment and only flew to Pebble Beach because it was a cheaper flight than flying home to his home in Augusta, Georgia and he hoped he could get into the event as an alternate. Taylor makes four birdies in a row starting on the 13th hole, capped with a 30-footer on the 16th hole, to shoot a final-round 65. "Just absolutely amazing," says Taylor of his victory.

1999 – Tiger Woods follows up his third-round 62 with a final-round 65 to win the Buick Invitational by two shots over runner-up Billy Ray Brown for his eighth career PGA Tour title. Woods makes an eagle on the final hole at Torrey Pines to clinch the victory, his first in nine months. "It was Tiger's tournament to lose," Brown, the runner-up, says. "All I could do was go free-wheel and he's the guy who had pressure on him. And you see how he responded to the pressure. An eagle on the last hole is just indicative of the kind of player he is."

1971 – Arnold Palmer ends a 14-month title drought and wins the Bob Hope Desert Classic for a fourth time for his 58th career

PGA Tour title. The 41-year-old Palmer rolls in a 25-foot birdie putt on the first playoff hole to beat 29-year-old Ray Floyd. "You know what a struggle it's been and all the chances I've had to win in the last 14 months and naturally all that was on my mind as I stood over the ball, but fortunately, I hit it good," Palmer says. "I gave it all I got and it's funny how all the hard work had to come down to just one putt."

February 15

2015 – Brandt Snedecker wins the AT&T Pebble Beach National Pro-Am for the second time in three years and breaks his own scoring record, shooting 22-under-par score of 265. Snedeker shoots a bogey-free five-under round of 67 in the final round and finishes three-shots clear of runner-up Nick Watney. "I feel like I'm relevant again," says Snedeker after winning for the first time in 18 months.

2004 – John Daly wins the Buick Invitational at Torrey Pines in San Diego – his first tournament victory in 189 starts over nearly nine years – winning a three-way playoff with Luke Donald and Chris Riley. Daly hits a 100-foot bunker shot on the par 5 18th hole that nestles to within four inches of the cup for birdie that wins him the tournament. The win is Daly's fifth PGA Tour title and the first since he won the Open Championship at St. Andrews in 1995.

February 16

2014 – Billy Payne, chairman of the Augusta National Golf Club, announces that due to damage sustained during an ice storm, the famed Eisenhower Tree that once guarded the 17th fairway was too damaged to preserve.

2003 – Tiger Woods wins the Buick Invitational at Torrey Pines in San Diego for the second time for his 35th career PGA Tour title, shooting a four-under par 68 to beat runner-up Carl Pettersson by four strokes. The win comes in the 2003 season debut for Woods, who returns to competitive play after a six-week recuperation from surgery on his left knee. Woods is paired with Phil Mickelson in the final group in the final round, giving the tournament the buzz of a major championship, but Mickelson is only able to shoot a final round of even par 72 to finish six shots back in fourth place. "He's the best in the world for a reason," Arron Oberholser, who ties for fourth with Mickleson, says to Tod Leonard of the *San Diego Union-Tribune* of Woods. "He's amazing…The guy took a month and a half off and dusted the field. I mean, c'mon."

February 17

1955 – Mike Souchak shoots a record-tying round of 60 in the first round of the Texas Open at Brackenridge Park in San Antonio. Souchak's round equals the record-low round shot by five other players, two on the very same course. Souchak's round ties the scores set by Al Brosch, also at Brackenridge Park in the third round of the 1951 Texas Open, Bill Nary at the El Paso Country Club in the third round of the 1952 El Paso Open, Ted Kroll, also at Brackenridge Park in the third round of the 1954 Texas Open, Wally Ulrich at the Cavalier Yacht & Country Club in the second round of the 1954 Virginia Beach Open and Tommy Bolt at the Wethersfield Country Club in the second round of the 1954 Insurance City Open in Connecticut. Souchak also shoots a record 27 on the back nine, a record that is broken by Corey Pavin, who shoots a 26 on his front nine in Milwaukee in 2006. The record round of 60 stands until 1977 when Al Geiberger shots a 59 at the Memphis Classic.

1974 – Dave Stockton wins the Los Angeles Open with one of the greatest approach shots ever hit at the famed Riviera Country

Club. Stockton holds a one-shot lead over Sam Snead on the 18th tee and Snead, in an act of gamesmanship, tells Stockton that he birdied the last two holes of the tournament in 1950 to beat Ben Hogan. Angered at Snead's behavior, Stockton mishits his tee shot left in the deep rough and faces a 244-0yard shot from a side-hill lie in deep rough. "I remember the ball was about eight inches below my feet," Stockton writes in his book *My Greatest Shot*, "and Sam was standing out on the fairway next to my caddie." Still incensed at Snead, Stockton proceeds to hit a three-wood approach to 12 feet from the hole. "After I hit it," Stockton writes, "I walked past Snead and said, 'I guess Hogan didn't hit it that close.'" Stockton makes birdie to beat Snead and John Mahaffey by two shots and register his seventh career PGA Tour title. The Riviera Country Club places a plaque where Stockton hit his famous shot. He said he has tried to replicate the shot at least 20 times since but has not come close.

February 18

1995 – Defending champion Scott Hoch participates in one of the most famous groupings in golf history in the first round of the Bob Hope Desert Classic as he plays with Bill Clinton, the sitting President of the United States, and former U.S. Presidents George H.W. Bush and Gerald Ford. Bush shoots a 92, despite hitting spectators with two of his shots, and beats Clinton by a stroke and Ford by eight shots. Hoch shoots a 70.

1968 – George Knudson of Canada wins his fifth career PGA Tour title at the Phoenix Open Invitational by three shots over runners-up Julius Boros, Sam Carmichael and Jack Montgomery. Knudson stays on a hot streak in the Arizona desert as he wins the following week at the Tucson Open shooting a final-round 65 to beat Frank Beard and Frank Boynton by one stroke. Knudson goes on to win eight times on the PGA Tour to become the most prolific Canadian winner on the PGA Tour until Mike Weir also wins eight titles. Weir, however, wins a major title at the Masters in 2003, while Knudson's best showing at a major comes at the 1969 Masters, where he finishes in second place, one stroke behind George Archer.

2007 – Charles Howell, III wins his second title on the PGA Tour beating Phil Mickelson on the third hole of a sudden-death playoff at the Nissan Open at Riviera Country Club in Los Angeles. Howell fires a final-round 65 and benefits from Mickelson making a bogey on the final hole to drop into the playoff. "I certainly felt like I had the tournament in control," says Mickelson, who won at Pebble Beach the week before and leads Howell by three shots entering the final round. "If I par the last hole, I win."

2001 – Joe Durant shoots a final-round 65 and sets a record for the lowest score under par in a 90-hole PGA Tour event while winning the Bob Hope Classic in La Quinta, Calif. Durant finishes at 324 and 36-under par, breaking the mark of 35-under par set in the same event in 1993 by Tom Kite. He finishes four shots better than runner-up Paul Stankowski. "It was really a magical week," Durant says. "It seemed like every time I needed to make a crucial putt, I did."

February 19

1967 – Tied for the lead on the final tee of the Tucson Open Invitational, Arnold Palmer hits his tee shot into the water, makes double bogey but still wins by one stroke over runner-up Chuck Courtney, who also hits his final tee shot into the water and makes triple bogey. "I have never made a double-bogey and won when it was this close, but you have to win both ways – with bad rounds and good ones," says Palmer. After shooting rounds of 66, 67 and 67, Palmer has a four-shot lead entering the final round, but is caught by Courtney on the ninth hole of the final round after he makes birdie and Palmer makes the first of his two double bogeys on the day. Courtney again ties Palmer on the 16th hole at Tucson National Golf Club with a birdie before he hits his drive into the water on the final hole. Palmer then incredibly follows Courtney into the water with his tee shot 70 yards farther down the fairway. After hitting his approach shot into the greenside trap and blasting 40 feet beyond the hole, Courtney misses his double-bogey putt while Palmer leaves his six-foot bogey putt on the lip for a tap-in putt for what is his 50th career PGA Tour victory. "What can you say?" says Palmer. "I thought after Chuck hit into the water that all I had to do was get it in the fairway. I thought I hit about as good a drive as I could hit but it rolled dead (into the water.)"

1978 – Dr. Gil Morgan, a licensed optometrist, shoots a final-round 70 at Riviera Country Club and beats Jack Nicklaus by two shots to win the Los Angeles Open for his second PGA Tour title. Nicklaus flubs a chip shot on the 15th hole and makes double-bogey which turns out to be the turning point in the final round. Says Morgan, "I never in my fondest dreams thought I'd ever beat Jack Nicklaus head to head on one of the greatest courses."

2017 – Dustin Johnson becomes the 20th man to earn the No. 1 world ranking after his decisive victory at the Genesis Open at Riviera Country Club in Los Angeles. Johnson leads by as many as nine-shots on the final day but finishes with a final-round 71 to finish at 17-under-par 267 to beat runners-up Thomas Pieters of Belgium and Scott Brown by five shots. When asked about how it feels to be the No. 1 ranked player in golf, Johnson says, "It sounds good."

February 20

1955 – Mike Souchak establishes a PGA Tour scoring record for 72 holes – shooting a 257 over four rounds – and wins the Texas Open in San Antonio. Souchak shots a six-under 65 in the final round to win by seven shots and earns him the first-prize paycheck of $2,200. Souchak's record stands until 2001 when Mark Calcavecchia shoots 256 at the Phoenix Open. Calcavecchia's record is subsequently broken when Tommy Armour III shoots 254 at the 2003 Valero Texas Open. Writes the Associated Press of Souchak, "Dressed in blue wind breakers and wearing deerskin gloves, the 27-year-old 210 pound former Duke University football star laughed at the elements it was near freezing and Brackenridge Park sobby 6,400 yards were swept by a raw wind."

1994 – Scott Hoch breaks out of a five-year winless drought and wins the Bob Hope Desert Classic, shooting a final-round 70 to give him a three-stroke win over Fuzzy Zoeller, Jim Gallagher, Jr. and Lennie Clements. Hoch had not won on the PGA Tour since the 1989 Las Vegas Invitational, his first tournament since he missed a short putt that would have won him the Masters in a playoff with Nick Faldo.

February 21

1993 – After winning his first career PGA Tour title as an amateur at the Northern Telecom Open in Tucson, Arizona in 1991, Phil Mickelson wins his first title as a professional at the Buick Invitational of California at Torrey Pines in his hometown of San Diego. Mickelson shoots a final-round 65 and wins by five shots over runner-up Dave Rummells. "When I was a kid, I used to come out here and watch the big guys play and dream of playing here someday," Mickelson says of Torrey Pines. "To win here gives me a really special feeling." While Mickelson was unable to accept the first-prize paycheck of $180,000 with his win at Tucson in 1991 while he was a junior at Arizona State, he was able to accept the prize money for his second tournament victory. Quips Mickelson, "This time I'm going to accept the check."

1982 – Tom Watson sinks a 30-foot birdie on the third hole of a sudden-death playoff with Johnny Miller to win his 29th career PGA Tour title at the Glen Campbell Los Angeles Open at Riviera Country Club. Watson, winless in eight months, benefits from Miller making bogey on the 17th and 18th holes to fall into the playoff. "I got lucky," says Watson, who wins again in California four months later at the U.S. Open at Pebble Beach.

February 22

1981 – Johnny Miller sets a new scoring record at the Riviera Country Club, posting a 14-under-par score of 270 to win the Los Angeles Open by two shots over runner-up Tom Weiskopf. Miller's 21st title of his career breaks the previous tournament record of 272 set by Hale Irwin in 1976, but his mark his upstaged by six shots four years later by Lanny Wadkins. Says Miller of winning at Riviera, "To me, winning here is as close to a major tournament as you can get."

1938 – "Lighthouse" Harry Cooper wins the Crescent City Open in New Orleans by four strokes over runner-up Harold "Jug" McSpaden. Cooper pockets $1,200 in winning the tournament that eventually is branded the New Orleans Open.

2009 – Amateur Danny Lee of New Zealand becomes the youngest ever winner on the European Tour at the time when he wins the Johnnie Walker Classic in Perth, Australia at the age of 18 years and 213 days (six months and 28 days). Lee is 77 days younger than Dale Hayes of South Africa when he won the 1971 Spanish Open. Matteo Manassero since wins the 2010 Castelló Masters Costa Azahar at the age of 17 years and 188 days to break Lee's record.

2015 – In her first start as the world's No. 1 golfer, 17-year-old Lydia Ko of New Zealand shoots a final-round two-under 71 and claims a two-stroke victory over South Korea's Amy Yang at the Women's Australian Open in Melbourne.

February 23

2014 – Jason Day finally beats Victor Dubuisson on the fifth extra hole of the 18-hole final match at the WGC-Accenture Match Play Championship in Tucson, Ariz., his second win on the PGA Tour. The Frenchman Dubuisson is two down with two holes to play, but makes birdie on the 17th hole and takes advantage of a Day bogey on the final hole. Dubuisson then amazingly negotiates halves on the first two extra holes hitting from against cactus bushes in the desert brush, but eventually succumbs on the 23rd hole of the match. "Vic, man, he has a lot of guts," Day says. "He has a great short game – straight out of the cactus twice. For a 23-year-old kid, he's got a lot of game. We're going to see a lot of him for years to come."

2003 – Mike Weir birdies the second hole of a sudden-death playoff and beats Charles Howell III to win the Nissan Open at the Riviera Country Club in Los Angeles. The win is the second for Weir in three weeks after also winning the Bob Hope Chrysler Classic in the California desert on February 2. Weir's strong play continues through the spring as he wins his first major championship at the Masters in April.

February 24

2008 – Brian Gay shots a one-under par 69 to win the first PGA Tour title of his career with a two-stroke victory over Steve Marino at Mayakoba Classic in Mexico. "Yeah, it has been a long time," says Gay of winning on his 292nd career start. "Obviously a lot of hard work. It took me longer to get out on the Tour after college than I thought. Even though I was doing really well on the mini-tours and had my chances through the years and wasn't able to get it done. So this is really a big, big relief to finally do it." Gay shoots a 62 in the third round to take a five-stroke leading heading into the final round. He wins twice the following year in 2009 at the Heritage Classic in Hilton Head Island, S.C. and the St. Jude Classic in Memphis and again in 2013 at the Humana Challenge in Palm Springs, Calif.

February 25

2007 – Fifty-year-old Fred Funk beats Argentina's Jose Coceres on the second playoff hole to win the Mayakoba Golf Classic in Mexico to become the fifth oldest winner on the PGA Tour. Funk, a two-time winner on the PGA Champions Tours, joins Craig Stadler as only the second man to win a PGA Tour event after winning on the Champions Tour. Stadler won the 2003 PGA Tour's B.C. Open in Endicott, N.Y., played the same week as the Open Championship, one week after winning the Ford Senior Players Championship "I think I validated how good the players are on the Champions Tour," Funk says. "Even though you are 50 or 51 through 55 ... age doesn't really mean anything. I just want to see how long I can last."

1957 – Arnold Palmer wins his fifth career PGA tour title beating Doug Ford by one stroke to win the Houston Open at Memorial Park golf course. Six weeks later, Ford shoots 10 shots better than Palmer in the final round of the Masters to win his second major by three shots with a final-round 66, Palmer shooting a final-round 76 to drop from a tie for second place into a tie for eighth, eight shots back of Ford.

1973 – Lee Trevino benefits from Forrest Fezler shooting a final-round 76, missing four-foot putts on the 17th and 18th holes, and wins the Jackie Gleason Inverrary Classic in Lauderhill, Fla., by one shot. Trevino trails Fezler by three shots entering the final round and needs only an even-par round of 72 to win his 16th PGA Tour title, earning $52,000.

February 26

1978 – Rookie pro Nancy Lopez wins the first of her 48 LPGA tournament titles at the Bent Tree Classic in Sarasota, Fla., shooting a final-round 73 to beat Jo Ann Washam by one stroke. Lopez goes on to win nine titles during the year including, at one point, five straight tournaments. She goes on to win LPGA Rookie of the Year, LPGA Player of the Year and is named Associated Press Female Athlete of the Year. The *Sarasota Herald-Tribune* calls the 1978 season for Lopez "arguably the greatest any golfer has experienced."

2006 – The women's World Golf Rankings are officially introduced and Annika Sorenstam is the first player to rank No. 1, a position she holds for a total of 60 weeks before her retirement from the game at the end of the 2008 season.

1978 – Jack Nicklaus incredibly birdies the final five holes in one of the greatest finishes in golf history and wins his 65th career PGA Tour title, successfully defending his title at the Jackie Gleason Inverrary Classic at the Inverrary Golf Club in Lauderhill, Fla. Nicklaus chips in from 80 feet away on the 14th hole, then sinks a 12-foot birdie on No. 15. Nicklaus then chips in again from 18 feet away on the 16th hole, before rolling in a 20-foot birdie on the 17th hole. On the final hole, Nicklaus sticks a nine-iron approach shot to four feet that he also makes for birdie. "The man's amazing," says Hale Irwin. "He birdied No. 16, walked across water to No. 17 and teed it up…All I've got to say is I saw the finest golf played today that I've ever seen played in my life."

2012 – Playing in only his fifth career PGA Tour event, John Huh wins an eight-hole sudden death playoff with Robert Allenby to win the Mayakoba Golf Classic in Mexico. The 21-year-old Huh gets into the playoff when Allenby blows a two-stroke lead on the final hole of regulation, hitting a driver off the tee into trees on the right side of the 18th hole and scoring a double-bogey. The eight-hole playoff falls three holes shy of the PGA Tour record of 11 set at the 1949 Motor City Open when Cary Middlecoff and Lloyd Mangrum are declared co-winners. The playoff is the fifth to go eight holes and first since the 1983 Phoenix Open.

February 27

1992 – Sixteen-year-old Tiger Woods makes his debut on the PGA Tour playing as an amateur at the Nissan Los Angeles Open at Riviera Country Club, shooting an opening round 72. Woods shoots a 75 in the second round to miss the cut by six shots.

1972 – Tom Weiskopf wins the Jackie Gleason Inverrary Classic by one shot over Jack Nicklaus to claim his fifth PGA Tour title. Weiskopf eagles the 15th hole, but nearly throws away the title on the 17th hole as he walks through a bunker to survey his approach shot to the green and rakes his tracks en route back to his ball. PGA rules state that it is against the rules to improve your line, but the PGA rules that Weiskopf didn't rake the portion of the bunker in his direct line and the two-shot penalty is not enforced. Weiskopf earns $52,000 for the championship.

2011 – Luke Donald beats Martin Kaymer to win the WGC-Accenture Match Play Championship in Arizona, but Kaymer, playing for his fifth title in his last 11 starts dating back to the 2010 PGA Championship, moves to the world No. 1 ranking with the runner-up finish. Kaymer becomes the 14th man to reach the No. 1 spot, and the second German to do so after Bernhard Langer.

1977 – Jack Nicklaus makes three birdies and an eagle on the back nine of the Inverrary Golf and Country Club in Fort Lauderdale and wins the Jackie Gleason Inverrary Classic by five shots over runner-up Gary Player. Nicklaus, Player and Gil Morgan are tied for the lead after the front nine, before Nicklaus makes his back-nine charge to shoot a final-round 70 while Player fades to a 73 and Morgan and 76. "I really don't think I'm a great front runner," says Nicklaus after claiming his 62nd career PGA Tour title. "Once I got behind, I just made up my mind and played more aggressive. I played better being behind at that point. I got confidence. I sort of steamrolled ahead."

February 28

1971 – In the only staging of the PGA Championship in February as the first major championship of the season, Jack Nicklaus wins his second PGA title at the original PGA National Golf Club in Palm Beach Gardens, Fla. Nicklaus wins the title by two strokes over runner-up Billy Casper to become the first player in golf history to win a double career Grand Slam – winning all four major titles at least two times. Nicklaus shoots a final-round 73 to hold off Casper, who shoots a final-round 68. Nicklaus earns $40,000 for the title.

1993 – Tom Kite wins his 19th and final PGA Tour title at the Nissan Los Angeles Open at the Riviera Country Club with a three-stroke victory over runners-up Fred Couples, Payne Stewart, Dave Barr and Donnie Hammond. Kite rallies from four shots back to make birdies on five of the last seven holes to shoot a final-round 67 in the rain-shortened 54-hole event. The 43-year-old Kite, two weeks removed from winning the Bob Hope Desert Classic also in Southern California, earns a first-prize paycheck of $180,000 making him the first golfer to earn $8 million in a career.

2015 – Lydia Ko sets the course record at the Clearwater Golf Club in Christchurch by firing an 11-under 61 in the second round of the New Zealand Women's Open, equaling the Ladies European Tour for lowest 18-hole score, held by six other players. Ko, 17, goes on to win the title the next day with a winning margin of four shots.

2016 – In only his third start since the new rule against anchored putters in put in effect, Adam Scott wins the Honda Classic at PGA National in Palm Beach Gardens, Fla., with a conventional putter. Scott fires a final round 70 to beat Sergio Garcia by one stroke for his 12th PGA Tour title. Scott uses the anchored putter the previous five years, including during his win at the Masters in 2013.

February 29

2004 – Heath Slocum wins his first PGA Tour title at the Chrysler Classic of Tucson shooting a final-round 65 to beat runner-up Aaron Baddeley by one stroke. Slocum benefits by Baddeley three-putting the final hole, missing a five-foot par putt that would have forced a playoff. Slocum, from Baton Rouge, La., wins again the following year at the Southern Farm Bureau Classic in Mississippi and registers his biggest title at The Barclays during the FedEx Cup Playoffs in 2009 at Liberty National Golf Club just outside of Manhattan, beating golf titans Tiger Woods, Ernie Els, Padraig Harrington and Steve Stricker by one shot.

2004 – Tiger Woods wins the WGC-Accenture Match Play Championship with a 3&2 win over Davis Love, III in the 36-hole final at the LaCosta Resort and Spa in Carlsbad, Calif. Woods earns $1,200,000 for the title. Love actually leads Woods one-up after the first 18 holes but becomes rattled by a heckler starting on the 20th hole. After Love misses a par putt to even the match, the heckler yells out "Whoop" and then yells "No Love" on the tee of the 23rd hole of the day. Love steps away from his tee shot and demands the fan be identified and he refuses to play until he is kicked out. A man wearing a Tiger Woods hat is subsequently tossed out of the event and Love continues, but does not win another hole. "I wasn't going to play anymore until somebody got kicked out, because he had already cost me a hole," Love says. "I wasn't going to put up with it. I want to win and I want to play and I want to play fair." Woods takes the lead for good on the 25th hole with a 12-foot birdie putt. Says Woods of his victory, "It basically boils down to what my dad has always told me when it comes to match play. All you have to do is just be better than your opponent that day. That's it. All you have to do is win more holes than you lose. It's as simple as that."

MARCH

March 1

1998 – Tiger Woods loses for the first and only time in a playoff in an official PGA Tour event as little-known Billy Mayfair makes a five-foot birdie putt on the first extra hole to win the Nissan Open in Los Angeles, then played at the Valencia Country Club. Writes Clifton Brown in the *New York Times* of Mayfair taking down the No. 1 ranked Woods, the reigning Masters champion. "How much were the odds stacked against Mayfair? He had not won on the PGA Tour since 1995. He needed a birdie on the last hole of regulation just to force a playoff. The first playoff hole was a 566-yard par-5, an advantage for Woods because of his length. And Mayfair's career record in sudden death before today was 1-4, while Woods was 2-0." The Riviera Country Club, the usual venue for the storied event, is not used for the tournament due to the club also hosting the U.S. Senior Open that year, and the club's membership decline to have their course closed for two events during the season.

1991 – At the age of 51, Jack Nicklaus shoots a 63 at the famed "Blue Monster" at the Doral Country Club in the second round of the Doral Open in Miami, one off the course record. "That's the best round of golf I've ever seen him play," says playing partner Andy Bean. "I don't think he mis-hit one shot the entire day." Nicklaus agrees, saying, "I didn't miss one." Nicklaus is one off the lead of Kenny Perry and ends up finishing in a tie for fifth, his first top-five finish on the PGA Tour since he won the 1986 Masters. After shooting a second-round 65, Paul Azinger is surprisingly disqualified from the event when it is discovered via a television viewer who calls the PGA Tour that he illegally moved loose impediments after taking his stance in a water hazard on the 18th hole the previous day. After officials review the video, it is determined that Azinger did in fact violate the rule. Since he was not assessed a two-stroke penalty for the violation, he signed an incorrect scorecard for his first round score of 69 and is thus disqualified.

1992 – Fred Couples recovers from hitting his opening tee shot out of bounds to win the Los Angeles Open at Riviera Country Club for the second time, beating Davis Love III on the second hole of a sudden-death playoff. Couples makes a double-bogey 7 on the first hole, but rallies to shoot a final-round 70 that ties Love, who shoots a final-round 69. "I started out with an OB on the first hole and it got better," says Couples, who also won at event in 1990. The win is the seventh of 15 career titles for Couples, who wins his first and only major championship at the Masters six weeks later.

March 2

2014 – Paula Creamer sinks a 75-foot eagle on the second playoff hole with Azahara Munoz to win the HSBC Women's Championships in Singapore. Creamer shoots a final-round 69 and comes from four shots back of third-round leader Karrie Webb to win the title. "I could stand there all day long and putt that and not get it within six or seven feet, but it just happens sometimes," says Creamer of her incredible winning putt. The win is the first for Creamer since her victory at the 2010 U.S. Women's Open.

2015 – Forty-three-year-old Padraig Harrington wins his first PGA Tour event since the 2008 PGA Championship beating 21-year-old Daniel Berger in the second hole of a sudden-death playoff at the Honda Classic. Harrington holds a one-shot lead on the 17th hole, but hits his tee-shot on the par 3 into the water and double-bogeys the hole to fall one shot back of Berger, who is in the clubhouse at six-under-par. Harrington then birdies the final hole, sinking a 15-footer to tie Berger. After both players par the first playoff hole – the 18th hole – Harrington pars the 17th hole to win after Berger's tee shot lands in the water. Harrington becomes the second player in as many weeks to win on the PGA Tour with a world ranking of No. 297, following James Hahn's win the previous week in Los Angeles.

1975 – Jack Nicklaus leads the Jackie Gleason Inverrary Classic by six shots four holes into his final round, but double-bogeys the 12th, 14th and 15th holes and goes on to lose the title to Bob Murphy. "I gave the tournament away," Nicklaus says simply after the round.

1997 – Nick Faldo wins his ninth and final career PGA Tour title shooting a final-round 68 to win the Nissan Open at the Riviera Country Club in Los Angeles, three shots ahead of runner-up Craig Stadler.

March 3

2012 – Rory McIlroy wins the Honda Classic by two shots over Tiger Woods and Tom Gillis to clinch the No. 1 World Golf Ranking for the first time. McIlroy holds steady and shoots a final-round 69 to win his fifth career title, despite Woods charging to a final-round 62, including an eagle on the final hole. "It was tough today, especially seeing Tiger make a charge," says McIlroy. "I knew par golf would probably be good enough. To shoot one under in these conditions, when you go into the round with the lead, is very nice. And I was just able to get the job done." McIlroy becomes the 16th player to achieve the No. 1 ranking since the world rankings began in 1986.

2002 – Ernie Els holds off a charging Tiger Woods and wins his ninth PGA Tour title at the Genuity Championships at the Doral Country Club in Miami. Els starts the day with an eight-shot lead, but Woods blisters the "Blue Monster" and draws within one shot of Els on the 12th hole before finishing two strokes back after a final-round 66. "He has wiped out leads like that before," says Els, who shoots a final-round of even par 72, of Woods. "When he gets on a roll, it's hard sometimes for him to hit a bad shot. It's not a very comfortable feeling." Says Woods of Els and his victory, "I made him work for it."

1996 – Greg Norman shoots a final-round 66 and wins the Doral Ryder Open for a third time in seven years with a two-shot victory over runners-up Vijay Singh and Michael Bradley. "I feel comfortable here," Norman says of the "Blue Monster" at the Doral Country Club. "I'm comfortable on the greens and on the tees. I've played it in all wind directions. I love the layout. It makes you use every aspect of your game."

March 4

1991 – Rocco Mediate becomes the first player to win a PGA Tour event using a long putter when he beats Curtis Strange on the first hole of a sudden-death playoff in a weather-delayed Monday finish at the Doral-Ryder Open in Miami. Mediate wins the first of his six career PGA Tour titles using a 49-inch center-shafted putter that he pushes against his sternum. He makes birdie on the last two holes of regulation to tie Strange, then makes a six foot birdie putt on the first playoff hole for the win. Writes Jaime Diaz in the *New York Times* of the longer putters that eventually become banned in golf at the end of the 2015 season, "The longer putters are designed to help cure the yips – the involuntary jumping of a golfer's hands on short puts. By holding the tip of the putter against his chest, the player is able to turn the shaft into a pendulum, making the stroke longer and smoother." Mediate improves his putting standing on the PGA Tour from 165th to 36th since using the longer putter.

1990 – Greg Norman fires a course-record final-round 62 at the Doral Country Club in Miami, comes from seven-shots back to force a playoff with Paul Azinger, Tim Simpson, Mark Calcavecchia and wins the tournament by chipping in for eagle on the first playoff hole. The dramatic win exorcises some of the ghosts Norman had felt after losing the 1986 PGA Championship to Bob Tway on a hole-out from the bunker and the 1987 Masters on a miracle chip from Larry Mize on the second playoff hole. Writes Jaime Diaz in the *New York Times*, "It's a new decade, and today at the Doral Ryder Open Greg Norman played sensational golf to answer those who spent the 1980's labeling him the golfer who has done less with more than anyone else in the game's history." Says Norman after the win and his past heart-break losses, "I don't live in the past because I'm such a positive person...What goes around comes around. It's a lot easier to forget the 80's when a new decade begins. I've started this decade basically with a fresh mind."

March 5

2017 – Dustin Johnson wins in his first start as the world's No. 1 player at the World Golf Championship Mexico Championship in Mexico City by one shot over runner-up Tommy Fleetwood. The win is the 14th in Johnson's career and his fifth in his last 15 starts that also includes his win at the 2016 U.S. Open at Oakmont. Johnson defends the title he won a year earlier at the Trump National Doral in Miami.

2015 – J.B. Holmes fires an opening round 62, equaling the course record at the "Blue Monster" at the Doral Country Club in Miami, in the opening round of the World Golf Championships. The record-tying round is played when the scoring average for the day is 73.39, almost 11 and a half strokes off the Holmes score. Holmes equals the course record set by Greg Norman, set in the final round in 1990 and again in the third round of 1993. The Holmes round, however, is played on the new, tougher and longer redesigned "Blue Monster" course with water in play on four more holes, instituted by new owner Donald Trump in 2014.

March 6

1972 – Jack Nicklaus wins the Doral Eastern Open in Miami, earning a first-prize paycheck of $30,000 to put him ahead of Arnold Palmer on the all-time PGA Tour money list. The Nicklaus earnings in 11 years as a professional increases to $1,477,200.86 with the victory, moving past Palmer and his $1,471,226.83 in winnings in 18 years of professional golf. Nicklaus wins his 40th career PGA Tour event with a final-round 70 to beat Lee Trevino and Bob Rosburg by two strokes in the weather-delayed Monday finish. The day before, Nicklaus shoots a 64, equaling his then course record on the "Blue Monster."

1993 – Greg Norman ties his own course record of 62 at the Doral Country Club in Miami during the third round of the Doral Open. As when he closed with his final-round of 62 at the famed "Blue Monster" course en route to winning in 1990, Norman goes on to win again at Doral the following day for his 12th PGA Tour title, needing only a two-under par 70 to beat runners-up Paul Azinger and Mark McCumber by four shots.

March 7

2004 – Craig Parry holes out with a six-iron from 176 yards out to miraculously win the Ford Championship at Doral Country Club in Miami on the first hole of a playoff with Scott Verplank. Parry's miracle eagle on the 18th hole gave him his second of two career PGA Tour titles and earns him the first prize of $900,000. "It's amazing," Parry says. "I probably won't be able to put into words what actually happened." Writes the Associated Press of the event's crazy conclusion, "The 38-year-old Australian realized the ball was in the cup by the reaction of the packed gallery surrounding the green. Parry tossed his club, kicked his left leg up and pumped his right fist. Then he hugged his caddie, his brother Glenn."

1982 – Tom Kite holes an eight-iron chip from the fringe to beat Jack Nicklaus and Denis Watson in the first hole of a sudden-death playoff to win the Bay Hill Classic in Orlando. The win is Kite's fourth of his career and earns him $54,000. Kite posts his final-round 69 early in the afternoon and watches as Watson and Ray Floyd and third-round leader Nicklaus falter in their final rounds. Nicklaus shoots a final-round four-over-par 75, despite two late birdies that get him into the playoff. Says Nicklaus, "I'll totally forget this day, I hope."

March 8

1992 – Ray Floyd joins Sam Snead as the only men to win on the PGA Tour in four decades when he shoots a final-round 70 to win the Doral Ryder Open in Miami by two shots over runners-up Fred Couples and Keith Clearwater. The win for the 49-year-old Floyd is his 22d career win, also tying Snead for the longest span of winning titles on the PGA Tour at 29 years. Floyd wins his first PGA Tour title at the 1963 St. Petersburg Open at the age of 20 and also wins in all, five titles in the 1960s, six titles in the 1970s, 10 in the 1980s to go with what would be his final tour win at Doral in the 1990s. Floyd's win also makes him the oldest player to win a PGA Tour event since Art Wall won the 1975 Milwaukee Open at the age of 51 and he becomes the fifth oldest player to win a PGA Tour event at the time. Later in the year, Floyd also wins on the Champions Tour after he turns 50 years old on September 4, becoming the first player in golf history to achieve that feat in the same year.

2015 – Dustin Johnson shoots a final-round three-under-par 69 at the Trump National Doral and wins the Cadillac Championship by one shot over runner-up J.B. Holmes. The win for Johnson comes one month after he returns to the PGA Tour after a six-month absence from professional golf to work on personal issues.

1981 – Tom Kite wins his third PGA Tour title at the American Motors Inverrary Classic in Lauderhill, Fla., by one stroke over Jack Nicklaus. Kite birdies the 16th and 17th holes while Nicklaus misses a three-foot par putt on the final hole that would have forced a playoff. Curtis Strange, who holds a four-shot lead going into the final round, makes bogey on the final three holes to lose the title.

March 9

1964 – Gary Player wins a playoff for the first time in his career – a three-way 18-hole playoff with Arnold Palmer and Miller Barber – to win the Pensacola Open in Florida. Player shoots a one-under-par 71 to beat defending champion Palmer by one stroke and Barber by three strokes. Player was previously 0-7 in playoffs in his career.

1997 – Steve Elkington survives the new bunkers at Doral's "Blue Monster" course in Miami and wins the seventh of 10 PGA Tour titles at the Doral-Ryder Open, firing a final-round 69 to beat runners-up Larry Nelson and Nick Price by two strokes. Four-time major winner and Miami resident Ray Floyd is hired to remake the bunkering on the course to make it more difficult, but causes more havoc for players than anticipated. Writes Jaime Diaz in *Sports Illustrated*, "Floyd topped off his work with thousands of tons of fluffy white sand, and because it hadn't had time to settle and was therefore inconsistent, the pros played as if Gene Sarazen had never invented the sand wedge."

March 10

1963 – Arnold Palmer shoots a final-round 67 and overcomes a four-shot lead of little-known Harold Kneece and wins his 38th PGA Tour title at the Pensacola Open Invitational. Palmer earns a first prize of $3,500 for his second of two titles in Pensacola, after winning in the Florida panhandle city in 1960.

2002 – Four years after inspiring top 25 finishes at the Masters and the U.S. Open as a college sophomore from Georgia Tech, Matt Kuchar wins his first PGA Tour title at the Honda Classic, posting a 19-under-par score of 269 to beat Brad Faxon and Joey Sindelar by two strokes. After his high-profile showing at the Masters and the U.S. Open as the reigning U.S. Amateur champion, Kuchar elects not to turn professional and finish his degree at Georgia Tech and does not turn professional until 2000.

1985 – Playing in just the third event since undergoing back surgery the previous September, reigning U.S. Open champion Fuzzy Zoeller wins his seventh PGA Tour title with a final-round 67 to win the Bay Hill Classic in Orlando. "To be just three weeks out on the tour and get a win is a great feeling," says Zoeller, who earns the first-prize of $90,000. "I feel wonderful right now…I'm on cloud nine. Anytime you beat these guys it's exciting. I don't think you'll find four tougher finishing holes anywhere--they'll bring out the man in you."

March 11

1945 – Byron Nelson's record of 11 consecutive tournament victories begins at the Miami Four-Ball Championship at the Miami Springs Country Club. Nelson teams up with Harold "Jug" McSpadden and does not lose at another golf event for five months, winning the Charlotte Open, the Greensboro Open, the Durham Open, the Atlanta Open, the Montreal Open, the

Philadelphia Inquirer Invitational, the Chicago Victory Open, the PGA Championship, the Tam O'Shanter Open and the Canadian Open consecutively. The 11-win win streak ends in early August when he finishes fourth at the Memphis Open. He wins a total of 18 events during the year and earns $63,335.66. Nelson is not eligible to serve in the war due to a condition where his blood does not clot in a normal manner.

1979 – Larry Nelson wins the first of 10 career PGA Tour titles, claiming a three-stroke victory over runner-up Grier Jones at the Jackie Gleason Inverrary Classic in Lauderhill, Fla. Nelson goes on to win three major championships of his nine other PGA Tour events – the 1981 and 1987 PGA Championships and the 1983 U.S. Open.

1984 – Tom Kite shoots a final round of seven-under par 65 and birdies four of the last six holes to beat Jack Nicklaus by two shots to win the Doral-Eastern Open in Miami. Kite sinks a 30-foot birdie putt on the final hole to clinch his sixth career PGA Tour title. "Yes it is fun to beat Jack," jokes Kite of beating Nicklaus. "You know it's ironic. Of the three tournaments I've won in Florida, Jack has finished second or tied for second. It's always fun to win on a good golf course and it's more fun to win on a good golf course over a classy field."

March 12

1978 – Tom Weiskopf withstands a furious challenge from Jack Nicklaus and edges the Golden Bear by one shot on the final green of a 36-hole final day at the Doral–Eastern Open in Miami. Nicklaus fires a back-nine 30, with only nine putts buoyed by chip-in eagles on the 10th and 12th holes – after chipping in for birdie on the ninth hole – and nearly chips in for a birdie on the final hole that would have tied Weiskopf and force a playoff. Says Nicklaus of his back nine charge, "It's a lot of fun holing wedges and all those other things that were happening.

I was just kind of waiting to see what would happen next. Tom deserved to win."

March 13

1960 – Arnold Palmer wins for the third consecutive week, winning the Pensacola Open, his 17th PGA Tour title. The previous two Sundays, Palmer wins the Texas Open and the Baton Rouge Open and wins eight events during the year, including his second Masters title and his first and only U.S. Open title.

2005 – Padraig Harrington, a winner of 10 previous events worldwide, wins the Honda Classic for his first PGA Tour title in the second hole of a sudden-death playoff with Vijay Singh at the Country Club of Mirasol in Palm Beach Gardens, Fla. Harrington wins the title when Singh, one week removed from relinquishing his six-month reign as the world's No. 1 golfer, misses a three-foot putt for bogey. "I thought it was a gimme," says Harrington, who shoots a final-round nine-under-par 63 to clinch his spot in the playoff.

2016 – Charl Schwartzel comes from five shots back in the final round and beats Bill Haas with a par on the first hole of a playoff to win the Valspar Championship in Palm Harbor, Fla., his first win in the United States since the 2011 Masters. Lee McCoy, a senior at the University of Georgia who grew up next to the Innisbrook Resort, finishes in fourth place to register the best finish by an amateur on the PGA Tour since 17-year-old Justin Rose finishes in a tied for fourth at the 1998 Open Championship at Royal Birkdale.

March 14

2004 – Todd Hamilton, a journeyman pro who was the all-time leading non-Japanese money winner on the Japan Tour, wins his first PGA Tour event at the Honda Classic in Palm Beach Gardens, Fla. Hamilton birdies the final two holes at the Country Club of Mirasol to beat Davis Love III by one stroke. Four months later, Hamilton shocks the world and wins the Open Championship at Royal Troon, beating Ernie Els in a four-hole playoff.

2014 – John Daly misses a four-foot par putt on the final hole to shoot a career-high round of 90 in the second round of the Valspar Championship in Palm Harbor, Fla. Daly's scorecard is "highlighted" with a 12 on the 16th hole – with four balls in the water – and 70 putts over two rounds. Says Daly of his 12, "I got two good drops and hit a heel-cut 3-wood into the water. Then I shanked a seven-iron, chili-dipped a chip, it was buried, didn't get that out... It was a good 12. I got up-and-down for 12."

1993 – Despite admitting "I choked like a dog coming in," Fred Couples hangs on to win the Honda Classic at Weston Hills Country Club in Weston, Fla. on the second hole of a playoff with Robert Gamez. Couples leads by four shots with eight holes to go in the final round but concludes with two birdies, two pars, three bogeys and one double-bogey. After making double-bogey on No. 16 by slicing his four-iron into the lake, Couples, trailing Gamez by one shot, holes a bunker shot for birdie from 20 feet away to regain a share of the lead. He wins the title with a par on the second playoff hole to win his 10th career PGA Tour title.

March 15

2015 – Jordan Spieth wins his second PGA Tour title when he holes a 28-foot birdie putt on the third playoff hole to win the

Valspar Championship in Palm Harbor, Fla. Spieth's birdie on the par-3 17th hole on the Copperhead Course at the Innisbrook Resort comes after Sean O'Hair misses from 40-feet away and Patrick Reed leaves his second shot from the bunker four feet from the hole. "Putts like that are luck, right?" the 21-year-old Spieth says of his winning putt. "If that doesn't hit the hole, it's four feet past. I guess it's just my day." Spieth becomes the fourth player since 1940 to win two PGA Tour events before turning 22, joining Tiger Woods, Sergio Garcia and Robert Gamez.

1987 – Payne Stewart wins the Hertz Bay Hill Classic in Orlando and donates his entire winner's check of $108,000 to charity. Stewart registers a three-stroke victory over David Frost for this third career PGA Tour victory and his first since the 1983 Walt Disney World Classic.

March 16

2001 – Annika Sörenstam becomes the first woman to score a 59 in competition as she shoots the magic number in the second round of the Standard Register Ping at Moon Valley Country Club in Phoenix. Her round on the 6,459 yard par 72 course features 13 birdies and five pars, and includes a missed 10 foot putt on the final hole for a 58. "It was an incredible day, obviously," Sorenstam says. "I had a lot of thoughts in my head. I was trying to stay calm and hit good shots, trying to hit it straight every time." Sorenstam's 59 is two shots better than the previous best score on the LPGA Tour, a 61 shared by Karrie Webb and Se Ri Pak.

1975 – Playing without a pitching wedge for six holes, Jack Nicklaus shoots a final-round 68 to win the Doral Eastern Open in Miami with a three-shot win over Forrest Fezler and Bert Yancey. The head of the Nicklaus pitching wedge flies off on the practice range before the round, causing Nicklaus to have a business associate find fast-drying glue to repair the club. "It had to set awhile, but I got it back on the seventh hole," says Nicklaus. Nicklaus caps the win by hitting a three-iron approach from out of a divot to within 20 feet on the final hole and subsequently making the birdie putt. The win is the first for Nicklaus in the 1975 season and the 55th of his career. A month later, he wins one of his most historic victories at the Masters with a final-round duel with Johnny Miller, who finishes fourth at Doral, and Tom Weiskopf.

March 17

1963 – Raymond Floyd wins his first PGA Tour title at the St. Petersburg Open Invitational at the age of 20 years, six months becoming the youngest player to win a PGA Tour event since 1928. A pro for only four months, Floyd fails to qualify for nine of his first 10 career PGA events and missing out on the money on the one tournament he did qualify into, the Lucky International in San Francisco. "Winning the St. Pete Open was the best, and most surprising thing, that ever happened to me," Floyd says days later to the *Miami News*. "I won for a couple of reasons. I used to take a rather negative approach toward the tournament, telling myself I'd be satisfied to finish high enough to make some money. Last week, I took an affirmative approach and told myself I would not be happy with anything short of first place. Also, of course, I never hit the ball better and had a keener putting touch." Floyds goes on to win a total of 22 PGA Tour titles, including the Masters in 1976, the U.S Open in 1986 and the PGA Championship in 1969 and 1982.

1985 – Seve Ballesteros wins his seventh PGA Tour title at the USF&G Classic in New Orleans, benefitting from John Mahaffey's double-bogey on the final hole. Ballesteros shoots a final-round 68 of the rain-shortened 54-hole event, but makes bogey on the final hole to drop into a tie with Mahaffey, playing the 17th hole at the time. Mahaffey, however, hits his tee shot into tree roots on the right side of the fairway, then his second into the trees to the left side. He then chips into the fairway, hits an approach to the green and two putts for a double bogey to finish two shots behind Ballesteros. "I made up my mind a long time ago – you don't win a golf tournament by backing off," Mahaffey says of being aggressive on the final hole of the tournament. "I gave it my best shot."

March 18

2001 – Hale Irwin wins his 30th career title on the PGA Champions Tour, breaking the record of 29 set by Lee Trevino, with a five-stroke win over Tom Watson and Allen Doyle at the Siebel Classic in Silicon Valley in California. Irwin goes on to win a total of 45 Champions Tour events, his final victory coming at the 2007 MasterCard Championship at Hualalai in Hawaii.

1990 – Jodie Mudd wins the biggest title of his career at the Players Championship by one shot over Mark Calcavecchia at the TPC at Sawgrass in Ponte Vedra Beach, Fla. Calcavecchia mounts a final-round charge and pulls within one shot of Mudd as both players reach the famed island-green 17th hole. After Calcavecchia hits safely into the middle of the green, Mudd places his shot right by the flagstick. Calcavecchia then looks right at Mudd and says, "Tell me you pushed that. I mean he's good, but he ain't that good." Mudd admits he had pushed it a little bit, then makes the birdie putt and holds on to win.

2001 – Des Smyth of Ireland, a two-time Ryder Cupper for Europe, becomes the oldest winner on the European Tour when he captures the Madeira Islands Open at Santo da Serra in Portugal at the age of 48 years and 34 days. His record subsequently, is broken twice by Miguel Angel Jiménez at the Hong Kong Open in 2012 and 2013, winning the latter at the age of 49 years, 337 days.

March 19

1989 – Tom Kite holds on to beat Chip Beck by one stroke to win the Players Championship at the TPC at Sawgrass in Ponte Vedra Beach, Fla., the biggest win at that point in his career. "There is so much talk about 'Tom Kite has done this and done that but he's never won a major,' so you are going to have a tough time convincing me that this isn't one," says Kite of his Players win, the 12th of his PGA Tour career. Kite finishes with a nine-under-par score of 279 and earns $243,000. He wins his elusive first – and only – major title at the 1992 U.S. Open.

1978 – Jack Nicklaus wins the Tournament Players Championship for the third time – or as he puts it "was the only one to survive" – shooting a final-round 75 at the Sawgrass Country Club in Ponte Vedra Beach, Fla., to beat Lou Graham by one shot. Nicklaus hangs on despite by the wind-swept conditions, not making a birdie in his final-round and posting a final, four-round score of one-over-par 289. "It looks like I tried to play the round without making a putt," says Nicklaus, who wins $60,000. "I'm just fortunate that no one else took much a run at me. I just held on to win."

1961 – Bob Goalby makes a string of eight straight birdies – a PGA tournament record at the time – en route to winning the St. Petersburg Open in Florida. Goalby makes birdie from the eighth through the 15th holes at the Pasadena Country Club as he shoots a final-round 65 to beat runner-up Ted Kroll by three shots. "Goalby's round was something to see" writes the Associated Press. "So accurate was his iron play that he left himself only short putts as he went through the 15th before his streak was checked." Goalby's record is equaled seven times but not broken until 2009 when Mark Calcavecchia makes nine straight birdies in the second round of the Canadian Open.

March 20

1982 – Ray Floyd endures one of the strangest routes to a third-round tee time in the history of golf at the Tournament Players Championship in Ponte Vedra Beach, Fla. After finishing his second round the previous day, not expecting to make the cut, Floyd leaves north Florida and returns to his home in Miami. After the second round of the tournament is completed early Saturday, due to being suspended the previous night due to darkness, Floyd is informed that his score of (78-70=148) is good enough to make the cut. Floyd then has to charter a jet from Miami to Jacksonville airport, then charter a helicopter 30 miles to Ponte Vedra Beach. He reaches his 12:34 pm tee time with two minutes to spare. With no warm-up or any kind of pre-round preparation, Floyd shoots a 70.

2016 – Needing only a bogey on the final hole to shoot a 59 and a two-shot win at the Australasian PGA Tour event in Toowoomba, Australia, Tim Hart hits his tee shot ball out-of-bounds, makes triple bogey and falls into a playoff, which he loses to David Klein of Germany on the first extra hole. "After hitting the driver so well, I put the worst swing of the week on it right there," Hart says. "Mate, it's easy to be disappointed, but if someone had said I'd be in a playoff for the title when starting the day 20th, I would have grabbed it. Even on the 18th tee, I wasn't trying to think too much about breaking 60. I just wanted to stay aggressive because I hadn't seen a leaderboard and wanted to keep pushing. If I'd known I was three or four shots in front, maybe the two-iron comes out."

2016 – Trailing Kevin Chappell by one stroke with two holes to play, Jason Day birdies the 17th hole at Bay Hill Country Club and benefits from Chappell making bogey on the final hole to win the Arnold Palmer Invitational. Day hits a bunker shot from 100 feet away to four feet on the final hole to save par and hold on for the victory. The win earns him $1.34 million and a congratulatory handshake from the tournament host, 86-year-old Arnold Palmer. "I was able to walk up there and have a special moment with the King," Day said. "That's something I always wanted to do." Day, unfortunately, becomes the final Arnold Palmer Invitational champion to have the pleasure of shaking hands with Palmer after winning the tournament as "The King" passes away six months later.

1977 – Mark Hayes shoots a final-round 72 to win the Tournament Players Championship by two strokes over Mike McCullough. Hayes posts a final score of one-under-par 289 over the wind-swept Sawgrass Country Club in Ponte Vedra Beach, Fla., the first time the course hosts the event. Tom Watson holds a two-shot lead at the start of the back nine, but falters with a 41.

2016 – Kim Sei-Young of South Korea matches Annika Sorenstam's record for the lowest 72-hole score in LPGA tournament history, posting a 27-under par score of 261 at the LPGA Founders Cup in Phoenix, Arizona, capped with a final round 62. "It's a dream come true," Kim says. "Today scoring 10 under, it was my best score ever. I didn't know it was best score ever. I asked caddie, 'Did I hit 10-under?' He said, 'Yeah.' Amazing. Dream come true." Sorenstam set her mark in winning the 2001 Standard Register PING tournament at Moon Valley Country Club, also in Phoenix.

March 21

1940 – Ben Hogan wins his first PGA title at the North-South Open on the famed Pinehurst No. 2 course in North Carolina. After building a seven-shot lead after opening rounds of 66 and 67, Hogan holds on to play the final 36-holes on the final day in 74 and 70 to beat Sam Snead by three strokes. Hogan had been winless in his first seven years on tour and was on the verge of retiring to be a full-time golf teaching professional due to his lack of success.

1982 – Jerry Pate wins the Tournament Players Championship at the new TPC of Sawgrass in Ponte Vedra Beach, Fla., and celebrates the victory by famously throwing Pete Dye, the architect of the golf course, and Deane R. Beman, commissioner of the PGA Tour into the lake on the 18th hole. Pate fires a final-round 67 to post an eight-under par 280 over four rounds, two strokes better than runners-up Brad Bryant and Scott Simpson. Pate birdies the difficult and intimidating 17th and 18th holes to win the championship, his eighth PGA Tour title.

March 22

1934 – The first edition of the Masters tournament begins at Augusta National Golf Club, then known as the "Augusta National Invitation Tournament." The course is played in reverse nine holes in the first staging of the event (and again in 1935) before it is played in its current manner in 1936.

1998 – John Daly makes an 18 on the 543-yard par 5 sixth hole in the final round of the Bay Hill Invitational in Orlando. Describing the scene as coming out of the Kevin Costner golf movie "Tin Cup," *Orlando Sentinel* golf writer Jeff Babineau writes, "Daly knocked a drive into the lake that runs along the left side of the hole. He walked forward 25 yards, dropped a ball, then tried to carry the lake – an estimated 270-yard shot – with his 3-wood. He missed by a few feet. He then dropped again and again and again and again, each time failing to clear the water." Says Paul Goydos, who was keeping Daly's score, of the scene, "After the fifth or sixth time, I just lost track. He just kept going. The crowd started yelling, Tin Cup, Tin Cup ... it was fun. It wasn't as if he wasn't trying." Daly clears the lake on his seventh attempt – his 13th shot – but his ball buries in a hazard. His 15th shot, a 6-iron from the fairway, lands in a greenside bunker. From there, Daly blasts out and two putts from 25 feet for an 18. Daly then birdies the next hole and pars the eighth and ninth hole to score 49 for the front nine and finishes with an 85. Daly's score, however, is not the record for the highest score on a hole. At the 1938 U.S. Open, Ray Ainsley makes a 19 on the par-4 16th hole at Cherry Hills in Denver. Says Daly, "It wasn't that I didn't care. I just lost my patience. I was more or less ... determined. I had the courage to do it. I just didn't have the wisdom to bail out. The way I look at it, it's progress before perfection. I'm not going to worry about it. I didn't do anything wrong. I just got a hell of a lot of practice with that 3-wood." Ernie Els wins the tournament title on the day, his sixth career PGA Tour title.

1992 – Fred Couples wins the Nestle Invitational in Orlando by nine strokes – the biggest margin of victory in his PGA Tour career – to win his eighth PGA Tour title. After a third-round 63 at the Bay Hill Country Club, Couples only needs a final round 70 for his comfortable nine stroke margin over runner-up Gene Sauers. Couples takes over the No. 1 ranking in the official World Golf Rankings with the victory.

1981 – Raymond Floyd wins for the second consecutive week claiming the Tournament Players Championship in Ponte Vedra Beach, Fla., the week after winning at the Doral Eastern Open in Miami. Floyd beats Curtis Strange and Barry Jaeckel on the first hole of sudden death to win his 14th PGA Tour title with a three-under-par score of 285 – and $72,000. Floyd's win closes the five-year chapter of the event being played at the Sawgrass Country Club as the following year, the event moves across the street to the Tournament Players Club.

March 23

1980 – Lee Trevino wins the Tournament Players Championship at the Sawgrass Country Club Oceanside course, shooting a final-round 70 to hold off Ben Crenshaw by one shot. Crenshaw fires a final-round course-record 66 to threaten to win the title. At one point during the day, a "who's who" in golf are tied for second behind Trevino – Jack Nicklaus, Gary Player, Tom Watson, Seve Ballesteros, Hubert Green and Crenshaw. The win is Trevino's 23rd on the PGA Tour and earns him $72,000.

1997 – Three shots behind with eight holes to go, Phil Mickelson makes an Arnold Palmer-like charge to cap off a final-round 65 to win the Bay Hill Invitational hosted by Palmer in Orlando, Fla. "Going into today, I was trying to think that this was Arnie's tournament and what would he do?" says Mickelson. "He'd put on a charge, so that's what I tried to do." Mickelson's three-shot win over Stuart Appleby is his 10th career PGA Tour victory and earns him $270,000.

March 24

2002 – Unheralded New Zealander Craig Perks is the surprise winner at The Players Championship, incredibly finishing the difficult final three holes at the TPC at Sawgrass eagle-birdie-par with only one putt. Perks first chips in for eagle at the 16th hole, then sinks a 28-foot birdie at the famous 17th island hole and caps his two-shot victory over Stephen Ames by chipping in for par on the 18th hole. The 35-year-old Perks becomes the first player to win their first PGA Tour event at The Players but it becomes his only career win on tour in 202 starts. After he makes only one cut on the PGA Tour during his 2006 and 2007, Perks retires from professional golf in November 2007.

1994 – Greg Norman shoots course record equaling 63 in the opening round of Tournament Players Championship at the TPC at Sawgrass. Norman's 63 ties the record set by Fred Couples, who shoots a 63 in the third round of the event in 1992. In 2013, Roberto Castro also ties the course record in the opening round of the tournament, then contested in May.

2001 – Tiger Woods faces a near impossible triple-breaking, downhill, lightning fast 60-foot birdie try at the island-green

17th hole at the TPC at Sawgrass in the third round of the Players Championship and what results is one of best golf calls in television history. As soon as Woods hits the putt, NBC golf announcer Gary Koch tells viewers that the putt is "better than most" and repeats the phrase until the ball drops in the hole for a birdie. The crowd explodes and Woods pumps his first in the air.

1952 – Doug Ford, a future Masters and PGA Championship winner, wins his first PGA Tour event at the Jacksonville Open in unusual fashion as Sam Snead forfeits the 18-hole playoff scheduled for the following day. Snead says his decision to forfeit the title to Ford is based hitting a ball out of bounds in the second round, but a rules official ruled that the ball was in bounds, citing that the starter did not tell the players that the stakes had been moved after the first round. Says Snead, "I want to be fair about it. I don't want anyone to think I took advantage of the ruling."

March 25

1934 – Horton Smith wins the inaugural staging of the Augusta National Invitation Tournament, now known as the Masters, in Augusta, Ga. Smith's 20-foot birdie putt on the 17th hole – now the eight hole – is the salient shot that vaults him to a one-shot victory over Craig Wood. Smith wins $1,500 first prize for his four-under-par score of 284. Bobby Jones, the tournament co-founder and host, finishes finished ten strokes back at 294 in a tie for thirteenth place.

1990 – Robert Gamez holes out from 176 yards for an eagle two on the final hole at the Nestle Invitational to beat Greg Norman by one shot at Bay Hill in Orlando, Fla. The seven-iron approach from Gamez bounces three times and into the hole for one of the most incredible conclusions to an event in PGA Tour history.

2001 – Despite a bogey on the final hole, Tiger Woods wins the Players Championship by one shot over Vijay Singh, finishing off a final-round 67 in a rain-delayed Monday finish. The win is the first of two victories at the Players Championship for Woods, who earns $1.08 million for his 26th career title on the PGA Tour. Woods also goes on to win a second Players title in 2013 to go with his 1994 win at the TPC at Sawgrass at the U.S. Amateur.

2012 – Tiger Woods wins the Arnold Palmer Invitational in Orlando, Fla., for a seventh time, beating runner-up Graeme McDowell by five strokes. The win is the 72nd career win on the PGA Tour for Woods and his first since he is rocked by a sex scandal at the end of 2009. "I think he really just kind of nailed home his comeback," says McDowell. "Great to have a front-row seat watching maybe the greatest of all time doing what he does best – winning golf tournaments."

1979 – Enduring winds up to 45 mph, Lanny Wadkins survives the difficult conditions and wins the Tournament Players Championship by five strokes over runner-up Tom Watson. Wadkins becomes the first player to win the event at the Sawgrass Country Club under par by posting a four-round total of five-under-par 283, six shots better than the winning scores of the previous two champions at Sawgrass Mark Hayes and Jack Nicklaus. Scores soar in the final round in the blustery conditions, highlighted by Bob Murphy, who cards a final-round score of 92, 20 over par for the round. Says Wadkins of his final-round of even-par 72, "This is probably the best I have ever played."

1974 – Johnny Miller shoots a final round 70 to cap a wire-to-wire win at the Sea Pines Heritage Classic at Harbour Town Golf Links in Hilton Head, S.C. Miller beats runner-up Gibby Gilbert by three shots to win his fourth of his eventual eight tournament titles in 1974 and his seventh of 25 career titles. Following the win, the red-hot Miller is asked if he considers himself better than Jack Nicklaus and answers, "Maybe when I've won 10 more major titles and he's 45. Maybe then I'll say I'm better than he."

1973 – In near darkness, Jack Nicklaus beats Miller Barber on the second hole of a sudden-death playoff to win the Greater New Orleans Open for his 47th PGA tour title. Nicklaus makes birdie on the second playoff hole – the 38th hole played on a marathon final day, and earns $25,000. Says Barber, "I got beat by what I consider to be the best," says Barber. Nicklaus, for many years the victim of fans overtly rooting against him, particularly when playing Arnold Palmer and his legions of "Arnie's Army" fans in the 1960s, is in an opposite role on this day as fans not only cheer vigorously for the Golden Bear, but against Barber. "I've never seen anything like it – people pulling against you," Barber says. "I know people wanted Jack to win and I probably would have pulled for him if I wasn't in it. But it really hurt me. I just wasn't brought up that way. I don't pull against anyone."

March 26

2000 – Hal Sutton stares down Tiger Woods and beats him by one shot at the Players Championship. "Be the right club today….Yes!" is the famous remark Sutton makes to himself as his five-iron to the final green lands safely on the green, after his playing partner Woods, trailing by one shot, misses the green.

1995 – Lee Janzen wins the Players Championship by one shot over runner-up Bernhard Langer, nearly hitting into the water on the famed island-green 17th hole, but getting up and down for par from the pot bunker. He makes a testy four-foot par putt on the final hole to seal the victory. Janzen wins the tournament using a putter that he had thrown into a creek on the seventh hole at the same TPC at Sawgrass course in 1992. After throwing the putter in the water, he had second thoughts, marked the area where he tossed the putter in the water and had it arranged to be retrieved.

1967 – Gay Brewer wins the Pensacola Open in Florida for the second straight year, posting a 26-under-par score of 262 to win by six shots. Brewer falls five shots shy of Mike Souchak's all-time scoring record from the 1955 Texas Open, but, the previous day, he sets the 54-scoring record with a 25-under par score. His attempt to break the 72-hole scoring record is dampened by a down-pour rain that he endures on the final four holes of play. Brewer's 54-hole PGA Tour record is matched in 2003 by Ernie Els at the 2003 Tournament of Champions, Steve Stricker at the 2010 John Deere Classic and Pat Perez at the 2009 Bob Hope Chrysler Classic and, eventually broken by Patrick Reed at the 2014 Humana Classic.

2006 – Stephen Ames wins the Players Championship by six strokes over runner-up Retief Goosen in the final edition of the event being played in March before its move to a May calendar slot.

2015 – Aaron Baddeley makes one of the most improbably birdies in golf history on the 336-yard par-4 17th hole at the TPC San Antonio in the first round of the Valero Texas Open. After hitting his first drive out of bounds, Baddeley is forced to re-tee, striking his third shot with a penalty. His second drive, improbably, falls into the hole for a birdie three.

March 27

1994 – Greg Norman dominates the Players Championship at the TPC at Sawgrass shooting a third consecutive round of 67 to post a 72-hole record score of 264 – 24-under-par – and registers a four-shot victory over Fuzzy Zoeller. Before Norman holes out for the win, Zoeller famously wipes Norman's brow with a towel. "In my 20 years out here, I don't think I've seen a player play as well for 72 holes," says Zoeller. "He just did everything extremely well. He drove the ball exceptionally, putted exceptionally. There wasn't any whimper in his swing, none at all." Writes Larry Dorman in the *New York Times*, "With a singular performance in the final round of the Players Championship, Norman turned the proceedings into the Player Championship. He was alone in this one."

2005 – Forty-eight-year-old Fred Funk becomes the oldest winner of the Players Championship, surviving brutally windy conditions for a one-stroke victory over Luke Donald, Tom Lehman and Scott Verplank. Funk three-putts three times during his one-under-par 71 final round that features a scoring average of 76.5. Wind gusts reach as high as 50 mph that, at one point, cause white-caps to form in the famous pond that surrounds the 17th hole at the TPC of Sawgrass. Bob Tway scores a nine-over-par 12 – that includes four shots hit in the water – on the famed 17th hole marking the worst ever score on the 140-yard par three.

1960 – Forty-seven-year-old Sam Snead wins his 79th PGA Tour title at the De Soto Open Invitational in Sarasota, Fla., with a one-shot victory over Jerry Barber. For the title, Snead earns $5,300 and the use of a new car for a year with the win.

1988 – Jacksonville native Mark McCumber shoots a final-round 68 and wins the Tournament Players Championship by four strokes over Mike Reid in a much-celebrated win for the hometown golfer. McCumber wakes up at 5 am and has to finish 14 holes of his delayed third round before starting his final round. He does not make a bogey on the day until the 18th hole – with victory all but assured – fighting back tears and emotions as he receives a standing ovation from his hometown fans. "You can debate whether this is a major or not, but I beat the best field we've ever had and that makes me very proud," says McCumber.

March 28

1999 – David Duval, a native of nearby Jacksonville, wins The Players Championship and vaults to the No. 1 ranking in the World Golf Rankings. Duval's two-shot win over runner-up Scott Gump occurs on the same day that his father Bob Duval wins the Emerald Coast Classic title on the Champions Tour in Sandestin, Fla. The Duvals are the only father-son duo to win on the Champions Tour and the PGA Tour in the same week.

1982 – Tom Watson survives cold and blustery conditions and a three-hole-playoff by unheralded Frank Conner to win the Sea Pines Heritage Classic at Harbour Town Golf Links in Hilton Head, S.C. Watson makes par on the third playoff hole – the famed 18th hole – to win his 30th career PGA Tour title and his second title at Harbour Town after also winning in 1979. The tournament features some of the worst weather in memory, with temperatures hovering in the high 40s and wind gusts up to 25 miles per hour causing Watson to wear nylon rain pants and a woolen ski cap pulled below his ears for the three playoff holes.

1993 – Nick Price shoots a final-round 67 and wins The Players Championship by five shots over Bernhard Langer at the TPC at Sawgrass in Ponte Vedra Beach, Fla. Price's signature shot of his round comes on the par-4 fourth hole when his tee shot rests on the lip of a fairway bunker. With one foot in the bunker, Price hits a baseball type swing at the ball that incredibly results in a tap-in birdie. Price calls the swing "the greatest shot of my life."

1983 – First-time competitor Hal Sutton wins The Tournament Players Championship by one shot over Bob Eastwood, shooting a final-round 69 and benefitting from John Cook's double-bogey on the final hole. "Every hole on this golf course is a potential disaster," says Sutton. "I was just fortunate I was able to steer clear of most of the trouble." Cook is tied for the lead on the

18th tee, but his tee shot finds the water and he makes double-bogey to finish two strokes back.

1940 – Ben Hogan, dubbed a serial runner-up in his very early career, wins his second career individual PGA tournament title at the Greensboro Open, one week after winning his first title at the North-South Open at Pinehurst. Hogan shoots a 66 in the morning round at Sedgefield Country Club and an afternoon round of 67 and beats runner-up Craig Wood by nine shots to earn the first prize of $1,200. Writes the Associated Press, "Hogan was so consistently brilliant that it is hard to describe the type of game he played."

2004 – Twenty-three-year-old Adam Scott becomes the youngest winner of the Players Championship beating Padraig Harrington by one shot, sinking a 10-foot bogey putt on the final hole, after pulling his second shot in the water. "I just didn't let myself think about anything else then but making the putt," says Scott of his winning stroke. Scott's record, however, is broken in 2017 when 21-year-old Si Woo Kim of South Korea wins the Players Championship by three strokes over Ian Poulter and Louis Oosthuizen.

1976 – Hubert Green wins his third straight tournament, needing only a closing two-over-par 73 to win the Heritage Golf Classic by five strokes over Jerry McGee at Harbour Town Golf Links in Hilton Head, S.C. Green becomes the first player to win three straight tournaments since Johnny Miller wins the first three PGA Tour events in 1974 and only the third since Arnold Palmer wins three straight in 1962. Green wins the Doral Eastern Open and the Jacksonville Open the previous two weeks.

March 29

1987 – Sandy Lyle beats Jeff Sluman on the third hole of a sudden-death playoff to win the Players Championship for his third PGA Tour title. On the second hole of the playoff, the famed island-green 17th hole, Sluman has a six-foot putt to win the championship, but just before he is going to strike the putt, he is distracted by a fan jumping into the lake that surrounds the hole. After the man is taken out of the water and into the hands of security, Sluman misses the putt. He then makes bogey on the third playoff hole, the 18th hole, and loses the title. "I was ready to pull the trigger when he jumped in," Sluman says of the distraction on the 17th hole. "I might have made the putt, but we'll never know."

1998 – Justin Leonard comes from five shots back and wins The Players Championship by two shots over Glenn Day and Tom Lehman. "There wasn't a lot of pressure on me, being five back," Leonard says after claiming the $720,000 first prize for his fourth career title. Jacksonville-native Len Mattiace threatens to win the title late in the round, but knowing he needs to birdie one of the last two holes, goes for the flag on the 17th hole. Mattiace, with his mother cheering for him in a wheelchair from the gallery, hits his nine-iron tee shot in the water and his penalty shot into the water and scores an 8 and finishes in a tie for fifth place.

2014 – Laura Diaz makes a hole-in-one for the second straight day in the Kia Classic in Carlsbad, Calif., becoming the second player in LPGA Tour history to make two aces in a tournament. Diaz aces the par-3 third hole in the third round, then holes out on the sixth in the final-round. "I went out today hoping I could get another one," Diaz says. "Just really using my head to see how wild and crazy it could get. Then it happened and I went nuts. It's pretty crazy." Jenny Lidback is the only other player with two holes-in-one at an event, turning the trick at the 1997 Tournament of Champions.

1981 – Bill Rogers nearly blows a five-stroke lead on the back nine holes, but shoots a final-round 70 and hangs on for a one-shot win at the Sea Pines Heritage Classic on Hilton Head

Island, S.C. Rogers makes two-putt pars on the final four holes and benefits from Gil Morgan lipping out a lead-tying birdie on the 17th hole and Hale Irwin barely missing a lead-tying putt on the 18th hole. "Winning came at a perfect time," says Rogers of his second career PGA Tour win after missing cuts in five of his last nine events. "It brings me from no confidence to the most confidence. On the tour we all believe you'll win when it's your time to win, but I wouldn't have won if Hale and Gil had made those putts." Rogers keeps his confidence for the rest of the season, winning his first and only major title at the Open Championship at Royal St. George's and also at the World Series of Golf and the Texas Open to earn PGA Tour "Player of the Year" honors.

1992 – Dottie Mochrie wins the first of her two titles at the Dinah Shore Championships on the first hole of a playoff with Juli Inkster in Rancho Mirage, Calif. Mochrie birdies the 18th hole to force a playoff, then wins her third of 17 career LPGA title with a par on first playoff hole. Mochrie says that she received extra motivation when a fan yells "loser" to her after she misses a birdie putt on the second-to-last hole. "That will get you fired up," says Mochrie who wins the Dinah Shore again in 1999 as Dottie Pepper.

March 30

1975 – Jack Nicklaus and Tom Weiskopf duel in the final round of the Sea Pines Heritage Classic on Hilton Head Island, S.C., but Nicklaus, adjusting his swing mid-round, wins his 56th PGA Tour title with a final-round 63 to win by three strokes. Says Nicklaus, "I had been swinging too loose and placing the ball too far right. Once I realized what I was doing wrong, I went right back to shooting right at the flag." Following the victory, Nicklaus says he is hitting the ball as good as he has in two or three years, anticipating the Masters in two weeks, fending off media suggestions that he is peaking too early for his appearance at Augusta National. "If anything, it would have been the other way around," says Nicklaus. "If I had lost, I'd feel maybe I'd peaked too soon." Nicklaus and Weiskopf duel again at the Masters, along with Johnny Miller, with Nicklaus remaining in top form winning his fifth Masters title.

2003 – Davis Love III shoots a final-round 64 and beats Pádraig Harrington and Jay Haas by six shots to win his second title at The Players Championship – 11 years after first winning at the TPC at Sawgrass. The final round is played in cold and windy conditions, that makes Love's final-round score even more incredible. "I've never seen a round like that," says Fred Couples, paired with Love in the final round. "To watch a round like that gets me jacked up. He put the hammer down." The signature shot of Love's round, one shot off the course record, comes on the 16th hole where, after hitting his tee shot into the trees and into the pine straw on the par 5, he hooks a six-iron to within 11 feet and sinks the eagle putt to extend his lead to five shots. For his 16th PGA Tour victory, Love earns a first-prize paycheck of $1.17 million – versus $324,000 for his win at the TPC in 1992.

1992 – Davis Love, III wins The Players Championship by four shots over Ian Baker-Finch, Phil Blackmar, Nick Faldo and Tom Watson. Love shoots a final-round 67 to post a 273 total, 15 under par. Starting play on the day is John Daly and Mark Calcavecchia, two of the fastest players on the PGA Tour, who finish their round in two hours, three minutes and shooting, 80 and 81, respectively, to finish second-to-last and last in the event. The two are "put on notice" by the PGA Tour for "failure to exert their best effort" and are fined an unknown amount.

1997 – Steve Elkington chips in for birdie on the 18th hole to cap a record seven-shot victory at The Players Championship at the TPC at Sawgrass. Elkington shoots a final-round three-under par 69 to win by the widest margin in the 24-year history of the event. "It was an unbelievable day," Elkington says. "I must say leading this tournament from wire-to-wire is the most difficult thing that I've ever had to do in golf…I'm sitting here trying to explain what it's like to win this tournament. I basically blew away the best field we ever had. And, I didn't know if I was capable." Elkington earns the $630,000 first-place check to also join Fred Couples as the only players at the time to win two titles at the Players Championship at the TPC at Sawgrass.

1986 – John Mahaffey improbably wins The Players Championship at the TPC at Sawgrass, benefitting from a faltering Larry Mize, to win the ninth of his 10 career PGA Tour titles. Mize leads the event by three-to-five shots for most of the final round, but, after a three consecutive bogeys starting on the 14th hole, Mize misses a five-foot birdie putt on the 17th hole and a three-foot par putt on the final hole and loses to Mahaffey by one shot. "I know exactly how Larry feels right now. I've been in those shoes. And I can tell you it's no fun," says Mahaffey, who twice let U.S. Open titles slip through his fingers, in 1975 and 1976. Says Mize after his final-round four-over-par 76, "Choke is a word a lot of us don't like, but, yeah, I guess I did. They say that every time you get in this position, you gain something, you learn something. I don't know right now. I'm too disappointed to think about it."

2006 – Lorena Ochoa birdies her final hole to tie an LPGA major championship record at 10-under 62, giving her a four-shot lead over Michelle Wie after the first round of the Kraft Nabisco Championship at Mission Hills Country Club in Rancho Mirage, Calif. The 62 ties the record in a major set by Minea Blomqvist in the 2004 Women's British Open at Sunningdale. Ochoa follows with rounds of 71, 74 and 72 and loses to Karrie Webb on the first round of a sudden-death playoff. Korea's Hyo-Joo Kim subsequently breaks the record score for lowest round at a major when she shoots a 61 in the opening round of the 2014 Evian Championship.

2014 – Ranked No. 339 in the world, Australia's Steven Bowditch wins the Texas Open for his first PGA Tour victory, shooting a final-round four-over 76 for a one-stroke victory. "I'm over the moon. I really can't believe it," says Bowditch, who attempted suicide in 2006 and has fought depression throughout his career. Bowditch's final-round score is the highest closing score by a winner since Vijay Singh finishes with a four-over 76 at the 2004 PGA Championship, and the highest in a non-major since Fred Couples shoots a five-over 77 in the 1983 Kemper Open.

1997 – Forty-one-year-old Betsy King overcomes a three-shot deficit over the last eight holes and wins the Nabisco Dinah Shore Championships in Rancho Mirage, Calif., for a third time. King, also the Dinah Shore winner in 1987 and 1990, shoots a final-round 71 to beat Kris Tschetter by two strokes.

March 31

1996 – Fred Couples wins his second title at The Players Championship firing a glorious final round 64 to win by four shots over Tommy Tolles and Colin Montgomerie. "It was the best round of golf I've played in a long, long time," says Couples after his round, where he eagles the par 5 16th hole and birdies the par 3 17th hole at the TPC at Sawgrass. The title is the 12th on the PGA Tour for Couples, also the TPC champion in 1984.

1985 – Calvin Peete makes five birdies on the final 10 holes – including a tap-in on the famed island-green 17th hole – and wins the Tournament Players Championship at the TPC at Sawgrass in Ponte Vedra Beach, Fla. "I have reached the mountain top," says Peete of his win and becoming the first African-American to win the event.

1991 – Steve Elkington shoots a final-round 68 and wins The Players Championship by one shot over Fuzzy Zoeller. Zoeller misses birdie putts on the final three holes – all from about 18 feet – and is unable to force the playoff. Says Zoeller after the round, "The ball just didn't want to go in." Phil Blackmar holds the lead when he reaches the island-green 17th hole, but hits his tee shot into the water to make double-bogey and finishes in third place with Paul Azinger and John Cook, two shots back.

1991 – Amy Alcott wins the Dinah Shore Championship with a record eight-shot victory over Dottie Mochrie. Alcott resumes the tradition that she started at the event three years earlier by jumping in the green-side pond at the Mission Hills Country Club, taking tournament host Dinah Shore along with her.

1974 – Lee Trevino wins the New Orleans Open by incredibly not making a bogey in the 72 holes of the event. Trevino birdies four of the first six holes en route to a final-round 65 to beat runners-up Ben Crenshaw and Bobby Cole by eight shots. "I knew it would be a good day when I cut (faded) a five-iron against the wind and stroked my first putt," Trevino says after his final-round. Trevino misses only three greens in regulation in his 72-hole tour of the Lakewood Country Club and finds only two bunkers.

APRIL

April 1

1984 – Twenty-four-year-old Fred Couples needs only a final-round 71 to win the Tournament Players Championship at the TPC at Sawgrass in Ponte Vedra Beach, Fla., for his second PGA Tour title. Couples, who shoots a second-round 64, then a course record, wins by one shot over Lee Trevino and holds off a cadre of other major champions including Seve Ballesteros, Tom Watson and Craig Stadler. "I'll bet that if I told Ballesteros and Watson I'd shoot 71 in the last round, they'd say 'take it' and figure they could beat it," Couples says after his win.

1979 – Tom Watson cruises to victory at the Sea Pines Heritage Classic at Harbour Town Golf Links in Hilton Head, S.C., only needing a final-round even par round of 71 for a five-shot victory over Tom Kite and Mike Morley. "The only pressure I felt was in trying to play defensively," says Watson who enters the final round with an eight-shot lead. "It's hard to play conservatively on this great golf course because it requires good golf shots."

2007 – Morgan Pressel, at the age of 18 years, 10 months, nine days, becomes the youngest major champion in LPGA Tour history when she shoots a final-round three-under 69 to win the Kraft Nabisco Championship in Rancho Mirage, Calif. Pressel benefits from Suzann Pettersen blowing a four-shot lead with four holes to play, but plays her final 25 holes at the Mission Hills Country Club without a bogey. Pressel's major record is broken in 2015 when Lydia Ko wins the Evian Championship at age 18 years, four months, 20 days.

2012 – I.K. Kim incredibly misses a one-foot putt on the final hole that would have clinched her first major championship at the Kraft Nabisco Championship but loses minutes later on the first hole of a sudden-death playoff to Sun Young Yoo. "I played straight, and it actually just broke to the right, even that short putt," Kim says of her missed putt. "On the playoff hole, it's just hard to kind of focus on what's going on right now, because I was still a little bit bummed (about) what happened on 18, honestly." Yoo makes an 18-foot putt on the first playoff hole – also the 18th hole the Mission Hills Country Club – to earn her second LPGA title and her first major.

April 2

1939 – Ralph Guldahl shoots a 70 and 69 over a 36-hole finale to win the sixth staging of the Masters by one stroke over Sam Snead. A runner-up at Augusta the previous two years, Guldhal says after winning the title in Greensboro the week before that he is "tired" of finishing second at the Bobby Jones created tournament. Guldahl, the 1937 and 1938 U.S. Open champion, shoots a 33 on the final nine holes, making eagle on No. 13 to go with birdies on No. 10 and No. 15 against a bogey at No. 17.

1959 – Nineteen-year-old Jack Nicklaus tees it up for his first round at the Masters and shoots an opening round 76. He then follows with a second-round 74 and misses the cut by one stroke.

1978 – Seve Ballesteros, at the age of 20 years, 11 months, wins his first PGA Tour title at the Greater Greensboro Open, shooting a final-round 66 to beat runners-up Fuzzy Zoeller and Jack Renner by one stroke.

2000 – Gary Nicklaus, the fourth of five children of Jack Nicklaus, falls just short of winning on the PGA Tour as he loses in a playoff at the BellSouth Open in Atlanta to Phil Mickelson. Heavy rains force the final round to be canceled and a playoff determines the championship between Nicklaus and Mickelson, the third-round co-leaders. Mickelson needs only two shots to earn his win, hitting a nine-iron shot to 18 feet on the par 3 16th hole at the TPC of Sugarloaf on the first playoff hole. "It would've been very nice for him to have been able to break through and get his first tournament win," says Mickelson of Nicklaus. "I didn't want it to be at my expense so I don't feel bad about that at all." Says Nicklaus, "I proved to myself that I can win out here. I was one shot away from winning the tournament against one of the best players in the world. It just lets me know that there are good things coming down the road." The best subsequent finish for Nicklaus on the PGA Tour came in 2001 at his father's Memorial tournament, where he finished fifteenth. He fails to keep his PGA Tour card in 2004 and he quits professional golf to focus on the family business.

April 3

1988 – Amy Alcott starts what becomes the biggest tradition in women's professional golf as she leaps into the greenside pond at the Mission Hills Country Club in Rancho Mirage, Calif., after winning the Nabisco Dinah Shore Championship. After Alcott taps in for a then record score of 14-under-par 274, beating runner-up Colleen Walker by two strokes, she is urged by her caddie Bill Kurre to leap in the pond and the two sprint and leap into the water. "I wanted to do it just to do it," Alcott says. "It was craziness and I had to talk myself into it." Alcott again dives into the pond after she wins again for her third Dinah Shore title in 1991, taking tournament namesake Dinah Shore along with her. The tradition does not entirely catch-on as annual ritual until 1994 when Donna Andrews takes the plunge. In 2006, the pond is named "Poppie's Pond" in honor of the event's tournament director Terry Wilcox, known to his grandchildren as "Poppie."

2011 – Stacy Lewis holds off defending champion Yani Tseng to win the Kraft Nabisco Championship in Rancho Mirage, Calif. by three strokes, earning her first LPGA Tour title in the year's first major. Lewis, whose grandfather dies on the eve of the tournament, shoots a three-under 69 to finish at 13-under 275.

1994 – Ben Crenshaw wins his 18th and second-to-last PGA Tour title at the Freeport McMoRan Classic in New Orleans beating Jose-Maria Olazabal by three strokes. Exactly one year and six days later, Crenshaw wins his 19th and final PGA Tour title at the Masters.

1988 – Sandy Lyle wins his fifth PGA Tour title at the Greater Greensboro Open, earning $180,000. Lyle's strong play continues into his next tournament the next week, the Masters, where he wins his second major championship.

April 4

1952 – The first-ever Masters champion's dinner is held at the Augusta National Golf Club, hosted by defending champion Ben Hogan. The dinner, held on the Friday night in the middle of the tournament, features nine Masters champions – Horton Smith, Gene Sarazen, Byron Nelson, Henry Picard, Jimmy Demaret, Craig Wood, Claude Harmon, Sam Snead and Hogan as well as Augusta National chairmen Bobby Jones and Clifford Roberts. The concept is thought up by Hogan, who ironically, was one of the most anti-social personalities ever in golf. Wrote Scott Michaux of Augusta.com of the champion's dinner, "Of all the enduring gifts left by Ben Hogan's golf legacy, the Masters Club might be the most cherished and unlikely."

1965 – Sam Snead wins his 82nd and final regular PGA Tour title winning the Greater Greensboro Open for an incredible eighth time. Snead, who also won at Greensboro in 1938, '46, '49, '50, '55, '56 and '60, also becomes the oldest player to win a title on the PGA Tour at the age of 52 years, 10 months and eight days. The win also comes 28 years, two months and 17 days after he won his first PGA Tour event at the Oakland Open on January 17, 1937, a record for the longest gap between first and last victories. In 1992, Ray Floyd breaks Snead's record tournament-win gap by nine months.

1937 – Byron Nelson makes up six strokes on Ralph Guldahl on the 12th and 13th holes in the final round and wins the fourth staging of the Masters by two strokes. Guldahl's makes a double-bogey 5 and a bogey 6, respectively, on No. 12 and No. 13, while Nelson plays the 12th and 13th holes with a birdie 2 and an eagle 3 respectively. The Nelson Bridge at the 13th hole at Augusta National is dedicated in 1958 to commemorate his feat.

1938 – Henry Picard fires a final round 70 to defeat Harry Cooper and Ralph Guldahl by two strokes and win the fifth staging of the Masters.

1940 – Lloyd Mangrum shoots an opening round eight-under-par 64 for a new course record at Augusta National Golf Club in the first round of the Masters. The course record stands for 46 years, until Nick Price shoots a 63 in 1986 and later equaled by Greg Norman in 1996.

April 5

1959 – Art Wall, Jr. birdies five of the last six holes and shoots a final round 66 to win the Masters by one shot over Cary Middlecoff. Wall passes 12 players on his final-day charge, including defending champion and third-round leader Arnold Palmer, who triple-bogeys the par-3 12th hole en route to a final-round 74, two strokes behind Wall.

1956 – Twenty-four-year-old amateur Ken Venturi opens the Masters with a first round 66, the best round to date at Augusta National by an amateur. Venturi holds the lead through the next two rounds, despite a third-round 75, but also shoots a final-round 80 and loses the championship to Jack Burke, Jr. by one stroke.

1957 – The first-ever 36-hole cut is made at the Masters as the field of 101 players is cut to 40 players after the first two rounds at 150, six-over par. The cut is changed to the low 44 players and ties in 1962 and then again in 1966 to include any player within 10 shots of the lead after two rounds. In 2013, the cut is again changed to include the top 50 players and ties and any player within 10 strokes of the lead.

2015 – Brittany Lincicome and Stacy Lewis play the 18th hole at the Mission Hills Country Club in Rancho Mirage, Calif., four times in a row, including three playoff rounds, before Lincicome makes a short par putt to win the ANA Inspiration for her second major title on the LPGA Tour. "It was nice to be out there with her to play this hole," Lincicome, the event's winner in 2009, says of Lewis. "Over and over again."

2009 – Brittany Lincicome hits a hybrid from 210 yards away to four feet to set up a winning eagle putt on the final hole to beat Cristie Kerr and Kristy McPherson by one shot and win the Kraft Nabisco Championship in Rancho Mirage, Calif., for her first major tournament victory.

April 6

1958 – Arnold Palmer wins his first of his four titles at the Masters – and his first major title – one stroke ahead of runners-up Doug Ford and Fred Hawkins. Palmer eagles the 13th hole in the final round, but three-putts on the final green for a final-round 73. Writes the Associated Press of the final day drama, "Arnold

Palmer, a mighty young man with a golf club or a rulebook, made the best use of both today and won the 22nd Masters tournament in a cavalry charge finish." The salient moment of the final round comes on the 12th hole when Palmer's tee shot on the par 3 imbeds in the wet ground on the back of the green. Palmer claims he is entitled to a lift, clean and place ruling due to a U.S. Golf Association "wet weather rule" but is denied by the rules official in his group. Palmer plays the embedded ball and makes a double-bogey, but drops a provisional ball utilizing the lift, clean and place rule and makes a par. The tournament rules committee later rule that Palmer was entitled to the free drop and Palmer's score of par on the hole is upheld. In his post-event reporting of tournament, *Sports Illustrated* writer Herbert Warren Wind first uses the term "Amen Corner" to describe the 11th, 12th and 13th holes at Augusta National in his story.

1960 – The Par 3 tournament is played for the first time at the Masters, Sam Snead winning the inaugural staging of the event played annually the day before the opening round. Snead shoots a four-under-par 23, edging Doug Sanders, Lew Worsham and Dick Knight by one stroke.

1936 – Due to inclement weather, the third and fourth rounds of the Masters are played on a Monday where Horton Smith chips in from 50 feet away at the 14th hole in the Monday afternoon final round and goes on to win his second title at Augusta National. After a morning round of 68, Smith shoots a 72 in the afternoon and beats Harry Cooper by one shot.

1947 – Jimmy Demaret joins Horton Smith and Byron Nelson as two-time winners of the Masters shooting a final-round 71 to beat Nelson and amateur Frank Stranahan by two shots. Demaret, who first won the Masters in 1940, becomes the first golfer to score four sub-par rounds in the same Masters tournament, shooting 69, 71, 70, 71 to win the first prize of $2,500. "It really has been a pleasure, as it always is, for me to play in Augusta but naturally I'm especially tickled with winning," writes Demaret in a first-person column on his victory to the International News Service. "I wanted to win this one more than anything I know. I kept thinking about what Walter Hagan used to say. He said if you win once you were lucky but if you win twice you're just plain good."

1952 – Sam Snead wins his second title at the Masters – and the sixth of his seven career majors – shooting a final-round 72 to beat runner-up Jack Burke, Jr. by four shots. Snead withstands strong winds over the final 36 holes, causing him to shoot a third-round 77. Snead, described by Charles Bartlett of the *Chicago Tribune* as "the gifted one with the 24-carat swing" and "a man who knows more ways to win or lose a golf tournament than most in the trade," benefits from third-round co-leader and defending champion Ben Hogan struggling to a final-round 79.

1950 – Ben Hogan returns to play major championship golf since his near fatal automobile accident in early 1949, teeing up for the first round of the Masters. Hogan moves himself into second place after 54 holes, but shoots a four-over-par 76 in the final round and falls back to tie for fourth place with Byron Nelson. Hogan, however, wins the next three majors he enters: the 1950 U.S. Open, the 1951 Masters, and the 1951 U.S. Open.

1986 – The first official World Golf Rankings are published and Bernhard Langer of Germany is the first player to be ranked No. 1 in the world. Langer is followed by two other European players – Seve Ballesteros of Spain at No. 2 and Sandy Lyle of Great Britain at No. 3. Tom Watson is the top-ranked American at No. 4. The rankings follow a method of calculations used by golf agent Mark McCormack in his *World of Professional Golf* annual since 1968.

2014 – Nineteen-year-old Lexi Thompson becomes the second-youngest player to win a LPGA major tournament at the time winning the Kraft Nabisco Championship in Rancho Mirage, Calif. Thompson shoots a four-under-par 68 at the Mission

Hills Country Club to win by three shots over fellow American Michelle Wie. At 19 years, one month and 27 days, Thompson becomes the second youngest LPGA women's major winner behind Morgan Pressel, who won the Kraft Nabisco in 2007 at the age of 18 years, 10 months and nine days. In 2015, Lydia Ko becomes the youngest women's major winner when she wins the Evian Championship at age 18 years, four months, 20 days.

April 7

1935 – Gene Sarazen hits what is called the "shot heard around the world," holing out from 235 yards away with a four-wood for double eagle on the 485-yard par-5 15th hole at Augusta National in the final round of the Masters. The shot helps Sarazen tie Craig Wood and force a 36-hole playoff to decide the second staging of the Masters, then called the "Augusta National Invitation Tournament." Sarazen is three shots off the lead at the time, tying for the lead with his one miraculous stroke. Sarazen wins the playoff with Wood the following day by five shots.

1963 – Twenty-three-year-old Jack Nicklaus makes a three-foot par putt on the final hole to clinch a one-shot victory over Tony Lema to win the first of his six titles at the Masters. Playing in soggy conditions, Nicklaus shoots a final-round even par 72 to become the youngest Masters winner at the time, holing a nine-foot putt for bogey on the dreaded twelfth hole, preventing disaster. Nicklaus, described by the Associated Press as "a judgy, 200-pound bundle of unshakable nerve," had won his first major title at the U.S. Open the previous summer in an 18-hole playoff with Arnold Palmer at Oakmont.

2005 – Seventy-three-year-old Billy Casper invokes his right as a past Masters champion and tees it up in the first round of the event and shoots a score of 106 (34-over-par), which unofficially is the worst record in Masters history by 11 shots.

The 1970 Masters champion does not hand in his scorecard and is disqualified from the event. His round is "highlighted" by a 14 on the par 3 No. 16 hole that includes five balls in the water. Says Casper following his round, "I was only going to play 18 holes – I just had to get it out of my system. I wanted to do it again. A lot of my grandchildren were here."

1940 – Jimmy Demaret wins the first of his three Masters titles, four strokes ahead of runner-up Lloyd Mangrum. Demaret makes par on the first 14 holes, two-putts for birdie on the 15th, then pars the final three holes to shot a 71 and earn the $1,500 first prize. Writes Tom Wall of the *Augusta Chronicle* of Demaret, "He clicked off the final round in machine-like precision despite tremendous pressure, never once appearing concerned about how it all might end."

1957 – Doug Ford shoots a bogey-free final-round 66, capped with a hole-out from the bunker on the final hole, and wins his only championship at the Masters by three strokes over three-time champion Sam Snead. Snead holds the lead entering the final round, but shoots a final-round even-par 72 that includes six birdies and six bogeys.

1946 – In the first staging of the Masters since 1942 due to World War II, Ben Hogan arrives at the 18th hole in the final round needing a birdie to win his first major title and a par to force a playoff with unheralded Herman Keiser, but three-putts from 12 feet to lose by one shot. The win is the only major title for Keiser, the native of Springfield, Missouri who, due to his serious nature, earned the nickname of "the Missouri Mortician."

1955 – Arnold Palmer tees it up at the Masters for the first time in his career. A pro for less than a year, Palmer shoots an opening round of 76 and eventually finishes tied for tenth place, earning $696.

April 8

2007 – Zach Johnson wins the Masters posting a tie for the highest score to win the tournament with a one-over-par 289, enduring cool temperatures and gusty winds. Johnson shoots a three-under par 69 in the final round to win by two strokes over Retief Goosen, Rory Sabbatini and Tiger Woods. Johnson, who famously lays up on every par 5 of the tournament, birdies three of his final six holes to win his first major title.

2012 – Bubba Watson wins the Masters on the second hole a sudden-death playoff with Louis Oosthuizen on Easter Sunday. The left-handed Watson hits one of the most famous shots in Masters history in the playoff, hooking his approach shot nearly 90 degrees from behind the trees in the pine straw off the right side of the 10th fairway to within 10 feet of the hole. Watson then two putts for par for the victory after Oosthuizen misses his par putt. Oosthuizen hits an incredible double eagle two on the par 5 second hole, only the fourth double eagle in Masters history and the first ever on the second hole.

1999 – Ninety-seven-year-old Gene Sarazen hits what ends up being the final shot of his life in his role as an honorary starter at the Masters. Appearing on the first tee with 87-year-old Byron Nelson, the 1937 Masters champion, and Sam Snead, the 86-year-old Masters champion in 1949, 1952 and 1954, Sarazen hits his shot down the middle of the fairway, using a Wilson woman's three-wood, while wearing two golf gloves. Sarazen calls it "the hardest day of my life. When you don't play golf at all, and you're afraid you're going to miss the ball and become the laughing stock of everybody, it's terrible. These hands are 97 years old. All the meat is gone. They're all skin and bones." Sarazen passes away 35 days later on May 13.

1935 – Gene Sarazen wins a 36-hole Monday playoff by five strokes over Craig Wood to win the Augusta National Invitation Tournament, earning $1,500. The title is the seventh and final major title for Sarazen, who becomes the first player to win a modern career "Grand Slam" by winning all four of golf's major championships.

1956 – Jack Burke, Jr. comes back from a record eight shots back to win his first major championship and only Masters, one stroke better than amateur Ken Venturi. Burke only shoots a one-under-par 71 in the final round, but he is one of only two players to break par in the final round due to windy conditions and benefits from Venturi, the third-round leader, shooting a final-round 80. Burke's final score of 289 is the highest winning total score in Masters history, along with Sam Snead in 1954 and Zach Johnson in 2007 who both also posted the one-over par score.

1990 – Nick Faldo wins his second consecutive Masters title – his third major of his career – beating 47-year-old Ray Floyd on the second hole of a sudden death playoff. After both Faldo and Floyd par the first playoff hole – No. 10 – Floyd hits his seven-iron approach shot into the water on No. 11 and Faldo two-putts from 18 feet to successfully defend his title. The previous year, Faldo also wins the Masters also in a playoff decided on the 11th hole, making a 25-foot birdie to beat Scott Hoch. Faldo joins 1965-66 Masters champion Jack Nicklaus as the only two players to win back-to-back Masters titles. Floyd, attempting to become the oldest Masters winner of all time, leads the tournament by four strokes with six holes to play, but is caught by Faldo, who makes birdie on No. 13, No. 15 and No. 16, while Floyd makes bogey at No. 17. Says Floyd of losing the chance to win his second Green Jacket, "This is the most devastating thing that's ever happened to me in my career. I've had a lot of losses, but nothing like this."

1951 – After eight top 10 finishes including two times as runner-up, Ben Hogan finally wins his first Masters title, shooting a bogey-free round of 68 in the final round to beat rookie pro Skee Riegel by two shots. The 38-year-old Hogan had previously won the U.S. Open in 1948 and 1950 and the PGA Championship in 1946 and 1948, but had yet been able to breakthrough at Augusta National, finishing as the runner-up in 1942 and 1946. The Associated Press describes Hogan's effort as a "sensational flourish to one of the great comeback sagas in sports today," saying "The gristly little man from Texas subdued Augusta National's treacherous acres with a grim and a meticulous last round 68, four under par golf that burned off all opposition."

2001 – Tiger Woods wins the Masters for the second time, and becomes the first golfer to hold all four professional major championships simultaneously. Woods finishes at 16-under par, two strokes better than David Duval, to win his sixth major title and earns $1,008,000 – the first time a major tournament awards a first prize of over $1 million. "To win four in succession, it's hard to believe," says Woods of his "Tiger Slam."

2004 – Arnold Palmer tees off in the first round at the Masters for a 50th and final time – not missing a tournament since his debut year in 1955. Palmer shoots 84 in his opening round and 84 the following day in the second round and misses the cut and ceases to claim his "Past Champion" exemption into the tournament. Palmer's 50 appearances is a Masters record until Gary Player breaks his record in 2008 (he finishes with 52 appearances, but Player's not consecutive starts as he missed the 1973 Masters due to illness.) Palmer does accept a role as an "honorary Starter" starting in 2007.

April 9

2017 – Sergio Garcia finally breaks through to win his first major championship at the Masters by beating Justin Rose on the first hole of a playoff on what would have been the 60th birthday of his fellow Spaniard, mentor and two-Masters champion Seve Ballesteros. Playing in his 74th major championships, Garcia blows his chance to win the title in regulation by missing a seven-foot birdie putt on the 72nd hole, but redeems himself by making a 12-foot birdie putt on the first playoff hole after Rose holes out for bogey after missing the 18th fairway off the tee. "Obviously, this is something I wanted to do for a long time but, you know, it never felt like a horror movie," says the 37-year-old Garcia of winning, despite his history of losing major championships, including lipping out a putt that would have won him the 2007 Open Championship at Carnoustie. "It felt like a little bit of a drama, but obviously with a happy ending." Garcia fights back after making bogey on No. 10 and No. 11 and having to take a penalty stroke for an unplayable lie after hitting into the woods on No. 13. Garcia, however, miraculously saves par on No. 13 and makes birdie on No. 14 and eagle on No. 15 to draw back even. Rose makes birdie on No. 16 and bogey on No. 17 to set up the final drama on the 18th hole in regulation and in the playoff.

1962 – Arnold Palmer wins his third Masters title, shooting a 68 to beat out Gary Player and Dow Finsterwald in a three-way Monday 18-hole playoff. Palmer trails Player by three shots at the turn, but shoots a 31 on the back nine to beat Player by three shots and Finsterwald by nine shots. The win is especially sweet for Palmer a year after he loses the Masters to Player on the final hole, needing only a par to win the title, but making double-bogey from the greenside bunker to give away the title. The turning point in the playoff comes on No. 10 when Palmer makes a 23-foot birdie and Player makes bogey, in a two-shot swing. Writes Bob Drum in the *Pittsburgh Press*, "Palmer was now in charge, even though Player was still a shot ahead. The famous Palmer come-from-behind move was in progress and everybody, including Finsterwald and Player, sensed it." Palmer also makes birdie on No. 12, No. 13, No. 14 and on No. 16 during his back-nine charge, while Player plays the final nine one over par.

1972 – Jack Nicklaus stumbles to a final-round 74, but hangs on to win his fourth Masters title, tying Arnold Palmer for the most Masters titles. Nicklaus finishes four shots ahead of Bruce Crampton, Tom Weiskopf and Bobby Mitchell to win his 10th professional major. "Nobody was doing anything. Nobody was making a move and nothing was happening," says Nicklaus of his mediocre play and lack of drama in the final round. "I usually play better when I'm behind or maybe tied. I kept looking at the scoreboards and I kept seeing a five shot lead, a five shot lead."

1978 – Gary Player comes from seven shots back to win his third Masters title and ninth major title at age 42, shooting a then-record tying round of 64. Player wins the title by one shot over Rod Funseth, defending champion Tom Watson and 54-hole leader Hubert Green. Player starts the day in 10th place and shoots 30 on the back nine and has to wait 40 minutes for the final group to finish. Watson misses an eight-foot par putt on the 18th hole to tie Player. Green, who starts the day with a three-shot lead, misses a three-foot birdie putt on the final hole to force a playoff.

1950 – Jimmy Demaret becomes the first three-time Masters champion, shooting a final-round 69 and benefitting from Jim Ferrier bogeying five of the last six holes at Augusta National in one of the great collapses in the history of the event. Ferrier, a naturalized American from Australia and the winner of the 1947 PGA Championship, begins the round with a two-shot lead but, as Demaret finishes his round, he hits his tee shot into Rae's Creek on the 13th hole. He three-putts for bogey on No. 13, No. 14, misses a short birdie putt on No. 15, makes bogey from behind the green on No. 16 and also from the front sand-trap on No. 17. On the 18th hole, he has a birdie putt to tie Demaret but three putts again for bogey to fall two shots back. Writes Charles Bartlett of the *Chicago Tribune* of the Ferrier collapse, "Today's strange climax illustrated dramatically the golfing axiom that championships are lost, not won." Says Demaret of the 13th hole at Augusta National, where the Ferrier collapse started, "That's the death hole of this tournament." Demaret plays the 13th hole at six-under par over his four rounds with two eagles and two birdies.

1967 – One year after his putt to win the Masters is left dangling on the edge of the cup on the final hole, Gay Brewer wins his one and only major title at the Masters with a one-shot victory over Bobby Nichols. The previous year, Brewer three putts on the final hole from 75 feet to fall into a three-way playoff with Tommy Jacobs and Jack Nicklaus that he loses to Nicklaus by shooting a 78. Brewer birdies the 13th, 14th and 15th holes in the final round and exorcises the ghosts of the previous year by safely two-putting from 20 feet for the victory on the final hole. "I blew it and I forgot it," says Brewer of his Masters meltdown the year before. "I don't worry about such things." The win by Brewer snaps a seven-year stranglehold on the Masters title by Jack Nicklaus, Arnold Palmer and Gary Player.

1973 – Tommy Aaron wins the Masters for his one and only major title, one stroke better than runner-up J.C. Snead in a rain-delayed Monday finish. Prior to his Masters victory, Aaron is best known as the player who incorrectly kept the final-round score of Robert de Vicenzo at the 1968 Masters, preventing the Argentine from winning at Augusta National in one of the biggest gaffes in the history of the sport. Ironically, Aaron catches a scoring mistake during his final round made by his playing partner Johnny Miller, who puts Aaron down for a par 5 on the 13th hole, when Aaron makes a birdie 4. "That is the reason you check those things," says Aaron after his final-round 68. "I know exactly what I shot. It happens quite often. I found the mistake, changed it, and signed it."

2000 – Vijay Singh wins his second major championships at the Masters, shooting a final-round 69 to win by three strokes over runner-up Ernie Els. "I think the hard work has paid off," says Singh, the 1998 PGA Championship winner known for his long sessions on the practice range. "You have to come here and believe in yourself."

1989 – Nick Faldo birdies the second hole of a sudden-death playoff with Scott Hoch to win his first of three Masters titles. Hoch famously misses a two-foot par putt on the first playoff hole at No. 10 that would have won him the tournament. Faldo then sinks his 25-foot birdie putt to win on the next hole, the 11th hole, the hole he makes bogey on during each round of the tournament. "You just stand there and watch," says Faldo of Hoch's missed putt to win the tournament. "You figure it's over. Then, as soon as he missed it, I said 'He's opened the door for me. I have new life.' Then it felt like destiny." Greg Norman and Ben Crenshaw both bogey the final hole to miss the playoff by one stroke. Faldo shoots a final-round 65 one day after shooting a third-round 77.

1995 – Just days after the death of his mentor Harvey Penick, Ben Crenshaw emotionally wins his second Masters title with a one-stroke victory over runner-up Davis Love, III. "I had a 15th club in my bag and it was Harvey," says the 43-year-old Crenshaw of Penick, Crenshaw's golf teacher since age 7 who passed away the previous Sunday at the age of 90. Crenshaw, in fact, flies from Augusta National to be a ball-bearer at Penick's funeral on Wednesday of the tournament. Crenshaw enters the final round tied with unheralded Brian Henninger, one shot ahead of five other players, but Crenshaw emerges victorious playing a steady round of 68. "I believe in fate," he says. "Fate has dictated another championship here. I played my heart out."

2006 – Phil Mickelson wins his second consecutive major title and his second Masters title shooting a final-round 69 for a two-stroke victory over Tim Clark. Mickelson makes only one bogey in the round, on the final hole when victory was almost all but assured. "It's been a long day but a wonderful day and I will cherish that final round and look back at some of the shots I was able to pull off and some of the putts I was able to make," says Mickelson, paired in the final group with 46-year-old Fred Couples, who finishes in a five-way tie for third place. Clark breaks out of a six-way tie for second place by holing out for birdie on the 72nd hole of the tournament.

April 10

1949 – The Green Jacket is awarded to the winner of the Masters for the first time as Sam Snead is the first recipient of the most coveted item of clothing in golf. Snead shoots his second consecutive 67 and wins his first of three Masters titles by three strokes over runners-up Johnny Bulla and Lloyd Mangrum.

1965 – Jack Nicklaus wins the second of his six Masters titles with a record-setting score of 17-under-par 271, three strokes better than Ben Hogan's 274 in 1953. The 25-year-old Nicklaus, described by the Associated Press as a "blond, youth Goliath with awesome power," shoots a final-round 69 – making bogey only at No. 4, his only bogey in a 29-hole stretch – and wins by an incredible nine shots over his fellow members of "The Big Three" Arnold Palmer and Gary Player. The nine-stroke victory is the biggest winning margin at Augusta National until Tiger Woods wins by 12 shots in 1997. The Nicklaus scoring record stands until it is equaled by Ray Floyd in 1976 and surpassed by one stroke by Woods in 1997.

1961 – Gary Player becomes the first international champion of the Masters with a one-shot victory over Arnold Palmer and amateur Charles Coe. Player enters Monday's rain-delayed final round with a four-shot lead over Palmer, but double-bogeys No. 13 and bogeys No. 15 to fall from the lead. Palmer holds a one-shot lead on the 18th hole, but his approach shot finds the bunker right of the green. With a bad lie, Palmer's bunker shot goes past the hole and off the green. Palmer putts the ball from off the green, but misses his 15-foot putt for bogey to lose to Player by one shot.

1977 – Tom Watson wins his second major championship and his first of two Masters titles by two shots over Jack Nicklaus. Watson starts the final round tied for the lead with Ben Crenshaw, but the tournament becomes a duel between he and Nicklaus, who starts the final round three shots back. Watson and Nicklaus are tied after 68 holes, but Watson makes a key birdie on the 17th hole at the same time that Nicklaus makes a bogey on the final hole. Watson, whose breakthrough major win came at the 1975 Open Championship, shoots a final-round 67 against the Nicklaus final-round 66. "I knew I had to make birdies to beat Jack, the way he was playing," says Watson, who again has a final-round duel with Nicklaus at the Open Championship at Turnberry later in the year.

1988 – Sandy Lyle hits a seven-iron to six feet from the fairway bunker on the 18th hole and makes birdie to win the Masters by one shot over Mark Calcavecchia. Lyle becomes the first British player to win the Masters and the first champion since Sam Snead in 1949 to win at Augusta after winning the week before. Lyle enters the tournament having won the Greater Greensboro Open the week before.

1994 – Jose Maria Olazabal wins the first of his two Masters titles, shooting a final-round 69 to beat runner-up Tom Lehman by two strokes. Olazabal makes a 35-foot eagle putt on the par-5 15th hole to take a two-shot lead over Lehman, who misses his eagle putt from 15 feet after Olazabal sinks his putt. Olazabal joins Seve Ballesteros, the 1980 and 1983 Masters champion, as Spanish winners at Augusta National.

2005 – Tiger Woods and Chris DiMarco duel down the stretch in a thrilling final round at the Masters that culminates in Woods sinking a 15-foot birdie putt on the first playoff hole to win his fourth green jacket. Woods makes a miraculous chip-in for birdie on the 16th hole – one of the most celebrated shots in Masters history – to take a two-shot lead but bogeys the final two holes to drop into the playoff with DiMarco. For the first time in Masters history, the playoff starts on No. 18. Says DiMarco of his final-day effort, "I went out and shot 68 around here on Sunday, which is a very good round, and 12-under is usually good enough to win. It was just that I was playing against Tiger Woods."

1975 – Lee Elder becomes the first African-American to compete at the Masters, shooting an opening round 74. The 40-year-old misses the cut the next day after shooting a 78.

2011 – In a wild final day at the Masters, where eight players hold a share of the lead including Tiger Woods and Rory McIlroy – and one player from every continent except Antarctica – Charl Schwartzel emerges as the victor by two shots over runners-up Adam Scott and Jason Day. Schwartzel birdies the last four holes to win his first major championship. McIlroy holds a four-stroke lead at the start of the day, but shoots a final-round 80 to finish 10 shots out of the lead. Others to hold the lead on the final day include Geoff Ogilvy of Australia, K.J. Choi of Korea and Angel Cabrera of Argentina.

April 11

2004 – Phil Mickelson slides an 18-foot birdie putt on the final hole to win his first major golf title at the Masters, one shot better than Ernie Els. Mickelson shoots a final-round 69 – with five birdies over the last seven holes – while Els fires a final-round 67, highlighted by eagles at No. 8 and No. 13. Mickelson, who enters the tournament winless in 46 career majors, finally fulfills the potential of becoming a major champion since he first won the PGA Tour as an amateur in 1991. "It's hard for me to explain how it feels," says Mickelson. "It's almost make-believe."

1966 – Twenty-six-year-old Jack Nicklaus becomes the first player to successively defend a Masters title by winning an

18-hole Monday playoff with Gay Brewer and Tommy Jacobs. Nicklaus shoots a 70 in the playoff, two strokes better than Jacobs and eight better than Brewer. Masters protocol dictates that the previous year's winner place the Masters green jacket onto the winner, but there was no established procedure for if a player defends the title. Bobby Jones, the tournament's founder, after a discussion with co-founder and tournament chairman Clifford Roberts, is reported to have told Nicklaus, "Cliff and I have discussed the problem, and have decided you will just have to put the coat on yourself."

1971 – Charles Coody wins his only major championship beating Jack Nicklaus and Johnny Miller by two strokes to win the Masters. Coody enters the final round tied with Nicklaus for the lead, but Miller blitzes to a two-shot lead on the back nine, shooting six-under-par through 14 holes. Miller, however, fades with bogeys on two of the last three holes. Coody, who bogeyed the final three holes in 1969 to lose by two strokes, birdies the 15th and 16th holes while Nicklaus shoots a back-nine 37 to fall back. The win is the third and final tournament victory for Coody in his career.

1976 – Ray Floyd ties the Masters tournament scoring record posting a 17-and-under score of 271 to finish off a wire-to-wire win at Augusta National. Floyd wins his only Masters title by eight shots over Ben Crenshaw, shooting a second consecutive weekend round of 70 after shooting 65 and 66 in the first two rounds. Floyd ties the tournament scoring record set by Jack Nicklaus in 1965 that is eventually broken by Tiger Woods with an 18-under-par 270 in 1997.

1996 – Greg Norman shoots a course-record tying round 63 in the opening round of the Masters, equaling the best-ever round at Augusta National shot by Nick Price in 1986 in the third round. "I just let it flow," says Norman. "When you get into the type of role that I got today… Hey let it happen. Let the reins of the horse go and let him run as fast as he wants to run."

1982 – Craig Stadler beats Dan Pohl on the first hole of a sudden-death playoff and wins the Masters, the one and only major championship that the player known affectionately as "the Walrus" wins in his career. Stadler builds a six-shot lead with seven holes to play, but bogeys four holes coming in, capped by a three-putt bogey on the final hole from 20 feet. After Stadler makes a two-foot par putt on the first playoff hole at No. 10 Pohl misses a six-foot par putt that clinches the championship for Stadler. Says Stadler of winning despite blowing his six-shot lead, "I'll take them anyway I can get them." Stadler opens the tournament with a 75 in the first round, the highest opening round score for an eventual Masters champion.

1983 – Seve Ballesteros wins his second Masters title and third major with a four-stroke victory over runners-up Ben Crenshaw and Tom Kite. Rain on Friday during the championship forces the tournament to be finished on a Monday for a first time since 1973. Ballesteros plays the first four holes in four-under par, making birdie on No. 1 and No. 4 and making a ten-foot eagle on No. 2 to take early command of the tournament and holding on for a final-round 69. "Ballesteros got off to such a good start, it kind of put a damper on everyone's spirits," says Kite. "Birdie. Eagle. Par. Birdie. It's like he was driving a Ferrari and everyone else was in a Chevrolet."

1993 – Bernhard Langer becomes a two-time winner of the Masters by shooting a final-round 70 to hold on for a four-stroke victory over Chip Beck. Langer, the 1985 champion at Augusta National, makes eagle on the 13th hole and makes five one-putts to save pars and is never threatened after starting the round with a four-shot lead over Beck and Dan Forsman.

1999 – Jose Maria Olazabal wins his second title at the Masters shooting a final-round 71 beating runner-up Davis Love III by two strokes and three ahead of Greg Norman. The Spaniard leads Norman by one stroke entering the final round but the Australian is never able to take control, make a charge, or get a break to seize the Masters title that proves so elusive to him. The 44-year-old Norman shoots a final-round 73 and never again contends at Augusta National. His career Masters career ends in 2002, finishing as the runner-up three times (1986, 1987 and 1996) and with nine top 10 finishes in 23 career appearances.

2010 – Phil Mickelson fires a final-round 67 and wins his third title at the Masters beating third-round leader Lee Westwood by three shots. The signature moment for Mickelson comes when he hits the par-5 13th hole in two from the pine straw behind a tree to within four feet. Mickelson misses the eagle putt, but the birdie gives him a two-shot lead.

2013 – Fourteen-year-old Tianlang Guan of China becomes the youngest player ever to compete in the Masters and shoots a 73 – two shots better than defending champion Bubba Watson and 37 other golfers.

1948 – Claude Harmon shoots a final-round 70 to win the Masters by five shots over runner-up Cary Middlecoff. Harmon becomes the last winner of the event to not be presented with the traditional green jacket, a custom that begins the following year. Harmon's three sons – Butch, Craig, and Bill – all became top golf instructors, most notably Butch, who mentored Masters champions Tiger Woods and Phil Mickelson.

April 12

1987 – Larry Mize hits one of the most miraculous shots in golf history, holing a 140-foot chip shot in the second hole of a sudden-death playoff to beat Greg Norman and win the Masters. Mize, an Augusta native, ties after 72 holes with Norman and Seve Ballesteros, but Ballesteros is eliminated after the first hole of the sudden-death playoff after failing to make par. On the second playoff hole, the 11th hole, Mize hits his approach shot well left, 140 feet from the hole, while Norman, playing conservatively after Mize's shot, hits his approach into the right fringe, 50-feet from the hole. "I took my sand wedge and I had to hit it low," says Mize of his winning chip. "I had to hit the green. I didn't dare hit a high shot. That rye grass around the green would grab it." Norman, obviously shaken by Mize's miracle shot, pushes his birdie attempt well past the hole. Says Norman of the dramatic loss, "It's a bitter pill but I'll have to swallow it."

1986 – Nick Price shoots an Augusta National course record 63 in third round of the Masters. Price has a 30-foot birdie putt on the 18th hole for a 62, which would have been the lowest round ever shot at a major tournament, but the putt lips out and Price taps in for 63. "I didn't want to leave that putt short," Price says. "I wanted to see if I could shoot 62. I didn't want to back off. I wanted to prove something to myself."

2009 – Angel Cabrera becomes the first Masters champion from Argentina and from South America when he wins a sudden death playoff with Kenny Perry and Chad Campbell. Perry, age 48 and attempting to become the oldest winner ever at a major tournament, birdies the 15th and 16th holes to take a two-shot lead, but bogeys the last two holes to fall into the playoff with Cabrera and Campbell. Cabrera salvages par from the trees on the first playoff hole on No. 18, but Campbell falls out with a bogey. Perry hooks his approach shot from the middle of the fairway on the second playoff hole at No. 10 and makes bogey as Cabrera two-putts for the title.

1998 – Mark O'Meara wins his first major championship, sinking a 20-foot birdie putt on the final hole to win the Masters by one stroke over David Duval and Fred Couples. O'Meara birdies three of the final four holes to shoot a final-round 67. He wins the tournament in his 15th appearance, setting a record for appearances before a victory. Jack Nicklaus, age 58, shoots a final-round 68 to finish in a tie for sixth. David Toms, playing in his first Masters, shoots a record-tying 29 on the back-nine–with birdies on holes 12-17, en route to a 64.

1992 – Fred Couples, aided by thick and wet blades of grass on the bank of Rae's Creek on the 12th hole at Augusta National, wins the Masters for his first and only major championship by two strokes over 49-year-old Ray Floyd. Couples is saved from potentially throwing away the golf tournament when his tee shot on the par 3 12th hole is lands short and trickles towards Rae's Creek. However, the ball gets caught up in a layer of wet, uncut grass and stays dry. Couples chips up and saves par, shoots a final-round 70 and goes on to victory. "The biggest break, probably, in my life," says Couples of the shot.

1953 – Ben Hogan breaks the Masters scoring record by five strokes, posting a 14-under-par score of 274 to win by five shots over runner-up Ed "Porky" Oliver. Hogan's scoring record holds until it is broken by Jack Nicklaus and his 17-under score of 271 in 1965. The title is Hogan's second at Augusta National and his seventh major title. It also marks the beginning of an historic year for Hogan, who plays only seven PGA Tour events, winning five of them, including the U.S. Open by six shots, and the Open Championship by four shots, claiming the first three legs of what was not yet called "The Grand Slam." Hogan, however, is prevented from attempting to win the PGA Championship because the dates and the time required traveling back from the Open Championship. Hogan remains the only player to win the first three legs of the Grand Slam in a calendar year.

1954 – In a battle of two 41-year-olds who had won the previous three Masters titles, Sam Snead defeats defending champion Ben Hogan 70-71 in an 18-hole Monday playoff to win his third Masters tournament and his seventh and final major victory.

1964 – Arnold Palmer becomes the first four-time Masters champion, needing only a final-round 70 to win by six strokes over Dave Marr and defending champion Jack Nicklaus. "I was never sure in past Masters that I had really won it on my own," the 34-year-old Palmer says of his victories at Augusta National in 1958, 1960 and 1962. "There was always the weather or some factor. But, I really won this one." While the immediate focus for Palmer and the golf world and media is whether Palmer can sweep all four major titles in the same year, the 1964 Masters becomes his final major victory.

1981 – Tom Watson wins his second Masters title and his fifth major championship with a two-stroke victory over runners-up Jack Nicklaus and Johnny Miller at Augusta National. "It's better the second time around," says Watson, also the 1977 Masters champion, after his final-round 71. "I was so nervous all day I felt like jumping out of my skin."

2015 – Twenty-one-year-old Jordan Spieth ties the Masters scoring record and becomes the second-youngest champion in the event's history needing only a final-round 70 to win by four shots over runners-up Phil Mickelson and Justin Rose. Spieth, playing in his second Masters, ties the Masters scoring record of 270, 18 under-par, set by Tiger Woods in 1997. After shooting an opening round 64 three days earlier, Spieth becomes the first to win at Augusta wire-to-wire since Raymond Floyd in 1976. "This was arguably the greatest day of my life," Spieth says. "To join Masters history and put my name on that trophy and to have this jacket forever, it's something that I can't fathom right now."

April 13

1986 – Forty-six-year-old Jack Nicklaus wins his record 18th professional major and his sixth green jacket with a historic one-stroke victory at the 50th staging of the Masters. Nicklaus shoots a final round 65 with a back nine score of six-under-par 30 to edge runners-up Tom Kite and Greg Norman. Nicklaus becomes the oldest ever winner at the Masters and the second oldest major championship winner after Julius Boros, who was 48 when he won the 1968 PGA Championship. "Obviously I'm not as good a golfer as I was 10, 15 years ago but then I don't play as much as I did then," says Nicklaus. "But I started feeling it come back again last week."

1997 – Tiger Woods completes what CBS TV commentator Jim Nantz historically calls "a win for the ages" as the 21-year-old breaks through to win his anticipated first major title at the Masters in historic fashion. Woods wins the title by a record 12 shots over runner-up Tom Kite with a record score of 18-under-par 270 and becomes the youngest Masters winner at the age of 21 years, three months. Culturally, Woods becomes the first non-white player to win at Augusta National and, despite the decisiveness of the victory, is the star in the most watched golf broadcast in television history with over 50 million Americans watching on CBS television in the United States. Writes Ron Sirak of the Associated Press, "Young, gifted, a black man in a white man's game, Tiger Woods seemed too good to be true. At the Masters, he was even better than advertised. In one of those rare instances when reality exceeds expectation, Woods won by a record 12 strokes Sunday at Augusta National Golf Club and suddenly the notion that he might be the greatest golfer ever doesn't seem far-fetched."

1975 – In one of the most dramatic Masters of all time, Jack Nicklaus beats out Tom Weiskopf and Johnny Miller by one stroke to win his fifth Masters title and his 13th major title. The signature shot and the stroke that ultimately wins the tournament for Nicklaus is a 40-foot putt for birdie that Nicklaus drains at the 16th hole, capping it with a leap and a trot around the green. "In all the time I have played golf, I thought this was the most exciting display I had ever seen," says Nicklaus of the final-round dramatics.

1980 – Twenty-three-year-old Seve Ballesteros wins his first Masters title by four strokes over runners-up Jack Newton and Gibby Gilbert to become the youngest winner at Augusta National at the time. Ballesteros leads by seven strokes at the start of the day and extends the lead to 10 shots in the front nine, reaching 16-under-par and threatening the Jack Nicklaus and Ray Floyd scoring record of 17-under-par. However, the Spaniard finds the water at No. 12 and No. 13 at Amen Corner but holds on for the victory.

1942 – Byron Nelson shoots five-under par in the final 13 holes of a Monday playoff to defeat Ben Hogan 69-70 and win his second Masters title. Nelson is buoyed by an eagle on the par-5 eighth hole than moves him one shot ahead of Hogan after trailing by three shots through six holes. Nelson leads by three shots through 13 holes and holds on for the one-stroke victory. Due to World War II, the event is not played again until 1946.

1969 – George Archer wins his only major championship at the Masters, one stroke ahead of runners-up Billy Casper, George Knudson and Tom Weiskopf. Weiskopf is tied for the lead on the 17th hole but makes bogey to fall back. Charles Coody, who would win the Masters two years later, bogeys the final three holes and finishes two shots back.

1970 – Billy Casper defeats Gene Littler 69 to 74 in an 18-hole Monday playoff to win his third and final major championship in the last 18-hole playoff at the Masters. The format is changed to sudden-death in 1976 and first used in 1979. Casper previously wins the U.S. Open in 1959 and 1966.

2003 – Mike Weir becomes the first Canadian to win a major title and the first left-hander to win the Masters beating Len Mattiace in the first hole of a sudden-death playoff. Mattiace shoots a final-round 65 and waits almost an hour to watch Weir make a seven-foot par putt on the final hole to force the playoff.

Weir's bogey on the playoff hole – the 10th hole at Augusta National – beats Mattiace, who scores a double-bogey.

2014 – Bubba Watson wins the Masters for the second time in three years, shooting a three-under-par 69 for a three-stroke victory over Jordan Spieth and Jonas Blixt. Watson starts the day tied for the lead with the 20-year-old Spieth, a first-time Masters participant seeking to become the youngest ever Masters champion. Watson trails by two strokes on the eighth hole, but makes two straight birdies as Spieth makes two straight bogeys. On the par-5 13th hole, Watson hits a 366-yard drive around the corner, hits a 56-degree sand wedge approach to the green and two-putts for an incredible final birdie of the day.

2008 – Trevor Immelman of South Africa wins the Masters, his first major championship, with an eight-under par score of 280, three strokes ahead of runner-up and four-time champion Tiger Woods.

April 14

1996 – Nick Faldo makes up six-shot deficit and wins his third Masters title by five shots over Greg Norman, shooting a final-round 67 while Norman collapses with a final-round 78. Norman seems poised to finally break through and win his elusive first Masters title but suffers through one of the worst collapses in sports history and finishes second for a third time at Augusta National. Norman's bogey on the final hole allowing Jack Nicklaus to win the Masters in 1986 and losing to Larry Mize's miracle hole-out chip shot in the second playoff hole in 1987 are just two of the heartbreaking losses Norman endures in his major tournament career that features two Open Championship titles and eight runner-up showings and numerous heartbreaks and lost opportunities. "Of all of those I let get away, this one I really let get away," says Norman. "It's not the end of the world for me. Nobody ever likes to lose major championships, and

I had a chance to win one this week. Losing is not the end of my world. My life goes on. You just put that one down to poor play."

1968 – Bob Goalby wins the Masters in one of the most unusual ways in golf history. After shooting a final round 66 and posting a score of 11-under par 277, Goalby appears to have tied Roberto DeVicenzo of Argentina, the reigning Open Championship winner, forcing an 18-hole Monday playoff. However, DeVicenzo signs an incorrect scorecard kept by his playing partner Tommy Aaron that shows him making a par 4 on the 17th hole, rather than the birdie 3 that he achieves. DeVicenzo does not catch the mistake and the score stands and, per U.S. Golf Association rules, the score signed for must stand and Goalby wins the tournament by one shot.

2002 – Tiger Woods successfully defends his title at the Masters posting a score of 12-under-par 276, three shots better than runner-up Retief Goosen. Woods is only the third player to successfully defend a title at the Masters, joining Jack Nicklaus in 1966 and Nick Faldo in 1990.

1974 – Gary Player wins his second Masters title and his seventh major title, posting a 10-under-par 278 score, two shots better than Dave Stockton and Tom Weiskopf. Player misses the Masters the previous year due to leg and abdominal surgery, the only Masters that he would miss in his 53 years span playing the event.

1985 – Bernhard Langer comes back from a four-shot deficit to win the Masters by two shots over Seve Ballesteros, Raymond Floyd and Curtis Strange. Langer birdies four of the last seven holes to win his first of two titles at Augusta National. Curtis Strange, despite shooting an opening-round 80, leads by three shots with six holes to play but bogeys the 13th hole, when his second shot lands in Rae's Creek, and also bogeys the 15th and 18th holes.

1991 – Ian Woosnam of Wales wins the Masters title emerging from a three-way tie for the lead on the final hole of the tournament to win his only major title. Woosnam is tied with Tom Watson and Jose Maria Olazabal on the final hole of the tournament and Olazabal, playing ahead of Woosnam and Watson, makes his first bogey of the day going from fairway bunker to greenside bunker and missing a 45-foot par putt. Watson hits his tee shot right on 18, then hits into a greenside bunker, where he chips out and three-putts for double-bogey. Woosnam then sinks a five-foot par putt to win the championship.

2013 – Adam Scott becomes the first Australian to win the Masters, and the first using a belly-putter, beating Angel Cabrera on the second hole of a sudden-death playoff. Scott shoots a final-round 69 and sinks a 15-foot birdie putt to win in fading light and a soft rain on the 10th green – after he and Cabrera scramble for pars on the 18th hole, the first hole of the playoff.

2011 – Kevin Na registers the worst par-4 hole score in PGA Tour history shooting a 16 on the 474-yard ninth hole at the Texas Open in San Antonio. Na's tee shot flies into the woods, but Na eventually finds the ball and calls it unplayable and tees off again, hitting it again into the woods, where his comedy of errors includes a whiffed stroke, another that ricochets off his inner thigh, two shots attempted left-handed and one that barely moves. Na first believes he makes a 15 on the hole, but after reviewing the hole on video, he signs for a 16 and finishes the round with an eight-over 80. Says Na to reporters after the round, "I got done with the hole and I said [to my caddie], 'I think I made somewhere between a 10 and a 15. But I think it's close to a 15. It's all a blur." John Daly holds the record for the worst single-hole score at a PGA Tour event with an 18 on the par-5 sixth hole at Bay Hill in 1998. Ray Ainsley scored a 19 on the par-4 16th hole at Cherry Hills in the 1938 U.S. Open, which is not a PGA Tour event.

April 15

1979 – Fuzzy Zoeller becomes the only player other than Horton Smith, the winner of the first Augusta National Invitation Tournament, to win in their debut appearance at the Masters. Zoeller sinks a six-foot birdie on the second hole of the first-ever sudden-death playoff at the Masters to beat out Ed Sneed and Tom Watson. Sneed is the tournament leader at the start of the day, but bogeys the final three holes to post a final-round score of 76.

1984 – Ben Crenshaw, long the victim of heartbreak at major championships, finally breaks through and wins the first of his two Masters titles with a two-shot victory over Tom Watson. Crenshaw, a 12-year-veteran of the PGA Tour, had previously finished runner-up at five previous majors, including twice at the Masters, but seizes his opportunity buoyed by sinking a 60-foot birdie putt on the 10th hole to take sole possession of the lead. "Today was my day. I was determined," says Crenshaw, who trailed third-round leader Tom Kite by two to start the day. "I was not going to let the shots slip away. I was determined to be in control of myself and my game. And I did a good job at it."

April 16

1978 – A week after winning his ninth major title at the Masters with a final-round 64, Gary Player wins in a come-for-behind fashion for a second straight week, firing a final-round 67 and coming back from seven strokes back in the final round to win the Tournament of Champions at the LaCosta Resort and Spa in Carlsbad, Calif. Player wins his 23rd career PGA Tour title by a two-stroke margin over runners-up Andy North and Lee Trevino and benefits from third-round leader Seve Ballesteros shooting a final-round 79. "The last two years of my career have been like wine," Players says after his win, the second-to-last of his PGA career. "My game has improved with age. That's the honest to goodness truth. I swing far better now than I have. If I knew in my 20s and 30s what I know now about the golf swing I would've doubled my tournament wins. The human being believes that he was supposed to be finished by the time he's 40. Well I think that's dead wrong. I believe the average human being could live until he's 120 years old if he lives with no pollution, no smoking, no drinking and no worries with plenty of rest and good food."

2007 – Thomas Brent "Boo" Weekley wins his first PGA Tour event in dramatic fashion, chipping in on the final two holes to edge two-time U.S. Open champion Ernie Els by one shot at the Verizon Heritage in Hilton Head, S.C. After Weekley makes bogey on the 16th hole, he muffs a chip behind the 17th green, but follows up his potentially tournament-costing mistake by holing his 40-foot, par-saving chip to hold on to a one-stroke lead. On the 18th hole, Weekley chips across the green on his third shot and once again rolls in a chip from 36-feet away to again save par and ultimately wins him the championship. After making bogey on 17 to fall two strokes behind Weekley, Els nearly holes his second shot on the final hole for eagle, the ball landing two feet from the hole. Says Weekley in his thick Southern accent of his win, "Right now, it feels good. It ain't all sunk in yet."

1995 – Bob Tway wins the MCI Classic at Harbour Town Golf Links in Hilton Head, S.C. with a par of the second hole of a sudden-death playoff with Nolan Henke and David Frost. Tway's win is the seventh of eight career PGA Tour wins and his first in five years. "This is better than the PGA Championship," Tway emotionally says after the win, referencing his incredible 1986 PGA Championship win where he holes a bunker shot for birdie on the final hole to beat Greg Norman. "This is better than any tournament. You been down so long, you start thinking you're never going to get back. Every time I start talking about it, I can hardly talk. Back then, it felt kind of easy. This was anything but easy, I can tell you that."

2001 – Jose Coceres becomes the first Argentine to win on the PGA Tour since Roberto De Vicenzo in 1968 when he beats Billy Mayfair in a playoff to win the WorldCom Classic at Harbour Town Golf Links in Hilton Head, S.C. Coceres and Mayfair play three of their five playoff holes in a Monday morning finish after they conclude regulation play – and two playoff holes – before darkness prevents further play the previous day.

April 17

1960 – Sam Snead birdies the last two holes at Starmount Forest Country Club, shoots a final-round 69 and wins his 80th PGA Tour title at the Greater Greensboro Open by two shots over runner-up Dow Finsterwald. Snead, who wins his record 82nd and final PGA tournament title again in Greensboro in 1965, earns $2,800 for the title.

1988 – Ian Baker-Finch wins the Bridgestone Aso Open on the Japan Golf Tour and wins a first-prize of 7.2 million yen (about $54,000 at the time) – and a cow. Rather than taking the cow, Baker-Finch actually negotiates with the tournament organizers to have them buy the cow back for $5,000.

1988 – Greg Norman comes from four shots back to claim a one-stroke win at the Heritage Classic at Hilton Head Island, S.C. Norman gains inspiration from Jamie Hutton, a 17-year-old stricken with leukemia, who walks all 18 holes with Norman during his final-round 66. "I just want to thank Jamie," Norman says after the win. "He showed me inspiration and courage. He told me he wanted me to shoot 64 and win. I shot a 66 and that was enough." Norman gives the winner's plaque to Hutton as well as the Heritage's signature tartan jacket given to the tournament's champion.

1994 – Forty-eight-year-old Hale Irwin wins his 20th and final PGA Tour title at the MCI Heritage Golf Classic in Hilton Head,

S.C., beating Greg Norman by one shot. Irwin shoots a final-round 68 wins at Harbour Town for the third time, 23 years after winning his first PGA Tour title on the same grounds in 1971.

2015 – Tom Watson becomes the second oldest player to make a cut on the PGA Tour at the RBC Heritage at Hilton Head, S.C. at the age of 65 years, seven months, 13 days. Watson makes a dramatic birdie on the 18th hole at the Harbour Town Golf Links, hitting his approach shot to four feet and sinking the birdie putt to make the cut on the number. The only player older than Watson to make a PGA Tour cut was 67-year-old Sam Snead at the 1979 Westchester Classic in N.Y. Says Watson of needing to make birdie on the final hole to make the cut, "First of all, I hit the best drive I've hit all week. Put it just short of the water, and then I had 156 yards to the hole and I hit a solid eight-iron that did exactly what I wanted it to do…didn't hit the greatest putt but the ball went into the hole and made 3 to make the cut."

April 18

2014 – Pablo Larrazabal experiences one of the most bizarre occurrences in the sport when he is attacked by hornets on the 14th hole at the Kuala Lumpur Country Club in the opening round of the Malaysian Open, forcing him to jump in a lake to fend off the dangerous insects. "They were three times the size of bees," Larrazabal says of his attackers. "They were huge and like 30 or 40 of them started to attack me big time. I didn't know what to do. My caddie told me to run, so I start running like a crazy guy, but the hornets were still there, so the other players told me to jump in the lake. I ran to the lake, threw my scorecard down, took off my shoes and jumped in the water. It was the scariest moment of my career, for sure. I've never been so scared." Larrazabal receives medical treatment, including injections, for multiple stings and, miraculously, birdies the hole where he is stung and shoots a 68.

2015 – In one of the most dramatic and improbable finishes in golf history, Sei Young Kim of South Korea wins the Lotte Championship in Hawaii by holing an eight-iron from 154 yards for eagle on the first sudden-death playoff hole with country-woman Inbee Park. Kim's shot comes after she dramatically chips in for par on the final hole of regulation to force the playoff after hitting her tee shot into the water. "I still can't believe what just happened," Kim says through a translator following her miracle victory.

1982 – Lanny Wadkins wins his ninth career PGA Tour title at the MONY Tournament of Champions in Carlsbad, Calif., when co-leader Ron Streck three-putts for bogey on the final hole. The one-stroke margin of victory for Wadkins is extended to three strokes, however, when Streck is assessed a two-stroke penalty after it is revealed by television viewers that Streck inappropriately moves branches away from his face after hitting his tee shot underneath a tree on the sixteenth hole. "He moved a branch with his hand. You cannot do that," PGA Tour official Claude Mangum says. "On several occasions he moved to branch which was in his face." The penalty moves Streck from solo second place into a four-way tie for second place with Craig Stadler, Andy Bean and David Graham, costing Streck $14,338 in prize money.

2010 – Jim Furyk wins the Verizon Heritage Classic in Hilton Head, S.C., when Brian Davis calls a two-shot penalty on himself on the first hole of a sudden-death playoff when Davis hits a reed of long grass with his backswing from the hazard to the left of the 18th green at Harbour Town Golf Links. The mistake is a violation of rule 13.4 in the rules of golf against moving a loose impediment during a takeaway. "It's just awkward to see it happen at such a key moment in the golf tournament," says Furyk, who wins his 15th career PGA Tour title. "Awkward for him to lose that way, and a little awkward for me to win…To have the tournament come down that way is definitely not the way I wanted to win. It's obviously a tough loss for him and I respect and admire what he did."

April 19

1987 – Davis Love III wins his first PGA Tour title at the MCI Heritage Golf Classic in Hilton Head, S.C., winning by one stroke over Steve Jones, who double-bogeys the final hole at the Harbour Town Golf Links with a drive off the tee that lands out of bounds. "Just one bad shot at the wrong moment," says Jones, who, like Love, was also in search of his first PGA Tour title. "It's a 70-yard fairway and I miss it. I was out of bounds by 10 yards." Ironically, the two men would become intertwined nine years later when Love would miss a three-foot par putt on the final hole at the 1996 U.S. Open at Oakland Hills that drops him one shot behind Jones, who goes on to win the tournament, his only major title.

1992 – Davis Love III wins the MCI Heritage Classic at Hilton Head Island, S.C. for a third time – his fifth PGA Tour title – with a 15-under-par score of 269, earning him $180,000. Love's final-round 68 leads him to a four-stroke victory over runner-up Chip Beck. The win comes just three weeks after Love wins the Tournament Players Championship just down I-95 in Ponte Vedra Beach, Florida.

1998 – Davis Love III wins the MCI Classic in Hilton Head, S.C. for a fourth time, firing a final-round of 65 at the Harbour Town Golf Links to win by seven shots over runner-up Glen Day.

2014 – Hawaii native Michelle Wie wins her first LPGA title in the United States, and her third career title, firing a five-under par 67 for a two-shot victory in the Lotte Championship in Kapolei, Hawaii, played on the Ko Olina golf course, her home course. "It feels good," says the 24-year-old. "I'm just so happy right now I can't think straight."

April 20

1958 – Gary Player wins on the PGA Tour for the first time in his career at the Kentucky Derby Open, shooting a final-round 69 to win by three strokes over runners-up Chick Harbert and Ernie Vossler.

1980 – Despite receiving a two-stroke penalty for giving his playing partner Lee Trevino putting advice, Tom Watson still wins the MONY Tournament of Champions by three shots over runner-up Jim Colbert. Watson originally wins the event by five shots, but officials announce the two-shot penalty 20 minutes after the conclusion of play. PGA Tour officials learn of the violation from a fan watching the live broadcast of the event on television, hearing Watson tell Trevino on the 13th hole that he needed to use a different putting stroke, and calls the tournament to report the violation. "I was wrong," Watson says of the infraction. "I simply was wrong. Rules are made to follow and I violated the rules. I told Lee about the ball placement as an act of friendship. Initially, I felt a little animosity towards the caller but now I realize it was my fault." The title is Watson's 21st of his PGA Tour career and earns him the first prize of $54,000.

2003 – Davis Love, III wins the MCI Heritage Classic for a fifth time in dramatic fashion, chipping in from 66 feet away on the final hole to tie the lead of Woody Austin, then hits the flag with his approach shot on the fourth playoff hole before tapping in for the victory. Love sinks the wedge shot on the final hole to tie Austin at 13-under par and to cap off a final round of 67. After Austin misses makeable six and three-foot birdie putts on the second and third playoff holes, Love hits a six-iron on the 18th hole that hits the flag and nestles three feet from the pin that he negotiates for the winning birdie. The win is the 17th career victory for Love, who earlier in the year wins at the AT&T Pebble Beach Pro-Am and The Players Championship.

2014 – Matt Kuchar dramatically chips in for birdie on the final hole to win the RBC Heritage by one stroke over Luke Donald at the Harbour Town Golf Links at Hilton Head, S.C. Kuchar trails Donald by four strokes at the start of the day but his chip-in birdie caps a final-round 64 to win his seventh career PGA Tour event.

1997 – Nick Price shoots a final round 66 to win the MCI Classic by six strokes over Brad Faxon and Jesper Parnevik at Harbour Town Golf Links at Hilton Head, S.C. After claiming his 16th career win on the PGA Tour, Price immediately acknowledges his long-time caddie and friend Jeff "Squeeky" Medlen who is recovering from a bone-marrow transplant in an attempt to beat leukemia. "It is important for me to win, but it is more important for me to know, for (Medlen) to know how many people are pulling for him," Price says after the win. "I think he knows that now." Medlen passes away from the disease two months later.

April 21

1963 – Bob Charles becomes the first left-handed player to win a PGA event when he wins the Houston Classic at Memorial Park, shooting a final-round 69 to beat Fred Hawkins by one stroke. Less than three months later, Charles becomes the first left-handed player to win a major when he wins the Open Championship title.

1974 – Lee Elder wins his first PGA Tour title at the Monsanto Open in Pensacola, Fla., and with it becomes the first black player to receive an invitation to play at the Masters. "I will definitely accept an invitation to the Masters and I will definitely play in the Masters," Elder tells the Associated Press after defeating Peter Oosterhuis with a birdie on the fourth hole of a sudden-death playoff at the Pensacola Country Club. Clifford Roberts, the chairman of the Augusta National Golf Club, issues a statement following Elder's win stating Elder will definitely be extended an invitation to play in the event, previously an all-white event. "He has earned his invitation and we are delighted he has done so," Roberts says. Responds Elder when hearing of the Roberts statement, "That's fine. Tell Mr. Roberts I'll see them at the Masters." Elder is not the first black player to win a PGA event as Charlie Sifford and Pete Brown both won events but before the Masters instituted its rule making all winners of regular tour events eligible for inclusion in the field.

1985 – One week after winning the Masters for his first win in the United States, Bernhard Langer wins again at the Sea Pines Heritage Classic in the first hole of a sudden-death playoff with Bobby Wadkins, the brother of Lanny Wadkins. Langer makes a tap-in par on the first hole of the playoff – the 16th hole – while Wadkins misses his 12-foot par attempt after escaping the greenside bunker. Langer, from West Germany, becomes the first man since Gary Player in 1978 to follow a win at the Masters with a victory the following week. Says Wadkins, ''I know he must have had a little letdown after winning last week. To come here, and play extremely well, like he did, my hat's off to him."

1995 – Loren Roberts, whose smooth putting stroke earns him the nick-name of "The Boss of the Moss," wins the MCI Heritage Classic in Hilton Head, S.C. making only 25 putts of his final 18 holes. Roberts follows a third-round 63 with a final-round 67 to beat Mark O'Meara by three strokes for the third of his eight career PGA Tour titles. The Roberts' 72-hole tournament score of 19-under-par 265 sets a new standard for the Harbour Town Golf Links. Ten months earlier, Roberts loses to Ernie Els on the 19th hole of an 18-hole playoff at the U.S. Open at Oakmont, Pa., that also included Colin Montgomerie.

April 22

1984 – Nick Faldo wins his first PGA Tour event at the Heritage Golf Classic at Harbour Town Golf Links on Hilton Head Island, S.C. to become the first Englishman to win on United States soil since Tony Jacklin at the 1972 Greater Jacksonville Open. Faldo shoots a final-round 69 for a one-shot win over Tom Kite, who birdies five of the first 12 holes in a final-round charge. "Tom made it a tough day," says Faldo of Kite and his bogey-free 66. "I knew I had to shoot under par. You can't shoot par or one over and win over here….It was my No. 1 goal for the season, to win in this country. I'm thrilled to bits."

1990 – Steve Elkington comes from seven shots back shooting a 31 on the back nine for a 66 to win his first PGA Tour title at the Kmart Greater Greensboro Open. Elkington is referred to as the "Other Australian" to media and fans as he sits in the shadow of his countryman Greg Norman, the No. 1 ranked golfer in the world. "I've just proven to everybody that there's more Australian players than the Baker-Finches and the Normans and the Gradys," says Elkington of Australian standouts Ian Baker-Finch, Wayne Grady and Greg Norman. Later that year, Grady wins the PGA Championship, while Baker-Finch wins the Open Championship the following year in 1991. Elkington also joins the Australian major winner club in 1995 when he wins the PGA Championship.

April 23

1978 – Gary Player wins his 24th and final event on the PGA Tour, shooting a final-round 69 to beat Andy Bean by one stroke at the Houston Open. The win caps an incredible three weeks of play for Player, who wins the Masters on April 9 and the Tournament of Champions in California the previous week. Player becomes the first player since Hubert Green in 1976 to win in three consecutive starts and the first foreigner player to do so on American soil since Bobby Locke, also from South Africa, in 1947. "I was very much aware of it," Player says of winning three weeks in a row. "It's a nice record to have. I have now won six of my last nine (including foreign events) – that's my hottest streak since 1974, which was my best year ever."

2000 – One month after staring down and beating Tiger Woods by a stroke to win the Players Championship, Hal Sutton wins again at the Greater Greensboro Chrysler Classic, shooting a final-round 71 to beat runner-up Andrew Magee by three strokes. The win is the 13th and second-to-last PGA Tour title for Sutton. Sutton, the winner of the 1983 PGA Championship, wins on the PGA Tour for a final time exactly 364 days later at the Shell Houston Open.

2007 – Lorena Ochoa of Mexico replaces Annika Sorenstam as the No. 1 women's golfer in the world. Ochoa holds the ranking for a record 158 weeks until May 3, 2010, the day after her last event as a professional player. She announces her retirement three years to the day of first achieving the No. 1 ranking in a 2010 press conference in Mexico City.

April 24

1927 – Bobby Jones makes his first career hole-in-one on the 170-yard 11th hole at his home course, the East Lake Country Club in Atlanta. Jones hits a half-swing seven-iron that bounces twice and falls into the hole.

2005 – Vijay Singh successfully defends his Shell Houston Open title beating John Daly on the first playoff hole to win his 26th career PGA Tour title. Singh only needs a par on hole No. 18 at the Redstone Golf Club after Daly hooks his drive into the water. It marks the third time Singh wins in Houston after winning in 2002 and in 2004.

1988 – Chip Beck shoots a final-round 64 and wins the USF&G Classic in New Orleans by seven strokes over runner-up Lanny Wadkins. Beck has a chance to tie the PGA Tour record of 27-under-par but leaves his 10-foot birdie putt short on the final hole. "I'm a little disappointed I left it short," Beck says. "(But) how can I be disappointed? To come through like this, it's overwhelming."

April 25

1999 – Jesper Parnevik, the eccentric-dressing Swedish golfer known for playing with a baseball hat with the front bill turned upwards, wins his second of his five career PGA Tour titles at the Greater Greensboro Open. Parnevik shoots a final-round 70 to beat runner-up Jim Furyk by two strokes. Earlier in the day, Swedish tennis player Magnus Norman wins the U.S. Clay Court Championship title in Orlando – televised in the United States on CBS, the same network covering the golf from Greensboro – and offers encouragement to Parnevik by wearing a baseball hat with the bill cap turned upwards like Parnevik with the words "Go Jesper" written on the inside bill of the hat.

1982 – Seve Ballesteros shoots a final-round 68 and wins the Cepsa Madrid Open in his native Spain by one shot over countryman Jose Maria Canizares. The win is the 17th of 50 tournament wins for Ballesteros on the European Tour.

April 26

2015 – Justin Rose makes birdie on the final two holes and claims a one-stroke victory over Cameron Tringale at the Zurich Classic in New Orleans. "Earlier this year it looked impossible to win," Rose says of his early season struggles. "I'm very happy to have turned my game around." Rose finishes a weather-delayed third-round of 65 earlier in the day before shooting a final-round 66 to win his seventh PGA Tour title.

1982 – Scott Hoch wins his second of 11 career PGA Tour titles, shooting a two-under par 70 to win a rain-delayed and shortened USF&G Classic in New Orleans by two shots over two-time defending champion Tom Watson and Bob Shearer. Heavy rains causes for the tournament to finish on a Monday and consist of only 54 holes. "I never knew I liked rain so much," quips Hoch of the soggy circumstances that allow for his victory.

1981 – Fresh off winning his second Masters title, Tom Watson wins his 27th PGA Tour title at the USF&G New Orleans Open shooting a final-round 68 to beat Bruce Fleisher by two strokes.

April 27

2014 – Three days after her 17th birthday, Lydia Ko wins her third career LPGA title – but first as a professional – making birdie on the final hole to beat Stacy Lewis and Jenny Shin at the Swinging Skirts LPGA Classic in Daly City, Calif.

2003 – Fred Couples, a former student at the University of Houston, wins his 15th and final PGA Tour title at the Shell Houston Open shooting his second consecutive 67 to win by four strokes over runners-up Mark Calcavecchia, Stuart Appleby and Hank Kuehne.

1997 – Frank Nobilo of New Zealand wins his first and only PGA Tour title at the Greater Greensboro Chrysler Classic in North Carolina. Nobilo, who nearly skips the event but is talked into playing by friend Ernie Els, birdies six of the final 11 holes in rainy conditions and scrambles for a par on the first hole of a sudden-death playoff with Brad Faxon to win the title.

Nobilo starts the final round five shots back of Faxon, the third round leader.

1986 – Seve Ballesteros becomes the second golfer to hold the No. 1 ranking in the official World Golf Rankings, taking over the top spot from Bernhard Langer. Ballesteros goes on to hold the No. 1 ranking for a total of 61 weeks during his career.

2008 – Australian Adam Scott birdies the third playoff hole and wins the Byron Nelson Championship for his first PGA Tour title in more than a year. Scott rolls in a birdie putt of 49 feet in defeating American Ryan Moore, who had a chance to extend the playoff, but misses his own birdie putt. Scott birdies the 18th hole in regulation to force the playoff then misses two chances to win before he drains his mammoth putt on the third playoff hole.

April 28

1974 – Mike Reasor records the highest score in PGA Tour history when he finishes the Tallahassee Open in Florida with a score of 93 over par. After making the 36-hole cut with an even par score of 144, Reasor scores weekend scores of 123 for the third round and 114 for the final round. The reason for Reasor's high score is injuries suffered when a horse he is riding for relaxation after his second round runs into a tree. Due to a rule at the time that exempts players from having to Monday qualify for events if they finish tournaments the previous week, Reasor must complete the final two rounds in Tallahassee, despite his injuries, in order to gain entry into the Byron Nelson Classic the following week, should be healthy enough to compete. Reasor suffers torn rib cartilage, damaged knee ligaments and a separated left shoulder, but plays the final two rounds of the tournament swinging only with his right arm with a five-iron. "You should have seen them laughing on the first tee. I stepped up with a five-iron and barely got it to the ladies tees," says

Reasor. "I think the fact that I made it around that course is commendable. I almost didn't make it going up the hill on 16. I was woozy there. I've got all kinds of medications in me... What a way to get recognition." Reasor's efforts are in vain as he does not recover in time to compete the following week at the Byron Nelson Classic. He dies in 2002 of a heart-attack while competing at the Pacific Northwest Section P.G.A. Senior Championship in Bend, Oregon.

1974 – Johnny Miller's torrid run of tournament wins continues as he wins his fifth tournament of the year at the Tournament of Champions at the LaCosta Resort in Carlsbad, Calif. Miller is tied for the lead on the final hole with John Mahaffey and John Allin and makes a four-foot par putt after his co-leaders make bogey giving him the one-stroke victory. Miller goes on to win three more titles during his stellar 1974 season, earning a then-record $353,201 in prize money and earning PGA Tour Player of the Year honors.

April 29

2007 – In his 21st attempt, Scott Verplank finally wins the Byron Nelson Golf Classic, shooting a final-round 66 to beat Luke Donald by one shot. Verplank, a Dallas native and long-time friend and pupil of Nelson, is the sentimental winner of the first staging of the tournament after the death of Nelson the previous year. "There's no question in my mind that the stars lined up and I got a little help from upstairs. I just haven't been playing that good," Verplank tells reporters afterward. "I think Byron had a hand in this week."

1990 – David Frost holes out from a bunker from 50 feet out on the final hole and wins the USF&G Classic in New Orleans by one stroke over Greg Norman. "What can you say? He hit a great shot," says a snake-bitten Norman.

1984 – Corey Pavin wins his first PGA Tour title by shooting a final-round 68 to win the Houston Open by one shot over runner-up Buddy Gardner. Pavin goes on to win 15 career titles on the PGA Tour, including the 1995 U.S. Open at Shinnecock Hills in Southampton, N.Y.

1973 – Dan Sikes misses a two-foot par putt on the first hole of a sudden-death playoff giving 23-year-old Lanny Wadkins his second career PGA Tour title at the Byron Nelson Classic. "I had accepted the fact he was going to make it and was thinking about the next hole," says Wadkins of the missed playoff putt from Sikes on the par-5 553-yard 15th hole at the Preston Trail Golf Club in Dallas. Wadkins birdies five of the last seven holes to shoot a final-round 67. Sikes, 42, makes an incredible 40-foot putt on the final hole to tie Wadkins and force the playoff. Sikes, a winner of six PGA Tour events from 1963 to 1968, never does win again the PGA Tour, while Wadkins wins 19 more times on tour, including the PGA Championship in 1977.

April 30

1978 – Gary Player falls just short of winning his fourth-straight PGA Tour title, faltering in the final round of the New Orleans Open as Lon Hinkle wins his first PGA Tour event. After Player wins the Masters, the Tournament of Champions and the Houston Open in his last three starts, he shoots a final-round 72 and, despite at one point being in a five-way tie for the lead, finishes in fifth place. "You can't go on winning every single week," says Player. "Winning three in a row in this day and age and against this competition it's something I'll remember all my life." Hinkle shoots a final-round 66 and birdies the final hole to beat out runners-up Fuzzy Zoeller and Gibby Gilbert. Says Hinkle of Player, "With everybody and his grandmother asking Gary if he thought he could win four in a row, it put tremendous pressure on him. I don't know how he played as well as he did."

1989 – Just two weeks after losing a heart-breaking playoff to Nick Faldo at the Masters, where he misses a two-foot par putt to win the title, Scott Hoch wins the Las Vegas Invitational in a playoff, beating Robert Wrenn for his fourth career PGA Tour title.

2000 – Robert Allenby wins his first PGA Tour title by incredibly surviving a four-hole playoff with Craig Stadler at the Shell Houston Open. Stadler misses putts to win the tournament in the playoff from four feet on the first hole, five feet on the second hole and 11 feet on the third hole. On the fourth playoff hole, Allenby makes a 10-foot putt for par before Stadler misses a slightly closer putt for par to lose the tournament.

MAY

May 1

1972 – Chi Chi Rodriguez wins the Byron Nelson Classic on the first hole of a sudden-death playoff with Billy Casper at the Preston Trails Golf Club in Dallas. The title is the sixth PGA Tour championship for Rodriguez and his first since the 1968 Sahara Invitational. As a child in Puerto Rico, Rodriguez worked for a dollar a day in the sugar cane fields, but earns $25,000 with the title. "They used to call me the hot dog pro when I was first on tour 12 years ago," Rodriguez tells reporters after his win. "Yes when spectators saw me down the fairway they commented 'He's nobody. Let's go get a hot dog.'"

2011 – Bubba Watson overcomes a three-stroke deficit over the final eight holes of regulation and beats Webb Simpson on the second hole of a sudden-death playoff to win Zurich Classic of New Orleans, his third PGA Tour victory. "My wife, my caddie and my trainer would say my attitude's in the right spot," Watson says. "This week, I won (by) not getting down on bad shots, just staying focused on what I'm supposed to be doing."

May 2

2010 – Eighteen-year-old Ryo Ishikawa shoots a 12-under-par round of 58 – the lowest score ever on a major tour – to win The Crowns golf tournament on the Japan Tour. Ishikawa nearly sinks a 15-foot birdie putt on the final hole that would have given him a 57, but settles for par. Ishikawa makes 12 birdies and no bogeys over the 6,545-yard Nagoya Golf Club course. "I always dreamed of getting a score like this but didn't think I would do it so fast," Ishikawa says. "It hasn't really sunk in yet, but I'm sure it will after a few days." Ishikawa breaks the Japan Tour record of 59 set by Masahiro Kuramoto in the first round of the 2003 Acom International. On the PGA Tour, Al Geiberger, Chip Beck and David Duval share the record at 59. Annika Sorenstam also had a 59 on the LPGA Tour. In 2000 in a U.S. Open qualifier, Shigeki Maruyama shot a 13-under 58.

1981 – Ron Streck becomes the first player to win on the PGA Tour with metal woods when he wins the Houston Open using the TaylorMade 'metal' woods. Streck shoots rounds of 68, 68 and 62 and leads the tournament entering the final round, but is declared the winner when the fourth round is washed out by six inches of rain and the course is flooded to an extent that makes play impossible on the course.

2010 – Twenty-year-old Rory McIlroy sinks a 40-foot birdie putt to cap a final-round 10-under-par 62 to win his first PGA Tour title at the Quail Hollow Championship in Charlotte, N.C. McIlroy's course-record score gives him a four-shot victory over runner-up Phil Mickelson. "I suppose I got into the zone," says McIlroy, who made the cut two days earlier on the number.

2010 – Lorena Ochoa of Mexico plays her final round of golf as a professional, shooting a final-round 71 to finish in sixth place at the Tres Marias Championship at Tres Marias Golf Club in Morelia, Mexico. Ochoa, who won the event three previous times among her 27 career LPGA victories, finishes seven shots back of winner Ai Miyazato of Japan. "It was a tough day with emotions, and now I'm only going to remember the fans, the good words, the support they gave me the last four days and, this, being here on the 18th green for the last time," Ochoa says upon the completion of her round.

May 3

1964 – Pete Brown becomes the first black player to win a PGA Tour event when he wins the Waco Turner Open in Burneyville, Oklahoma by one stroke over Dan Sikes.

1970 – Jack Nicklaus beats Arnold Palmer on the first hole of a sudden-death playoff to win the Byron Nelson Classic for his 29th career title. Playing the 555-yard par-5 15th hole in the playoff, Nicklaus reaches the green in two shots, while Palmer reaches the putting surface in three. Nicklaus two putts for birdie to win while Palmer misses his 12-footer for birdie. Says the 40-year-old Palmer of the playoff hole, "I used two drivers, one from the tee and the other from the fairway at the extra hole because I knew Jack could probably get home in two, but I was short and then I hit a bad chip."

1987 – Paul Azinger, tied for the lead with Hal Sutton and Curtis Strange, sinks a 30-foot breaking eagle putt on final hole to win the Las Vegas Invitational at the Las Vegas Country Club. "I wasn't thinking of eagle, but trying to make a birdie," Azinger says following the round. "I can't believe that putt went in." Azinger wins $225,000, the largest first-place check in PGA Tour history at the time.

2010 – Jiyai Shin of South Korea becomes the third woman to achieve the world No. 1 ranking – and the first from her nation – as she takes over the top spot from Lorena Ochoa. She holds the ranking for a total of 25 weeks.

May 4

1986 – After finishing second to Jack Nicklaus at the Masters and Fuzzy Zoeller at the Heritage Classic in his last two starts, Greg Norman breaks through and wins the Las Vegas Invitational, shooting a final-round 65 at the Las Vegas Country Club, earning $207,000. "It just goes to show it just takes patience," says Norman of the win, his first in two years. "If you keep knocking at the door, sooner or later it's going to open. I guess this week I took it right off its hinges."

1959 – Ben Hogan wins his fifth title at the Colonial Invitational with a four-shot win in an 18-hole playoff over Fred Hawkins. Hogan shoots a 69 to 73 from Hawkins. The title is the 65th PGA Tour title for the 46-year-old Hogan and his first since the 1956 Canadian Open.

2003 – David Toms is so dominant at the inaugural staging of the Wachovia Championship at Quail Hollow Golf Club in Charlotte, N.C. that he wins the tournament by two strokes after making a quadruple bogey 8 on the final hole.

2003 – Hale Irwin wins his 37th PGA Champions Tour title in one of the most unusual rounds of his career. On the front nine at the Kinko's Classic in Austin, Texas, Irwin makes a double-bogey and whiffs a tap-in putt that results in a triple bogey, but recovers with four back-nine birdies and wins the tournament on the second hole of a playoff with Tom Watson. Irwin also whiffs a tap-in putt at the 1983 British Open, where he loses by one stroke to, ironically, Watson. "I guess he got me back today," Watson says after the playoff loss.

2014 – Three years after undergoing two brain surgeries, J.B. Holmes, ranked No. 242 in the world golf rankings, wins the Wells Fargo Championship at Quail Hollow in Charlotte, N.C. by one shot over runner-up Jim Furyk. Holmes, who described the surgeries as "low risk" to help alleviate Chiari malformations that cause vertigo-like symptoms, shoots a final-round 71 and holds on for the victory, despite making bogey on the 16th and 18th holes.

2008 – Twenty-two-year-old second-year PGA Tour pro Anthony Kim wins his first PGA Tour event at the Wachovia

Championship at Quail Hollow in Charlotte, N.C. Kim posts a 16-under-par score of 272, the lowest 72-hole score in the event's history – five shots better than runner-up Ben Curtis. Kim wins again later in the year at the AT&T National and again in 2010 at the Houston Open, before an injury forces him off the tour in 2012.

May 5

1978 – Mark James registers a score of 111 in the second round of the Italian Open in Sardinia – the highest 18-hole score in the history of the European Tour. James ends his round playing one-handed due to an injured left wrist, but refuses to withdraw after being fined 50 pounds by the European Tour in 1977 after pulling out of a tournament with a wrenched knee. This remains the highest 18-hole score in the history of the European Tour.

2002 – K.J. Choi becomes the first South Korean winner in PGA Tour history, shooting a final-round five-under 67 for a four-stroke victory in the Compaq Classic in New Orleans. "I believe it will influence a generation of Korean golfers to come to the U.S. and try out for the PGA," Choi says through an interpreter. "In that sense, the win is very special."

1991 – Eight years after winning his first PGA Tour title at the World Series of Golf in 1983, Nick Price finally wins his elusive second title with a one-stroke win over runner-up Craig Stadler at the Byron Nelson Classic. Price wins again later in the year at the Canadian Open and a total of 13 times in the next three-and-a-half years, including the PGA Championship twice in 1992 and 1994 and the Open Championship in 1994.

1985 – Tom Kite runs away from the field at the MONY Tournament of Champions, claiming a six-stroke win over runner-up Mark McCumber at the LaCosta Resort & Spa in Carlsbad, Calif. Tom Watson, the defending champion, and his playing partner Scott Hoch are the first players off in the final round and finish 18 holes in two hours, nine minutes and each shoot a two-under-par 70s.

May 6

2012 – Rickie Fowler wins his anticipated first PGA Tour title at the Wells Fargo Championship at Quail Hollow in Charlotte, winning on the first hole of a sudden-death playoff with world No. 1 Rory McIlroy and D.A. Points. Fowler hits his approach shot on the 18th hole to four feet and makes a birdie to win in his 67th start as a professional. "I didn't want to play it safe," says the 23-year-old Fowler of his approach on the playoff hole. "I had a good number (133 yards), and I was aiming right of the hole with the wind coming out of the right, and if I hit a perfect shot, it comes down right on the stick…I hit a perfect shot at the right time, and I was going for it."

2001 – David Toms, an LSU graduate and a native of Shreveport, La., wins his home-state PGA Tour title at the Compaq Classic of New Orleans by two shots over runner-up Phil Mickelson. Toms holes out for eagle at the par-5 11th hole during the final round en route to winning his fifth career PGA Tour title. Toms and Mickelson duel again later in the year at the PGA Championship at the Atlanta Athletic Club, Toms again victorious by one shot.

2007 – Tiger Woods beats runner-up Steve Stricker by two strokes and wins the Wachovia Championship at Quail Hollow in Charlotte for his 57th career PGA Tour title. "Over the course of my career, I've won a few tournaments here and there, and it's been nice," says Woods. "This one, considering the field and the golf course and the conditions, ecstatic to have won here."

1990 – Five years after blowing a three-shot lead on the final hole to lose the Byron Nelson Classic, Payne Stewart exorcises his bad memories at the even with a two-stroke win over Lanny Wadkins to win his seventh PGA Tour title. Stewart fires a final-round 67 to hold off Wadkins, who shoots a 65. "I didn't start well today and in the past I might have lost my composure," Stewart says. "But I didn't today. I think I am in better shape to handle the pressure than I was a few years ago."

May 7

2006 – Jim Furyk wins his 11th PGA Tour title at the Wachovia Championship at Quail Hollow Golf Club in Charlotte beating Trevor Immelman on the first hole of a sudden-death playoff. Immelman needs only to two-putt for par from 50 feet on the final hole of regulation to earn his first tournament win in the United States, but misses his 10-foot par putt. His tee shot on the 18th hole in the playoff finds a bad lie in the deep rough and he makes bogey after hitting his approach shot 80 yards shy of the green. Furyk makes a six-foot putt for par to earn the title and the $1.134 million first prize. Immelman does break through to win his first title on U.S. soil later in the year at the Western Open in Chicago and then again in 2008 at the Masters.

1995 – Mark Calcavecchia shoots a final-round six-under-par 66 at the Atlanta Country Club and wins the BellSouth Classic by two shots over runner-up Jim Gallagher, Jr. Calcavecchia says after his round that when he starts the back nine four shots behind Gallagher that he thought he would have to shoot 31 on the back nine in order to win. "Lo and behold, I shot 31," he says. "It was amazing."

2017 – John Daly wins his first event on the PGA Champions Tour at the Insperity Invitational at The Woodlands in Texas, closing with three straight bogeys to win by one shot over Tommy Armour III and Kenny Perry. "It wasn't pretty at the end," says the 51-year-old Daly of his three-bogey finish. "But I got it done and that's all that matters." The win is the tour win for Daly since he last won on the PGA Tour at the 2004 Buick Invitational at Torrey Pines.

May 8

1988 – Gary Koch shoots a five-under-par 67 to score his first PGA Tour victory in four years with a one-stroke win over runners-up Mark O'Meara and Peter Jacobsen at the Las Vegas Invitational at the Las Vegas Country Club. Koch finishes 175th on the money list the previous year and only gets into the tournament on a sponsor exemption. Koch earns $250,000 for the title – more than he did one in all but one of his 12 previous seasons on the PGA Tour. "It's a long way to go from 175th on the money list to thinking about winning a tournament," says Koch.

1994 – John Daly wins the third of his five PGA Tour titles at the BellSouth Classic in Atlanta beating runners-up Nolan Henke and Brian Henninger by one shot. Writes Larry Dorman in the *New York Times* of the win, "John Daly took another giant step on the long road back today. He took an emotional walk across the minefield, from alcoholism, from suspension and, ultimately, from self-doubt, all on one cool, spectacular afternoon, and he won the BellSouth Classic at the Atlanta Country Club the way he has never won a golf tournament in his life. He won it sober." Says Daly, "Nothing could mean more than that. To win again is a great feeling. But the best feeling is that I know I can win a golf tournament sober. You always wonder. You always think, 'Hey, can I do that?'"

2005 – Sergio Garcia blows a six-stroke lead entering the final-round of the Wachovia Championship at Quail Hollow in Charlotte as Vijay Singh wins a three-way playoff to win his 27th career PGA Tour title. Garcia leads by six shots with only 12 holes to play, but falters with a final-round 72 and is eliminated on the first hole of the playoff with Singh and Jim Furyk. Singh wins the title on the fourth playoff hole with a par on the 18th hole. "Sometimes it's harder to play with a big lead," Singh says of Garcia losing his large lead. "You don't want to lose the tournament. If the guys are catching up... you start to get a little nervous. But we played well." Garcia's six-stroke collapse is a margin that only four other players in PGA Tour history have wasted, none since Greg Norman at the 1996 Masters.

May 9

1971 – Jack Nicklaus shoots final round 66 to win Byron Nelson Classic, his 33rd career PGA Tour title. The 31-year-old Nicklaus birdies three of last four holes and shoots a back-nine 32 on the Preston Trails Country Club to beat out Jerry McGree and Frank Beard by two shots.

1999 – Carlos Franco becomes the first player from Paraguay to win on the PGA Tour winning the Compaq Classic of New Orleans by two shots over runners-up Steve Flesch and Harrison Frazar. Franco's win comes in his first start after an impressive sixth-place finish at the Masters that caused for a national parade in his native country. "They have probably already started to celebrate," says Franco, a PGA Tour rookie, after shooting a final-round 66 to become the first South American to win on the PGA Tour since Roberto De Vicenzo in Houston in 1968. "I'm pretty sure I'll get a parade, maybe more than that." Franco grows up in poverty, living as a child in a one-room, dirt-floored shack with a family of nine in Asuncion, Paraguay, a country with only three golf courses. Franco learns to play the sport barefoot with borrowed clubs.

2013 – Roberto Castro shoots a nine-under 63 in his debut round at The Players Championship to match the course record at the Stadium Course at the TPC of Sawgrass. Castro's bogey-free round includes seven birdies and an eagle at the par-5 second hole. Castro misses a 13-foot birdie putt on the par-5 ninth hole

– his 18th hole – that would have broken the course record. Castro becomes the third player to shoot 63 on the famed Pete Dye-designed course, joining Fred Couples (third round, 1992) and Greg Norman (first round, 1994). Castro shoots 78 in his next round and goes on to finish in 19th place.

2010 – Tim Clark of South Africa, in his 206th start on the PGA Tour, finally loses the moniker of being the most successful player on the PGA Tour without a tournament victory when he wins his maiden title at the Players Championship, one stroke better than runner-up Robert Allenby. Entering the event, Clark had won $14.7 million in his career without a title, the most of anyone without a win, but makes only one bogey over the last two rounds and shoots a final-round 67 to finally reach the winner's circle. "You do start to wonder when it is going to happen for me," says the 34-year-old Clark. "I guess that's the nature of this game. Sometimes you don't have to play your best to win tournaments. Luckily for me, this week I did play my best. That's about as good as I can play."

May 10

2015 – Rickie Fowler birdies the famed island-green 17th hole at the TPC at Sawgrass three times in a matter of 90 minutes and dramatically wins The Players Championship in a playoff with Sergio Garcia and Kevin Kisner. Fowler goes six-under-par on the final six holes of regulation, making eagle on the par 5 16th hole, birdie on the famed par 3 17th and birdie on the final hole. Fowler's final-round 67 places him in a three-hole aggregate score playoff with Garcia and Kisner and makes birdie with Kisner on 17th hole again. After he and Kisner finish tied at one-under-par for the three holes – eliminating Garcia – the two again return to the 17th hole where Fowler sinks a winning four-foot-putt to win his second career PGA Tour event.

1929 – In an early May staging of the world's oldest golf championship, Walter Hagen successfully defends his title at the Open Championship at Muirfield in Scotland, winning by six strokes ahead of runner-up Johnny Farrell. The title is Hagen's fourth at the Open and his eleventh and final major title.

1998 – Tiger Woods wins his seventh career PGA Tour title at the BellSouth Classic in Atlanta, beating runner-up Jay Don Blake by one shot. The title is the only PGA Tour event he wins during the 1998 season, his least productive season of golf between his rookie year in 1996 and his winless 2010 season following his sex scandal that breaks in November of 2009.

2009 – Henrik Stenson wins the Players Championship shooting a final-round 66 to win the biggest title of his career at the time. Stenson's 12-under-par total is four better than runner-up Ian Poulter. Third-round leader Alex Cejka shoots a final-round 79 to finish in a tie for ninth place.

May 11

1928 – Walter Hagen wins a rare May staging of the Open Championship, beating Gene Sarazen by two strokes at Royal St. Georges. The win is the third of four Open Championship titles for Hagen, who benefits when defending champion Bobby Jones decides not to make the trip to Britain to defend his title.

2008 – Sergio Garcia wins the biggest title of his career at the time by defeating Paul Goydos on the first playoff hole to win The Players Championship. For the first time in tournament history, the playoff begins at the famed 17th hole. Goydos hits first, but finds the water and Garcia hits his shot to within four feet of the hole. Garcia misses the birdie putt but taps in for par and the victory, the seventh of his PGA Tour career and first in almost three years. "It's been a lot of work," Garcia says of his winless streak. "It feels like the last three years I've been playing well. Unfortunately, I haven't been able to come around and win. This week, I played so nicely. It felt like everything was so hard. I'm just thrilled the week is over and I managed to finish on top."

2014 – Martin Kaymer of Germany sinks a dramatic 28-foot par putt – with six feet of break – on the famed island green 17th hole at the TPC of Sawgrass and pars the 18th hole in virtual darkness to win the Players Championship by one stroke over Jim Furyk. "What a putt at No. 17," Kaymer says. "It was very, very tough to read because it was already very dark. But I don't care anymore. It went in. There's always a bit of luck involved. But it was a good putt." Plays is suspended for 93 minutes due to rain and lightning and Kaymer almost immediately throws away his three-shot lead with a double-bogey on No. 15, before recovering with pars on the final three holes to close out the victory. Three days earlier, Kaymer shoots 63 in the first round, equaling the course record held by Fred Couples in 1992, Greg Norman in 1994 and Roberto Castro in 2013.

1980 – Tom Watson wins Byron Nelson Classic for a third straight year, playing 36 holes in the sweltering hot conditions and shooting 69 and 71 to win by one shot over Bill Rogers, the same player he beats in a playoff to win the title the previous year.

May 12

2013 – Tiger Woods wins his second title at The Players Championship in a back-nine dual with Sergio Garcia at the TPC at Sawgrass. Woods and Garcia are tied for the lead as Garcia, playing in the last group, reaches the 17th tee and hits two balls into the water on the famous island-green par 3 hole. Garcia gets a 7 on the hole, and double-bogeys the 18th hole after his tee shot also lands in the water. Woods wins the title by two shots over David Lingmerth, Kevin Streelman and Jeff Maggert. Woods, also the 2001 Players champion, joins Fred Couples, Davis Love III, Hal Sutton and Steve Elkington as the only two-time winners of the event at TPC Sawgrass. It also marks his 78th career win on the PGA Tour, four short of the record held by Sam Snead. A public snipping between Woods and Garcia from a controversy the day before add to the final-day drama. Garcia complains in a TV interview the day before that on the second hole of the third round, his shot was disrupted by cheers from the crowd around Woods, away in the trees 50 yards away from Garcia, after he selected a wood to hit his second shot. "Not real surprising that he's complaining about something," Woods says. Counters Garcia, "At least I'm true to myself. I know what I'm doing, and he can do whatever he wants." After the round is postponed due to the weather, Garcia also volunteers that Woods is "not the nicest guy on tour."

1996 – Bolstered by a 30-foot chip-in eagle on the 16th hole, 25-year-old Phil Mickelson wins the Byron Nelson Classic shooting a final-round 66 to beat Craig Parry of Australia by two shots. Says Mickelson, "When I made that eagle I felt like I had it." Mickelson was scheduled to take a vacation during the tournament, but decides to play after receiving a personal invitation from the 84-year-old Nelson.

1985 – Leading the Byron Nelson Classic by two shots on the final hole, Payne Stewart makes double-bogey, then double-bogeys the first hole in a sudden-death playoff, allowing Bob Eastwood to win the title. "He had the tournament wrapped up, but it's a funny game," says Eastwood, who sinks a 45-foot birdie putt on the final hole to draw within two shots of Stewart. Eastwood only needs to make a bogey on the first playoff hole to win his third and final PGA Tour event. "I hate to win it with a bogey, but I will take it anytime," Eastwood says.

2012 – Rhein Gibson, a 26-year-old pro from Australia, shoots a 55 at River Oaks Golf Club in Edmond, Okla., the lowest score ever recorded for a full length 18-hole course. Gibson, playing in a friendly Saturday morning round, makes 12 birdies and two eagles for a 16-under round on the 6,698 yard par 71 course, shooting 26 on his front nine and 29 on his back nine.

2012 – Carlos del Moral takes only 20 putts in a third-round score of 63 at the Medeira Islands Open in Portugal, setting a new European Tour record. Del Moral makes nine one-putts on his back nine, the last three for birdies. Del Moral actually uses the putter 22 times, two times from off the green not officially counting as putts.

May 13

1962 – Bruce Crampton goes down in infamy at the Colonial National Invitational, hitting his approach shot in the greenside lake on the 18th hole to make double bogey to finish one shot out of a playoff. The previous day, Crampton also makes double bogey on the 18th hole at the Colonial Country Club after hitting in the same lake having a chance to break Ben Hogan's then course record of 65. Arnold Palmer beats Johnny Potts in an 18-hole playoff the following day to win the tournament and the lake on the 18th hole comes to be known as "Crampton's Lake." Crampton goes on to win the tournament two years later in 1965 and again faces the 18th hole, this time with a three-shot lead. "I thought about using an iron off the tee and just laying up to the hole so I wouldn't be taking any chances," Crampton says after his 1965 win. "But then I thought this was not the way a champion should play; I'd say this was being chicken I wanted to prove to myself that I could whip this hazard. So I played it a straightaway and won."

1973 – Bruce Crampton makes a double bogey on the 18th hole and loses the Colonial Invitational by one shot to Tom Weiskopf.

Crampton hooks his tee shot into a ditch on the 18th hole, then hits into a lateral water hazard, then in the bunker and misses his bogey putt by four inches. The final-hole drama harkens back to Crampton famously hitting into the Colonial Country Club's 18th hole greenside lake at the end of the third and fourth rounds of the event in 1962. Weiskopf's final-round 69 earns him his sixth PGA Tour win.

2007 – Phil Mickelson wins The Players Championship by two shots over Sergio Garcia in the first staging of the tournament in May after its traditional March date in the calendar. Sean O'Hair, trailing Mickelson by two shots on the island-green par 3 17th hole, hits a daring attacking shot to the pin, but hits his nine-iron over the green and into the water and, after hitting another ball into the water from the drop zone, settles for a quadruple bogey 7 and falls from second place to 11th place, costing him $747,000. "You've got to make something happen," O'Hair says. "I didn't bust my butt for four days to get second place. Obviously, I paid for it."

1978 – Frenchman Philippe Porquier takes a 20 on the 511-yard 13th at La Baule in the second round of the French Open, the highest score for a single hole ever recorded on the European Tour. After a first round of 82, Porquier shoots a second-round of 98, including his 20 that includes several shanks and lost balls.

1941 – Vic Ghezzi wins his only major title at the PGA Championship at Cherry Hills Country Club in Colorado beating defending champion Byron Nelson in a 38-hole match-play final. The event is the last "full field" staging of the PGA Championship until 1946 due to World War II. The match-play bracket for the event is scaled back from 64 competitors to 32 for 1942, when the PGA and the Masters are the only majors held. The PGA Championship is the only major contested in 1944 and 1945; none are played in 1943 and the other three return in 1946.

2005 – After a record 142 consecutive tournaments, Tiger Woods misses a cut on the PGA Tour at the Byron Nelson Classic in Irving, Texas. Woods misses the cut by one shot when his 15-foot par putt slips past the 18th hole at Cottonwood Valley Course and he settles for a two-over-par score of 72, coupled with his opening round 69. It is the first missed cut for Woods since the 1998 AT&T Pebble Beach National Pro-Am, but that missed cut was under unusual circumstances as the event was shortened to 54 holes due to rain, but the last 18 holes were played in August, six months later. Woods, who was not in contention after 36 holes, did not return to play the event and the withdrawal is counted as a missed cut. The only other prior missed cut in Woods' pro career was the 1997 Canadian Open.

1979 – Tom Watson hits a bunker shot to within 10 inches and sinks the birdie putt on the 15th hole of the Preston Trail Golf Club to beat Bill Rogers in the first hole of sudden death to win the Byron Nelson Classic. Watson becomes the first three-time winner of the event.

May 14

1989 – Bob Tway wins on the PGA Tour for the first time since his 1986 PGA Championship victory beating runner-up Fuzzy Zoeller by two shots to win the Memorial tournament. Tway birdies three of the last four holes to win his fifth career PGA Tour title and receives a high-five from Zoeller after he sinks a 25-foot birdie on the final hole. Says Tway of his victory drought, "For three years, I've been hounded by questions: `What's wrong? Why aren't you winning?' It was very frustrating. I didn't have any answers."

1978 – Lee Trevino wins the Colonial National Invitational for the second time shooting a four-under 66 to win by four strokes over Jerry Pate and Jerry Heard. The title is Trevino's 21st of his career and marks the 11th straight year that he wins a tournament in the United States. He receives a standing ovation from fans as he walks down the 18th fairway.

May 15

1998 – Notah Begay becomes the third player to shoot a 59 on a U.S. pro tour, scoring a hole-in-one on his 12th hole to break 60 at the Nike Dominion Open in Richmond, Va. Begay joins Al Geiberger and Chip Beck, both of whom turned the trick on the PGA Tour, with his 59 at the time. Begay shoots a 27 on the front nine and makes nine birdies and two eagles on the 7,020-yard, par-72 Dominion Club course. "After the hole-in-one, 59 came into my mind," he says. "I guaranteed myself a piece of immortality." Geiberger shot his 59 at the Memphis Classic in 1977 and Beck got his at the Las Vegas Invitational in 1991.

1994 – Neal Lancaster wins the largest sudden-death playoff in the history of the PGA Tour, beating five others to win the storm-shortened Byron Nelson Classic in Irving, Texas. Lancaster sinks a four-foot birdie putt on the first extra hole to beat David Ogrin, David Edwards, Japanese rookie Yoshi Mizumaki, Tom Byrum and Mark Carnevale. All six players only completed one round on each of two rain-soaked courses at the Tournament Players Club at Los Colinas in nine-under-par 132. The tournament is reduced to a 36-hole format following a series of rainstorms.

2011 – South Korean K. J. Choi defeats David Toms on the first hole of a sudden-death playoff to win the Players Championship and become the event's first champion from Asia. Choi benefits when Toms misses a short par putt on the famed island-green 17th hole, the first hole of the playoff. Leading by two shots on the par-15 16th hole, Toms goes for the green in two and hits it into the water. However, Toms ties Choi with a 20-foot birdie on the final hole to force the playoff.

May 16

2004 – Lorena Ochoa wins her first pro event, posting a four-under-par 68 for a one-stroke victory over Wendy Ward at the inaugural Franklin American Mortgage Championship in Franklin, Tenn. Ochoa's win comes on the same day that her 27-year-old brother Alejandro completes a climb of Mount Everest.

1982 – Jack Nicklaus wins his 71st title on the PGA Tour claiming a three-stroke win over runner-up Andy North at the Colonial National Invitational in Fort Worth, Texas. The win, his third-to-last PGA Tour title, is his first title since he wins the PGA Championship in 1980. "Since early this year, I've been saying I've been playing well, even though I haven't been hitting the ball well," Nicklaus says after his win. "Then I missed a few cuts. But when you feel you're playing well with no results, then people ask: 'What's he saying? Look at the scoreboard.'"

1976 – Lee Trevino wins in his home state of Texas for the first time in his career when he wins the Colonial Invitational in Fort Worth by one stroke. Trevino, who was born in Dallas, makes birdie on the 200-yard par-3 16th hole that provides him his winning margin over runner-up Mike Morley.

May 17

2009 – One day after matching the La Cantera course record of 10-under-par 60, Zach Johnson repeats as Valero Texas Open champion in San Antonio beating James Driscoll on the first hole of a playoff. Johnson sinks a 12-foot birdie on the first playoff hole to win his sixth career PGA Tour title. Johnson shoots a final-round 70, ten shots worse the previous day's course record score, but hangs to win, fighting off Driscoll, who surges from eight strokes back to force the playoff.

2015 – One day after shooting a course record 61 – and the lowest round of his pro career – Rory McIlroy wins his 11th PGA Tour title at the Wells Fargo Championship at Quail Hollow in Charlotte, N.C. McIlroy shoots a final-round 69 and wins by seven strokes over runners-up Patrick Rodgers and Webb Simpson. McIlroy's four-round score of 21-under-par 267 also sets a new tournament record. Says McIlroy, "Everything is firing on all cylinders for me."

2009 – Shane Lowry, a 22-year-old Irish amateur, wins the Irish Open at County Louth in Baltray, defeating Robert Rock on the third hole of a sudden-death playoff. Lowery, buoyed by a second-round score of 62 two days earlier, wins the title in his first appearance at a European Tour event and becomes the third amateur to win on the European Tour, joining Danny Lee, earlier in the year at the Johnnie Walker Classic in Perth, Australia, and Pablo Martin in 2007 at the Portugal Open in 2007. "What am I feeling? Mostly shock," Lowry says of his unexpected win while being showered with champagne by former amateur partner Rory McIlroy of Northern Ireland. Writes Bill Elliott in *The Guardian* newspaper "Finally, with the sun long gone, the rain lashing and the crowd singing, Shane Lowry created his own little bit of local history."

May 18

1997 – Playing in his first event since his historic first win at the Masters a month earlier, Tiger Woods wins the Byron Nelson Classic by two shots over runner-up Lee Rinker. It marks the fifth win for Woods in his 16 PGA Tour appearances as a pro, making him the fastest to reach that benchmark. Horton Smith previously was the quickest to reach five titles, doing so in 27 tournaments. Woods wins despite playing a self-described "C-plus game" and calls in his swing coach Butch Harmon to take a four-hour drive from Houston the morning of the final round to help him prior to the final round. "Winning like this means a lot," says Woods. "It shows if you think well and have a short game, you can win a lot out here. This was a learning experience. I hung in there and relied on my chipping and putting." Quips Rinker of the Woods form, "I think he's closer to his A-game than he's letting on. What's his A-game, 40 under par?"

1975 – Billy Casper wins his 51st and eventually his last PGA Tour title at the New Orleans Open. Casper shoots a final-round two-under par 70 at the Lakewood Country Club to beat runner-up Peter Oosterhuis by two shots.

2013 – After hitting his tee shot into a hazard on the par 4 10th hole at Thracian Cliffs course in Bulgaria during the Volvo World Match Play Championship, Nicolas Colsaerts is given "relief" and a drop in a nearby bathroom in his quarterfinal match with Graeme McDowell. Writes golf blogger Shane Bacon, "The ball was dropped inside the toilet, and Colsaerts then was able to take relief from that spot, which means he was able to re-drop his ball close by without penalty because it lay in an unplayable position. Colsaerts then hit his approach shot on the green and rolled in the putt for par. It was enjoyable watching Colsaerts and the rules official having a chuckle about the whole situation, and even cooler that he still made par despite the penalty stroke, but his hopes of winning the match were, ahem, flushed by McDowell who won 2 & 1." Says Colsaerts of the episode, "I was laughing because I was going to look like a clown. I'm sure it's going to make the news, some Belgian dude dropping the ball in a toilet. It's fun to be recognized for stupid stuff like that."

1947 – Ben Hogan wins the second staging of the Colonial National Invitational, repeating as tournament champion by shooting a final-round 69 to beat Tony Penna by one shot.

May 19

2014 – Lucy Li, age 11, becomes the youngest person ever to qualify for the U.S. Women's Open when she wins the sectional qualifier at Half Moon Bay in California. Li breaks the previous record held by Lexi Thompson, who was 12 when she qualified for the field at the 2007 Women's Open.

1996 – Reigning U.S. Open champion Corey Pavin wins the 50th Colonial National Invitational by two strokes over Jeff Sluman. Pavin shoots a final-round 69 to win at Colonial for a second time. Pavin's first win at Colonial comes exactly 11 years to the day earlier when he shoots a no-bogey final-round two-under-par 68 to win by four shots over runner-up Bob Murphy. Says Pavin after his first win at Colonial, "To win at Colonial, in only my second year on the tour, to do it at 14 under par, this is something I'll always cherish."

1946 – Ben Hogan shoots a final round 65 to win the first edition of the Colonial National Invitational in Fort Worth, Texas beating Harry Todd by one stroke.

May 20

2012 – Jason Dufner drains a 25-foot birdie putt on the final hole of the Byron Nelson Championship to win by one shot over runner-up Dicky Pride. The win is the second title in three weeks for Dufner, who also gets married three weeks earlier. "You probably couldn't dream it any better than what's been going on here," says Dufner who wins his first PGA Tour title on April 29 in New Orleans. "The wedding has been in the works for close to a year, so we know that's been coming around the corner. And there's been a lot of good golf since then, but to win two events and get married in the span of 22 days, pretty remarkable."

2010 – At age 16, Jordan Spieth, the reigning U.S. junior amateur champion and a student at nearby Jesuit College Preparatory School, becomes the youngest player to compete in the Byron Nelson Classic in Irving, Texas, courtesy of a sponsor's exemption. Spieth plays 11 holes at even par before play is suspended, but returns the next day to make two birdies and shoots an opening round 68. After a half-hour break for lunch, he shoots a second-round 69 to make the cut, becoming the sixth youngest player in PGA history to make a cut. "I don't want to think of myself as the amateur out here," Spieth says after making the cut. "I want to think of myself as a contender." Spieth eventually finishes 16th at the event.

2001 – Twenty-one-year-old Sergio Garcia wins his first title on the PGA Tour firing a final-round seven-under-par 63 to win the Colonial National Invitational in Fort Worth, Texas. Garcia finishes two strokes ahead of runners-up Brian Gay and defending champion Phil Mickelson. Garcia starts the day five strokes behind Mickelson, but quickly threatens the lead shooting a six-under 29 on the front nine at the Colonial Country Club. "I don't feel like it should have taken so much time," Garcia says of his maiden PGA Tour win. "I felt like I played good enough to win before this. It's been hard, but I think it's even sweeter now. They always say the first one is the toughest, so hopefully I'll start doing some nice things."

1990 – Ben Crenshaw shoots a final-round 66 and wins the Colonial National Invitational by three strokes over Corey Pavin, John Mahaffey and Nick Price. Crenshaw doesn't miss any putt under 15 feet on the round and sinks two 30-foot birdies on the seventh and ninth holes. Says fifth-place finisher Curtis Strange of Crenshaw, "The man's amazing. I can't even carry his putter."

May 21

1989 – Nancy Lopez wins her third LPGA Championship – all at the Jack Nicklaus Sports Center Grizzly Course in Mason, Ohio – shooting a final-round six-under-par 66, winning by three shots over Ayako Okamoto. The win is the 40th of Lopez's career. "It's hard to compare them," Lopez says of her three LPGA crowns. "All have been special for me. The first year (as a rookie in 1978), being so young, winning with my dad here and all of that pressure at such a young age – it meant a lot."

1995 – Seve Ballesteros wins what becomes his final pro victory – and the 50th of his European Tour career – at the Peugeot Spanish Open at Valderrama, beating fellow Spaniards Ignacio Garrido and Jose Rivero by two strokes.

1989 – Ian Baker-Finch closes out a wire-to-wire win at the Colonial National Invitational, shooting a final-round 70 to win by four shots over runner-up David Edwards. The win is the only win on U.S. soil for Baker-Finch, the Australian who would win the Open Championship two years later.

2000 – Phil Mickelson makes five birdies on the back nine and shoots a final-round 63 to win the Colonial National Invitational by two shots over runners-up Davis Love, III and Stewart Cink. "I got off to a good start and was thinking a lot about winning," says Mickelson, who starts the day six shots off the lead. "When I made the turn, I tried not to think about winning. I tried to hit some good golf shots because I was too far behind to win. I ended up making a few birdies. When I birdied 10, 11 and 12, I looked up at the board and saw I was only two back. That's when I knew I had a chance to win."

May 22

2003 – Annika Sorenstam becomes the first woman in 58 years to play in a PGA Tour event at the Colonial National Invitational in Fort Worth, Texas and shoots an opening round of one-over-par 71. The 32-year-old Sorenstam pars 12 of her first 13 holes, hits 13 of 14 fairways and 14 of 18 greens and makes one birdie. "I'll remember this day for the rest of my life," Sorenstam says following the round. Sorenstam is the first woman to play in a PGA Tour event since Babe Didrikson Zaharias plays the Tucson Open in 1945. Sorenstam shoots a four-over-par 74 the next day and misses the cut, but finishes 96th out of 111 players in the field.

1994 – Tom Lehman wins his first PGA Tour title at the Memorial Tournament at Muirfield Village Golf Club in Ohio, posting a record low score of 20-under-par in a five-shot win over Greg Norman. Says the 35-year-old Lehman of his first PGA Tour title, "I had made a career of beating myself. Whether it was not getting up and down for birdie at a par-five or three-putting from 15 feet or whatever, I never seemed to get it done. Today, I didn't beat myself. That was key." Says tournament founder Jack Nicklaus of Lehman, "Bobby Jones once said at Augusta that I played a game with which he was not familiar. Well, this week Tom Lehman played a game with which I am not familiar."

1988 – Lanny Wadkins makes a three-foot birdie on the final hole to win the Colonial National Invitational in Fort Worth, Texas by one stroke over Mark Calcavecchia, Ben Crenshaw and Joey Sindelar. Prior to his winning week in Fort Worth, Wadkins had played 35 competitive rounds at Colonial Country Club but had never broken par. He shoots a final-round five-under-par 65 to win the 18th of his 22 career PGA Tour titles.

2005 – Kenny Perry wins the Colonial Invitational for a second time, posting a 19-under-par score of 261, equaling his own record-setting low score. Perry is on pace to break his 72-hole scoring record at the Colonial Country Club, but makes double-bogey on the 17th hole en route to a seven-stroke win over runner-up Bill Mayfair. Says Perry, "I wanted to finish 20 under. But that's OK, I tied my own record. That's pretty special. I just wanted to win again." The win is the ninth of 14 career PGA Tour titles for Perry, who also won at Colonial in 2003.

2005 – One week before her high school graduation, 18-year-old Paula Creamer makes a 15-foot birdie putt on the final hole and wins her first LPGA title at the Sybase Classic at New Rochelle, N.Y. Creamer finishes one stroke better than runners-up Jeong Jang and Gloria Park.

2011 – A week after losing a heart-breaking playoff to K.J. Choi at the Players Championship, David Toms emotionally wins the Colonial National Invitational with a final-round 67 to beat runner-up Charlie Wi by one shot. "I didn't know if this day would ever come again," says the 44-year-old Toms of his first PGA Tour win in five years and the 13th of his career. Toms actually leads the event by seven shots after two rounds, after shooting consecutive rounds of 62, but shoots a 74 in the third round to trail Wi by one shot entering the final round.

———

May 23

———

1977 – Calling it "my biggest thrill in golf," Jack Nicklaus wins the second staging of his own tournament, the Memorial Tournament, by two shots over runner-up Hubert Green in a rain-delayed Monday finish at the Nicklaus-designed Muirfield Village in Dublin, Ohio. "I had a shot at winning the first tournament last year, but in a way I'm happy I didn't if you know what I mean," says a humble Nicklaus of winning his own tournament, won by Roger Maltbie in its inaugural staging the year before.

2010 – Twenty-two-year-old Jason Day becomes the youngest Australian to win a PGA Tour event when he wins the Byron Nelson Golf Classic by two shots over runners-up Blake Adams, Jeff Overton and Brian Gay. "To finally come through with a win, I'm just so happy," Day says. "I've got no words for it."

2004 – Left-handed Steve Flesch celebrates his 37th birthday by shooting a final-round 67 to win the Colonial National Invitational by one stroke over runner-up Chad Campbell. The win is the second of four career PGA Tour titles for Flesch, who is only surpassed by Phil Mickelson, Mike Weir, Bubba Watson and Bob Charles as left-handed players with more PGA Tour victories.

2015 – Miguel Angel Jimenez sets a European Tour record when scores his 10th career hole in one on the par-3 second hole at Wentworth in England in the third round of the BMW PGA Championship. Jimenez breaks out of a tie for the distinction with Colin Montgomerie, whom he tied the previous week with his ninth hole-in-one. On the PGA Tour, Hal Sutton and Robert Allenby share the record for most holes-in-one also with 10 each.

May 24

1998 – Forty-eight-year-old Tom Watson wins his 39th and final PGA Tour event at the MasterCard Colonial in Fort Worth, Texas shooting a final-round 66 to beat runner-up Jim Furyk by two shots. "It's a surprise. Winning at my age is a rarity," says Watson. "I didn't know if I was going to win another tournament on tour or not."

1953 – Ben Hogan, described by the Associated Press as "golf's mighty stretch-runner," wins his fourth title at the Colonial National Invitational, finishing five strokes ahead of runner-up Doug Ford and Cary Middlecoff.

1992 – Bruce Lietzke wins his 12th PGA Tour title – and first in four years – winning the Colonial National Invitational by beating Corey Pavin with a 12-foot birdie on the first hole of a sudden-death playoff. Lietzke, known as one of the most consistent players on the PGA Tour having never finishing lower than 74th on the PGA Tour money list, wins his 13th and final PGA Tour title in 1994 at the Las Vegas Invitational, but he falls short of winning a major title. His best major finish comes when he ties for second at the 1991 PGA Championships, won by John Daly. However, on the PGA Champions Tour, after winning six events in his first two years on the "over-age-50" tour, he finally wins a senior major when he out-duels Tom Watson to win the U.S. Senior Open in 2003 at Inverness in Toledo, Ohio on June 29. Lietzke shoots a final-round 73 – nine shots worse than his third-round 64 – to beat Watson by two shots. "I'm not sure I feel like a champion as much as a survivor," he says after his breakthrough win.

May 25

1948 – Ben Hogan wins the PGA Championship for a second and final time beating Mike Turnesa 7&6 in the match-play final at the Norwood Hills Country Club in St. Louis, Mo. The win is the second of Hogan's eight major titles – his third coming just weeks later at the U.S. Open at the Riviera Country Club in Los Angeles. Due to Hogan's near fatal car accident the following year, Hogan does not play in the PGA until 1960 when it changed its format from a five-day 36-holes-a-day format to a 72-hole stroke play format due to the grueling nature of the event would have on his injured body.

2014 – Playing during the week where he breaks off his marriage to tennis star Caroline Wozniacki, Rory McIlroy wins the BMW PGA Championship at Wentworth, shooting a final-round six-under-par 66 to claim a one-shot victory over Shane Lowry. "I'm not exactly sure how I'm feeling right now, to be honest,"

McIlroy says of his emotional week. "I'm happy that I won, obviously….mixed emotions." McIlroy comes from seven shots back of third-round leader Thomas Bjorn to win.

2014 – Playing for the first week as the world's No. 1 golfer, Adam Scott make it an even more memorable week by winning the Colonial National Invitational in Fort Worth, Texas on the third hole of a sudden-death playoff with Jason Dufner. Scott makes a seven-foot birdie on the third hole of the playoff for his 11th PGA Tour title. Scott also becomes the first player to win all four PGA Tour events played in the Lone Star State, also winning at the Byron Nelson Championship in Dallas, the Texas Open in San Antonio and the Houston Open. There are 13 other players with wins at three of the four Texas tour events, including Sam Snead, Arnold Palmer, Byron Nelson, Ben Hogan and Nick Price.

2008 – Phil Mickelson makes a dramatic final-hole birdie – after hitting his tee-shot well left of the fairway – and wins the Crowne Plaza Invitational at the Colonial Country Club in Fort Worth, Texas by one stroke over Rod Pampling and Tim Clark. Tied with Pampling on the final tee, Mickelson hits his tee shot into the heavy rough, under the trees on the left side of the fairway, but rather than punching out into the fairway, lofts a wedge under one tree and over another from 140 yards away to eight feet, where he makes birdie to win. Mickelson calls the approach shot "probably top five" in his career. "If there is at all a chance, I'm going for it," says Mickelson. "You have to take some risks to win."

1952 – Ben Hogan fires a final-round 67 and comes from six shots back to win his third title at the Colonial National Invitational in Fort Worth, Texas. Hogan benefits from third-round leader Raymond Gafford shooting a final-round 80 and finishes four shots clear of runner-up Lloyd Mangrum. Writes the Associated Press of the win, "Hogan never had a better finish in his glamorous golf career."

2008 – Miguel Angel Jimenez of Spain scores a hole-in-one with a four-iron from 187 yards away on the fifth hole at Wentworth in England en route to winning the BMW PGA Championship. Jimenez beats Oliver Wilson with a birdie on the second hole of a sudden-death playoff to win the biggest title of his career.

1997 – David Frost wins for the first time in three years and prevents Tiger Woods from winning his third-straight tournament, winning the Colonial Invitational in Fort Worth, Texas by two strokes over the first-time Masters champion. Frost, who shoots a final-round 67, benefits from Woods making double-bogey on the 17th hole to win his 10th and final PGA Tour title.

1980 – David Graham wins the Memorial Tournament with a dramatic 30-foot birdie on the final hole to beat Tom Watson by one shot. After Graham's birdie, Watson misses a 20-foot putt to tie. Graham never holds sole possession of the lead until Watson misses his final putt. "Of all the tournaments I have won, this means the most to me," says Graham, who won the PGA Championship the previous year.

2003 – Kenny Perry shoots a final-round 68 to win the Colonial National Invitational in Fort Worth, Texas by six shots over runner-up Justin Leonard. Perry leads by seven shots entering the final round after shooting a course record 61 during Saturday's third round. Leonard equals Perry's course record with a final-round 61, missing a par putt on the final hole. Perry's anti-climactic winning effort is overshadowed during the week by Annika Sorenstam becoming the first woman in 58 years to compete on the PGA Tour. Says Perry, "I'll probably be remembered as the guy who won Annika's event, but that's OK with me."

May 26

1974 – Gary Player shoots final round 67 and wins the Danny Thomas Memphis Classic by two shots over runners-up Hubert Green and Lou Graham. Player holes a sand shot for birdie on the 12th hole to take the lead for the first time and holds on to win for the 20th time on the PGA Tour. "My bunker play has won many, many tournaments for me," says Player. "I have spent countless hours practicing in bunkers as a boy in South Africa. I threw a bucket of balls in a bunker and stayed in until I holed one."

2013 – Boo Weekley adds a third Tartan jacket to his wardrobe, winning the special jacket given to the winner of the Colonial Invitational. Weekley shoots a final round 66 to win by one stroke over runner-up Matt Kuchar. Weekley's other two PGA Tour titles come at the 2007 and 2008 Heritage Classics in Hilton Head, S.C., an event that also awards a Tartan jacket to its winner.

May 27

1984 – Jack Nicklaus wins his 72nd and the second-to-last PGA Tour title at his home tournament that he created – the Memorial Tournament – on the third hole of a sudden-death playoff with Andy Bean. "Winning the Memorial means more to me than the majors, in a way," Nicklaus says of the event he started in 1976 at Muirfield Village, the course he designed. "It's because of the town, the people who put in so much time, the course we built and the effort I've put in on this tournament." After Nicklaus and Bean both finish 72 holes at eight-under par – Bean missing a four-foot putt for par and the win on the final hole – Nicklaus wins on the third playoff hole with a par as Bean misses another four-foot putt for a par. "I've said I'll play this game as long as I can compete the way I feel I should," says the 44-year-old Nicklaus after his first PGA Tour win since the 1982 Colonial.

"I've even thought maybe I was getting too old. Now, I just happen to think I'm going to win some more majors." Nicklaus wins his 73rd and final tour victory two years later, at a major, with his dramatic win at the Masters.

2012 – Zach Johnson nearly throws away his championship at the Colonial National Invitational after being assessed a two-stroke penalty for failing to properly re-mark his ball on the 72nd green after putting out for what he thought was a three-stroke victory. Johnson moves his original ball mark out of the line of his playing partner Jason Dufner, but forgets to move it back before making his five-foot putt for par on the final green. The penalty is assessed after Johnson celebrates his win and does a TV interview, but before he signs his scorecard. "There's a number of adjectives I'm calling myself right now. And lucky would be the biggest one," Johnson says. The win is the eighth career title for Johnson, the 2007 Masters champion, whose last win was at the Colonial two years earlier.

May 28

1950 – Sam Snead shoots a final-round 73 and holds on to win the Colonial National Invitational in Fort Worth, Texas by three shots over runner-up Skip Alexander. Snead shoots a 66 in the first and third rounds of the event and holds on to win the $3,000 first-prize paycheck. "I'm sure glad it's over," Snead says after four three-putt greens and his only birdie on the day coming on a chip-in on the first hole.

2006 – Jeff Maggert shoots a final-round 65 and wins the St. Jude Classic in Memphis by three strokes over runner-up Tom Pernice, Jr. The win is the third and final PGA Tour title for Maggert, a player known for his strong play in major championships, finishing in the top 10 seven times at the U.S. Open, three times at the PGA, twice at the Masters and once at the Open Championship.

May 29

2005 – Justin Leonard starts his final round at the St. Jude Classic in Memphis with an eight-stroke lead, but shoots a final-round three-over 73, making a three-foot putt for bogey on the final hole to hang for a one-shot victory over runner-up David Toms. "It's a good thing I had an eight-shot cushion because I was able to stay out just enough in front of a great round by David," Leonard says after winning his 10th career PGA Tour title.

1988 – Curtis Strange wins the Memorial Tournament by two strokes over runners-up Hale Irwin and David Frost and is immediately lauded as "the best player in the world right now" by Irwin. The win is the fifth PGA Tour title in 10 months for Strange, who goes on to win his first major title three weeks later at the U.S. Open.

2011 – Keegan Bradley wins his first PGA Tour title at the Byron Nelson Championship, making a par on the first hole of a sudden-death playoff with Ryan Palmer. Says Bradley of his maiden win, "I don't know what to say. I'm so happy, I can't believe this just happened. This is a dream come true. I've waited for this my whole life." Three months later, Bradley nets his second pro win and his first major title at the PGA Championship in Atlanta.

2015 – Torrential rain in Texas cause PGA Tour officials at the Byron Nelson Classic to change the 406-yard par-4 14th hole at the TPC Four Seasons Resort at Las Colinas to a 108-yard par 3 for the second round and for the remainder of the championship. The change makes the course into a par 69, marking the first time since PGA Tour records were kept in 1983 that a Tour course had a par of under 70.

2000 – Tiger Woods shoots a two-under-par 70 in a weather-delayed Monday finish to claim a five-stroke victory over runners-up Ernie Els and Justin Leonard at the Memorial

Tournament. The win marks the first time Woods successfully defends a title in 10 tries and becomes the first repeat champion in the 25-year history of the tournament. He also joins Jack Nicklaus, Tom Watson, Hale Irwin and Greg Norman as the only players to win the Memorial twice. Says Nicklaus, the tournament founder, of the dominance of Woods, "When you have the ability to outdistance your opponents by 30 or 40 yards and know exactly what you're doing and where it's going to go, you're playing for second every week, unless he doesn't play well."

May 30

1976 – Roger Maltbie wins the inaugural staging of the Memorial Tournament, the Jack Nicklaus-conceived event at the course he designed, Muirfield Village in Dublin, Ohio. Maltbie beats Hale Irwin in a first-of-its kind three-hole aggregate playoff, which extends to a fourth hole. Maltbie scrambles for an incredible par on the third hole after he hooks his approach shot that bounces on to the green off a metal stake that holds up the gallery ropes. He then wins the playoff on the next hole with a 15-foot birdie. "When you think of the size of that pole 180 yards away and the bounce it took to the green, it has to be some sort of destiny," Maltbie says of his fortunate bounce. "I was terribly scared I hit somebody on the head because of the way came back to the green. I was terribly relieved I didn't hit anybody but I'm not going to be ashamed for the way I played for four days and for four extra holes because of that one hole." Says Irwin of the Nicklaus created event, "Jack has made a magnificent effort. He has taken a lot of time and worked hard on this tournament. He has put his name in the record books in another category. We play a lot of first-time tournaments and for first-time tournaments, none even none come close to this one. If they didn't change a thing it would have to be one of the great tournaments we play in, but it is going to get better. I don't know how but it will."

1937 – Denny Shute wins his second consecutive PGA Championship in a span of less than seven months defeating Harold "Jug" McSpaden in a 37-hole match play final at the Pittsburgh Field Club in Fox Chapel, Pa. Shute also wins the 1936 PGA at Pinehurst the previous November. McSpaden leads two-up with three holes to play, but Shute makes a birdie on the 34th hole and McSpade makes a bogey on the 35th to level the match. McSpaden also misses a four-foot birdie putt on the 36th hole for the win, then lips out his par putt from eight feet on the 37th hole to lose the match. No player successfully defends their PGA Championship title until Tiger Woods in 1999 and 2000. The win is the third and final major for Shute, who also wins the Open Championship in 1933.

May 31

1942 – Sam Snead wins his first major title at the PGA Championship at Seaview Country Club in Galloway, N.J., just north of Atlantic City. Snead wins the match-play final 2 & 1 over Jim Turnesa, capped by a 60-foot chip in birdie on the 35th hole to clinch the match. Snead begins his service in the U.S. Navy immediately after the event, joining Turnesa, on leave from active service in the U.S. Army at the time. Due to the war, the Masters and the PGA are the only major championships played. No majors are played in 1943 while the PGA returns in 1944 and the other three in 1946.

1949 – Sam Snead wins the second of his three PGA Championships beating Johnny Palmer 3 & 2 in the match-play final at the Hermitage Country Club in Lakeside, Va., just north of Richmond. The 27-year-old Snead earns $3,500 for the win in becoming the oldest PGA Championship winner at the time.

2013 – Andrew Dodt of Australia makes history at the Scandinavian Masters becoming the first player on the European Tour to record two holes-in-one in a single round.

Dodt first aces the 11th hole when playing the back nine first, then the seventh hole en route to a seven-under-par 65. "The shot at the 11th, my second hole, kick-started things," Dodt tells reporters after the round. "I made a few more birdies in between, then a couple of bogeys and I was heading the wrong way when I got to the seventh. That was an eight-iron, it felt a little bit heavy at the start but it was right on line and went in. I can't get my head around it – I'm pretty proud to be the first one to do it. I didn't putt very well today so I'm glad I was able to hole with a long club."

2015 – Four years after marrying his wife Amanda at the TPC Four Seasons Las Colinas golf course – and posing for wedding photos on the 18th green – Steven Bowditch wins there for his second career PGA Tour victory at the Byron Nelson Classic. Bowditch shoots a final-round 64 to claim a four-shot win over runners-up Jimmy Walker, Charley Hoffman and Scott Pinckney. "We took some wedding pictures here at TPC so it is a special place and I get to take some more pictures here," Bowditch says shortly after his win of his September, 2011 wedding. "It's such a special place to me and I just wanted to stay patient out there."

JUNE

June 1

2003 – Kenny Perry wins for the second consecutive week holding on for a two-stroke victory over Lee Janzen at the Memorial, one week after winning at the Colonial National Invitational. "This is the time of my life," Perry says of winning two of the most prestigious events on the PGA Tour. "I've never played golf like this." The victory, coupled with his victory at Muirfield Village in 1991, puts Perry in the company of tournament founder Jack Nicklaus, Tiger Woods, Greg Norman and Hale Irwin as multiple winners of the championship.

2008 – Kenny Perry joins Tiger Woods as the only three-time winner of the Memorial by shooting a final-round 69 for a two-shot victory at Muirfield Village. The 47-year-old Perry becomes the oldest winner at the tournament Jack Nicklaus built. "Magic always happens here," says Perry, who also won the Memorial in 1991 for his first-ever PGA Tour title and in 2003.

June 2

1996 – "It's like winning all over again for the first time," says 46-year-old Tom Watson after winning his first PGA Tour event in nine years, a two-shot victory at the Memorial Tournament. "God, it feels good. It feels so good to win again. Nine years. Half of that, I wasn't playing good and the last half I was. But it feels good to be the last person off the golf course, the guy who knocked the last putt in." Watson last wins on the PGA Tour at the 1987 Nabisco Championships prior to winning his second title at Muirfield Village, his 38th and second-to-last PGA Tour title.

2013 – Matt Kuchar sinks a 20-foot birdie putt on the 18th hole to cap off a two-shot victory over late-charging Kevin Chappell at the Memorial Tournament at Muirfield Village. Kuchar enters the event having finished in second place the week before at Colonial and winning the World Match Play Championship in February. "There are a couple of things I thought were missing from my pedigree," says Kuchar. "A major championship is on the list, and a multiple-win season was on the list. That's something that at the beginning of the year when I set goals, I wanted to have a multiple-win year. And making the Presidents Cup team was on the list…To have kind of sealed the deal with winning this tournament feels really good. Having a multiple-win season is nice to be able to check that one off the list."

1997 – Vijay Singh wins a 54-hole, rain-shortened Memorial Tournament by two shots over Greg Norman and Jim Furyk with the final-round of the tournament taking three days to complete. Singh sleeps Sunday night facing a 240-plus yard second shot into the par-5 11th hole and hits it within 18 inches of the hole on his first shot of the day to tap in for eagle. "Coming over here, I didn't have that much expectation of doing that well," says Singh, a native of Fiji. "I haven't won {on the U.S. tour} in two years. I can't be any more pleased than I am now." Tournament founder Jack Nicklaus, 57, finishes in a tie for eighth place.

———

June 3

———

2012 – Tiger Woods ties Jack Nicklaus for career PGA Tour victories with 73 by winning Jack's own tournament, the Memorial at Muirfield Village. Woods birdies three of the last four holes – including a chip-in on No. 16 that Woods calls one of the toughest shots he has ever made – to shoot a five-under 67 to post a two-shot win over Rory Sabbatini and Andres Romero. Says Nicklaus of Woods' chip-in on the par-3 16th hole, "Under the circumstances – the circumstances being Tiger has been struggling – it was either fish or cut bait. He had one place to land the ball. He's playing a shot that if he leaves it short, he's going to leave himself again a very difficult shot. If he hits it long, he's going to probably lose the tournament. He lands the ball exactly where it has to land. Going in the hole was a bonus. But what a shot! I don't think under the circumstances I've ever seen a better shot." At age 36, Woods is 10 years younger than Nicklaus when he wins his 73rd tournament at the 1986 Masters. Sam Snead holds the PGA Tour record with 82 wins.

1984 – Greg Norman wins his first PGA Tour title, holding on for a five-shot victory over runner-up Mark O'Meara at the Kemper Open at Congressional Country Club in Bethesda, Md. Norman starts the day with a seven-shot lead and shoots a final-round 73 to coast to the victory. Norman pockets the first-prize paycheck of $72,000 for what is his 30th world-wide win after claiming 29 other titles outside of the United States.

2001 – Karrie Webb of Australia wins the U.S. Women's Open Golf Championship at Pine Needles Lodge and Golf Club in Southern Pines, N.C. by eight shots over Se Ri Pak of South Korea.

2001 – Tiger Woods fires a six-under-par 66 and wins the Memorial for a third year in a row, claiming a seven-shot victory over Paul Azinger and Sergio Garcia. Azinger, paired with Woods, says that he actually apologizes to Woods for the non-competitiveness of the tournament. "I would say he's probably the most dominant athlete in the history of sports," Azinger says to reporters. Says Woods of his victory, "I'm amazed by some of the shots I was able to pull off this week. If I wanted to step up there and hit a two-iron 250 yards in the air and I was able to do it, I did it consistently. That, to me, is kind of cool."

June 4

2017 – One day after shooting a 77 to turn a five-shot second-round lead into a four-shot deficit entering the final round, Jason Dufner sinks a 32-foot par putt on the final hole to clinch what becomes a three-shot win at the Memorial in Dublin, Ohio. Dufner wins his fifth PGA Tour with his final-round 68 and joins tournament host and founder Jack Nicklaus as the only Ohio-born winners of the event. Dufner also becomes the first player to shoot 77 in a third round and still win on the PGA Tour since Nick Faldo at the 1989 Masters. "Yesterday was not my best day," Dufner says of his third-round 77. "But I had to get over it quick. It's a 72-hole tournament. There's a lot of things that can happen out there. I knew I was still in the mix."

1995 – Greg Norman shoots a final-round 66 and beats Mark Calcavecchia, Steve Elkington and David Duval by four strokes to win the Memorial at Muirfield Village. It is Norman's second Memorial Tournament victory and his 13th PGA Tour victory. Perhaps the most crucial shot for Norman comes when he safely hits his ball through the trees on the 12th hole and salvages par. Says Norman, "I never even saw those trees. It was like they weren't there. I was just concentrating on where I wanted to hit it."

June 5

2011 – Steve Stricker shoots a final-round four-under 68 to claim a one-shot victory over Matt Kuchar and Brandt Jobe at the Memorial at Muirfield Village. "You've seen so many guys do that over the years, the winners coming off the green and getting greeted by Mr. Nicklaus," Stricker says of the annual winner's handshake from the tournament founder and chairman Jack Nicklaus. "And you always think one day that could be you. And it turned out it was me this year. It's a great thrill. It's a dream come true."

1925 – Willie Macfarlane of Scotland defeats Bobby Jones by one stroke on the final hole of a 36-hole playoff to win his only major championship at the U.S. Open at the Worcester Country Club in Worcester, Mass. After both players shoot 75 in the 18-hole playoff, held in the morning, another 18-hole playoff is held to break the tie. Jones, the 1923 U.S. Open champion, takes a four-shot lead after nine holes in the second playoff round, but falters on the back nine and both players are tied on the 18th hole. Macfarlane two-putts for a par while Jones fails to get up and down from the greenside bunker to lose the championship by one shot. During the first round of play on June 3, Jones calls a one-shot penalty on himself – a decision that ultimately costs him the championship – when he says his club causes his ball to move in the rough on the 11th hole. Says Jones when he is lauded for his sportsmanship, "You might as well praise me for not robbing a bank."

1931 – Scottish-born American Tommy Armour fires a then course record 71 in the final-round to outlast José Jurado of Argentina by a single stroke to win his only Open Championship title at Carnoustie. Jurado misses a nine-foot putt on the final hole that would have tied Armour.

1941 – Tyrell Garth, a month shy of his 16th birthday, establishes a new U.S. Open record for youngest competitor at the Colonial Country Club in Fort Worth, Texas. Garth shoots an 80 in the first round and withdraws during the second round. His record stands until 2006, when Tadd Fujikawa, at the age of 15 years, six months, and seven days old, tees off at Winged Foot in Mamaroneck, N.Y. In 2012, Fujikawa's mark is broken when Andy Zhang of China, at 14 years, six months, competes at the Olympic Club in San Francisco.

June 6

1924 – Cyril Walker, a little known British golfer, wins the 1924 U.S. Open at Oakland Hills Country Club in Birmingham, Mich., by three shots over Bobby Jones. Walker never achieves any notoriety again in golf and ends up working as a dishwasher and dies in a New Jersey jail cell in 1948 at the age of 56.

1993 – In one of the most improbable endings in PGA Tour history, Paul Azinger holes out for birdie from the bunker on the 72nd hole giving him a one-shot win over Payne Stewart at the Memorial Tournament. Azinger calls the shot "a miracle" and "the bunker shot of my life." Stewart leads by one shot against his good friend Azinger when the final pair play the 18th hole. Stewart hits his birdie putt eight feet past the hole before Azinger makes his incredible birdie. Stewart then misses his par putt – and the one coming back – to finish two shots back in third place behind Corey Pavin.

1999 – Tiger Woods holds off Vijay Singh by two strokes to win the Memorial Tournament in Dublin, Ohio, his first tournament victory at the Jack Nicklaus-founded tournament. Woods is bailed out by his short game – highlighted by a chip-in par at the 14th hole – enabling him to post a final-round 69. "The short-game shots, I've always loved hitting them. I've always loved chipping and scrambling," says Woods. "I was so wild when I was younger, I had to hit those shots."

2010 – Justin Rose fires a final-round 66 to come from four strokes back to win the Memorial Tournament for his first career PGA Tour victory. Rose trails tour rookie Rickie Fowler by four strokes entering the final round, but registers six birdies and no bogeys and beats Fowler by three shots.

1936 – Little-known Tony Manero wins the U.S. Open on the Upper Course at the Baltusrol Golf Club in Springfield, N.J., overtaking third-round leader Harry Cooper and winning by two shots. Cooper leads Manero by four strokes entering the final round, but Manero shoots a final-round 67, a course record at the time. Manero is lucky to even be in the tournament, needing a chip-in on the final hole of sectional qualifying just to qualify for the tournament.

1999 – In her 20th attempt, Juli Inkster finally wins the U.S. Women's Open Golf Championship at Old Waverly Golf Club in West Point, Miss. by five shots over Sherri Turner. The 38-year-old Inkster breaks the tournament's under-par scoring record of 16-under and becomes the oldest U.S. Open champion since 40-year-old Fay Crocker wins the title in 1955.

2015 – Tiger Woods plays the worst round of his professional career, shooting a 13-over-par 85 in the third round of the Memorial Tournament at Muirfield Village. The horrid round for Woods is capped with a quadruple bogey 8 on the 18th hole that allows his score to eclipse his previous worst of 82 at the Phoenix Open earlier in the year.

June 7

1941 – Reigning Masters champion Craig Wood claims his second consecutive major with a three-stroke win over runner-up Denny Shute at the U.S. Open in sweltering heat at the Colonial Country Club in Fort Worth, Texas. Wood nearly withdraws from the tournament after scoring a 7 on his opening hole and still feeling the effects of a nagging back injury suffered two weeks earlier. He is, however, convinced to stay in the tournament by his playing partner Tommy Armour. The staging of the U.S. Open at Colonial marked the first time the event is played south of the Mason-Dixon Line and is so successful that the club launches its own annual tournament – the Colonial National Invitation Tournament – in 1946.

2009 – Tiger Woods birdies the last two holes to win the Memorial by one shot over Jim Furyk, his fourth career victory at the tournament founded by Jack Nicklaus. Woods comes from four shots back with a final-round 65, hitting every fairway on the course. Woods hits nine-iron to nine feet on the 17th hole and a seven-iron to a foot on the final hole to win his 67th PGA Tour title.

June 8

1935 – Sam Parks, Jr., a 25-year-old club pro at nearby South Hills Country Club with no prior tournament victories, wins the U.S. Open at Oakmont Country Club in Oakmont, Pa. Parks shoots a 76 in the final round to beat Jimmy Thompson by two strokes. Parks benefits from frequent visits to Oakmont for practice rounds before returning to his own club to work.

1950 – Lee Mackey establishes a new U.S. Open record by shooting a 64 in the first round at the Merion Golf Club in Ardmore, Pa. Mackey holds a three-shot lead after the first round, but follows his record round with an 81 in the second and, eventually, finishes in 25th place. Mackey's score of 64 is not be bettered in any other major championship until Johnny Miller shoots his famous final-round 63 at the 1973 U.S. Open.

June 9

1934 – Olin Dutra overcomes an eight-stroke deficit after 36 holes and wins the U.S. Open at Merion Golf Club in Ardmore, Pa. by one stroke over runner-up Gene Sarazen. Dutra falls ill just before the tournament and loses 15 pounds and cannot practice for 10 days. He nearly withdraws before the start of the tournament but is convinced to tough it out by his brother Mortie, who finishes in 28th place.

1940 – Lawson Little, the winner of both the U.S. and British Amateur Championship in 1934 and 1935, wins his first and only professional major when defeats Gene Sarazen by three shots in an 18-hole playoff at the U.S. Open at Canterbury Golf Club in Beachwood, Ohio.

1919 – Willie Chisholm set an unfortunate tournament record in the first round of the U.S. Open making an 18 on the 185-yard par-3 eighth hole at the Brae Burn Country Club in West Newton, Mass. Chisholm's tee shot is hit fat and lands in a rocky ravine in front the green. Rather than taking an unplayable lie penalty, Chisholm tries to slash the ball out with a niblick club, but needs 14 strokes to get the ball onto the green, his playing partner Jim Barnes counting his strokes. Chisholm then three putts for the highest score recorded on a hole in U.S. Open history.

June 10

1977 – Al Geiberger shoots the first 59 in PGA Tour history in the second round of the Danny Thomas Memphis Classic at the 7,193 yard par 72 Colonial Country Club in Tennessee. Geiberger makes 11 birdies, an eagle and six pars in his famous round, clinched with a 10-foot putt on his 18th hole, the ninth hole of the course. Says Geiberger of his last, history-clinching putt, "I said to myself, 'Whatever you do, don't leave it short. You may never get this chance again.'"

1950 – Ben Hogan hits one of his most famous shots in golf history – made more famous by the photograph of him hitting the shot – as he hits a one-iron approach shot to 40 feet on the final hole of the U.S. Open at the Merion Cricket Club in Ardmore, Pa. Hogan two-putts for par to force a three-way playoff the next day with George Fazio and Lloyd Mangrum, that he wins by four strokes. Hogan has a chance to win the tournament outright but misses a short par putt on the 15th hole and also bogeys the 17th hole, before his pressure shot from the 18th fairway. Mangrum leads the tournament by two shots over Hogan at the start of the final 18 holes, but shoots a six-over-par 76 to post a final-round score of seven-over-par 287 along with Hogan and Fazio.

1932 – Gene Sarazen wins the Open Championship for the first and only time, beating runner-up Macdonald Smith by five strokes at Prince's Golf Club in Sandwich, England. Two weeks later, Sarazen wins the U.S. Open to join Bobby Jones as the only players to win the British and U.S. Opens in the same year, subsequently joined by Ben Hogan (1953), Lee Trevino (1971), Tom Watson (1982) and Tiger Woods (2000).

1939 – Needing a par on the final hole to win the U.S. Open at the Philadelphia Country Club, Sam Snead believes that he needs a birdie and plays aggressively, finds two bunkers and scores a triple-bogey eight and loses the title, missing out on a playoff with Byron Nelson, Denny Shute and Craig Wood by two shots.

1933 – Amateur Johnny Goodman beats Ralph Guldahl by one stroke to win the U.S. Open at the North Shore Country Club in Glenview, Ill., becoming the eighth and last amateur to win the title. Bobby Jones, the greatest amateur player of all time, wins four U.S. Open titles, the last in 1930 as part of his "Grand Slam." Goodman starts the final round with a six-shot lead and begins his round with an eagle and a birdie but fades dramatically down the stretch, registering a par on the final hole for a final-round 76 and the one-stroke victory. Guldahl misses a four-foot putt on the final hole that would have forced a playoff.

1938 – In the second round of the U.S. Open at Cherry Hills Country Club in Englewood, Colo., Ray Ainsley scores a 19 on the par-4 16th hole. Ainsley's ball lands in a creek, and rather than taking a drop, he continues to try and play the ball out. He ends up shooting a 25-over-par score of 96 and misses the cut.

June 11

1950 – Ben Hogan wins an 18-hole playoff over Lloyd Mangrum and George Fazio to win the second of his four U.S. Open titles at Merion Golf Club in Ardmore, Pa. The turning point in the round comes on the 16th hole when Mangrum picks up his ball on the green to remove a bug and is assessed a two-stroke penalty due to a violation of the rules. Hogan goes up by three strokes and wins by four strokes as Fazio bogeys four of the last five holes. The win for Hogan comes just 16 months after being severely injured in a car accident.

1938 – Ralph Guldahl wins his second straight U.S. Open title beating runner-up Dick Metz by six strokes at Cherry Hills Country Club in Englewood, Colo. Guldahl becomes the fourth player to successfully defend at the U.S. Open, joining Willie Anderson, John McDermott and Bobby Jones. Subsequent players to repeat as U.S. Open champion are Ben Hogan in 1951 and Curtis Strange in 1989.

1949 – Cary Middlecoff wins the first of his two U.S. Open titles, beating out runners-up Clayton Heafner and Sam Snead at Medinah Country Club in Medinah, Ill. Heafner, who holds the lead several times in the final round, misses a six-foot birdie putt on the final hole that would have forced a playoff. Snead also misses a chance to force a playoff, needing birdie on the final hole, but misses the green on his approach shot and settles for par. It marks the third of four second-place finishes for Snead at the U.S. Open, the only major championship he never wins. Defending champion Ben Hogan misses the tournament after being severely injured in an automobile accident in February.

1953 – Arnold Palmer, a 23-year-old from nearby Latrobe, Pa., makes his debut at the U.S. Open at Oakmont Country Club in Oakmont, Pa. and shoots an 84. He shoots a 78 the next day in the second round and misses the cut by nine shots. Seven years later, he wins his only U.S. Open title in 1960 and plays his last U.S. Open at Oakmont again in 1994.

June 12

1948 – Ben Hogan wins the U.S. Open for the first time by shooting a final-round 69 to beat runner-up Jimmy Demaret by two strokes at the Riviera Country Club in Pacific Palisades, Calif. Hogan beats the U.S. Open scoring record by five strokes and his three rounds in the 60s is a tournament first. Hogan's scoring record stands for 19 years until Jack Nicklaus breaks it in 1967. Hogan's U.S. Open win at Riviera, coupled with his wins there at the Los Angeles Open earlier in the year and in 1947, cause the course to become known as "Hogan's Alley."

1937 – Ralph Guldahl wins the first of his two consecutive U.S. Opens, two strokes ahead of runner-up and tournament debutant Sam Snead at the Oakland Hills Country Club in Birmingham, Mich. Guldahl is two years removed from temporary leaving golf to become a carpenter. Oakland Hills is set at 7,037 yards by the U.S. Golf Association, marking the first time a U.S. Open venue surpasses 7,000 yards.

1939 – Byron Nelson wins his first and only U.S. Open title closing out Craig Wood in a second 18-hole playoff at the Philadelphia Country Club in Gladwyne, Pa. Nelson takes control of the playoff on the third hole with a birdie while Wood makes double-bogey. On the next hole, Nelson then holes out for an eagle to take a five-stroke lead and holds on to shoot a 70 to Wood's 73 to win the championship. The previous day, Nelson, Wood and Denny Shute play the first 18-hole playoff, Nelson and Wood each carding scores of 68, necessitating another 18-hole playoff, and Shute shooting a 76 to be eliminated.

1919 – In the first U.S. Open since 1916 due to World War I, Walter Hagen defeats Mike Brady by one stroke in an 18-hole playoff to win his second and final U.S. Open at Brae Burn Country Club in West Newton, Mass.

1980 – Jack Nicklaus and Tom Weiskopf open the U.S. Open at Baltusrol Golf Club in Springfield, N.J. by shooting a U.S. Open and major tournament record-tying 63 in the first round. Weiskopf, however, does not shoot better than 75 in any other round and finishes in 37th place while Nicklaus goes on to win his fourth U.S. Open title.

1957 – Jack Nicklaus, a 17-year-old amateur, tees it up at the U.S. Open for the first time at the Inverness Club in Toledo, Ohio. The future four-time tournament winner shoots an opening round of 80 and shoots another 80 the next day to miss the cut.

1988 – Seve Ballesteros shoots a final-round 67 and birdies the first hole of a four-man sudden-death playoff with Greg Norman, David Frost and Ken Green and wins the Westchester Classic at the Westchester Country Club in Harrison, N.Y. The win ultimately becomes the last win in the United States for Ballesteros. Exactly five years earlier to the day, Ballesteros also wins at Westchester by two strokes over runners-up Andy Bean and Craig Stadler. Ballesteros first wins in the United States at the 1978 Greater Greensboro Open and, after wins at the Masters in 1980 and 1983, wins twice at Westchester and also in New Orleans in 1985.

2003 – Bruce Edwards, the longtime caddie for Tom Watson diagnosed with amyotrophic lateral sclerosis (Lou Gehrig's disease) for five months, carries the bag for his 53-year-old boss who shoots an opening round 65 to tie for the opening day lead at the U.S. Open at Olympia Fields with Brett Quigley. Writes Thomas Boswell in the *Washington Post*, "At times, sports defies time, mocks age. Or, makes us cherish time. Watson and Edwards did all of that – evoking their storied 30-year golf past together, then creating a new moment as moving as any before it." Says Edwards, his voice slurred by the effects of his disease,

"We turned back the clock today. It was wonderful. It was a blast. Not bad for old folks, eh?" Watson's magical play only lasts for one day as she shoots 72, 75 and 72 to finish in a tie for 28th place.

June 13

1953 – Ben Hogan wins a record-tying fourth U.S. Open title, six strokes ahead of runner-up Sam Snead at the Oakmont Country Club in Oakmont, Pa. Hogan's fourth title equals the record of Willie Anderson and Bobby Jones and is later equaled by Jack Nicklaus, who wins his fourth U.S. Open title in 1980.

1982 – Ray Floyd wins his 17th PGA Tour title at the Danny Thomas Memphis Classic and becomes the sixth golfer to accumulate $2 million in career earnings. The 39-year-old Floyd birdies the last three holes for a final-round 69 and a six-shot win over Mike Holland. Floyd earns $72,000, increasing his career winnings to $2,022,597, trailing only Jack Nicklaus, Tom Watson, Lee Trevino, Hale Irwin and Tom Weiskopf on the all-time earnings list at the time.

2010 – Robert Garrigus blows a three-stroke lead on the final hole of regulation with a triple bogey, and bogeys the first playoff hole that allows Lee Westwood to win his second career PGA Tour victory at the St. Jude Classic in Memphis. Westwood prevails in the three-way playoff on the fourth hole, outlasting Robert Karlsson of Sweden.

1993 – Thirty-year-old Vijay Singh of Fiji wins his first PGA Tour title at the Buick Classic at the Westchester Country Club in Harrison, N.Y., making birdie on the third hole of a sudden-death playoff with Mark Wiebe. Singh goes on to win 34 career PGA Tour titles, including an incredible 22 in his 40s.

2003 – Vijay Singh equals a U.S. Open and major tournament record by shooting 63 in the second round of the U.S. Open at Olympia Fields in Illinois, sharing the second-round lead with eventual champion Jim Furyk. Singh shoots a 29 on the back nine, equaling the U.S. Open record for lowest score over nine holes, tying Neal Lancaster who shot 29 on the back nine twice at the U.S. Open, in 1995 and 1996. Singh fades in the final two rounds, shooting 72 and 78 and finishes in a tie for 20th.

June 14

1952 – Julius Boros wins the first of his three major titles – and his first PGA Tour event – winning the U.S. Open at the Northwood Club in Dallas, Texas, four strokes ahead of runner-up Ed Oliver. Two-time defending champion Ben Hogan leads entering the final 36 holes, but shoots consecutive rounds of 74 in the morning and afternoon rounds in the Texas heat and finishes in third place, five strokes behind Boros. Hogan was looking to join Willie Anderson (1903-1905) as the only players to win three straight U.S. Open titles.

1959 – Billy Casper wins the first of his two U.S. Open titles and his first major title, a stroke ahead of runner-up Bob Rosburg on the West Course at Winged Foot Golf Club in Mamaroneck, N.Y. Casper shoots a final-round 74 to hold off Rosburg, who shoots a 71, Rosburg missing a 40-foot birdie putt on the final hole that would have forced a Monday 18-hole playoff. Casper begins the final round with a three-stroke lead over 46-year-old Ben Hogan, who shoots a 76 and finishes eighth.

1958 – Native Oklahoman Tommy Bolt wins his only major championship at the U.S. Open at Southern Hills Country Club in Tulsa, Okla. with a four-stroke win over U.S. Open debutant Gary Player.

1985 – Jack Nicklaus misses the cut at the U.S. Open at Oakland Hills Country Club in Birmingham, Mich., snapping a streak of consecutive U.S. Open cuts made at 21. Nicklaus shoots a 73 that places him at nine-over-par for the tournament after a first round 76.

June 15

1980 – Jack Nicklaus sets a new tournament scoring record and wins his fourth U.S. Open championship at Baltusrol Golf Club in Springfield, N.J. Nicklaus sets a new tournament record of 272, breaking his own record of 275 set in 1967, also at Baltusrol, and beating Isao Aoki of Japan by two shots. Nicklaus also ties Willie Anderson, Bobby Jones and Ben Hogan by winning his fourth U.S. Open title. Nicklaus enters the tournament having not won a tournament since 1978 and, at age 40, many questioning whether his best days were over. But, one of the manual scoreboard operators writes what everyone was thinking at the end of this U.S. Open – "Jack is Back." Says Nicklaus as he accepts his championship trophy, being showered with applause by thousands of fans, "If you don't mind, I'm just going to stand here for a minute and enjoy this."

1986 – At 43 years, nine months and 11 days, Ray Floyd becomes the oldest winner of the U.S. Open at the time emerging from a crowded final-round leaderboard to claim a two-stroke victory over Chip Beck and Lanny Wadkins at Shinnecock Hills Golf Club in Shinnecock Hills, N.Y. At one point during the frenzied final-day nine players share the lead, including third-round leader Greg Norman, who famously holds the 54-hole lead at every major tournament during the 1986 season. Norman shoots a final-round 75 to finish in 12th place. "I felt if I couldn't handle it this time it wouldn't happen," Floyd says. "Realistically, I felt today I had to do it. It was probably my last chance." Floyd is five months older than Ted Ray, who wins the 1920 U.S. Open at the age of 43 years, four months, 16 days. Wadkins and Beck each card course record 65s to finish in second place. Hale Irwin breaks Floyd's record as the oldest U.S. Open winner in 1990 when he wins at Medinah at the age of 45 years, 15 days.

1969 – Orville Moody wins his first and only PGA Tour event when he captures the U.S. Open by one shot over Deane Beman, Bob Rosburg and Al Geiberger at Champions Golf Club in Houston, Texas. Moody advances into the tournament by advancing through local and sectional qualifying. Miller Barber begins the final round with a three-stroke lead, but shoots a final-round 78 and finishes in sixth place. Not only does Moody not win another PGA Tour event, but he only has one more top 10 finish at a major tournament. However, after he turns 50 years old, he wins 11 titles on the PGA Champions Tour.

1997 – Ernie Els wins his second U.S. Open, holding off Colin Montgomerie by one shot at the Congressional Country Club Blue Course in Bethesda, Md. Tom Lehman is the third-round leader for the third straight year at the U.S. Open, but falters with a final-round 73 to finish two shots behind Els. Lehman's chances for victory die when he hits a seven-iron shot into the water on the 71st hole while trailing Els by one shot. "That was a perfect yardage to a perfect pin for me, I was definitely thinking about a birdie," Lehman says. "I feel an incredible amount of pain." Els, the 1994 U.S. Open champion, culminates his victorious effort with a knee-knocking four-foot par putt on the par-3 18th hole. "I was really, really tense over that last putt," says Els, who shoots a final-round 69. "Maybe my exterior is calm, but inside I'm pretty tense."

2003 – Jim Furyk stays steady and holds on for a three-shot victory over Stephen Leaney at the 2003 U.S. Open Championship at Olympia Fields Country Club in Olympia Fields, Ill., a suburb south of Chicago. Furyk's four-round total of 272 ties the record for the lowest 72-hole score in U.S. Open history, also achieved in 2000 by Tiger Woods and 1980 by Jack Nicklaus (and since broken when Rory McIlroy shoots

268 in 2011). "It's a proud day, it's beyond some dreams," says Furyk. "I liked the way I was playing…I really felt comfortable with my game and I came here with a good mind-set. I love being the front-runner and hitting solid shots and putting the pressure on the other guy."

2008 – Tiger Woods dramatically sinks a 12-foot birdie putt on the final hole to force an 18-hole Monday playoff with Rocco Mediate at the U.S. Open at Torrey Pines in San Diego. Woods shoots a final-round 73, played in pain on a surgically repaired left knee that left some to question whether or not he would pull out of the tournament. Needing a birdie on the final hole to tie Mediate, Woods hits his tee shot on the final hole in a fairway bunker. He then lays up in the right rough and pitches to 12 feet from 105 yards away before making one of the most dramatic putts in major championship golf. "That was actually one of the worst parts of the green," Woods says of his tying putt. "It's so bumpy down there. And I just kept telling myself two and a half balls outside the right, but make sure you stay committed to it, make a pure stroke, and if it plinkos in or plinkos out it doesn't matter, as long as I make a pure stroke. And I did. I hit it good. It took forever to break, but it finally snuck in there at the end."

1957 – Dick Mayer beats defending champion Cary Middlecoff in an 18-hole playoff to win the U.S. Open at the Inverness Club in Toledo, Ohio. Mayer cards a 72 to Middlecoff's 79 in the playoff, played in temperatures in the 90s and high humidity.

1923 – Arthur Havers holes a bunker shot on the 72nd hole and wins the Open Championship at Troon by one shot over defending champion Walter Hagen. After Havers' chip-in for a final-round 76 and a three-over par score of 295, Hagen finds himself in the same bunker on the final hole of the championship and needs to hole out to force a 36-hole playoff. However, Hagen narrowly misses. The championship marks the first time the event is held at Troon.

1947 – Lew Worsham beats Sam Snead in an 18-hole playoff to win the U.S. Open at St. Louis Country Club in Ladue, Mo. Snead leads Worsham by two strokes with three holes to play, but after Worsham birdies the 16th hole and Snead bogeys the 17th hole, the two players are tied on the 18th hole. After both players reach the fairway, Snead hits an approach shot to 15 feet, while Worsham is long and 40 feet away in the fringe. Worsham's chip rolls into the hole and bounces out, ending up 29 inches from the hole. Snead's subsequent birdie putt to win the championship is left well short. As Snead prepares to hole out, Worsham asks for an official to determine who is farther away and, with a tape measure, it is determined that it remains Snead's turn. Upset at the delay, Snead then misses the 30.5 inch putt. Worsham then sinks his 29-inch putt to win the playoff by one stroke.

1997 – Tiger Woods, at the age of 21 years and 167 days, becomes the youngest golfer to rank No. 1 in the world. Woods achieves the top ranking in his just his 42nd week as a professional golfer. The first No. 1 run for Woods lasts only one week as Ernie Els follows his win at the U.S. Open with a win at the Buick Classic the following week, taking over the top spot.

1962 – Dave Hill famously takes six putts on the sixth green at the Oakmont Country Club in Oakmont, Pa., in the second round of the U.S. Open. Hill then immediately withdraws from the tournament.

2014 – Martin Kaymer of Germany finishes a dominating wire-to-wire victory at the U.S. Open at Pinehurst No. 2 in Pinehurst Village, N.C. by eight shots over runners-up Erik Compton and Rickie Fowler. Kaymer becomes the first player from Germany and continental Europe to win the U.S. Open.

1995 – Eldrick "Tiger" Woods, the U.S. Amateur champion, plays his first ever U.S. Open round and cards a four-over-par 74 in the first round of the U.S. Open at Shinnecock Hills Golf

Club in Southampton, N.Y. Nick Price, the reigning Open and PGA Champion, describes some of the shots coming of the club of the 19-year-old as "amazing." Says Price, "He is up there with John Daly. He hits the ball so far. I mean, I can't see where he gets all his power from, but the ball just takes off like a rocket. He outdrove me three times today by about 50 yards, and I think I'm in the top 10 or top 15 in driving distance." Says Woods of what he learned from his first U.S. Open round. "What I learned is basically you've got to manage your game well. Nick Price is a perfect example. He plays very conservatively, very much within himself."

June 16

1968 – Lee Trevino wins his first major championship – and his first PGA Tour victory – with a four-shot victory over Jack Nicklaus at the U.S. Open at the East Course of Oak Hill Country Club in Rochester, N.Y. Trevino enters the final round trailing Bert Yancey by one stroke, but Yancey balloons to a final-round 76 to finish in third place, while Trevino fires a 67. Trevino's 275 total score ties the tournament record set by Nicklaus the previous year. Fifty-six-year-old Sam Snead finishes in a tie for ninth place, his final top-10 finish at the U.S. Open.

1951 – "I'm glad I brought this course – this monster – to its knees," says Ben Hogan as he wins his second consecutive U.S. Open title – and his third title in his last three attempts – with a two stroke victory over Clayton Heafner at Oakland Hills Country Club in Birmingham, Mich. Hogan won the 1948 U.S. Open and missed the 1949 championship due to injuries suffered in a serious car crash, before returning and winning the U.S. Open again in 1950. Hogan fires a final-round 67 – one of the two rounds under par at "the monster" during the tournament.

1946 – Lloyd Mangrum, a World War II veteran and recipient of two Purple Hearts, wins the first U.S. Open title held since 1941 defeating Byron Nelson and Vic Ghezzi in a 36-hole playoff at Canterbury Golf Club in Beachwood, Ohio. All three players shoot an even-par 72 during the first 18 holes, which, according to U.S. Open rules at the time, force another 18-hole playoff in the afternoon, as there was no sudden-death playoff at the time. Mangrum, despite a bogey-bogey finish, shoots a 72 in the second 18 holes, beating Nelson and Ghezzi by one stroke.

1985 – Andy North wins his second U.S. Open title by a stroke over runners-up Dave Barr, Tze-Chung Chen and Denis Watson at Oakland Hills in Birmingham, Mich. The signature moment of the final round comes when third-round leader Tze-Chung "T.C." Chen, leading by four shots, accidentally "double hits" a chip shot from the thick greenside rough on the fifth hole. Chen is assessed a stroke penalty, then three-putts for a quadruple-bogey 8. Chen then bogeys the next three holes and North narrowly hangs on, tapping in for bogey on the final hole to close out his one-shot victory. In his final round, North hits only four fairways and makes just one birdie. For the entire tournament, he makes only nine birdies, the lowest by a champion in post-World War II U.S. Open history. Curiously, North's U.S. Open title is his third and final PGA Tour victory, his only other victories being his 1978 U.S. Open victory and at the 1977 Westchester Classic.

2002 – Tiger Woods wins his second U.S. Open title and his eighth major championship, three shots ahead of runner-up Phil Mickelson at the Black Course at Bethpage State Park in Farmingdale, N.Y. It marks the first time that the U.S. Open is played on a public golf course. The victory for Woods marks the first time in 30 years that the winner of the Masters also wins the U.S. Open, a feat last accomplished by Jack Nicklaus in 1972, and also by Arnold Palmer (1960), Ben Hogan (1951, 1953), and Craig Wood (1941).

1996 – Steve Jones edges runners-up Tom Lehman and Davis Love III by one stroke to win the U.S. Open at Oakland Hills Country Club in Birmingham, Mich. Jones goes through sectional qualifying to enter the U.S. Open field, becoming the first champion to do so since Jerry Pate in 1976. Jones is off the tour for three years from 1992 until 1994 recovering from a dirt bike accident where he separates his shoulder and suffers ligament damage in his index finger that threatens his career.

1974 – Hale Irwin survives the "Massacre at Winged Foot" winning the U.S. Open at Winged Foot Golf Club in Mamaroneck, N.Y. with a winning score of seven over par, two better than runner-up Forest Fezler. Irwin's seven-over score is the second-highest in post-World War II history, after Julius Boros' score of nine-over at the 1963 U.S. Open. Many speculated that the U.S. Golf Association makes the course setup extra difficult in response to Johnny Miller's record-breaking score of 63 the year before.

2008 – Tiger Woods win his third U.S. Open title – and his 14th major championship – in the 19th hole of a playoff with Rocco Mediate at Torrey Pines in San Diego, Calif. Woods, hobbled by what is eventually diagnosed as anterior cruciate ligament tear, blows a three-shot lead with eight holes to play and needs to birdie the 18th hole of the playoff to extend the playoff. The forty-five-year-old Mediate has an opportunity to win the tournament, and register one of the greatest upsets in golf history, with a 20-foot birdie putt on the 18th hole, but pulls it slightly and misses. Woods pars the sudden-death 19th hole of the playoff while Mediate bogeys, ending the contest. "I think this is probably the best ever," Woods says of his victory. "All things considered, I don't know how I ended up in this position, to be honest with you. It was a long week. A lot of doubt, a lot of questions going into the week. And here we are, 91 holes later." Says Mediate, "Obviously, I would have loved to win. I don't know what else to say. They wanted a show, they got one."

1956 – Cary Middlecoff wins his second U.S. Open title by one stroke over Julius Boros and Ben Hogan at Oak Hill Country Club in Rochester, N.Y. Despite making bogey on the 16th and 17th holes, Middlecoff finishes with his third straight round of 70 and waits as Hogan, Boros and Ted Kroll all fail to match or better his score.

2013 – Justin Rose wins the U.S. Open by two shots over Phil Mickelson and Jason Day at the Merion Golf Club in Ardmore, Pa., becoming the first English winner of the event since Tony Jacklin in 1970. For Mickelson, it marks his record sixth runner-up finish at the U.S. Open, the major event that he treasures the most. He leads or co-leads after the first three rounds of the event and is the leader by one shot entering the final round. "This is tough to swallow after coming so close," says Mickelson on his 43rd birthday. "I felt like this was as good an opportunity I could ask for and to not get it…it hurts."

1989 – During the second round of the U.S. Open at Oak Hill in Rochester, N.Y., four players – Jerry Pate, Nick Price, Doug Weaver and Mark Wiebe – make holes-in-one at the downhill 167-yard sixth hole. All four players hit a seven-iron past the flag for their aces.

2006 – Tiger Woods misses the cut in his first professional major after shooting consecutive rounds of 76 – the highest consecutive rounds of his pro career at the time – at the U.S. Open at Winged Foot in Mamaroneck, N.Y. Woods plays the event six weeks after the death of his father Earl. Says Woods, "What's happened off the course, I don't know if it gives you a different type of perspective. But I don't care if you had what transpired in my life of recent or not, poor execution is never going to feel very good."

June 17

1962 – Twenty-two-year-old Jack Nicklaus wins an historic 18-hole Sunday playoff with Arnold Palmer at the Oakmont Country Club in Oakmont, Pa., and wins the 1962 U.S. Open, his first career major championship. Nicklaus shoots a 71 to Palmer's 74 to win the title and disappoint many of the 10,000 fans decidedly in favor of Palmer, from nearby Latrobe, Pa. Nicklaus leads by four shots after just six holes, but Palmer is able to chip away at the lead and draws within one shot with a birdie on the 12th hole. However, a three-putt bogey on the 13th hole again swings the momentum back to Nicklaus. Nicklaus becomes the youngest winner of the U.S. Open since Bobby Jones in 1923, and becomes the first since Jones to hold the U.S. Open and the U.S. Amateur championship at the same time. Nicklaus had won the U.S. Amateur the previous year before turning pro.

2012 – Webb Simpson birdies four holes in a five-hole stretch and shoots a two-under-par 68 to win the U.S. Open at the Olympic Club in San Francisco, holding off former champions Jim Furyk and Graeme McDowell. "I never really wrapped my mind around winning," says Simpson, who finishes at one-over 281, one stroke better than McDowell and Michael Thompson. "This place is so demanding, and so all I was really concerned about was keeping the ball in front of me and making pars."

1973 – In what many regard as the greatest ever round of golf, Johnny Miller shoots a final-round 63 – the lowest round ever at a major championship at the time – to win the U.S. Open at the Oakmont Country Club. After shooting a five-over-par 76 in the third round, the 26-year-old Miller starts the final round six strokes back, in a tie for 13th place at three over par. He birdies the first four holes, and, after a bogey at the eighth hole, he birdies four of the next five holes. After a par at No. 14, he sits in a tie for the lead with Arnold Palmer, Julius Boros and Tom Weiskopf. Miller's birdie from 10 feet away on the 15th hole places him in the lead by himself. Miller barely misses his birdie attempt on the 18th hole for a 62 and has to wait for an hour before John Schlee's 40-foot putt for birdie on the 18th hole misses for him to clinch the championship. Miller hits all 18 greens in regulation and needs only 29 putts. Ten of his approach shots land within 15 feet of the hole, while five are within six feet. Only three other players manage to even break 70 on the day.

1979 – Hale Irwin wins his second U.S. Open title, beating Jerry Pate and Gary Player by two strokes at the Inverness Club in Toledo, Ohio. Irwin shoots a final-round 75, equaling the post-World War II tournament record for highest final round score by the champion. He finishes the tournament with a double-bogey, bogey on his final two holes.

1991 – Payne Stewart beats Scott Simpson in an 18-hole Monday playoff to win the U.S. Open at Hazeltine National Golf Club in Chaska, Minn. Simpson leads Stewart by two strokes on the 16th hole, but makes bogey while Stewart birdies to even the contest. On the par-3 17th hole, Simpson's tee shot finds the water, leading to another bogey, while Stewart pars to take a one-shot lead into the 18th hole, where Simpson makes another bogey to lose the playoff by two strokes. The previous day, Simpson leads the tournament by one stroke on the 72nd hole, but bogeys the final hole to force the playoff.

1961 – Gene Littler win the U.S. Open – his sole major title – by one stroke over Bob Goalby and Doug Sanders at Oakland Hills Country Club in Birmingham, Mich. Littler only needs to bogey the final hole to stay ahead of Goalby, who was already in the clubhouse, and bogeys while Sanders, his playing partner, nearly chips in for birdie that would have forced a playoff.

1927 – Tommy Armour wins the first of his three major championships by beating Harry Cooper in an 18-hole playoff to win the U.S. Open at the Oakmont Country Club in Oakmont,

Pa., the first time the U.S. Open is held at the famed Pennsylvania course. While Armour goes on to win two more majors – the PGA Championship in 1930 and the Open Championship in 1931 – Cooper never wins one, his 31 PGA Tour victories being the most by a player without a major win, often earning him the moniker as the "best player to never win a major."

2007 – Angel Cabrera becomes only the second player from South America to win a major championship when he wins the U.S. Open by one shot ahead of Tiger Woods and Jim Furyk at the Oakmont Country Club. Cabrera joins fellow Argentine Roberto De Vicenzo, the winner of the 1967 Open Championship, as the only South American winners in majors. Cabrera, who finishes with a five-over-par score of 285, fires a final-round one-under-par 69 and is one of two players to shoot under par on the final day. In fact, of the 437 rounds played in the entire event, only eight are under par. "I feel great. I hope (Argentina) is enjoying it. This is for them," says Cabrera through a translator.

1994 – Sixty-four-year-old Arnold Palmer plays his final U.S. Open round at the Oakmont Country Club, site of his U.S. Open debut in 1953 and near his hometown of Latrobe, Pa. Palmer shoots an 81 in the second round to miss the cut at 16-over-par and holds an emotional press conference where he cannot gain his composure. After only five minutes, with a few words and tears shed in his towel, he walks away from the microphone ending the press conference and receives a standing ovation from the press corps.

June 18

1978 – Andy North bogeys the final hole but still edges Dave Stockton and J.C. Snead by one stroke to win the U.S. Open at Cherry Hills Country Club in Englewood, Colo. North needs only 114 putts over 72 holes, tying the record set by Billy Casper in 1966, to win his second PGA event. North does not win again until the 1985 U.S. Open for his third and final victory.

1960 – Arnold Palmer mounts the greatest comeback in U.S. Open history, overcoming a seven-stroke deficit during the final round to win his only U.S. Open title at Cherry Hills in Englewood, Colo. Palmer trails leader Mike Souchak by eight strokes after 36 holes and by seven shots after 54 holes. While eating lunch after his morning 18 holes on the 36-hole U.S. Open finale, Palmer becomes annoyed when golf writers Bob Drum and Dan Jenkins laugh at his chances to win the tournament. Palmer then proceeds to famously drive the green at the 346-yard par 4 first hole and shoots a final-round 65 to win his only U.S. Open title. Amateur Jack Nicklaus finishes in second place, two shots behind Palmer. Ben Hogan, at age 47, is tied for the lead with Palmer on the 71st hole and goes for the par 5 in two only to find the water. He finds the water again on the final hole and finishes in a tie for ninth place. Souchak double-bogeys the final hole to finish in a tie for third.

1967 – Jack Nicklaus wins his second U.S. Open title at Baltusrol Golf Club in Springfield, N.J. and breaks Ben Hogan's U.S. Open scoring record with a four-round total of 275. Nicklaus beats Arnold Palmer by four shots by shooting a final-round 65, capped with an incredible birdie on the final hole to break Hogan's record by one shot. After hitting his tee shot into the trees on the 543-yard par-5 18th hole, Nicklaus pitches out where he faces a 230-yard uphill shot to the green. Nicklaus stripes a one-iron to 22 feet and sinks the putt for birdie to break the Hogan record. "I wasn't thinking about records," Nicklaus says to reporters of his final-hole heroics. "Records come. They're made to be broken. I just wanted to win this tournament." Nicklaus references Palmer's final-round U.S. Open collapse the previous year when he was attempting to break the Hogan record and also Dick Mayer making double-bogey on the same hole at the 1954 U.S. Open to fall out of a playoff.

1972 – Jack Nicklaus wins his third U.S. Open title with a three-stroke win over runner-up Bruce Crampton in the first ever major championship played at the Pebble Beach Golf Links in Pebble Beach, Calif. The signature shot of the Nicklaus win comes on the 17th hole where he hits a one-iron that bounces off the green and hits the flagstick, settling inches from the hole for a tap-in birdie that gives him a four-shot lead heading into the final hole. The win for Nicklaus is his 11th career major championship, tying him with Walter Hagen in second place behind Bobby Jones with 13 majors that includes his five U.S. Amateur and one British Amateur titles.

1995 – In the 100th anniversary staging of the U.S. Open, Corey Pavin wins his only major championship, two strokes ahead of runner-up Greg Norman at Shinnecock Hills Golf Club in Southampton, N.Y. Pavin starts the day three shots back of third-round leader Tom Lehman and shoots a final-round 68, highlighted by a four-wood approach to the 18th hole that skirts past the flag and, after a two-putt par, caps his triumph.

1984 – Fuzzy Zoeller defeats Greg Norman in an 18-hole Monday playoff to win the U.S. Open at Winged Foot Golf Club in Mamaroneck, N.Y. Zoeller shoots a 67, eight shots better than Norman, to win his second major championship after winning the 1979 Masters. A day earlier, Norman holes a 45-foot putt to save par on the final hole, but Zoeller believes it's a birdie to take a one-shot lead and playfully waves a white towel to Norman in mock surrender from the fairway. At the conclusion of the Monday playoff, it is Norman who waves a white towel in mock surrender in an excellent display of sportsmanship.

2001 – Retief Goosen wins the first of his two U.S. Open titles in an 18-hole Monday playoff, two strokes ahead of runner-up Mark Brooks at Southern Hills in Tulsa, Okla. The conclusion of the final round the day before features one of the most unusual occurrences ever at the U.S. Open. Brooks three putts for bogey on the final hole to drop a shot back from co-leaders Goosen and Stewart Cink, playing in the final pairing. Goosen hits the final green, 10 feet from the hole for birdie, while Cink misses the green long. After Cink misses his 15 foot par putt that he thinks would keep him alive, he hurries his 18-inch bogey putt and misses to make double bogey. Goosen then has two putts to win from 10 feet and hits his birdie putt two feet by the hole. Goosen then incredibly misses his par putt that forces the Monday playoff with Brooks, but not Cink, whose hurried miss to get out of Goosen's way costs him a chance to join the playoff. "I definitely had to work hard for this one," says Goosen. "It's been a long week, it feels like a year out here." The tournament ends defending champion Tiger Woods's run of four consecutive major championship wins, or the "Tiger Slam."

1990 – Hale Irwin becomes the oldest U.S. Open champion at the age of 45 years, 15 days by defeating Mike Donald on the 91st hole of the championship, the first sudden-death hole after an 18-hole Monday playoff, at the Medinah Country Club in Medinah, Ill. Irwin and Donald tie after 18 holes of the playoff and Irwin birdies the first extra hole to win his third U.S. Open title, also winning in 1974 and 1979. Donald, a journeyman pro, leads the playoff by two shots on the 16th tee, but Irwin birdies the 16th hole and Donald misses a 15-foot par putt to win the title on the 18th hole of the playoff. The day before, Irwin sinks a 45-foot birdie on the final hole to cap a final-round 67 that gets him into the playoff. Irwin famously takes a "victory lap" after his famous putt, high-fiving fans while running alongside the ropes surrounding the green.

1989 – Curtis Strange wins his second consecutive U.S. Open, one stroke ahead of runners-up Chip Beck, Mark McCumber, and Ian Woosnam at Oak Hill Country Club in Rochester, N.Y., and becomes the first player to successfully defend a U.S. Open title since Ben Hogan in 1951. During a steady final round, Strange makes 15 consecutive pars until he makes a birdie at the 16th hole. Despite a three-putt bogey on the final hole, Strange hangs on for the one-stroke victory. Strange does not win again on the PGA Tour.

1898 – Scotland's Fred Herd wins the U.S. Open title by seven strokes over runner-up Alex Smith at the Myopia Hunt Club in South Hamilton, Mass. The tournament is the fourth ever staging of the championship and the first time the event is played over 72 holes. Competitors play eight loops of Myopia's nine-hole course.

2000 – Tiger Woods wins his first U.S. Open by a record fifteen strokes over runners-up Ernie Els and Miguel Ángel Jiménez at Pebble Beach Golf Links in the most dominating performance in any major golf championship. Woods shoots a final-round 67 to post a 12-under-par score of 272, becoming the first player in the 106-year history of the U.S. Open to finish at double-digits under par and tying what was then the lowest score ever in a U.S. Open set by Jack Nicklaus, Lee Janzen and Jim Furyk, all achieved on par-70 courses. "Records are great, but you don't really pay attention to that," Woods says. "The only thing I know is I got the trophy sitting right next to me. To perform the way I did, and on one of the greatest venues in golf, it doesn't get much better than that."

1915 – Four-time U.S. Amateur champion Jerome Travers wins his only U.S. Open title by one stroke over runner-up Tom McNamara at the Baltusrol Golf Club in Springfield, N.J. Shortly after his win, Travers announces his retirement from competitive golf and never again plays in the U.S. Open.

2006 – Needing only a par on the final hole to win his first U.S. Open title, Phil Mickelson makes double bogey giving Geoff Ogilvy the title at Winged Foot Golf Club in Mamaroneck, N.Y. Mickelson's tee shot on the final hole hits a hospitality tent off the left side of the fairway and, rather than pitching out and trying to get par, he goes for the green only to hit a tree, advancing the ball only 25 yards. He then hits his third shot into a greenside bunker. With a plugged lie in the bunker, Mickelson blasts out past the hole and off the green and misses his bogey chip that would have forced a playoff with Ogilvy. "I still am in shock that I did that. I just can't believe that I did that," Mickelson says after the final round. "I am such an idiot." Mickelson, who leads by two shots with four holes to play, hits only two fairways in the final round, none on the back nine. Ogilvy finishes with a bit of retrospective drama as he chips in from the rough on the 17th hole to save par, then, after his tee shot on the final lands in a divot, he gets up and down from the hill in front of the 18th green, his approach shot landing on the false front of the green. He sinks a six-foot par putt which, at the time, he thought secured him a runner-up finish. "I think I was the beneficiary of a little bit of charity," says Ogilvy, the first Australian to win the U.S. Open since David Graham in 1981.

June 19

2005 – Michael Campbell of New Zealand holds off a charging Tiger Woods and wins the U.S. Open by two strokes at Pinehurst No. 2 in North Carolina. Campbell benefits from third-round leader and defending champion Retief Goosen ballooning to a final-round 81, trailing him by four shots at the start of the day.

1977 – Playing in the fear of an assassination attempt, Hubert Green hangs on to win the U.S. Open at Southern Hills Country Club in Tulsa, Okla. by one shot over 1975 U.S. Open champion Lou Graham. With four holes to play, Green needs to par in to win the championship, but as he steps on the 14th green, he is approached by tournament officials and Tulsa police officers, who inform him they had received a phone call threatening to assassinate him as he played the 15th hole. Green decides to play on, hits a tree with this drive, but manages to safely par the hole without incident. After he birdies the 16th hole, Green makes a four-foot putt for bogey on the final hole to clinch the championship. The final round of golf marks the first time that the final 18 holes of U.S. Open golf are broadcast on television.

1955 – Jack Fleck, a municipal course pro from Iowa, registers one of the greatest upsets in golf history beating Ben Hogan in an 18-hole playoff to win the U.S. Open at the Olympic Club in San Francisco. Fleck leads Hogan by a single stroke on the 18th hole of the playoff but Hogan drives into thick rough and takes three strokes to get to the fairway. Hogan makes a 25-foot putt to save double-bogey while Fleck make par to win the playoff by three shots. The win for Fleck, who uses golf clubs manufactured by Hogan's company to win the tournament, prevents Hogan from winning the U.S. Open for a fifth time. The day before, after NBC television signed off the air and commentator Gene Sarazen congratulating Hogan on winning the tournament, Fleck makes an eight-foot birdie putt on the final hole to force the playoff.

2011 – Rory McIlroy wins the U.S. Open in emphatic fashion, posting four-day totals of 268 and 16-under-par – both U.S. Open records – and wins his first major title by a eight strokes. The 22-year old McIlroy becomes the youngest U.S. champion since Bobby Jones in 1923. "Overall, the week has been incredible," McIlroy says when asked of breaking Tiger Wood's previous U.S. Open record under-par score of 12-under. "I knew how good Tiger was in 2000 and I was trying to go out there and emulate him in some way. Right now, I couldn't ask for anything more."

1954 – Ed Furgol wins his only major title at the U.S. Open at the Baltusrol Golf Club in Springfield, N.J. beating runner-up Gene Littler by one stroke. Furgol makes an amazing recovery for par the final hole, hitting his second shot from the trees into the fairway of Baltusrol's other golf course, en route to managing a par 5 to win by one stroke. The tournament is the first U.S. Open to be televised nationally and the first in which ropes are used to control galleries.

2014 – Lucy Li, age 11, becomes the youngest player to compete in the U.S. Open Women's Open and shoots an impressive 78 at Pinehurst's No. 2 course in North Carolina. "I'm happy with how I played," says the 5-foot-1 sixth grader to the press while eating a watermelon flavored ice cream bar. "I mean, it's eight over, it's not bad. But I was seven over in three holes, so that's one over in 15 holes. I just need to get rid of the big numbers. … I learned that you've got to be patient. One shot at a time. Try to get rid of the big numbers. And, yeah, I learned a lot."

June 20

1982 – Tom Watson hits one of the most memorable shots in golf history when he chips in for birdie on the 17th hole at Pebble Beach Golf Links en route to winning his first and only U.S. Open title. Tied with Jack Nicklaus for the lead, Watson hits a two-iron on the par-3 17th hole into thick greenside rough and is encouraged by caddie Bruce Edwards telling him to "Get it close." Watson retorts to Edwards, "Get it close? Hell, I'm going to sink it." Watson then, incredibly, sinks the chip and runs around the green before pointing at Edwards, acknowledging his prediction. Watson then birdies the 18th hole to beat Nicklaus by two shots.

1983 – In a rain-delayed Monday finish, Larry Nelson wins the U.S. Open for his second major title with a one-stroke victory over Tom Watson at Oakmont Country Club in Pennsylvania. Nelson's 62-foot birdie putt on the 16th hole proves to be the signature stroke of his victory. Watson bogeys the 17th hole to drop one shot behind Nelson and fails to birdie the final hole to force a playoff.

1976 – Needing a par on the final hole to win the U.S. Open at the Atlanta Athletic Club in Duluth, Ga., Jerry Pate hits one of the greatest shots in championship history, striking a five-iron from 194 yards away from the rough to within three feet of the hole. Pate makes the putt to win the U.S. Open by two shots over runners-up Al Geiberger and Tom Weiskopf. Writes Dan Jenkins in *Sports Illustrated,* "In the end, with the Sunday evening sky beginning to match the brooding darkness of the Atlanta Athletic Club's sprawling water hazards, it was Pate who struck the winningest shot on the final hole that any Open has ever produced."

1966 – Billy Casper completes one of the greatest comebacks in golf history as he finishes his comeback from seven strokes down on the final nine holes from the day before to beat Arnold Palmer in an 18-hole playoff to win the U.S. Open at The Olympic Club in San Francisco. Casper shoots a 69 to Palmer's 73 and, for a second day, mounts a back nine comeback. Palmer leads by two strokes after the first nine holes of the playoff, but Casper birdies No. 12 while Palmer makes bogey to draw even. Palmer then bogeys No. 14 and No. 15 and double-bogey on No. 16 to fall off and finish with a back-nine 40 to lose in a U.S. Open playoff for a third time (1962, 1963, and 1966). The day before, Palmer leads Casper by seven shots on the 10th tee and has an eye on Ben Hogan's U.S. Open scoring record, needing to only shoot 36 (one over par) for the back nine for the record. However, Palmer bogeys No. 10, bounces back with a birdie at No. 12, then bogeys No. 13. At the par-3 15th hole, Casper makes birdie to Palmer's bogey, shrinking the lead to three shots. After another bogey-birdie swing at No. 16, Palmer drops even to Casper with a bogey at No. 17. Both men par the 18th hole to force the playoff, Palmer needing an up-and-down from the thick rough.

1988 – Curtis Strange defeats Nick Faldo in an 18-hole Monday playoff to win the U.S. Open at The Country Club in Brookline, Mass. Strange cards a 71 to Faldo's 75 to win the first of his two U.S. Open titles. It also marks the third time the U.S. Open is held at The Country Club – all of which end in playoffs – Julius Boros, age 43, defeating Arnold Palmer and Jacky Cupit in 1963, and 20-year-old amateur Francis Ouimet upsetting Brits Harry Vardon and Ted Ray in 1913.

1994 – Ernie Els wins his first major title on the second sudden-death playoff hole over Loren Roberts at the U.S. Open at Oakmont Country Club in Oakmont, Pa. Els, Roberts and Colin Montgomerie compete in an 18-hole playoff and Els and Roberts remain tied after both shoot a 74, Montgomerie being eliminated with a 78. After Els and Roberts both par the first sudden-death hole, their 19th of the day, Roberts lips out on his par putt after hitting his approach into the greenside bunker. The 24-year-old Els then two-putts for par to win the championship.

1993 – Lee Janzen ties the U.S. Open scoring record and wins his first of two U.S. Open titles by two strokes over runner-up Payne Stewart at Baltusrol Golf Club in Springfield, N.J. Janzen's total of 272 ties the U.S. Open scoring record set by Jack Nicklaus in 1980, also at Baltusrol. It marks the third consecutive time at Baltusrol that the scoring record is tied or broken. Nicklaus also won in 1967 with a 275, one stroke better than Ben Hogan's 276 at Riviera in 1948. Rory McIlroy sets a new U.S. Open scoring standard with a 268 while winning the title in 2011.

1964 – In one of the most courageous efforts in the history of sports, Ken Venturi withstands heat-stroke in 100-degree temperatures over the final-day 36-hole trudge at Congressional Country Club in Bethesda, Md. and wins the U.S. Open by four strokes over runner-up Tommy Jacobs. Before he plays his final round on Saturday afternoon, Venturi is advised by doctors to withdraw from the tournament due to dehydration, warning him he could die. Venturi, however, presses on and shoots a final round of 70 to win his only major title. The next year, the tournament is expanded to four days. Venturi's effort not only helps him earn the PGA Player of the Year award, but also the prestigious "Sportsman of the Year" honor from *Sports Illustrated*.

2009 – Matteo Manassero becomes the youngest-ever winner of the British Amateur Championship at the age of 16 years, two months and two days, defeating Sam Hutsby 4&3 in the match-play final at Formby Golf Club in Liverpool. Manassero, also the first Italian to win the Championship, receives an invitation to the 2010 Masters as the tournament champion where he becomes the youngest player ever to make the cut at the time. After turning pro, he becomes the youngest winner on the European Tour when he wins the title in Valencia, Spain in 2010 at the age of 17.

1992 – After making a birdie at the third hole of the third round of the U.S. Open at Pebble Beach, Gil Morgan becomes the first player in U.S. Open history to reach double-digits under-par at 10-under par. Morgan gets as low as 12-under after a birdie at the seventh hole, but then collapses. He makes three double-bogeys the rest of the round, but still maintains the third-round lead at four-under par after a third-round 77. Morgan shoots a final-round 81 the next day and finishes in 13th place, playing his final 29 holes in 17-over par.

1930 – Bobby Jones wins his third Open Championship title with a two-stroke win over runners-up Leo Diegel and Macdonald Smith at Royal Liverpool Golf Club at Hoylake. The win for Jones gives him the second leg of the Grand Slam of golf, having won the British Amateur the week before. Later in the summer, he wins the U.S. Open in July and the U.S. Amateur in September. After completing the Grand Slam, Jones, at age 28, retires from the game.

2010 – Graeme McDowell becomes the first man from Northern Ireland to win the U.S. Open championship, beating runner-up Gregory Havret of France by one stroke at Pebble Beach. McDowell, the first European to win the U.S. Open since Tony Jacklin in 1970, trails third-round leader Dustin Johnson by three strokes entering the final round, but survives shooting a 74, the highest closing round by a U.S. Open winner in 25 years.

Johnson fires a final-round 82 to finish in a tie for eighth. "I am just so thrilled to get over the line," the 30-year-old McDowell says. "I can't believe I'm standing here looking at this trophy. It is absolutely a dream come true. I've dreamed of this all my life, and all of a sudden I have a 20-foot putt for it."

1999 – Payne Stewart dramatically wins his second U.S. Open and third major championship with a 15-foot par putt on the final hole to defeat Phil Mickelson by one stroke at Pinehurst No. 2 in Pinehurst, N.C. Stewart, the 1991 U.S. Open champion, shoots a final-round even-par 70 in the steady drizzle to beat Mickelson, who plays the final round with a beeper, awaiting word when his wife Amy is ready to give birth to their first child. Mickelson says he will withdraw from the tournament as soon as hears from his wife that she is going into labor, adding to the drama of the afternoon. After pumping his fist into the air after making his winning putt, Stewart grabs Mickelson with both hands and tells him "You're going to be a great father." Tragically, Stewart is killed in a plane crash four months later.

2004 – Retief Goosen wins his second U.S. Open title by two strokes over runner-up Phil Mickelson at Shinnecock Hills Golf Club in Shinnecock Hills, N.Y. Goosen shoots a one-over-par 71 in the final round to finish at four-under 276. Conditions on the Long Island links-style course are so brutal in the final round that the average score is 78.7 and not a single golfer finishes their round under par. Mickelson, who also shoots 71, finishes second for a third time at the U.S. Open, a three-putt double-bogey on the 17th hole costing him the championship.

1910 – Alex Smith wins an 18-hole playoff over his brother Macdonald Smith and 18-year-old American John McDermott to win his second U.S. Open title at the Philadelphia Cricket Club in Chestnut Hill, Pa.

June 21

2015 – Jordan Spieth wins an historic U.S. Open at Chambers Bay in University Place, Wash. by one shot over runners-up Dustin Johnson and Louis Oosthuizen, benefitting from Johnson three-putting the par-5 final hole from 12 feet to lose by one stroke. After holding a three-shot lead after making birdie on the 16th hole, Spieth three putts the 17th hole for a double bogey, but two putts the final hole for a birdie to post a five-under-par score. Johnson, playing in the final group behind Spieth, makes birdie on the 17th hole to draw to within one shot of Spieth and hits his second shot to the final hole to 12 feet for an eagle putt to win the tournament. Johnson, however, slides the putt three feet past the hole and misses the return putt that would have forced an 18-hole Monday playoff. Spieth, who won his first major at the Masters two months earlier, becomes the youngest player in golf history to win the Masters and the U.S. Open at age 21. He also becomes the youngest U.S. Open champion since Bobby Jones, a younger 21, in 1923. Spieth also is the first player to make birdie on the final hole of the U.S. Open to win by one since Jones in 1926.

1971 – Lee Trevino wins his second U.S. Open, defeating Jack Nicklaus by three strokes in an 18-hole playoff at Merion Golf Club in Ardmore, Pa. Trevino shoots 68 to a 71 from Nicklaus, not relinquishing the lead after making bogey on the first hole. Trevino famously throws a rubber snake out of his bag at Nicklaus at the first tee prior to the start of the playoff. Trevino had acquired it at a zoo gift shop and used it earlier in the week during a whimsical photo shoot emphasizing Merion's thick and penal rough.

1992 – Tom Kite breaks through and wins his elusive major championship, surviving brutal final-round conditions at Pebble Beach Golf Links in California and beating runner-up Jeff Sluman by two shots. Kite shoots an even par 72 and finishes with a three-under par 285 as his main rivals card high scores in the high winds and fast, dry greens. Third-round leader Gil Morgan shoots an 81. Ian Woosnam, starting the day one shot out of the third-round lead, shoots a 79 and Nick Faldo, two shots out of the lead, shoots a 77.

1981 – David Graham wins his second major title and becomes the first Australian to win the U.S. Open, claiming a three-stroke victory over runners-up George Burns and Bill Rogers at Merion Golf Club in Ardmore, Pa. Graham trails Burns by three strokes entering the final round, but shoots a 67 to a 73 from Burns to take the title.

1998 – Lee Janzen comes back from seven strokes back and wins his second U.S. Open at the Olympic Golf Club in San Francisco, one stroke ahead of runner-up Payne Stewart, the same player he beats out for his first U.S. Open in 1993. Janzen becomes the second winner at a U.S. Open at the Olympic Club to come back from seven strokes behind in the final round joining 1966 champion Billy Casper.

1965 – Gary Player of South Africa defeats Kel Nagle of Australia in an 18-hole playoff at the Bellerive Country Club in St. Louis, Mo. to win his only U.S. Open title and complete his career Grand Slam at age 29. The win for Player makes him the first foreign-born winner of the U.S. Open since Tommy Armour of Scotland in 1927. With his win, Player joins Gene Sarazen and Ben Hogan as the only players to win all four professional major championships, the career Grand Slam. Jack Nicklaus completes the feat himself the next year at the 1966 British Open and Tiger Woods at the 2000 British Open.

1907 – Arnaud Massy wins the Open Championship at Royal Liverpool Golf Club at Hoylake to become the first (and to this date, only) Frenchman to win a major Championship.

1970 – Tony Jacklin shoots under-par in all four rounds and finishes his wire-to-wire win at the U.S. Open at Hazeltine

National Golf Club in Chaska, Minn. Jacklin becomes the first Englishman to win the U.S. Open since Ted Ray in 1920 with his seven-shot win over runner-up Dave Hill.

1907 – Alex Ross, brother of famed golf course designer Donald Ross, wins his first U.S. Open title by two strokes over Gilbert Nicholls at the Philadelphia Cricket Club in Chestnut Hill, Pa.

1987 – Scott Simpson stays steady and shoots a final-round 68 to beat Tom Watson by one shot to win his one and only major title at the U.S. Open at the Olympic Club in San Francisco.

June 22

2009 – Lucas Glover sinks a three-foot par putt on the 18th hole to clinch a two-shot win at the U.S. Open at Bethpage Black in Farmingdale, N.Y. Glover shoots a final-round 73 in the rain and darkness-delayed Monday finish to beat runners-up Phil Mickelson, David Duval and Ricky Barnes. Glover, a 29-year-old who entered the U.S. Open field via qualifying, only won one previous time on the PGA Tour at the Funai Classic at Walt Disney World four years earlier. His previous best finish at a major was a tie for 20th place at the 2007 Masters and he had never previously even made a U.S. Open cut. "I hope I don't downgrade it or anything with my name on there," Glover quips of earning the U.S. Open trophy. "It's an honor, and I'm just excited and happy as I can be to be on here." The Associated Press describes Glover's final hole out as "an anticlimactic finish to five dreary days at a U.S. Open filled with more delays than drama." Each of the four rounds of tournament are started and finished on different days due to the rainy weather.

2014 – Michelle Wie wins her first major championship claiming the U.S. Women's Open at Pinehurst in North Carolina, firing a final-round 70, two shots better than runner-up Stacy Lewis. Wie leads by three strokes on the 16th hole, but makes double-bogey to see her lead shrink to one. A birdie on No. 17 gave her a two-shot cushion on the final hole. "I just had a lot of fun out there," says Wie. "I woke up so excited. I was so grateful for this opportunity."

1997 – One week after winning his second U.S. Open title at Congressional Golf Club in Maryland, defending champion Ernie Els wins for a second straight week, winning the Buick Classic at Westchester Country Club in Harrison, N.Y. and takes over the world No. 1 ranking from Tiger Woods. Els ties the tournament's 72-hole record on a par-71 course (16-under 268) and becomes the first repeat wire-to-wire winner since Tom Watson at the 1979 and '80 Tournament of Champions. Els also becomes the fourth player and the first since Hale Irwin in 1990 to win the week after winning the U.S. Open. He also joins Jack Nicklaus, Seve Ballesteros and Vijay Singh as two-time winners at Westchester. Says Els of becoming the world's No. 1 golfer, "I don't know what to say. I've been struggling for six months, then win two tournaments and you're No. 1. I guess I won the two at the right time."

2014 – Kevin Streelman dramatically birdies the last seven holes and shoots a final-round 64 to win the Travelers Championships in Hartford, Conn. Streelman's final-round charge gives him a one-stroke victory over K.J. Choi and Sergio Garcia. Streelman's birdie streak breaks a PGA Tour record previously held by Mike Souchak at the 1956 St. Paul Open. Streelman fires a back-nine 28 and one-putts every green on the back nine.

2015 – Patrick Wills, a 59-year-old veteran from Woodbridge, Va., shoots a 14-under-par 57, including three holes-in-one, in an amateur tournament round at the 6,021-yard Laurel Hill Golf Club in Lorton, Va. Incredibly, two of the holes-in-one from Wills come on par 4 holes – the 289-yard seventh hole and the 334-yard 10th hole. He also aces the 187-yard fourteenth hole with a five-iron. The score was verified by Laurel Hill PGA Director Gene Orrico. "People are allowed to believe what they want to believe – I fought for that freedom," Wills tells Yahoo Sports about skepticism towards his score. "But I know what I shot, my playing partners know what I shot and the people at the tournament do as well."

June 23

1975 – Lou Graham defeats John Mahaffey by two strokes in an 18-hole Monday playoff to win the U.S. Open at the Medinah Country Club in Medinah, Ill. Graham shoots a 71 to Mahaffey's 73 but makes five fewer putts – 30 to 35 – which proves to be the difference in the playoff. "I hit the ball good and I putted pretty good," says Graham. "My goal was to keep making pars, just like I was trying to do all week. The main thing was that John didn't make any putts."

1963 – Julius Boros wins his second U.S. Open title in an 18-hole Sunday playoff with Jacky Cupit and Arnold Palmer at The Country Club in Brookline, Mass. Boros wins the playoff shooting a 70 to Cupit's 73 and Palmer's 76. He leads by three strokes after the front nine and benefits from Palmer making triple bogey on the 11th hole and Cupit making bogey. At age 43, Boros becomes the second-oldest winner in U.S. Open history, being only a month younger than Ted Ray, the 1920 champion. For Palmer, it is the second consecutive year he loses in a playoff at the U.S. Open, falling to Jack Nicklaus the year before at Oakmont. Boros earns $16,000 for the win, and each of the three playoff participants receive a bonus of $1,500 from the playoff gate receipts.

1922 – Walter Hagen becomes the first American-born winner of the Open Championship, winning the Claret Jug at Royal St. George's by one stroke over runners-up Jim Barnes and George Duncan. It is the first of Hagen's four Open Championships and the fourth of his eleven major titles.

2013 – Journeyman Ken Duke, age 44 and ranked No. 144 in the world, wins his first PGA Tour title at the Travelers Championship in Connecticut in the second playoff hole over Chris Stroud. A two-time runner-up on the PGA Tour and making his 187th tour start, Duke becomes the oldest first-time winner on the PGA Tour since Ed Dougherty, who was 47 years old when he won the 1995 Deposit Guaranty Classic. "You gotta believe in yourself in everything you do," Duke says. "That's why those guys at the top are winning week in, week out because they believe they can do it. It's kind of one of those things once you finally do it might come easier the next time. That's kind of the way I feel." Luck plays a big role in the final round as on the 10th hole, Duke's ball ricochets off a tree and onto the green five feet from the pin, allowing him to make birdie. He appears to be the winner outright at the event, but Stroud chips in from 51 feet for birdie on the final hole to force the playoff.

1996 – John Cook falls one shot shy of Mike Souchak's 72-hole PGA Tour scoring record shooting a final-round 69 to post a four-round total of 258, 26 under par, and wins the St. Jude Memphis Classic. Cook's birdie chip on the final hole hits the pin, preserving the Souchak record achieved at the 1955 Texas Open.

2002 – Phil Mickelson comes from five strokes back and shoots a six-under-par 64 to become the first repeat winner in the 51-year history of the Greater Hartford Open. Mickelson makes a four-foot birdie on the final hole and beats Jonathan Kaye and Davis Love III by one stroke.

June 24

1921 – Nineteen-year-old Bobby Jones famously quits the Open Championship at St. Andrews, picking up after taking four shots to get out of the bunker on the 11th hole and tearing up his scorecard in the third round of the tournament. The tantrum is not forgotten by Jones who goes on to become perhaps the greatest golfer in the sports history, winning the amateur Grand Slam nine years later and earning the highest merits of sportsmanship.

1928 – Johnny Farrell defeats amateur Bobby Jones in a 36-hole playoff to win his only major title at the U.S. Open at Olympia Fields Country Club in Olympia Fields, Ill. For Jones, a two-time champion in 1923 and 1926, it was his second playoff loss at the U.S. Open in four years and his fourth finish as a runner-up. He goes on to win the next two stagings of the event in 1929 and1930.

1947 – Jim Ferrier wins the PGA Championship at the Plum Hollow Country Club in Southfield, Mich., winning the match-play final 2 & 1 over Chick Harbert. The win is the only major title for Ferrier, a naturalized U.S. citizen born in Australia, described as an "apple-cheeked par blaster from Down Under" by Willie Hoare of the *St. Petersburg Times*.

1909 – David Hunter becomes the first player to break 70 in a round at the U.S. Open in the tournament's opening round at Englewood Golf Club in Englewood, N.J. He follows up the historical round with an 84 and finishes in 30th place.

1990 – One week after winning his third U.S. Open title at Medinah Country Club in Illinois in a 19-hole Monday playoff – and becoming the oldest player to win the event at age 45 – Hale Irwin wins for the second straight week at the Buick Classic at Westchester Country Club in Harrison, N.Y. for his 19th PGA Tour title. Irwin beats Paul Azinger by two shots, firing a final-round 65 that is capped with a six-foot birdie on the final hole. Prior to his U.S. Open win, Irwin was winless on the PGA Tour since 1985.

June 25

1926 – Bobby Jones wins the first of his three Open Championship titles beating runner-up Al Watrous by two strokes at Royal Lytham & St. Annes Golf Club and becomes the first amateur to win the title in 29 years. Jones, at age 24, wins his first Open Championship in just his second appearance – the first being five years earlier when he famously walks off the Old Course at St. Andrews in 1921 in frustration. Jones famously hits a 175-yard mashie from a bunker over deep rough to the middle of the 17th green – a shot commemorated by a plaque at the course. The 1926 Open Championship marks the first time an admission fee is charged for spectators.

1923 – Gene Sarazen wins his second U.S. Open championship, and the fifth of his seven major titles, with a three-shot win at Fresh Meadow Country Club in Flushing, N.Y. Sarazen wins by three strokes and shoots a final-round 66 – the best final-round score by a champion at the U.S. Open at the time, not to be beaten until Arnold Palmer shoots a final-round 65 in 1960.

1952 – Jim Turnesa wins the PGA Championship at Big Spring Country Club in Louisville, Ky., winning in the match-play format one-up over Chick Harbert in the final. The win is the only major for Turnesa, who loses to Sam Snead in the PGA final in 1942. Turnesa, a native New Yorker, is one of seven golfing brothers, but the only one to win a major championship.

1911 – Nineteen-year-old John McDermott becomes the youngest U.S. Open champion in tournament history and the event's first American-born champion beating Mike Brady and George Simpson in an 18-hole playoff at the Chicago Golf Club in Wheaton, Ill.

1921 – Former St. Andrews resident Jock Hutchison triumphs on the famed course of his old hometown winning his only Open Championship in a 36-hole playoff over amateur Roger

Wethered at the Old Course at St. Andrews. Wethered almost does not make it to the playoff, as he is scheduled to play for his cricket team that day but is persuaded to stay and play golf, but loses the playoff by nine shots. Although a native of St. Andrews, Hutchison became a United States citizen and is thus recognized as being the Open's first American champion. The following year, however, Walter Hagen becomes the first U.S.-born winner of the tournament.

1909 – George Sargent wins his first U.S. Open title at Englewood Golf Club in Englewood, N.J., beating runner-up Tom McNamara by four strokes and setting a new U.S. Open tournament scoring record of 290 – breaking the old mark by five shots. McNamara leads Sargent by two strokes heading into the final round after becoming only the second player in tournament history to shoot below 70 when he records a 69 in the second round, after David Hunter records the same score in the first round.

June 26

1982 – Bob Gilder scores one of the most famous shots in PGA Tour history, scoring a double-eagle two on the 509-yard, par-5 18th hole at the Westchester Country Club to cap a six-shot lead after the third round of the Manufacturers Hanover Westchester Classic. From the fairway of the 18th hole, Gilder hits his second shot, a three-wood, 251 yards into the cup. The ball takes three hops and rolls into the hole. "From the reaction of the crowd I couldn't be sure the ball went in," Gilder says. "After all, on the ninth green I hit my approach 10 feet from the pin and there wasn't a single clap." Gilder wins the title the next day, his fourth of six career PGA Tour titles, by five strokes over Tom Kite and Peter Jacobsen.

2005 – Birdie Kim holes out for a birdie out from a greenside bunker on the 72nd hole and wins her only major title at the U.S.

Women's Open at Cherry Hills Country Club in Denver, Colo. Kim's dramatic shot gives her a two-stroke win over runners-up Brittany Lang and Morgan Pressel, both teenage amateurs. "I can't believe it," says Kim of her dramatic winning-shot, the only birdie on the 459-yard par 4 18th hole in the last two days of the competition. "I don't think I was going to make it. I was trying my best to make par." Prior to her win, that earned her $560,000, the largest payout in women's golf at the time, Kim had only won $79,832 and had made only 10 cuts in 34 career starts. She played the previous season under her real name Jun-Yun Kim but changed her name to "Birdie" to stand out more from the five other players on the LPGA Tour with the same surname.

1925 – Jim Barnes wins the Open Championship at Prestwick Golf Club in Prestwick, Scotland, his only Open title, one stroke ahead of runners-up Ted Ray and Archie Compston. The win is the fourth and final major title for Barnes, after winning the first two PGA Championships in 1916 and 1919, and the U.S. Open in 1921.

June 27

2010 – Bubba Watson wins his first PGA Tour event beating Corey Pavin and Scott Verplank in a playoff at the Travelers Championship in Hartford, Conn. Watson overcomes a six-stroke deficit to force a playoff with Pavin and Verplank and beats Verplank with a par on the second playoff hole. "I'm a very emotional guy," Watson says after crying and hugging his wife Angie after winning the playoff. "I cry all the time. When I go to church on Sunday, I cry at church. I couldn't get the 'Yes' out of 'I do' at my wedding. The pastor said, 'You got to say it. You can't just nod. You can't nod. Everybody has issues. My family had some issues. My dad is battling cancer. My wife last year thought she had a tumor in her brain. We got lucky with that one, and now, we're battling with my dad. It's emotional."

2004 – "This is probably the best golfing day I will ever have," says Craig Stadler after winning the Bank of America Championship in Concord Mass., on the PGA Champions Tour, then watching his son Kevin win for the first time on Nationwide Tour at the Lake Erie Charity Classic in Findley Lake, N.Y. "I don't think another win will ever come close to this. This is incredible. I am so happy for him and so proud for him."

1936 – Alf Padgham wins his only major title at the Open Championship at Royal Liverpool in Hoylake, England, one stroke ahead of runner-up Jimmy Adams.

1950 – Chandler Harper wins the PGA Championship at the Scioto Country Club in Upper Arlington, Ohio with a 4&3 win over Henry Williams, Jr. in the match-play final. The PGA Championship is held in a tight schedule of major championship played just two weeks after the U.S. Open and two weeks before the British Open.

1924 – Walter Hagen sinks a six-foot putt on the final hole to win his second Open Championships golf championship with a one-shot win over Ernest Whitcombe at the Royal Liverpool Golf Club.

June 28

1981 – Jerry Pate celebrates his first victory in almost three years at the Danny Thomas Memphis Classic by leaping into the lake in front of the 18th green. After holing out after recording a final-round 69 – good enough for a two-stroke victory – Pate does not even sign his scorecard before diving, fully clothed, into the lake. "I hadn't won in so long," Pate says. "I wanted to be sure this one soaked in. I just wanted to be sure to remind myself how much fun winning really is. I feel that I should win more tournaments than I do. This was very important to me." The following year, Pate also famously dives into the water on the 18th green after winning the Tournament Player's Championship at the TPC at Sawgrass in Florida.

2009 – Forty-eight-year-old Kenny Perry wins his 14th and final career PGA Tour title shooting a final-round 63 to post a tournament record 258 and win the Travelers Championship in Cromwell, Conn., three strokes better than Paul Goydos and David Toms. Perry wins his 11th tournament in his 40s just two and a half months following his bogey-bogey finish that prevents him from winning the Masters in April, but credits his mistake at Augusta to helping him with in Connecticut. "I knew that I had to keep making birdies," he says. "I wasn't going to let up. I wasn't going to play defensive golf. I learned something from that mistake."

1975 – Lee Trevino is struck by lightning during the second round of the Western Open at Butler National Golf Club in Oak Brook, Ill. Trevino and playing partner Jerry Heard are both knocked unconscious and subsequently require spine operations

June 29

1906 – Alex Smith of Carnoustie, Scotland wins his first U.S. Open title by seven strokes over his brother Willie, the 1899 champion, at the Onwentsia Club in Lake Forest, Ill. Willie Anderson, the three-time defending champion and the club pro at Onwentsia, is the heavy favorite entering the tournament, but shoots a final-round 84 and finishes in fifth place. Smith finishes with a score of 295, a new tournament record, to become the player to record a sub-300 winning score at the U.S. Open. While Smith's brother Willie finishes in second place, his brother-in-law James Maiden finishes in tied for third.

1903 – Scottish immigrant Willie Anderson beats David Brown by two shots in an 18-hole playoff at the Baltusrol Golf Club in

Springfield, N.J., to win his second U.S. Open championship. After Anderson and Brown both post a 307 total, eight-strokes clear of the rest of the tournament field, the players compete in a playoff delayed by a day due to Sunday being reserved exclusively for member play at the course. In the playoff, played in a heavy rainstorm, Anderson shoots an 82 to Brown's 84. Anderson, also the champion in 1901, wins the next two U.S. Open championship in 1904 and 1905 to become the only man to win three straight U.S. Open titles.

1934 – Leading by 10 shots entering the final round of the Open Championship at Royal St. George's, Henry Cotton holds on for a five-shot victory over Sid Brews, despite shooting a final-round 79.

2008 – Nineteen-year-old Inbee Park wins the U.S. Women's Open at the Interlachen Country Club in Edina, Minn. by four strokes over runner-up Helen Alfredsson.

1980 – In the first staging of the U.S. Senior Open, Roberto de Vicenzo wins the championship at Winged Foot Golf Club in Mamaroneck, N.Y. by four strokes over runner-up, amateur William Campbell.

1997 – Greg Norman birdies the last three holes to shoot a final-round 66 and win the St. Jude Classic in Memphis by one shot over Dudley Hart "I think it is more elation than relief," says Norman who eclipses $11 million in prize money for his career, the first player to do so. The win vaults Norman back into the world No. 1 ranking, taking over the spot from Ernie Els, who debuted in the top spot the previous week. Two weeks earlier, Tiger Woods assumed the No. 1 ranking for the first time, but holds the top spot for only a week, surrendering it to Els the following week.

June 30

1974 – Tom Watson wins his first PGA Tour event at the Western Open at Butler National Golf Club in Chicago, shooting a final-round 69 in blustery winds to beat runners-up J.C. Snead and Tom Weiskopf by two strokes. Watson finally breaks through to win his first title after having numerous chances to win earlier in the year, including two weeks earlier at the U.S. Open where he shoots a final-round 79 after holding a one-shot lead through three rounds. "It finally happened," says Watson of his first win. "I knew it was just a matter of time. I never doubted that I could win. I always knew I would." Writes the Associated Press of Watson's win, "The young man with the bulging forearms of the blacksmith had plenty of reason to wonder he'd come so close so often as recently as two weeks ago only to be thwarted in his quest for his first professional victory." Watson is six shots out of the lead of Weiskopf to start the day and benefits from Weiskopf shooting a final-round 77.

1929 – Bobby Jones wins his third U.S. Open championship winning a 36-hole playoff by 23 strokes over Al Espinosa at the West Course of the Winged Foot Golf Club in Mamaroneck, N.Y. Jones shoots a 72 in the morning playoff round to open up a 12-shot lead over Espinosa, who shoots an 84. In the afternoon round, Jones shoots a 69 to Espinosa's 80. The previous day, Jones leads the tournament by four shots with four holes to go, but triple-bogeys the 15th hole, bogeys the 16th hole but sinks a 12-foot par putt on the final hole to force the playoff.

1916 – Amateur Chick Evans closes out a wire-to-wire victory at the U.S. Open at the Minikahda Club in Minneapolis, Minnesota, two strokes ahead of runner-up Jock Hutchison. Evans' total of 286 established a new U.S. Open scoring record that stands for two decades, until 1936. The win for Evans is also the last time the tournament is played over two days, 36-holes per day. When the tournament resumes play in 1919, after the 1917 and 1918 tournaments are canceled due to World War I, the tournament is held over three days, with 18 holes on the first two days and 36 holes on the third day.

1991 – Meg Mallon wins the LPGA Championship at the Bethesda Country Club in Bethesda, Md., on the final hole, breaking a three-way tie with playing partners Pat Bradley and Ayako Okamoto with a 10-foot-birdie putt. "What a way to finish a golf tournament," Mallon says. "It's a dream being in that situation, and I felt like I was in a dream. It's the type of thing you think about as a kid…I was concentrating so hard, I guess, that I didn't really realize the magnitude of what was going on."

JULY

July 1

1956 – Arnold Palmer wins his first U.S. PGA Tour event at the Insurance City Open in Hartford, Conn., beating Ted Kroll on the second hole of a sudden death playoff. Palmer wins the event, ironically, using a putter that Kroll gave him months earlier. Says Palmer "Ted is a great guy – he even gave me the putter that beat him." Palmer's first win on the PGA Tour came the previous year when he won the Canadian Open.

2007 – Cristie Kerr wins her first major championship at the U.S. Women's Open at the Pine Needles Lodge and Golf Club in Southern Pines, N.C. with a two-shot victory over runners-up Lorena Ochoa and Angela Park. "When I stepped on the grounds this week, it was just magic," says Kerr. "Going head-to-head with Lorena and beating her ... it was special memories. You can't make this stuff up. These are thing you take to the grave and you just smile about."

1920 – In the first Open Championship played after a six-year hiatus due to World War I, George Duncan overcomes a 13-stroke deficit after the first 36 holes and wins his only major title at Royal Cinque Ports Golf Club in Kent, England. Duncan's shoots a final-round 72 for a four-round score of 303, two strokes better than runner-up Sandy Herd, the 1902 Open champion.

1984 – Greg Norman benefits from out-of-bounds stakes and a car being removed in an errant shot into a parking lot on the 17th hole of the final round of the Canadian Open at Glen Abbey in Oakville, Ontario and beats Jack Nicklaus by two shots for his second career PGA Tour victory. Leading by three shots on the 17th hole, Norman hits his approach shot over the green and into a grassy parking area that had been previously designated as out of bounds but the out-of-bounds stakes had been removed. A car has to be moved in order for Norman to play his third shot and the Australian salvages bogey and holds on for victory. Norman shoots a final-round five-under-par 67 and makes up four shots from third-round leader Nick Price. It is the sixth of seven times that Nicklaus finishes as the runner-up at the Canadian Open, a tournament that he famously does not win in his illustrious career. Nicklaus finishes as the bridesmaid the following year in 1985 while also finishing second in 1965, 1968, 1975, 1976 and 1981.

2001 – One day after firing a then career-best round of 61, Phil Mickelson fires a two-under par 68 to claim a one-shot victory over Bill Andrade to win the Greater Hartford Open in Connecticut. Mickelson says he did not pick up a club after shooting a final-round 75 to fall out of contention at the U.S. Open at Southern Hills in Tulsa, Okla., choosing to only work on his mental approach to the game using visualization techniques. "I felt much more comfortable, much more relaxed, and worked from a positive frame of mind," Mickelson says. "Changing my mental approach and my outlook has allowed me to perform at a higher lever to perform at my best. I feel if I can start to work on that and refine that and get better at it, I should be able to close more on the opportunities that I have been giving myself."

July 2

1967 – Catherine Lacoste of France becomes the first foreigner and the first amateur to win the U.S. Women's Open when she claims a two-shot victory at the Cascades Course at The

Homestead in Hot Springs, Va. Lacoste wins the title on the 63rd birthday of her father Rene Lacoste, the legendary French tennis champion who won the U.S. national title in tennis 40 years earlier. Lacoste shoots a final-round 79 but is still able to hold on for the victory.

1926 – Bobby Jones becomes the first individual sportsman to be honored with a ticker-tape parade in New York City after he wins the Open Championship at Royal Lytham & St. Annes on June 25th. Eight days after the parade, Jones goes on to win the U.S. Open, becoming the first golfer, amateur or professional, to win both national Opens in the same year.

1930 – Bobby Jones becomes the only sporting personality ever to be honored with a second ticker-tape parade in New York City – four years from the day from his first parade down lower Manhattan's "Canyon of Heroes." On June 20th, Jones wins the Open Championship for the third time at Hoylake, just one week after winning the British Amateur Championship at St. Andrews. Ten days later, Jones would win the third leg of his eventual historic Grand Slam, clinched by winning the U.S. Amateur at Merion Cricket Club in September.

1948 – Forty-one-year-old Henry Cotton wins his third and final Open Championship title with a five-shot victory over defending champion Fred Daly at Muirfield Golf Links.

2000 – Notah Begay, best known as the Stanford college teammate of Tiger Woods, wins for a second consecutive time on the PGA Tour winning the Greater Hartford Open. Begay, the winner at the St. Jude Classic the previous week in Memphis, Tenn., holes a 25-foot birdie putt on the final hole to claim a one-stroke victory over Mark Calcavecchia. Begay earns the distinction of being the first player to win consecutive tournaments on the PGA Tour since Woods won the final two events the previous year. "It's beyond words for me," says Begay.

2006 – J.J. Henry, from nearby Fairfield, Connecticut, becomes the first Connecticut player to win the 55-year-old Hartford Open with a three-shot victory, his first PGA Tour title. "Every time I'd leave here I'd go back to the putting green or the driving range and pretend I was winning the tournament," Henry says of his childhood visits to the tournament. "I thought how cool that would be someday if I could be one of those guys and play against the best players in the world. It means the world to me."

July 3

1959 – Gary Player shoots a final-round 68 and wins the Open Championship for the first time at Muirfield Golf Links. Player finishes two strokes ahead of runners-up Fred Bullock and Flory Van Donck.

1951 – Sam Snead wins the PGA Championship for a third time with a 7&6 match-play win over Walter Burkemo at the Oakmont Country Club in Pennsylvania. The 39-year-old Snead earns $3,500 for the title, his sixth career major title. The tournament at Oakmont marks the first time that the PGA Championship is contested at Oakmont since 1922. Curiously, the Open Championship is also held the same week as the PGA and its mandatory two-day qualifier is held the same days as the PGA's semifinals and finals, preventing participation in both events.

2005 – Ron Streck wins the Commerce Bank Championship at Eisenhower Park, N.Y. to become the first player to record wins on all three major American professional tours, the Nationwide (1993 Nike Yuma Open), the PGA (1978 San Antonio Texas Open & 1981 Michelob Houston Open) and now the Champions Tour. In addition, Streck also claims a tournament victory at the 1983 Hassan II Golf Trophy in Morocco, although the event only becomes an official European Tour event in 2010. Streck is also known as the first PGA Tour player to use metal woods and the first to use them in a tournament victory at the 1981 Houston Open.

2014 – Tyler Raber makes one of the most rare shots in golf – a hole-in-one on the par-4 – holing out for a double eagle on the 279-yard 17th hole of the eGolf Pro Tour's ArrowCreek Open in Reno, Nev. "We heard it hit the pin," Raber says to the Golf Channel. "We couldn't see it, but we looked at each other and said, 'That hit the pin.' We looked all around the green before finally looking in the hole, and there it was. It was the craziest thing ever. My first hole-in-one or double-eagle in a tournament, so I guess I killed two birds with one stone." The only hole-in-one on a par 4 in PGA Tour history came in 2001 by Andrew Magee at the FBR Open in Phoenix.

July 4

2006 – Annika Sorenstam wins the U.S. Open for a third time, beating Pat Hurst in an 18-hole Monday playoff at the Newport Country Club in Newport, R.I. Island. Sorenstam shoots a 70 to Hurst's 74 to win her 10th and what ends up being her final major title. Writes Doug Ferguson of the Associated Press of Sorenstam, "Walking briskly between shots, leaving Hurst behind on the fairways and on the scorecard, Sorenstam turned the playoff into a snoozer at Newport Country Club." Sorenstam's 10th major title ties her with Babe Zaharias for fourth all-time, five major shy of Patty Berg's LPGA record of 15.

2004 – Meg Mallon shoots a final-round 65 and wins her second U.S. Women's Open title beating runner-up Annika Sorenstam by two shots at the Orchards Golf Club in South Hadley, Mass. Mallon shoots the lowest final-round by a champion in the 59-year history of the U.S. Women's Open with her six-under par closing effort that allows her to beat Jennifer Rosales, whom she trails by three shots to start the day, and Sorenstam. The win comes 13 years after Mallon's first U.S. Women's Open victory in 1991 at Colonial Country Club in Fort Worth, Texas. "I'm 41 years old, and you've got to enjoy your days, enjoy when things like this happen," Mallon says. "I was going to go out and have a fun time and play a great golf course and just do the best I can. And it was all that. I'm incredibly proud that I have my name on that trophy again."

1947 – Fred Daly becomes the first Irish winner of the Open Championship, claiming a one-stroke victory over runners-up Reg Horne and amateur Frank Stranahan at first-time venue Royal Liverpool Golf Club in Hoylake, England.

July 5

1946 – In the first post-World War II staging of the Open Championship, Sam Snead wins his only Open title by four strokes over runners-up Johnny Bulla and Bobby Locke at the Old Course at St. Andrews. Snead, however, doesn't quite endear himself to the Scottish crowds after he says that the historic home of golf looks "like an old abandoned kinda place." Snead only plays the Open Championship five times in all, his first in 1937 and then again not until 1962 following his victory in 1946.

1975 – Art Wall, Jr., at the age of 51 years, seven months and 10 days, wins the Greater Milwaukee Open by one shot over runner-up Gary McCord to become the second oldest winner on the PGA Tour. Wall is one year and three months younger than Sam Snead when he won the 1965 Greater Greensboro Open at age 52. The win is Wall's 14th and final title of his PGA Tour career, highlighted by his victory at the 1959 Masters.

1964 – For the second time – and for one of only three times in the history of golf – the "Big Three" of golf – Arnold Palmer, Gary Player and Jack Nicklaus finish in first, second and third place at a PGA Tour event or major championship at the Whitemarsh Open Invitational in Philadelphia. Jack Nicklaus wins the title, the 11th PGA title of his career, by one shot over Player, with Palmer finishing in third place. The only other time where the "Big Three" finish in the top three of an event comes at the 1963 Phoenix Open Invitational (Palmer winning, Player finishing second and Nicklaus finishing third) and at the 1965 Masters (Nicklaus winning and Palmer and Player finishing in a tie for second).

1958 – Peter Thomson wins his fourth Claret Jug in five years with a four-stroke win at the Open Championship over Dave Thomas in a 36-hole Saturday playoff at Royal Lytham & St. Annes Golf Club. It is the first playoff at the Open Championship since 1949 and marks the seventh consecutive year that Thomson, age 28, finishes either as the tournament's champion or runner-up.

1957 – Bobby Locke wins his fourth and final title at the Open Championship with a three-shot victory over three-time defending champion Peter Thomson at the Old Course at St. Andrews.

July 6

1931 – Billy Burke wins the longest playoff in U.S. Open history – 72 holes – to win his only major title at the Inverness Club in Toledo, Ohio. Burke and George Von Elm tie after 72 holes of regulation at 292, after Von Elm bogeys four of the last seven holes, making birdie on the final hole to force the 36-hole playoff. After the two players remain tied after the 36-hole playoff, rules at the time dictate that they must play another 36-hole playoff, which Burke wins by one stroke. Both playoff days feature temperatures in excess of 100 degrees and legend has it that Burke smoked 32 cigars during the course of the tournament.

1956 – Peter Thomson of Australia wins his third straight Open Championship title with a three-stroke victory over Flory Van Douck of Belgium at Royal Liverpool in Hoylake, England. Thomson wins 1,000 British pounds for his victory.

1998 – Se Ri Pak of South Korea wins a 20-hole Monday playoff over amateur Jenny Chuasiriporn of the United States at the U.S. Women's Open Golf Championship at Blackwolf Run in Kohler, Wis. Pak and Chuasiriporn, both 20 years old, finish the 18-hole playoff round tied at 73, and both make par on the first extra hole. Pak, who won the LPGA Championship earlier in the year, then makes an 18-foot birdie putt on the 92nd hole of competition to become the youngest woman to win two major championships in the same year. The day before, on the 72nd hole, Chuasiriporn sinks an incredible 40-foot birdie putt to get into the playoff.

1986 – "For the dreamers of the world, the people whose spirits have been fragmented along the yellow brick road, this is a day I share with them," says Mac O'Grady in winning his first career PGA Tour victory at the Canon Sammy Davis, Jr. Greater Hartford Open on the first hole of a sudden death playoff with Roger Maltbie. The unique O'Grady, a left-hander playing on tour on appeal from a six-week suspension for allegedly berating a tournament official at the USF&G Classic in New Orleans in 1984, shoots a final-round 62 to get into a playoff with Maltbie. O'Grady misses a four-foot birdie putt on the first playoff hole, but Maltbie misses an even shorter par putt to give O'Grady the title. "There are times when you spread your wings and your molecules rise higher than they ever have before," O'Grady says. "Playing on the tour comes down to being like a test pilot on the X-15. You have to perform, you have to be adaptable."

1951 – Max Faulkner wins the first-ever staging of the Open Championship in Northern Ireland when he wins his only major title by two strokes over Antonio Cerda of Argentina at Royal Portrush Golf Club.

July 7

1985 – Curtis Strange wins the Canadian Open at Glen Abbey Golf Course in Oakville, Ontario winning by two strokes over defending champion Greg Norman and Jack Nicklaus, who finishes as the event's runner-up for a seventh time. The Canadian Open is the biggest title that Nicklaus never wins in his career, finishing second in 1965, 1968, 1975, 1976, 1981, 1984 and 1985.

2003 – Hilary Lunke is a surprise winner of a topsy-turvy U.S. Women's Open at Pumpkin Ridge Golf Club in Oregon, winning a three-way Monday playoff over Angela Stanford and Kelly Robbins. The three players post 72-hole scores of one-under-par 283, one stroke ahead of two-time champion Annika Sorenstam, who bogeys the final hole to miss the playoff. Lunke makes birdie on the final hole of the playoff to edge Stanford by one stroke and Robbins by three shots. Lunke becomes the first player to go through local and sectional qualifying to win the U.S. Women's Open. Her U.S. Open victory is her one and only LPGA tournament triumph.

2002 – Juli Inkster wins her second U.S. Women's Open title, beating Annika Sorenstam by two strokes at Prairie Dunes Country Club outside of Hutchinson, Kan. The 42-year-old Inkster shoots a final-round 66 to earn her seventh and final major championship and join Babe Zaharias as the only women to win two majors after age 40.

1950 – Bobby Locke of South Africa wins the second of his four Open Championship titles by two strokes over runner-up Roberto de Vicenzo of Argentina at Troon Golf Club in Scotland.

1939 – Dick Burton of England wins the Open Championship at St. Andrews, beating out runner-up Johnny Bulla by two shots. Burton's title is the last Open Championship for seven years due to the outbreak of World War II.

1953 – Walter Burkemo wins the PGA Championship with a 2&1 match-play victory over Felice Torza at the Birmingham Country Club in Birmingham, Mich. Burkemo earns $5,000 for the title, his only major victory.

July 8

1955 – Peter Thomson wins the second of his five Open Championship titles beating runner-up John Fallon by two strokes at the Old Course at St. Andrews. The tournament marks the first time the famous No. 17 "Road Hole" at St. Andrews is changed from a par 5 to a par 4, changing the par of the course from 73 to 72.

1938 – Gale force winds blowing across Royal St. George's Golf Club in Sandwich, England disrupt the Open Championship, ripping apart a large exhibition tent on site, and playing havoc on competing golfers. Reg Whitcombe prevails in the elements to win his only major title, claiming the title by two strokes over runner-up Jimmy Adams.

1933 – Denny Shute defeats fellow American Craig Wood by five strokes in a 36-hole Saturday playoff to win his only Open Championship title at the Old Course at St. Andrews. It is the first playoff at the Open since 1921, also won by an American at St. Andrews; Jock Hutchison, a naturalized U.S. citizen born in Scotland.

2010 – Paul Goydos becomes the fourth player to shoot 59 on the PGA Tour when he fires the magic score in the first round of the John Deere Classic at the 7,268-yard and par 71 TPC Deere Run in Silvis, Ill. Goydos makes 12 birdies and six pars in his round, but, three days later, finishes second to tournament victor Steve Stricker.

1956 – Amateur Doug Sanders wins his first PGA tournament title at the Canadian Open with a par on the first hole of a sudden-death playoff with Dow Finsterwald at the Beaconsfield Golf Club in Montreal. Sanders becomes the first amateur to win a PGA event since Gene Littler two years earlier in San Diego. An amateur does not win again on the PGA Tour until 1985 when Scott Verplank wins the Western Open. Sanders goes on to win 19 more PGA events, all as a professional.

2012 – Na Yeon Choi wins her first major championship at the U.S. Women's Open at Blackwolf Run in Kohler, Wis., four strokes ahead of runner-up Amy Yang.

July 9

1977 – Tom Watson wins the epic "Duel in the Sun" at the Ailsa Course at Turnberry, Scotland, beating Jack Nicklaus by one shot to win his second Open Championship title. After both co-leaders shoot 65 the previous day, Watson shoots another 65 in the final-round, one shot better than the 66 turned in by Nicklaus. After Nicklaus pulls ahead by three strokes after four holes with two early birdies, Watson draws even with birdies on three of the next four holes. After Watson makes bogey on No. 9 and Nicklaus makes birdie at No. 12, the "Golden Bear" takes a two-shot lead. Watson then birdies No. 13 and No. 15 to draw even. Watson pulls one stroke ahead on No. 17 with a two-putt birdie on the par 5, while Nicklaus can only make par. On the final hole, after Watson hits his tee shot in the middle of the fairway, Nicklaus cuts the ball into the right rough. Watson hits a seven-iron approach to within two feet of the hole, seemingly guaranteeing him the title. Nicklaus then slashes out of the rough and manages to get the ball to slither on the green, 35 feet from the hole. Nicklaus then incredibly sinks the long-distance birdie to pressure Watson to make his final two-foot putt. Watson, however, makes his short birdie putt to conclude one of the most dramatic duels in major championship history.

1954 – Twenty-three-year-old Peter Thomson wins the first of his five Open titles by one stroke over runners-up Bobby Locke, Dai Rees, and Syd Scott at Royal Birkdale Golf Club in Southport, England. Thomson is the first Australian to win the Open Championship, and the youngest champion since Bobby Jones.

1904 – Willie Anderson shoots a final-round 72 – the lowest round U.S. Open history at the time – and wins his second consecutive, and third overall, U.S. Open title winning by five strokes over runner-up Gilbert Nicholls at Glenview Club in Golf, Ill.

1966 – Jack Nicklaus completes the career Grand Slam of golf when he wins the first of his three Open Championship titles beating runners-up Doug Sanders and Dave Thomas by one stroke at Muirfield Golf Links in Gullane, Scotland. The Associated Press writes that Nicklaus "stormed his final citadel" in winning the only major title he had yet to win. Nicklaus virtually seals the title on the 528-yard par-5 17th hole when he hits a three-iron off the tee, a five-iron approach to 15 feet and two-putts for birdie.

1965 – Peter Thomson wins the Open Championship for a fifth time, claiming a two-shot victory over runners-up Brian Huggett and Christy O'Connor Sr. at Royal Birkdale Golf Club in Southport, England. Thomson's five titles are one shy of the Open Championship record of six, set by Harry Vardon. Tom Watson equals Thomson's five titles when he wins his fifth Open Championship in 1983.

1960 – Australian Kel Nagle edges Arnold Palmer by a stroke to win the Open Championship at the Old Course at St. Andrews in the 100 anniversary staging of the oldest championship in golf. Palmer enters the event having won both the Masters and the U.S. Open, looking to win first three legs of the Grand Slam but falls just short. He trails Nagle by four shots at the start of the back nine but starts one of his famous charges, making birdie at No. 13, No. 15 and a closing birdie on No. 18. At the time of Palmer's birdie on 18, that is met with a roaring ovation from the gallery, Nagle is putting for par on the famed 17th "Road Hole." Nagle backs away from the putt and waits for the ovation to die down, then makes the putt and pars the final hole to seal the one-shot victory. Palmer goes on to win the Open Championship the next two years.

1937 – Playing the final 36 holes in a cold, steady rain, Henry Cotton wins the second of his three Open Championship titles at Carnoustie Golf Links in Scotland. The conditions are so wet that 54-hole leader Reg Whitcombe has his club slip out of his hand on the seventh tee, the ball only traveling 40 yards. The tournament is played the week after the Ryder Cup matches and features a strong field of Americans who stay the next week to play in the event, including Sam Snead, Byron Nelson and Walter Hagen.

1949 – Bobby Locke of South Africa wins the first of his four Open titles in a 36-hole Saturday playoff at Royal St. George's Golf Club in Sandwich, England, beating runner-up Harry Bradshaw of Ireland by 12 strokes.

July 10

1953 – In his only Open Championship appearance, Ben Hogan wins his third major championship of the year at Carnoustie Golf Links, winning by four strokes over runners-up Peter Thomson of Australia, Dai Rees of Wales, Antonio Cerda of Argentina and American amateur Frank Stranahan. The win marks the ninth and final major championship of Hogan's career. Having already won the Masters and the U.S. Open earlier in the year, Hogan arrives at Carnoustie two weeks before the event to practice with the smaller British golf ball. Since the staging of the PGA Championship conflicts with the Open Championship,

Hogan is not able to try and complete a single-season "Grand Slam." During his 1953 season, Hogan plays only six events, winning five of them, including three majors.

1926 – Bobby Jones becomes the first player to win the U.S. Open and British Opens in the same year when he wins the 30th U.S. Open at the Scioto Country Club in Columbus, Ohio. Jones wins his second U.S. Open championship by one stroke over runner-up Joe Turnesa, who leads Jones by three strokes entering the final round. Needing a birdie on the par-5 18th hole to win, Jones smashes a 310-yard drive and hits his second shot to 15 feet and two putts for the win with a final-round 73.

1976 – Johnny Miller wins the Open Championship at Royal Birkdale in Southport, England by six shots over runners-up Seve Ballesteros and Jack Nicklaus. Miller shoots a final-round 66 to overtake Ballesteros, the 19-year-old Spanish sensation who leads by two shots to start the day, but falters with a final-round 74. "I felt good and strong and I knew somehow I could do it," says the 29-year-old Miller.

1971 – In the 100th staging of the Open Championship, Lee Trevino caps an incredible four weeks of play adding the Open Championship title to the U.S. Open title he wins at Merion. Trevino finishes one stroke better around the links of Royal Birkdale than Lu Liang-Huan of Taiwan and becomes the fourth player to win both the U.S. Open and the Open Championship in the same year, joining Bobby Jones (1926, 1930), Gene Sarazen (1932) and Ben Hogan (1953).

2010 – Rory McIlroy ties a major championship record with a round of 63 in the opening round of the Open Championship at the Old Course at St. Andrews. It marks only the eighth 63 in Open Championship history and the 22nd time a 63 has been carded in major championship history.

1964 – Tony Lema wins his only major championship at the Open Championship at the Old Course at St. Andrews beating runner-up Jack Nicklaus by five strokes. Lema leads by seven strokes to start the day and only needs a final-round 70 to win in his first-ever event in Britain.

July 11

1970 – Doug Sanders misses a 30-inch, downhill, left-to-right putt on the 18th at the Old Course at St. Andrews to win the Open Championship. Instead, Saunders ties Jack Nicklaus and loses in an 18-hole playoff the next day by one shot. Years later when asked if he ever thinks of missing the putt, Sanders replies "Only once every four or five minutes."

1973 – Gene Sarazen, age 71, makes a hole-in-one on the 123 yard par-3 eighth hole at Troon – the famous "Postage Stamp" hole – in the first round of the Open Championship. Sarazen uses a five-iron for his famous ace. The following day on the same hole, he holes out from the bunker for a 2, using a sand wedge, a club he invented and first uses to win the 1932 Open Championship.

1952 – Bobby Locke wins the third of his four Open Championship titles, one stroke better than runner-up Peter Thompson at Royal Lytham & St. Annes.

2010 – Paula Creamer, playing in only her fourth tournament after surgery to her left thumb, wins her first major championship at the U.S. Women's Open at Oakmont, Pa. Creamer wins by four shots over runners-up Na Yeon Choi and Suzann Pettersen. The win allows Creamer to lose the tag of the best woman golfer without a major title. "I believed I could do this. I believed I could do this even when I had a cast on," Creamer says of winning, despite her wrist issues.

2011 – So Yeon Ryu of South Korea defeats compatriot Hee Kyung Seo in a three-hole aggregate playoff to win the U.S. Women's Open at The Broadmoor East Course in Colorado Springs, Colo. Both players finish the regulation 72 holes at three-under-par 281, two strokes ahead of Cristie Kerr. Seo finishes her final round on Sunday and Ryu on Monday morning and Ryu wins the playoff by three strokes with birdies on the last two holes. It is the first U.S. Women's Open to use the three-hole aggregate playoff. The playoff was formerly 18 holes, last played in 2006. The format was changed starting in 2007.

July 12

1930 – Bobby Jones wins his second consecutive and record-tying fourth U.S. Open title – and the third leg of the Grand Slam – at Interlachen Country Club in Edina, Minn. Jones, who already won the British Amateur and the British Open in June, completes the Grand Slam with his victory in September at the fourth and final leg, the U.S. Amateur. Jones shots a 68 and a 75 on his final 36 holes and needs to two putt from 40 feet on the final green to win the tournament. He only needs one putt and makes birdie to seal the two-shot win over Horton Smith, the man who four years later would win the inaugural Jones-created "Augusta National Invitation Tournament" otherwise known as the "Masters." Jones becomes the first player to successfully defend his U.S. Open title since John McDermott in 1911–12. He ties Willie Anderson with four U.S. Open titles, but does not attempt to win a fifth, retiring from golf after winning the Grand Slam at the U.S. Amateur in September.

1970 – Jack Nicklaus wins the second of his three Open Championship titles at the Old Course at St. Andrews in an 18-hole Sunday playoff over Doug Sanders, who the previous day misses an 18-inch putt to win the title. Nicklaus shoots a 72 to a 73 from Sanders in the first Open Championship playoff since 1963 and the first that is staged over only 18 holes. Nicklaus leads Sanders by as many as four shots during the playoff but the lead shrinks to one shot on the 18th hole. Nicklaus then famously takes off his yellow sweater and rips a tee-shot over the green on the 360-yard home hole. He chips onto the green and curls in an eight-foot birdie putt to win the championship, heaving his putter into the air in celebration.

2015 – Gee Chun of South Korea becomes the third youngest U.S. Women's Open champion at 20 years, 11 months and three days when she claims a one-shot win over runner-up Amy Yang in Lancaster, Pa. Chun becomes the first player to win in their U.S. Open debut since Birdie Kim in 2005 and wins the title when third-round leader Yang makes bogey on the final hole. "Everything I faced and I did here was completely new," says Chun, who shoots a final-round 66. "So all I did was enjoy the new stuff ... I enjoyed it and had a lot of fun. Even though I'm Korean, here American fans supported me a lot and they gave a lot of claps. That has put me in the great rhythm of play, and I enjoyed that tournament rhythm."

2009 – Eun-Hee Ji wins the U.S. Women's Open at Saucon Valley Country Club in Bethlehem, Pa. sinking a 20-foot birdie putt on the 72nd hole to finish with an even-par 71, one stroke ahead of runner-up Candie Kung.

2015 – One day after shooting a 61 for the lowest round of his PGA Tour career, Jordan Spieth wins the John Deere Classic in Silvis, Ill. for his fifth career PGA Tour win and fourth of the season. Spieth, the Masters and U.S. Open champion, wins on the second hole of a sudden-death playoff over 46-year-old Tom Gillis, seeking his first career PGA Tour victory.

July 13

1975 – Tom Watson wins an 18-hole playoff by one stroke over Jack Newton to win the Open Championship at Carnoustie Golf

Links, the first of his eight major titles. Watson and Newton are tied at the 18th tee of the playoff and Watson hits the green par-4 "Home" hole in two, while Newton's approach lands in the front bunker. Newton's sand shot runs ten feet past the hole and he misses his par putt, while Watson two-putts for par and the title.

1963 – Bob Charles becomes the first left-handed player to win a major championship when he wins his only major title at the Open Championship at Royal Lytham & St Annes Golf Club. Charles, from New Zealand, wins a 36-hole playoff with Phil Rodgers by eight strokes to achieve his historic victory. The 36-hole playoff is the last to take place at the Open Championship as it is changed to 18 holes the following year and first used in 1970.

1962 – Arnold Palmer wins his second consecutive Open Championship at Troon Golf Club, six strokes ahead of runner-up Kel Nagle. The title is Palmer's sixth of seven major titles and his second of the year after he wins the Masters for a third time. Jack Nicklaus finishes his first Open Championship in 34th place.

1968 – Gary Player wins the second of his three Open Championship titles at Carnoustie Golf Links, two strokes ahead of runners-up Bob Charles and Jack Nicklaus. In a curious fact, the inaugural Greater Milwaukee Open is held in the United States during the same week, with a first prize of $40,000, over five times the winner's share of the Open Championship, which is $7,200. Dave Stockton wins that event, concluded the next day, to win his third PGA Tour title.

1974 – Gary Player wins his third Open Championship at Royal Lytham & St. Annes Golf Club, four strokes ahead of runner-up Peter Oosterhuis. It marks the eighth of his nine major titles and his second of the year after winning at the Masters earlier in the year.

2014 – Mo Martin hits one of the most clutch shots in major championship history, nearly holing out from 240 yards with a three-wood for a double-eagle on the final hole of the British Women's Open at Royal Birkdale, but taps in for eagle to win her first major and her first LPGA title. The eagle is the first for the year for Martin, one of the shortest hitters on the LPGA Tour and winless in 63 previous events. "An absolutely perfect three-wood," Martin says after her one-shot victory over Shanshan Feng of China and Suzann Pettersen of Norway. "When it was in the air, I said, `Sit.' And then I said, `Stop.' And then when it was going toward the hole, I said, `OK, I don't have anything more to say to that ball.' I actually heard it hit the pin. It's definitely one to remember." Writes Shane Bacon of the *Devil Ball Golf* blog, "There are certain golf shots hit at major championships that don't need explaining. Sarazen at the 1935 Masters. Jack Nicklaus' 1-iron at Pebble Beach in '72. Tiger's chip on the 16th at Augusta National in 2005. Mo Martin's second shot on the 18th at Royal Birkdale should make that list."

July 14

1973 – Tom Weiskopf closes out a wire-to-wire win at the Open Championship at the Troon Golf Club, shooting a final-round 70 to claim a four-stroke win over runners-up Neil Coles and Johnny Miller.

2013 – Nineteen-year-old Jordan Spieth becomes the youngest player to win a PGA Tour event in 82 years when he survives a five-hole, sudden-death playoff with defending champion Zach Johnson and David Hearn to win the John Deere Classic at Silvis, Ill. Spieth becomes the youngest winner on the PGA Tour since 19-year-old Ralph Guldahl wins the Santa Monica Open in 1931. Spieth gets into the playoff when he holes a bunker shot on the final hole of regulation, a shot he calls "the luckiest shot I've ever hit in my life," as he finishes with a final-round 65.

2013 – Will Wilcox fires a 12-under 59 in the final round of the Web.com Tour's Utah Championship at Willow Creek Country Club in Sandy, Utah. Wilcox becomes the fourth player in the history of the Web.com Tour at the time to shoot 59 joining Notah Begay III, Doug Dunakey and Jason Gore. Wilcox shoots a seven-under 29 on the back nine, making birdie at his first four holes and then notching an eagle at the par-5 17th. In all, he records 10 birdies and an eagle. Wilcox, however, finishes one shot out of a playoff, won by Steven Atker of New Zealand over Ashley Hall of Australia.

2013 – Phil Mickelson wins the Scottish Open at Castle Stuart in Inverness, Scotland in a playoff over Branden Grace, his 48th career worldwide win and his first in Europe since 1993. Mickelson starts the day with a double-bogey, but then makes a barrage of birdies only to three-putt the final hole from 20 feet to fall into a playoff with Grace. In the playoff, Mickelson hits a third-shot pitch on the par-5 18th hole to within six inches for a tap-in birdie and the victory. The win was the first for Mickelson in Europe since he won in Paris on the European Challenge Tour in 1993. The following week, he wins the Open Championship at Muirfield.

July 15

2005 – Jack Nicklaus makes a 15-foot birdie putt on the final stroke of his professional career in the second round of the Open Championship at the Old Course at St. Andrews. On his walk up to the final green, he receives a ten-minute standing ovation, posing for photographs on the iconic Swilcan Bridge. Nicklaus shoots an even-par 72 in his final competitive round, but misses the cut by three strokes with a three-over-par score of 147.

1923 – Amateur golf legend Bobby Jones wins his first major championship at the age of 21 winning an 18-hole playoff with

Bobby Cruickshank at the Inwood Country Club in Inwood, N.Y. Jones and Cruickshank are tied on the 18th hole of the playoff and each drive into the rough. After Cruickshank lays up short of the green, Jones stiffs a two-iron to within eight feet. After Cruickshank fails to get up-and-down, Jones two-putts and wins the title.

1961 – Arnold Palmer wins the Open Championship for the first time shooting a 69 and a 72 over the final day's 36 holes to beat Dai Rees of Wales by one shot at Royal Birkdale Golf Club in Southport, England. In only his second appearance at the Open Championship, Palmer wins the fourth of his seven major titles and is the first American to win the Claret Jug since Ben Hogan in 1953.

1927 – Twenty-five-year-old amateur Bobby Jones successfully defends the title at the Open Championship at the Old Course at St. Andrews with a six-stroke victory over runners-up Aubrey Boomer and Fred Robson. The win for Jones exorcises ghosts of his first experiences on the course six years earlier when he walks off the course in the third round of the 1921 Open Championship. Jones takes four swings at his ball in a deep bunker on the 11th hole, failing to get the ball out. He then picks up the ball and walks off.

1967 – Forty-four-year-old Roberto De Vicenzo of Argentina wins his only major championship at the Open Championship at the River Liverpool Golf Club at Hoylake. DeVicenzo shoots a final-round 70 and finishes two strokes ahead of runner-up and defending champion Jack Nicklaus.

1972 – Lee Trevino successfully defends his Open title and prevents Jack Nicklaus from winning the third leg of a possible Grand Slam by edging "The Golden Bear" by one shot at Muirfield. Trevino becomes the first player to win consecutive Open titles since Arnold Palmer in 1961-1962. Nicklaus, who won his first Open title at Muirfield in 1966, charges from six strokes back on the final day shooting 65, but plays the final three holes at one over par. Trevino shoots a final-round of even-par 71 and fortuitously chips in for par on the 17th hole to preserve his one-stroke lead.

1978 – Jack Nicklaus wins his third and final Open Championship, winning by two strokes ahead of runners-up Ben Crenshaw, Raymond Floyd, Tom Kite and Simon Owen at the Old Course at St. Andrews. Owen actually leads the event by one shot after chipping in for birdie on the 15th hole from 25 feet away. However, the New Zealander flies the green and makes bogey on No. 16 while Nicklaus makes a six-foot birdie putt to take the lead. He then pars the final two holes to win the 15th of his 18 major championships.

1922 – Twenty-year-old Gene Sarazen wins the first of his seven major championships winning the U.S. Open at the Skokie Country Club in Glencoe, Ill., one stroke ahead of runners-up John Black and amateur Bobby Jones. Sarazen shoots a final-round 68 to become the fourth American-born champion of the U.S. Open, joining John McDermott, Francis Ouimet, and Walter Hagen.

1945 – Byron Nelson wins the PGA Championship at Moraine Country Club in Kettering, Ohio winning the match-play final 4 & 3 over Sam Byrd, a former major league baseball player. The win was the fifth and final major title for Nelson and his second win at the PGA Championship. Nelson, also the 1940 PGA Champion, wins $5,000 in war bonds. Due to World War II, the PGA Championship is the only major championship played in 1944 and 1945.

July 16

1901 – Willie Anderson win his first of four U.S. Open titles winning the first-ever playoff in U.S. Open history over Alex

Smith at the Myopia Hunt Club in South Hamilton, Mass. The playoff is postponed from Sunday to Monday to allow for member play at the club. Smith leads the playoff by five strokes with five to play, but Anderson draws even after 17 holes. Smith misses a four-foot par putt on the final hole to lose the championship. Anderson's playoff round of 85 and Smith's 86 ensures that for the only time in U.S. Open history no player manages to break 80 in any round. Both Anderson and Smith's 331 total score after 72 holes is the highest winning score in U.S. Open history. Anderson goes on to win another three U.S. Open titles, the most ever along with Jack Nicklaus, Ben Hogan, and Bobby Jones.

1938 – Paul Runyan wins his second PGA Championship beating Sam Snead 8&7 in the final of the match-play format at the Shawnee Country Club in Smithfield Township, Pa. It is the largest margin of victory ever in the match-play format of the PGA Championship.

1983 – Hale Irwin performs a "whiff" on a two-inch par putt on the 14th hole of the third round at Open Championship at Royal Birkdale. After missing his 12-foot birdie putt, an upset Irwin tries to backhand the tap-in and misses the ball completely. He then takes another stroke to sink the two-inch putt and takes a bogey on the hole. The following day, Irwin shoots a final-round 67 and finishes in second place behind Tom Watson…. by one stroke.

1995 – Annika Sorenstam wins the first of her 72 LPGA Tour career titles at the U.S. Women's Open at the East Course at the Broadmoor Golf Club in Colorado Springs, Colo. Sorenstam wins the first of her ten major titles shooting a final-round 68 to win by one shot over third-round leader Meg Mallon, whom she trailed by five strokes at the start of the day.

July 17

1983 – Tom Watson wins his fifth Open Championship, and second consecutive, one stroke ahead of runners-up Andy Bean and Hale Irwin at Royal Birkdale in Southport, England. Watson joins an elite group of five-time Open Championship winners – J.H. Taylor, Harry Vardon, James Braid and Peter Thomson, the most recent five-time winner who sends Watson a telegram immediately following his two-putt par on the final hole reading "Delighted and thrilled to welcome you to the five-times club."

2005 – Tiger Woods wins his second Open Championship title, and his 10th career major, posting a five-shot victory over runner-up Colin Montgomerie at the Old Course at St. Andrews. Woods shoots a two-under par 70, the only round under par among the final 14 players competing in the field. Montgomerie finishes second at a major championship for a fifth time.

1994 – Nick Price wins the second of his three major championships and only Open Championship title, one stroke ahead of runner-up Jesper Parnevik at Turnberry. Price shoots a final-round 66, going three-under par over the final three holes, highlighted by a 50-foot eagle putt on the 17th hole. Parnevik makes bogey on the final hole to miss a playoff.

2011 – At the age 42, with his chances to win a major championship seemingly behind him, Darren Clarke of Northern Ireland secures a popular victory at the Open Championship at Royal St. Georges with a three-shot victory over Americans Phil Mickelson and Dustin Johnson. Writes Lawrence Donegan of *The Guardian* of Clarke, "He had won more than 20 tournaments around the world, but never won the big one. He had played a distinguishing role in five Ryder Cup teams, never more so than in 2006 at the K Club, when he performed brilliantly for Europe just a few weeks after the death of his wife, Heather. Yet for all that he had never gained entry into the exclusive club reserved for major champions – a rotten injustice for a golfer acknowledged by his peers as one of the most naturally gifted of his generation." Clarke, who leads the tournament by one shot heading into the final round, pays respect to his deceased wife in the Claret Jug presentation ceremony saying, "In terms of what's going through my heart, there's obviously somebody who is watching down from up above there, and I know she'd be very proud of me. She'd probably be saying, I told you so."

1997 – Ian Baker-Finch shoots a 21-over-par round of 92 in the first round of the Open Championship at Troon. Baker-Finch, just six years removed from winning the 1991 Open Championship title, had not made a cut in 31 consecutive events dating back three years. "Horrendous," says Baker-Finch of his round that features five pars, six bogeys, six double bogeys and a triple bogey. Baker-Finch, a 36-year-old Australian, uses Wimbledon tennis doubles champion Todd Woodbridge as his caddie.

July 18

1999 – In the most dramatic and tragic final-hole disaster in major tournament golf, Jean van de Velde of France blows a three-shot lead on the final hole of the Open Championship at Carnoustie Golf Links and loses in a three-man, four-hole aggregate playoff to Paul Lawrie. Leading by five shots at the start of the day, van de Velde stands on the 18th tee needing only a double-bogey to win the Claret Jug, but hits his drive into the right rough. His approach shot bounces off the grandstand, off a rock in the Barry Burn and into knee-high rough, where, incredibly, van de Velde then hits his third shot into the burn in front of the green. After a long delay where he takes off his shoes and socks and considers playing the ball out of the burn, van de Velde takes a drop with a penalty stroke and hits his fifth shot into a greenside bunker. After pitching out, he then makes an eight-foot putt for a triple bogey 7 to join Lawrie and Justin Leonard in the four-hole aggregate play-off. Lawrie makes birdie on the third hole and the final playoff hole, capped with a four-iron to four feet, to win the playoff by three shots. Lawrie begins the day 10 shots out of the lead, making his victory the biggest comeback in major championship history.

2004 – Todd Hamilton becomes one of the most unlikely winners of a major championship when he defeats three-time major champion Ernie Els in a four-hole aggregate playoff to win the Open Championship at Royal Troon. A 500-to-one long-shot to win the title at the start of the week, Hamilton makes four pars on the four playoff holes to win by one stroke over Els, who makes three pars and a bogey. Hamilton, age 38 and ranked No. 56 in the World Golf Rankings, played on the Asian Tour for 15 years winning 11 times, but fails to qualify for the PGA Tour eight times before earning his card. Says Hamilton after his upset victory, "Not to be conceited or anything, but I think it's a pretty neat story." Hamilton won his first PGA Tour event earlier in the year at the Honda Classic, but does not win again and his 187 subsequent tour starts where he misses the cut 111 times and posts only three top-10 finishes.

1988 – In a first-ever Monday finish at the Open Championship, Seve Ballesteros shoots a final-round 65 to capture his third Open Championship and fifth major title at Royal Lytham & St. Annes Golf Club. Ballesteros, also the winner of the 1979 and 1984 Open Championship, finishes two strokes ahead of runner-up Nick Price, the 54-hole leader. Heavy rain on Saturday causes flooding on the course and the third round is cancelled after play is started and postponed until Sunday.

1993 – Greg Norman shoots a final-round 64 to win his second Open Championship, two strokes ahead of runner-up Nick Faldo at Royal St. George's Golf Club in Sandwich, England. "Today I did not mis-hit a shot," says Norman. "I hit every shot perfect, every iron perfect. I'm not a guy to brag about myself, but I was just in awe of myself."

1982 – Tom Watson wins his fourth Open Championship title at Royal Troon Golf Club, posting a one-stroke win over runners-up Peter Oosterhuis and Nick Price. It is Watson's second consecutive major victory after winning the U.S. Open at Pebble Beach a month earlier. Watson becomes the fifth to win the U.S. Open and the Open Championship in the same year, joining fellow Americans Bobby Jones (1926, 1930), Gene Sarazen (1932), Ben Hogan (1953), and Lee Trevino (1971). Tiger Woods later turns the trick in 2000.

2010 – Louis Oosthuizen shoots a final-round 71 and wins his first major championship by seven shots at the Open Championship at St. Andrews in Scotland. Oosthuizen finishes with a 16-under-par total of 272, seven strokes ahead of runner-up Lee Westwood.

1896 – James Foulis wins the second staging of the U.S. Open, held at Shinnecock Golf Club in Southampton, N.Y., three strokes ahead of runner-up Horace Rawlins, the defending champion. Foulis shoots rounds of 78-74 in the 36-hole event, his round of 74 being a U.S. Open record until 1903. Shinnecock Hills plays at a distance of 4,423 yards, the shortest course in U.S. Open history.

July 19

1987 – Nick Faldo pars all eighteen holes in the final round of the Open Championship at Muirfield and wins his first of three Open Championships by one stroke over runner-up Paul Azinger. "It might look conservative by the scoreboard but I think it was aggressive," Faldo says of his final-round score. "It's a tough golf course." Azinger leads by one shot entering the final round, but bogeys four of the last nine holes, including the 17th and 18th and loses by one stroke. "I don't feel like I succumbed to the pressure," Azinger says. "I felt in complete control and I really felt like I would win…I liked the way it (the pressure of leading) felt, and I handled it well. I came out of the box like a trooper. I was not at any time any more nervous than on the PGA Tour." Faldo is the first Englishman to win The Open since Tony Jacklin in 1969.

2009 – Tom Watson nearly becomes the oldest player to win a major championship, but the 59-year-old lets a record-tying sixth Claret Jug slip from his fingers, missing an eight-foot putt on the 72nd hole for victory and loses the four-hole aggregate playoff to Stewart Cink at the Open Championship at Turnberry. "It would have been a hell of a story, wouldn't it?" Watson says to the press, and then repeats, "It would have been a hell of a story. It wasn't to be. And yes, it's a great disappointment. It tears at your gut, as it always has torn at my gut. It's not easy to take. I put myself in position to win, didn't do it in the last hole." Says Cink of his breakthrough win at a major, "I don't feel ashamed. I don't feel disappointed. I'm pleased as punch that I've won this tournament, and also proud of the way Tom Watson played because he showed, not only did he show how great a golfer he is, but he showed what a great game we all play, the longevity that can exist for a guy to come out and compete."

1981 – Bill Rogers wins his lone major championship at the Open Championship with a four-stroke victory over runner-up Bernard Langer in the first staging of the event at Royal St. George's since 1949. "If somebody would have told me at the beginning of the week that I'd be doing this I'd tell them they were a liar," Rogers tells the crowd as he is handed the Claret Jug. "I could never have dreamed of the recognition I've gained from winning or the things it has opened up for me," Rogers says a year after his triumph. "All of the sudden, I am the guy they're coming to see. I'm the drawing card."

1998 – Three months after dramatically winning his first major championship at the Masters, 41-year-old Mark O'Meara collects a second major title in a four-hole playoff over Brian

Watts at the Open Championship at Royal Birkdale. O'Meara starts the day two shots out of the lead of Watts, a 32-year-old American who plays on the Japanese Tour, but shoots 68 to force the Open Championship's four-hole aggregate score playoff that he wins by two shots. Says O'Meara of winning two major titles in one year at the age of 41 – the oldest to turn that calendar-year double, "The golf ball doesn't know how old you are." Seventeen-year-old Brit Justin Rose holes out a 45-yard pitch shot for birdie on the final hole to tie for fourth, the best finish by an amateur at the Open Championship since Frank Stranahan finished second at Carnoustie in 1953.

1992 – Nick Faldo rallies to win his third Open Championship title by one stroke over John Cook at Muirfield Golf Links, the site of his first Open title five years earlier. Cook, playing one group ahead of Faldo, leads the tournament by two shots after he birdies the 16th hole, but three putts for par on the 17th hole and bogeys the 18th hole. Faldo birdies the 15th and 17th hole and taps in for par on the 18th hole for victory, exploding into tears of disbelief and happiness. "The first time I cried in joy in this game was in 1987 when I won here," Faldo says. "I cried when I won the second time at Augusta (1990 Masters) and now here. I am just an emotional little petal."

1964 – Bobby Nichols caps a wire-to-wire win at the PGA Championship at the Columbus Country Club in Columbus, Ohio, shooting a final-round 67 to beat runners-up Jack Nicklaus and Arnold Palmer by three strokes. "I couldn't believe them myself, but I have witnesses," says Nichols of many of the incredible shots he hits while posting a then PGA Championship record low score of nine-under-par 271. Nicklaus, playing in his hometown, shoots a final-round 64 to tie Palmer for second place. "It was probably the finest round of golf I have ever played. It just wasn't good enough," says Nicklaus. The win is the first and only major title for Nichols, who wins 12 career titles in his PGA Tour career. The PGA Championship is played the week after the Open Championship is staged at St. Andrews, won by Tony Lema.

1996 – Fifty-six-year old Jack Nicklaus shoots a five-under-par 66 in the second round of the Open Championship at Royal Lythm and St. Anne's, placing him one shot out of the lead. Nicklaus then flippantly predicts how the tournament will end up for him when asked by media how he thinks the rest of the tournament will unfold for him. "Who knows?" he says. "I might play great or I might go out the next two days and shoot 150." Nicklaus then shoots 77 and 73 in his next two rounds for exactly a 150, which gives him a T-44 finish.

2008 – Fifty-three-year-old Greg Norman becomes the oldest golfer ever to hold at least a share of the 54-hole lead at the Open Championship, leading Padraig Harrington and K.J. Choi by two shots at Birkdale. Norman's record which would last just one year, as a 59-year-old Tom Watson leads the tournament after three rounds in 2009.

July 20

2003 – Ben Curtis, ranked No. 396 in the world, becomes the most unlikely winner of a major golf tournament in history winning the Open Championship at Royal St. George's in Sandwich, England. Playing in a major championship for the first time in his career and without even a top 10 finish on the PGA Tour, Curtis defeats runners-up Thomas Bjorn and Vijay Singh by one shot and becomes the first player to win in his maiden major since Francis Ouimet at the 1913 U.S. Open. "Oh, man, that's about all I can say now," says Curtis to open up his press conference with reporters. "I came in here this week just trying to play the best I could and hopefully make the cut and compete on the weekend. And obviously I did that and went out there and probably played the best weekend of my life." Bjorn leads the tournament by three shots with four holes to play and by two shots with three holes to play, but needs three shots to get out of the greenside bunker on the 16th hole and falters.

1980 – Tom Watson claims his third Open Championship title winning by four strokes over Lee Trevino at Muirfield Golf Links in Scotland. Says Watson of his victory, "Winning in Scotland is a different feeling to all my wins elsewhere. I am a sentimentalist and something of a traditionalist, and this, after all, is the birthplace of the game. And one cannot but think of the champions whose footsteps you are following in on a course like Muirfield." The tournament is the first Open that is scheduled to start on a Thursday and end on a Sunday – previous Opens beginning on Wednesday and ending on a Saturday and prior to 1966, the final 36 holes being scheduled for a Friday.

1986 – Greg Norman finally secures his elusive first major championship winning the Open Championship at Turnberry by five shots over runner-up Gordon J. Brand. After losing in a playoff at the 1984 U.S. Open and blowing 36-hole leads at the 1986 Masters and at the U.S. Open at Shinnecock Hills in New York, Norman finally is able to call himself a major champion. "You get a monkey on your back not from yourself but from people around you," says Norman of his unfulfilled expectations. "I woke today and was a little jumpy and nervous. All I said was that I wouldn't let myself have a letdown like I did at Shinnecock." Despite shooting a major tournament equaling 63 in Friday's second round, Norman wins with a score of even par, 12 shots off the pace set the last time the Open was held at Turnberry in 1977 when Tom Watson's winning score was 12 under par. "I played better today than I did when I shot the 63," Norman says of his final-round 69. "I hit some iron shots on the back nine that I was even impressed with."

1997 – Five shots out of the lead entering the final round, Justin Leonard fires a final-round 65 and wins the Open Championship at Troon by three strokes over third-round leader Jesper

Parnevik and Darren Clarke. The title was Leonard's first at a major championship and gives him the distinction of being the fifth straight American to win the Open title at Troon.

2008 – Padraig Harrington defends his Open Championship title – becoming only the fifth golfer to repeat as champion in 50 years – surging past 53-year-old third-round leader Greg Norman to win at Royal Birkdale in Southport, England. Harrington finishes with a final-round 69 for a three-over-par total of 283, four shots better than second-place finisher Ian Poulter. Norman, who shoots a final-round 77, finishes in a tie for third with Henrik Stenson. Says Norman, "Obviously I'm disappointed. That would be an understatement if I didn't say I was disappointed. But I can walk away from here with my head held high because I hung in there. It wasn't meant to be." Writes Hank Gola in the *New York Daily News*, "A Norman conquest would have been one of the greatest stories in the history of golf, as the 53-year-old would have become the oldest major champion by five years. But he began his round with three straight bogeys and had eight bogeys on the day, and although he held the lead at the turn, he seemed simply to be hanging on the whole way." Harrington almost withdraws from the tournament the night before its start with severe pain in his wrist. "Beware the injured golfer," he quips after hoisting the Claret Jug.

2015 – Zach Johnson wins his second major title at the Open Championship, winning a three-man, four-hole aggregate playoff over Louis Oosthuizen and Marc Leishman at St. Andrews. Johnson, the 2007 Masters champion, holes a 30-foot-birdie on the 72nd hole to post his 15-under-par 273 score and wins the playoff over Oosthuizen by one shot and Leishman by three shots. Twenty-one-year-old Jordan Spieth, the reigning Masters and U.S. Open champion, falls one shot out of the playoff and in his attempt of becoming the first player since Ben Hogan in 1953 to win three legs of Grand Slam of golf in one season. Due to high wind delays at the rain-delayed finish of the second round two days earlier, the final round is played on a Monday for the first time since 1988.

1979 – At age 67, Sam Snead becomes the first player to shoot his age on the PGA Tour, shooting a 67 in the second round of the Ed McMahon Quad Cities Open in Illinois. Two days later, Snead beats his age again with a final-round 66 and finishes in a tie for 36th place, 11 shots behind winner D.A. Weibring. "I don't feel any different than I did 10 years ago," Snead says after his final-round 66. "Except maybe a little heavier. When you get up around 67, most of them have either quit or are dead. There's not many of them still around."

1958 – Dow Finsterwald wins the first staging of the PGA Championship as a stroke-play event, shooting a final-round 67 to win his only major title at the Llanerch Country Club in Havertown, Pa. Finsterwald, the runner-up at the PGA in 1957 when a match-play event, beats runner-up Billy Casper by two shots.

2003 – Fifty-year-old Craig Stadler shoots a nine-under-par 63 and comes from eight strokes back to win the BC Open in Endicott, N.Y. by one shot over runners-up Steve Lowery and Alex Cejka. Stadler, winless on the PGA Tour since 1996, enters the tournament having won the previous week for the first time on the Champions Tour at the Senior Players Championship. Stadler becomes the sixth oldest player to win the PGA Tour, two years and nine months younger than Sam Snead, the oldest to win on the PGA Tour at the age of 52 years, 10 months and eight days at the 1965 Greater Greensboro Open.

July 21

1979 – Twenty-two-year-old Seve Ballesteros wins his first major championship with three-shot victory over Jack Nicklaus and Ben Crenshaw at The Open Championship at Royal Lytham &

St. Annes. The Spaniard shoots a final-round one-under round of 70 to finish at one-under 283. Reigning U.S Open champion Hale Irwin, the third-round leader by two shots over Ballesteros, shoots a final-round 78 to fall out of contention. John Radosta in the *New York Times*, who describes Ballesteros as one "with the face of an altar boy and the style of a blade-swinging corsair" writes of the final scene on the final hole, "After he had sunk a par putt of three feet on the 18th green, two of his brothers, Vincente and Baldomero, rushed out and surrounded him in an emotional embrace. Their eyes were filled with tears."

2013 – Phil Mickelson cards a final round 66 – his best final-round score at a major championship – and wins the Open Championship for the first time at Muirfield. Mickelson birdies four of the last six holes, including hitting an incredible 302-yard three-wood into the wind on the par-5 17th hole that sets up a two-putt birdie. Mickelson caps his memorable win with a 12-foot birdie putt on the final hole. "This is such an accomplishment for me because I just never knew if I'd be able to develop the game to play links golf effectively," Mickelson says of winning the third leg of a career Grand Slam. "To play the best round arguably of my career, to putt better than I've ever putted, to shoot the round of my life ... it feels amazing to win the Claret Jug."

1996 – Tom Lehman breaks through and finally wins his elusive major title at the Open Championship at Royal Lytham & St. Annes Golf Club by two strokes over runners-up Mark McCumber and Ernie Els. After losing majors in heart-breaking fashion to Jose-Maria Olazabal at the 1994 Masters, to Corey Pavin at the 1995 U.S. Open and, on the final hole, to Steve Jones at the U.S. Open just a month before the Open Championship, Lehman joins the elusive club of major tournament winners. Says Lehman as he is presented with the Claret Jug, "I may not swing the prettiest or look the prettiest, and I may do some things kind of funny but I have a lot of heart." Lehman, who leads by six shots entering the final round, becomes the first

American to win the Open at Lytham & St. Annes since Bobby Jones seventy years earlier.

1985 – Sandy Lyle becomes the first British champion at The Open Championship since Tony Jacklin in 1969 with a one-shot victory over Payne Stewart at Royal St. George's. Lyle shoots a final round of even par 70, capped with a heart-stopping bogey on the 18th hole, the Scotsman hitting a greenside chip shot that rolls back in front of him. Lyle drops to his knees in anguish and slams his club into the ground before two putting to end his championship. Lyle then waits in the clubhouse as third-round co-leaders Bernard Langer and David Graham are not able to catch him. Writes Mike Littwin in the *Los Angeles Times* of the celebration of the end of the British drought at the Open championship, "The crowds cheered. BBC-TV positioned its cameras on the Union Jack atop the clubhouse. British reporters roared their approval. It wasn't V-E day, but there was definitely a night of celebration ahead." The other highlight from the day comes when a streaker runs onto the 18th green and is famously tackled by Peter Jacobsen. "He streaked into my line and I got a little hot, so I tackled him," Jacobsen says.

1991 – Ian Baker-Finch fires a front nine 29 en route to a final-round 66 – hitting every fairway and every green – to win his only major title at the Open Championship at Royal Birkdale Golf Club in Southport, England. Baker-Finch stands at two-over par in 28th place after the second round, but shoots 10 under par for the weekend to win by two shots over Mike Harwood. Says Baker-Finch, "The Open to me is the most special event in my life. To play in it is a thrill. To win it is a dream."

1968 – Forty-eight-year-old Julius Boros wins the 50th staging of the PGA Championship at the Pecan Valley Golf Club in San Antonio and becomes the oldest player to win a major championship. Boros shoots a final-round 69 to beat runners-up Arnold Palmer and Bob Charles by one shot. Palmer misses an eight-foot putt on the final hole that would have tied Boros, but settles for the second of his three runner-up finishes at the PGA, the only major tournament he does not win in his career.

1963 – Jack Nicklaus wins the first of his five PGA Championship titles at the Blue Course at the Dallas Athletic Club in Dallas, Texas, beating runner-up Dave Ragan by two shots. The win is the third of 18 career major titles for Nicklaus, who won his first Masters title in April and his first U.S. Open the previous year.

1957 – In the last staging of the PGA Championship as a match-play event, Lionel Hebert beats Dow Finsterwald 2&1 at the Miami Valley Golf Club in Dayton, Ohio to win his first PGA Tour event. Herbert's brother Jay wins the PGA three years later in 1960 when it is a stroke-play event.

1921 – Jock Hutchison defeats James Douglas Edgar one-up in the match-play final to win the third staging of the PGA Championship at the Flossmoor Country Club in Flossmoor, Ill.

July 22

1984 – Seve Ballesteros wins his fourth major title at the Open Championship at St. Andrews, two strokes ahead of runners-up Bernhard Langer and five-time champion Tom Watson. Ballesteros makes birdie on the final hole to shoot a final-round 69, pumping his fists in the air in what becomes the signature gesture and moment in the Spaniard's career. As Ballesteros makes birdie on the final hole, third-round leader Tom Watson makes a bogey on the Road Hole, the 17th hole, to fall out of the lead.

2013 – Adam Scott holds a four-shot lead with four holes to play, but falters down the stretch and loses the Open Championship by one stroke to Ernie Els at Royal Lythm St. Annes. Els makes a 15-foot birdie on the final hole to shoot a final-round two-under-par 68, while Scott makes bogey on the final four holes. Scott misses a seven-foot par putt on the 18th hole, after hitting his three-wood off the tee into a pot bunker, to lose the title. "I know I let a really great chance slip through my fingers today," Scott says. "I had it in my hands with four to go." The win is the second Open Championship title for Els and his fourth career major.

2001 – David Duval wins his only major championship at the Open Championship at Lytham St. Annes in England, shooting a final-round 67 to post a three-stroke victory over runner-up Niclas Fasth. After not converting on four great chances to win at Augusta National, two chances at the U.S. Open and the previous year at the Open Championship at St. Andrews, Duval finally is able to break through and win his elusive first major title. "It's kind of a big relief," he says. "It's so pressure-packed in major championships, and then you put it on a golf course like this, where any minor mistake is magnified and it makes the pressure even greater. You just can't let up, and I didn't let up today." Duval becomes the sixth American in the past seven years to claim golf's oldest championship. "I knew it was there, I just needed to play good," says Duval of winning his first major. "I don't know if I can savor this any more than I do now. I imagine what it would do is intensify my desire to do it again." Duval, curiously, does not win again on the PGA Tour. In one of the unusual circumstances in major golf history, former Masters champion Ian Woosnam birdies the first hole, but realizes on the second tee that he has an extra club in his bag and is assessed a two-stroke penalty, eventually finishing four strokes back of Duval.

2007 – Pádraig Harrington defeats Sergio García in an aggregate four-hole playoff to win a wild-ending Open Championship at Carnoustie Golf Links for his first major championship title. Harrington holds a one-shot lead on the final hole, but hits two balls into the Barry Burn and makes double bogey, giving Garcia a one-shot lead. Playing the final hole needing par to win his elusive first major title, Garcia hits his approach shot into a greenside bunker and lips out a 10-foot putt for par and for the championship. In the playoff, Harrington birdies the first hole, while Garcia makes bogey, and Harrington holds on to win the four-hole playoff by one stroke to become the first Irishman to win Open Championship in 60 years. Earlier in the final round, Andres Romero of Argentina rushes to a two-shot lead with two holes to play, but finishes double-bogey, bogey to finish one stroke out of the playoff. Eighteen-year-old Rory McIlroy finishes in 42nd place to win low amateur honors.

1962 – Gary Player wins the first of his two PGA Championships, one stroke ahead of runner-up Bob Goalby at the Aronimink Golf Club in Newton Square, Pa. The win is the third of Player's nine major titles. The win comes one week after Player misses the cut at the Open Championship at Troon in Scotland, won by Arnold Palmer, who finishes 10 strokes back of Player at the PGA in a tie for 17th.

1990 – Nick Faldo wins his second Open Championship title – and his second major title of the year after winning the Masters – winning by five-shots over runners-up Mark McNulty and Payne Stewart at the Old Course at St. Andrews.

1921 – Jim Barnes closes out a wire-to-wire victory at the U.S. Open at Columbia Country Club in Chevy Chase, Md., nine strokes ahead of runners-up Walter Hagen and Fred McLeod. President Warren G. Harding is in attendance for the final round and presents the championship trophy to Barnes, the only time a U.S. President hands out the national championship trophy for golf for the nation. The nine-shot win for Barnes stands as a U.S. Open record until Tiger Woods breaks it in 2000, winning by 15 shots.

2017 – Branden Grace of South Africa shoots a 62 in the third round of the Open Championship at Royal Birkdale, the lowest round by a man in the history of major championship golf.

Grace makes eight birdies and no bogeys but has to be told by his caddie, Zack Rasego, that he became part of golf history after he pulled his ball from the cup on the 18th hole. "What a special day," says Grace. "It's always nice shooting a low number, whether it's any day of the week, whether it's in a tournament or with friends. And then finishing the round and then finding out what you've done makes it even better." Previously, 31 players held the record of 63, the first being Johnny Miller in the final round of the 1973 U.S. Open at Oakmont and most recently Justin Thomas in the third round of the U.S. Open at Erin Hills in Wisconsin 35 days earlier.

July 23

2000 – Tiger Woods completes his career Grand Slam by winning the Open Championship for the first time, eight shots better than runners-up Ernie Els and Thomas Bjorn at the Old Course at St. Andrews. Woods, 24, becomes the youngest player to win all four of golf's majors, beating Jack Nicklaus by two years, and sets a 72-hole scoring record in relation to par at a major championship with his 19-under score over 72 holes. Woods also becomes the fifth player to accomplish the feat, joining Gene Sarazen, Ben Hogan, Jack Nicklaus and Gary Player.

2006 – Tiger Woods wins the first major title since the May death of his father Earl Woods at the Open Championship at Royal Liverpool Golf Club at Hoylake. Woods beats runner-up Chris DiMarco by two shots to win his 11th major championship, his second consecutive Open Championship title and his third overall. Writes the Associated Press of the emotional Woods after he holes out for his victory, "Woods buried his head in the shoulder of caddie Steve Williams, sobbing uncontrollably, his chest heaving. Then he found his wife, Elin, and hugged her for the longest minute, tears still streaming down his face." Says Woods of his reaction after winning the first title without his father, "I'm kind of the one who bottles things up a little bit and moves on. But at that moment, it just came pouring out. And of all the things that my father has meant to me and the game of golf, I just wish he would have seen it one more time."

1995 – John Daly wins his second major championship at the Open Championship at St. Andrews, winning an aggregate four-hole playoff with Constantino Rocca of Italy. Rocca provides one of the most dramatic moments in Open Championship history on the final hole of regulation where, trailing Daly by one shot, he holes a 65-foot birdie putt through the "Valley of Sin" to force the playoff. Rocca falls to the ground and pounds the turf with his fists in excitement. Rocca, however, loses the four-hole playoff by four shots.

1989 – Mark Calcavecchia wins his only major championship at the Open Championship at Royal Troon Golf Club in Troon, Scotland in a playoff over Greg Norman and Wayne Grady. The playoff is the first at the Open in fourteen years and the first to use a four-hole aggregate playoff format, adopted in 1985. The playoff was formerly an 18-hole playoff and, prior to 1964, a 36-hole playoff.

2000 – Karrie Webb of Australia registers a five-shot win over Cristie Kerr and Meg Mallon to win the U.S. Women's Open at The Merit Club in Gurnee, Ill.

2017 – Twenty-three-year-old Jordan Spieth dramatically wins the Open Championship at Royal Birkdale for this third major championship, joining Jack Nicklaus as the only player to win three of the four legs of a career Grand Slam before his 24th birthday. Spieth scrambles for an incredible bogey on the 13th hole after hitting his tee shot 60 yards off-line, taking an unplayable lie and working with officials on his best possible drop. Spieth eventually drops in the driving range and, after 29 minutes, makes bogey and drops one shot out of the lead of his playing partner Matt Kuchar. Spieth, however makes birdie on the next hole, drains a 50-foot eagle putt on No. 15 and goes five-under-par over the final five holes to win the title by three shots over Kuchar.

July 24

1967 – Don January wins his only major title at the PGA Championship at Columbine Country Club in Colorado, winning an 18-hole playoff over Don Massengale. January shoots a 69 to Massengale's 71 to win the title. The 18-hole Monday playoff is the second and last such playoff at the PGA, which was a match-play format through 1957. The next PGA playoff comes ten years later in 1977 when it is decided by sudden-death.

1966 – Al Geiberger, described by Dan Jenkins in *Sports Illustrated* as the man "who looks like the new guy they've hired at the bank to handle home improvement loans," wins his biggest championship and only major title at the PGA Championship at the Firestone Country Club in Akron, Ohio. Geiberger wins the championship by four strokes over runner-up Dudley Wysong. He, however, gains even more recognition in golf history for being the first player in PGA Tour history to break 60, shooting a 59 in the second round of Danny Thomas Memphis Classic in 1977.

1966 – "Champagne" Tony Lema, the winner of the Open Championship in 1964 at St. Andrews and the winner of 11 other PGA Tour titles, is tragically killed in a light aircraft accident following the 1966 PGA Championship at Firestone Country Club in Akron, Ohio. He and his wife are en route to an exhibition when his plane runs out of fuel and crashes in a water hazard close to the seventh green of the Lansing Country Club in Illinois, less than a mile from their destination airport. All four people on board the plane are killed.

1956 – Masters champion Jack Burke, Jr. wins his second major championship of the year, beating Ted Kroll 3&2 in the match-play final at the PGA Championship at the Blue Hill Country Club in Canton, Mass.

1960 – Three years after his younger brother Lionel Hebert wins the PGA Championship, Jay Hebert joins him as a PGA Champion, winning the title at the Firestone Country Club in Akron, Ohio, one stroke ahead of runner-up Jim Ferrier.

July 25

2009 – Mark Calcavecchia birdies nine straight holes in the second round of the Canadian Open at Glen Abbey to break the PGA Tour record. Calcavecchia breaks the record set by Bob Goalby in his 1961 St. Petersburg Open victory and matched by Fuzzy Zoeller (1976 Quad Cities Open), Dewey Arnette (1987 Buick Open), Edward Fryatt (2000 Doral-Ryder Open), J.P. Hayes (2002 Bob Hope Classic) and Jerry Kelly (2003 Las Vegas Invitational). Calcavecchia shoots a seven-under 65, with his nine birdies all being within 15 feet. Says Calcavecchia after his feat, "Records are made to be broken. Could somebody make 10 in a row? Sure…It wouldn't surprise me if some guy whips out 10 birdies in a row sometime this weekend. Really wouldn't. These guys are good."

1976 – One month removed from his dramatic break-through win at the U.S. Open, twenty-two-year rookie Jerry Pate wins his second PGA Tour title by firing a final-round 63 to beat runner-up Jack Nicklaus by four shots and win the Canadian Open at the Essex Golf & Country Club in Windsor, Ontario.

July 26

2013 – Russell Knox shoots a 59 in the second round of the Web. com Tour's Albertson's Boise Open at the par-71, 6,698-yard Hillcrest Country Club in Idaho. After playing the first five holes at one under par, Knox plays the next 11 holes at 11 under par to become the fifth player to shoot 59 in Web.com history. Knox also becomes the second player in three weeks to break 60 after Will Wilcox shots 59 at the Utah Championships. Others to shoot 59 on the Web.com are Jason Gore in 2005 and Doug Dunakey and Notah Begay III in 1998.

1955 – Doug Ford posts a 4&3 win over Cary Middlecoff in the match-play final of the PGA Championship at the Meadowbrook Country Club in Northville Township, Mich., northwest of Detroit. The victory is the first of two major titles for Ford, who also wins the Masters in 1957.

1998 – Eight years after becoming the oldest man to win the U.S. Open at the age 45, Hale Irwin wins the U.S. Senior Open at the Riviera Country Club in Los Angeles for the first of two times. Irwin also goes on to win the U.S. Senior Open in 2000 after winning three U.S. Opens on the PGA Tour in 1974, 1979 and 1990.

2015 – Jason Day birdies the final three holes to win the Canadian Open at Glen Abbey, including a 20-foot birdie putt on the par-5 18th to post a four-under 68 to beat runner-up Bubba Watson by one stroke. David O'Hearn, the third-round leader attempting to become the first Canadian to win the Canadian Open since 1954, finishes in third place, two strokes back.

July 27

1975 – Tom Weiskopf wins the Canadian Open for a second time, beating Jack Nicklaus in the first hole of a sudden-death playoff at the Royal Montreal Golf Club. Nicklaus leads by one shot on the final hole but hooks his three-wood off the tee into the water and makes bogey to fall into the playoff. Weiskopf makes a three-foot birdie putt on the first playoff hole after Nicklaus misses his birdie from six feet. Weiskopf says the win helps ease the pain he feels after losing the Masters to Nicklaus by one shot in dramatic fashion earlier in the year. "I thought I would get over that disappointment in maybe a couple of weeks but I really didn't – that's the reason I haven't played a lot since then," says Weiskopf of the Masters discontent. "My desire and concentration was not the same as it was working up to Augusta. I was very disappointed – as disappointed as I've ever been but this kind of takes care of that, especially since I beat Jack."

2003 – Tom Watson wins the Senior British Open for the first time beating Carl Mason with a par on the second hole of a sudden death playoff at Turnberry. Watson shoots a final-round 64 while Mason makes a double bogey on the final hole to drop into the playoff. Watson famously wins five Open Championships in his career, his most famous victory coming at Turnberry in 1977 in his "Duel in the Sun" with Jack Nicklaus.

2013 – Hunter Mahan, leading the RBC Canadian Open at Glen Abbey by two shots over John Merrick entering the third round, withdraws from the tournament suddenly when on the range when he receives word that his wife Kandi has gone into labor with their first child. Brandt Snedeker takes advantage, shooting 63 and 70 on the weekend to claim a two-shot win for his sixth career PGA Tour title.

1954 – Chick Harbert claims a 4&3 match-play final win over defending champion Walter Burkemo to win the PGA Championship at the Keller Golf Club in St. Paul, Minn.

2014 – Bernard Langer wins the Senior British Open by a record 13 shots at Royal Porthcawl, the largest margin of victory ever on the senior tour. Langer shoots a final-round 67 to post an 18-under-par score of 266. Colin Montgomerie finishes in second place after finishing with a two-under-par final-round 69. Langer's margin over victory beats Hale Irwin's 12¬stroke win in the Senior PGA Championship in 1997 and almost doubles Bob Charles' Senior British record of seven strokes set at Turnberry in 1989.

July 28

1985 – On his 37th hole of play of the day, 6-foot-7, 260 pound, Phil Blackmar, the largest player on the PGA Tour, sinks a 10-foot putt on the first hole of sudden death playoff with Jodie Mudd and Dan Pohl and wins the Greater Hartford Open in Connecticut, his first career PGA Tour victory. The 36-hole final day was necessitated by rain during Friday's second round. Due to a PGA rule that forbids playing more than 27 holes on the day of a 36-hole cut, the final two rounds of the tournament had to be played on the final Sunday.

2013 – Brandt Snedeker wins the RBC Canadian Open, his sixth PGA Tour title, shooting a final-round two-under-par 70 for a three-shot win over runners-up Dustin Johnson, Matt Kuchur, Jason Bohn and William McGirt. Snedeker benefits from shooting a nine-under-par 63 the previous day, and the withdrawal of second round leader Hunter Mahan, who flies home to be with his wife Kandi during the birth of their first child, Zoe, born in the morning. "Zoe will be getting a very nice baby gift from me," says Snedeker. "I can't thank Kandi enough for going into labor early. I don't know if I'd be sitting here if she hadn't, but that is way more important thing than a golf tournament. I missed a golf tournament when my first was born and it was the best decision I ever made. I'm sure Hunter would say the same thing."

1991 – Jack Nicklaus wins his first PGA Seniors' Championship wire to wire beating runner-up Bruce Crampton by six shots at the PGA National Golf Club Champion Course. The runner-up showing for Crampton marks the fifth time he finishes second in a major championship – on the regular tour and the senior tour – losing on all occasions to Nicklaus. Crampton is also the bridesmaid to Nicklaus at the 1972 Masters and U.S. Open and the 1973 and 1975 PGA Championship.

2006 – Forty-six-year-old Corey Pavin sets a PGA Tour's scoring record for nine holes in the first round of the U.S. Bank Championship in Milwaukee by shooting a 26 on the front nine at the par 70 Brown Deer Park golf course. Pavin, who finishes with a 61, breaks the previous record of 27 set by Mike Souchak at the 1955 Texas Open and equaled by Andy North at the 1975 B.C. Open, Billy Mayfair at the 2001 Buick Open and Roberts Gamez at the 2004 Bob Hope Chrysler Classic. Says Pavin of his record score "It seemed like it was a misprint up there maybe. It was just one of those nine holes, once in a lifetime for me so far, anyway." Pavin goes on to shoot 64, 68 and 67 the next three days to win the tournament by two shots over Jerry Kelly for his 15th and final PGA Tour title.

July 29

1984 – Peter Jacobsen wins the Greater Hartford Open at the new TPC of Connecticut by two shots at over Mark O'Meara. The title is Jacobsen's third PGA Tour title, earning $72,000. "I imitated my favorite golfer today….that as me winning," quips Jacobsen. Jacobsen wins the event again on July 27, 2003 at age 49 for his seventh and final PGA Tour victory.

2007 – A hole-in-one at the 209-yard fourth hole at Angus Glen in Markham, Ontario helps Jim Furyk successfully defend his title at the Canadian Open. The fourth hole proves pivotal in Furyk's one-shot victory over runner-up Vijay Singh, playing the hole at five-under-par for the week, while Singh goes three-over-par on the hole for the week. "Eight strokes, that's a huge turn-around on one hole," Furyk says. "It's pretty special to play the hole five under on the week. You usually do that on a par 5 and rarely or never see that on a par 3. A pretty darn good hole, too. It's not like a wedge or a nine-iron shot."

2013 – Resuming a sudden-death playoff postponed after two holes the previous night due to darkness, Mark Wiebe beats Bernhard Langer to win the British Senior Open at Royal Birkdale on the fifth hole of the playoff with a par. Langer leads by two shots on the final hole of the storm-delayed final round, but makes double-bogey to fall into the playoff. Langer has a chance to win the title on the 8 am resumption of play on Monday morning with a 12-foot birdie, but fails to convert and makes bogey on the fifth playoff hole to lose the title. "Obviously not what I wanted, but the major mistake was again yesterday, the 72nd hole,'' Langer, a two-time Masters champion, says of the loss. ''In the playoff anybody can win. It comes down to one good shot or one bad shot. And that's what happened. Mark is a very deserving champion.''

July 30

1978 – Rod Funseth, the golfer known for his self-deprecating approach to golf, wins his third and final PGA Tour event at the Sammy Davis Jr. Greater Hartford Open in Connecticut at age 45. Funseth shoots a final round 64 to beat runners-up Dale Douglass, Lee Elder and Billy Kratzert by six shots. Funseth says following the win that he will use the $42,000 first prize to pay for a newly-constructed horse barn at his house in Napa, Calif. Earlier in the year, Funseth finishes one shot back of

Gary Player at the Masters, his best career showing at a major championship.

2015 – Rickie Fowler finishes his first round at the Quicken Loans National with a hole-in-one at the par-3 ninth hole at Robert Trent Jones Golf Club in Gainesville, Va. Fowler then promptly treats the attending media to beers, sending a bucket of beverages to the media room following the round. Fowler, who uses a seven-iron on the 200-yard downhill hole, goes on to finish second in the event, three shots behind first-time PGA Tour winner Troy Merritt.

July 31

1961 – Forty-five-year old Jerry Barber wins his only major title beating Don January by one shot in an 18-hole Monday playoff at the PGA Championship at Olympia Fields Country Club outside of Chicago. Both players are tied on the 18th hole in the playoff, but January is unable to get up-and-down from a greenside bunker and makes bogey for a 68. Meanwhile, Barber two-putts from 18 feet for a 67 and the victory. At the time, Barber was the oldest winner of the PGA Championship (eclipsed by forty-eight-year-old Julius Boros in 1968), with only Old Tom Morris winning a major at an older age at the 1867 Open Championship at the age of 46.

1988 – Two weeks after winning the Open Championship for a third time, Seve Ballesteros wins his 37th title on the European Tour at the Scandinavian Enterprise Open in Stockholm by five shots over runner-up Gerry Taylor. After the win, Ballesteros announces he will donate his irons to a charity. "I will not be disposing of my driver, three wood, sand wedge, wedge and putter – the ladder which I have used for 15 years but the grooves on the irons are getting a bit worn but hopefully they can raise some money for people in need."

AUGUST

August 1

2010 – Stuart Appleby becomes the fifth player to shoot a 59 on the PGA Tour, making birdie on the final three holes in the final round of the Greenbrier Classic in West Virginia to claim a one-shot victory. Appleby's score-card on the 7,020-yard par 70 Old White course at The Greenbrier resort features nine birdies and one eagle. Appleby's round comes less than a month after Paul Goydos shoots a 59 at the John Deere Classic. Appleby joins the PGA Tour's "59" club that at the time also features Goydos, Al Geiberger at the 1977 Memphis Classic, Chip Beck at the 1991 Las Vegas Invitational and David Duval at the 1999 Bob Hope Classic. Appleby is the first to shoot the score on a par 70 course.

2014 – Brady Schnell holes out with a 52-degree gap wedge from 122 yards away for eagle on his final hole to shot a 59 at the ATB Financial Classic at the Sirocco Golf Club in Calgary, Canada on the PGA Tour Canada. Schell's 13-under par round is only the second sub-60 round in the history of the Canadian Tour, but is one shot shy of the tour record of 58 set by Jason Bohn on a par 71 course at the 2001 Bayer Championship.

1999 – Brent Geiberger, the son of Al Geiberger, wins his first PGA Tour event with a three-stroke victory over Skip Kendall at the Greater Hartford Open in Connecticut. Says Brent of his father, the first player to break 60 in a PGA tournament, and his famous achievement, "I shoot 59 every time I go out and play, but I always have at least a couple of holes to play."

Al Geiberger shoots a 59 en route to winning the Memphis Classic in 1977.

August 2

1959 – Bob Rosburg shoots a final-round four-under 66 and comes from six shots back to win his only major championship at the PGA Championship at the Minneapolis Golf Club in Minnesota. Rosburg finishes one stroke ahead of runners-up Jerry Barber and Doug Sanders.

1912 – Twenty-year-old John McDermott successfully defends his U.S. Open title with a two-stroke victory over Tom McNamara at the Country Club of Buffalo in Williamsville, N.Y. McDermott trails Mike Brady by three shots entering the final round but McDermott shoots a final-round 71, while Brady struggles to a 79. The tournament features a par-6 hole – the 10th hole that measures 606 yards – the only time that a hole is given a par more than five.

2015 – Inbee Park wins the Women's British Open at Turnberry – her fourth different major championship in women's golf – coming from three shots behind to beat fellow South Korean Jin-Young Ko by three-shots. Park becomes the seventh female player to win four different majors, joining Louise Suggs, Mickey Wright, Pat Bradley, Juli Inkster, Karrie Webb and Annika Sorenstam. The LPGA calls Park's achievement a career Grand Slam, although her win at the Evian Championship, the fifth LPGA major, was in 2012, one year before the event is designated as major championship. "This is something I have been dreaming of all my life and all my career," Park says following her win. "To finally reach my goal is just a relief...I don't know what else to go for."

2013 – Tiger Woods flirts with shooting 59, going nine-under par through 13 holes, but settles for a 61 in the second round of the Bridgestone Invitational at the par 70 Firestone Country Club in Akron, Ohio. The score equals his lowest round of his PGA Tour career, a score he shoots four other times, including at Firestone in 2000. "I could have done it," Woods tells Golf Channel of potentially breaking 60. "I felt pretty relaxed, if I hadn't ever shot 59 before it would have been a different story. It wasn't out of the realm of being uncomfortable."

August 3

1979 – Sam Snead sets the record as the oldest player to make the cut in a major championship when at 67 years, two months, and seven days he makes the cut at the PGA Championship at Oakland Hills in Michigan. Snead, a three-time PGA Championship winner, ends up finishing 42nd with an eight-over score of 288.

2008 – Twenty-year-old Jiyai Shin of South Korea wins her first major championship – and her first LPGA Tour title – at the Ricoh Women's British Open at Sunningdale Golf Club with a three-shot win over runner-up Yani Tseng of Taiwan.

2014 – Two weeks after winning the Open Championship at Royal Liverpool, Rory McIlroy wins in consecutive events with a two-shot win at the Bridgestone Invitational in Akron, Ohio, returning him to the world No. 1 ranking. McIlroy trails third-round leader Sergio Garcia by three shots to start the day, but shoots a four-under 66 to Garcia's 71. "It feels like a long time since I lost that No. 1 spot, but it feels good to be back on top," McIlroy says. "Hopefully, I can keep it for a while."

August 4

2013 – Tiger Woods wins the Bridgestone Invitational by seven shots to claim a record-extending eighth title at the Firestone

Country Club in Akron, Ohio. The win is his 79th PGA Tour title – three shy of Sam Snead's record of 82 – and is his 20th in the week before a major championship. With the win, Woods collects five or more PGA Tour titles in a year a record-extending 10 times. Earlier in the year, he wins the Arnold Palmer Invitational also for an eighth time to tie the mark for the most victories in a single PGA Tour event set by Snead at the Greater Greensboro Open in 1965.

2013 – Stacy Lewis birdies the final two holes at the Old Course at St. Andrews and wins the Women's British Open by two shots for her second major championship on the LPGA Tour. Lewis shoots a final-round 72 to end a record streak of 10 straight majors won by Asian players. "It's unbelievable," Lewis says of her win. "It all happened so fast at the end. You're afraid for every shot, and all of a sudden you make a couple of birdies and it's over."

1985 – Amateur Scott Verplank defeats Jim Thorpe in a playoff to win the Western Open at Butler National Golf Club in Oak Brook, Ill. Verplank becomes the first amateur to win a PGA Tour event since Doug Sanders at the 1956 Canadian Open.

1958 – Ken Venturi wins his fourth tournament of the year at the Gleneagles Chicago Open Invitational, shooting a final-round 72 to beat runners-up Julius Boros and Jack Burke, Jr. by one stroke. Venturi's most prolific season of professional golf also includes wins at the Thunderbird Invitational, the Phoenix Open and the Baton Rouge Open. Six years later, he wins his first and only major at the U.S. Open at Congressional Country Club in Maryland.

August 5

1979 – David Graham wins the PGA Championship for his first major title in the third-hole of a sudden-death playoff with Ben Crenshaw at Oakland Hills in Birmingham, Mich. Graham double-bogeys the final hole to drop into the playoff with Crenshaw and drains a 25-foot putt for par on the first playoff hole and a ten-foot putt for birdie on the second playoff hole to stay alive. Crenshaw then misses a 25-foot par putt on the third playoff hole to finish second at a major championship for the fifth time in his career and for the fourth consecutive tournament, including his second consecutive major. "I guess I probably didn't deserve to be in the playoff," says Crenshaw after the loss. "I didn't expect to be. I thought I had him on the first and second playoff holes, but I came up short again. I don't like second worth a damn."

1982 – Ray Floyd shoots an opening round 63, equaling the lowest round ever at a major championship at the time, and takes the first-round lead at the PGA Championship at Southern Hills in Tulsa, Okla. Floyd misses only three fairways and two greens and shoots 33-30 on the par 70 set-up in 102 degree temperatures. "It's the best round of golf I've ever played," Floyd admits.

1990 – Tom Kite becomes the first player to win $6 million in career earnings on the PGA Tour when he sinks a 15-foot birdie putt on the first playoff hole to defeat John Cook and win the St. Jude Memphis Classic. Kite wins the first prize of $180,000 that pushes his career earnings to $6,144,890.

2012 – Down six shots to Jim Furyk with 13 holes to play, Keegan Bradley wins the Bridgestone Invitational at Firestone Country Club in Akron, Ohio benefitting from Furyk's double bogey on the final hole. "I don't think I've let one slip nearly as bad as this one," Furyk says. "This was my worst effort to finish off an event. I'm just disappointed. The thing I love about golf and this sport is that I have no one else to blame but myself."

2007 – Tiger Woods birdies four of the first six holes and shoots a five-under 65 in rainy conditions and wins the Bridgestone

Invitational in Akron, Ohio by eight strokes. Woods actually trails third-round leader Rory Sabbatini by one shot at the start of the day, but Sabbatini shoots a final-round 74. The win is the fourth for Woods on the season and his sixth in eight years at Firestone Country Club.

August 6

1978 – John Mahaffey sinks a 12-foot birdie putt on the second hole of a sudden-death playoff with Tom Watson and Jerry Pate to win the PGA Championship at Oakmont Country Club in Pennsylvania. The win is Mahaffey's only major championship and exorcises ghosts of him losing an 18-hole playoff with Lou Graham at the 1975 U.S. Open and being the 54-hole leader at the 1976 U.S. Open, won by Pate. The tournament is Watson's best opportunity to win the PGA, the only major he does not win in his career. He leads the tournament after each day and holds a five-shot lead entering the final round. However, he shoots a final-round 73 against Mahaffey's final-round 66. Pate actually has a four-foot par putt on the final hole to win the tournament, but the putt lips out.

1972 – Gary Player hits perhaps the signature shot of his career en route to winning the PGA Championship at Oakland Hills in Michigan. Having lost his lead to Jim Jamieson with three holes to play, Player hits a nine-iron blind approach shot over water and trees on the 16th hole to within four feet, which he makes for birdie. He goes on to win by two strokes over runners-up Jamieson and Tommy Aaron. The win is the sixth of Player's nine major titles. Sam Snead, age 60, finishes in fourth place and says of his finish "I guess I am just too dumb to quit."

2017 – Hideki Matsuyama of Japan fires a course-record tying 61 to win the Bridgestone Invitational by five shots over Zach Johnson at the Firestone Country Club in Akron, Ohio.

August 7

2016 – Jim Furyk shoots a 58, the lowest-ever round in PGA Tour history, in the final-round of the Travelers Championship at the TPC of River Highlands in Connecticut. Furyk makes 10 birdies, one eagle, hits every green in regulation and putts only 24 times in the historic round. Furyk, who makes the tournament cut on the number two days earlier, actually misses a birdie putt on the final hole for a 57. The 46-year old becomes the first player to ever shoot two rounds under 60 after having shot a 59 in the third round of the BMW Championship in 2013, becoming one of six players at the time to shoot 59 on the PGA Tour. The round allows Furyk to move up 65 places on the final day to finish in fifth place, three shots behind event winner Russell Knox.

1983 – Hal Sutton holds off Jack Nicklaus by one shot and wins the PGA Championship at Riviera Country Club in Los Angeles. Sutton leads by five shots during the final round but bogeys three holes in a row, while Nicklaus makes a final-day charge, carding a final-round 66 to Sutton's even par round of 71. Sutton settles down and pars the final four holes for the narrow win, his first and only major tournament title. "It was my thinking, not my game, that fell apart," Sutton says of his near collapse. "I went from aggressive to conservative, and I was hitting too easy. It was not intentional. If I could answer why I changed my thinking, I'd be sure not to do it again. I think I let up a bit." Nicklaus finishes second a major tournament for the 18th and final time in his career. "The opportunity to have a chance to win, that's really what this game is all about," says Nicklaus, a five-time PGA champion. "It's a game. Keep it a game."

1960 – Arnold Palmer wins the Insurance City Open in Hartford, Conn., beating Jack Fleck and Bill Collins in a playoff. Palmer shoots a final-round five under par 66 to rally from five shots back at the start of the day. Collins is eliminated in the first hole, carding a par to Fleck and Palmer's birdies, and after the remaining two par the second hole, Fleck misses a four-footer for par on the third extra playoff hole, giving Palmer the title.

1977 – Billy Kratzert beats Larry Nelson and Grier Jones by three shots to win the Sammy Davis Jr. Greater Hartford Open in Connecticut. Two years earlier, Kratzert had quit golf and gone to work as a forklift operator.

2006 – Tiger Woods beats Jim Furyk by three strokes to win the Buick Open in Grand Blanc, Mich., becoming the youngest player to win 50 tournaments on the PGA Tour. "As far as enjoying this type of golf tournament, no, it's not my favorite," says the Buick-sponsored Woods after posting his fourth consecutive round of six-under-par 66 at the Warwick Hills Golf Club. "If you look at my tournament schedule, I usually don't play events that are like this. I enjoy playing where single digits is a good winning score; if you shoot 70 or 69, that will shoot you up the board. Here, you'll get run over with spike marks all over your back."

2011 – Steve Williams, the ex-caddie of Tiger Woods, is thrust into the spotlight when he caddies for Adam Scott in his win at the Bridgestone Invitational calling it "the best win of my life." Fired by Woods a month earlier, Williams is greeted by chants of "Ste-vie Will-iams" as Scott walks up the 18th fairway en route to four-shot win over runner-up Luke Donald, the world's No. 1 ranked golfer, and Rickie Fowler. Williams also conducts interviews after Scott's win and says to CBS television, "I've caddied for 33 years – 145 wins now – and that's the best win I've ever had." Scott shoots a final-round 65 at the Firestone Country Club in Akron, Ohio.

August 8

1982 – Ray Floyd finishes a wire-to-wire win at the PGA Championship, his third major victory, at Southern Hills

Country Club in Tulsa, Okla. After opening with a major championship-record-tying low score of 63, Floyd shoots a final-round 72 and hangs on to win by three-shots over runner-up Lanny Wadkins. ''The trick when you get an early lead in a tournament is to avoid playing safe," Floyd says after his win. "Somebody else turns hot, you try to shift gears – and the gears are stuck. I think I'm a good player from in front because I don't just try to make pars and protect my lead. If I'm hot, I keep trying to make birdies. If I had putted well at all, I would have put the tournament away Saturday. I only made one long putt all week."

1976 – Eighteen-year-old Seve Ballesteros wins his first pro title at the Dutch Open, winning by eight shots over runner-up Howard Clark of England. Ballesteros goes on to win 50 titles on the European Tour and another nine titles on the PGA Tour.

1991 – A spectator is killed by lightning walking to his car during a weather delay in the first round of the PGA Championship at Crooked Stick, Ind., the second lightning death to occur at a major championship in 1991. At the U.S. Open at Hazeltine in Minnesota two months earlier, lightning strikes six fans standing under a tree, killing one.

August 9

1981 – Larry Nelson wins the PGA Championship with a four-stroke victory over Fuzzy Zoeller at the Atlanta Athletic Club in Duluth, Ga. Both Nelson and Zoeller shoot final-rounds of 71, Zoeller not able to muster a charge to challenge Nelson, who is steady and consistent for the entire final round. "I hit more good tee shots than I have in two and a half years," says Nelson. "I hit it where I wanted to on every hole but the 14th." Says Zoeller of Nelson and his consistency, "When you see a player hitting fairways like Larry does, it's pretty to watch."

1987 – Larry Nelson wins his second PGA Championship title – and his third career major title – when Lanny Wadkins misses a six-foot par putt on the first playoff hole at the Champions Course at PGA National in Palm Beach Gardens, Fla. Nelson sinks a seven-foot par putt before the miss from Wadkins that clinches his victory. "That was one of the greatest putts of my career, that last little one," says Nelson. Mark McCumber and D.A. Weibring enter the final round as co-leaders and Seve Ballesteros, Scott Hoch, Bobby Wadkins and Raymond Floyd also contend in the final round but fade in the windy conditions and the 97-degree temperatures. Writes Tom Boswell from the *Washington Post*, "Nelson, who also won the 1981 PGA, captured this title just as he has won his others-with straight driving, marvelous iron play, an utterly imperturbable temperament and a hunt-and-peck putting game."

2013 – Jason Dufner leaves a 12-foot birdie putt on the 18th hole inches short of breaking the record for lowest round ever at a major championship, settling for a 63 at the Oak Hill Country Club in the second round of the PGA Championship. Dufner's round ties him with 23 other players for the lowest round ever shot at a major championship at the time, but breaks the Oak Hill course record of 64 set by Ben Hogan in 1942, Curtis Strange in 1989 and Webb Simpson, from earlier in the day. "I obviously had a fantastic day today in a major championship, chased a little bit of history," says Dufner. "Came up a little short on that last putt, but all in all I'm excited. The position I'm in, the golf course has obviously yielded some low scores, and I'm looking forward to continuing good play here on the weekend. … It's tough when you're chasing history. You will be the first one to do something. I don't think I've been the first to do anything in my life. So it was a little nerve-racking for a Friday. It's usually the pressure you might fell towards the end of the tournament. But I got through it." Dufner goes on to win the title two days later, his first major championship, beating Jim Furyk by two shots and redeeming himself from blowing a five-shot lead with four holes to play at the PGA two years earlier.

2009 – Tiger Woods wins his 70th PGA Tour title with his seventh victory at the Firestone Country Club at the Bridgestone Invitational – the first time a player wins that many times at a single PGA Tour venue. Woods wins by four strokes over runners-up Padraig Harrington and Robert Allenby. The title is mostly decided on the par-5 16th hole when Woods hits an eight-iron to within a foot of the pin, while Harrington hits his fourth shot, a greenside chip, into the water and settles for an 8.

1953 – Lew Worsham, the 1947 U.S. Open champion, holes a wedge shot for an eagle 2 from 135 yards on the 410 yard final hole to win the Tarn O'Shanter World Championship of Golf by one shot over Chandler Harper. The event is the first tournament that is televised nationally in the United States. The tournament also features the first ever $100,000 purse, of which Worsham wins $25,000, the biggest prize in golf at the time.

August 10

1980 – Jack Nicklaus wins his record tying fifth PGA Championship and his 17th major championship with a seven-shot victory over Andy Bean at Oak Hill Country Club in Rochester, N.Y. The win for the 40-year-old Nicklaus gives him the distinction of being the third player to win the U.S. Open and the PGA in the same year, joining Gene Sarazen in 1922 and Ben Hogan in 1948 and, later, Tiger Woods in 2000. The seven stroke win is also the largest ever at the PGA, not broken until 2012 when Rory McIlroy wins by eight strokes. Nicklaus leads by three shots over Lon Hinkle entering the final round and shoots a 69 and is not challenged. Says Nicklaus, "Nobody made a run at me today so it was not an exciting day but it was exciting enough for me."

2008 – Padraig Harrington wins his second consecutive major championship at the PGA Championship beating Sergio Garcia and Ben Curtis by two strokes at Oakland Hills in Michigan.

Just three weeks after winning his second Open Championship title, Harrington shoots a final-round 66, capped with a 18-foot par putt on the final hole to clinch victory. Garcia leads for most of the day, not making a bogey in the final round until the 16th hole. "I don't know how other people are going to feel; I know I love the idea of the back nine of a major on a Sunday," says Harrington. "I love it so much that I'm actually disappointed I'm seven months away from the next major, and I don't know what I'm going to do." Harrington, the winner in three of the last six majors, becomes the first European to win the PGA since Tommy Armour in 1930 and becomes the first European to win the British Open and the PGA in the same year, and the first European ever to win two consecutive majors.

1975 – Jack Nicklaus wins his fourth PGA Championship – and the fourteenth of his 18 major titles – beating runner-up Bruce Crampton by two-shots at the Firestone Country Club in Akron, Ohio. "I think I'm probably playing my best golf," says Nicklaus, who won his fifth Masters title earlier in the year. "And there's no reason to think my game shouldn't improve. This was probably my best of the year."

2014 – Rory McIlroy wins the PGA Championship at Valhalla Golf Club in Louisville, Ky., putting out on the final hole in near darkness to beat runner-up Phil Mickelson by one shot. Leading by two shots on the final tee in the near dark, McIlroy is given permission to have he and playing partner Bernd Weisberger play into Mickelson's penultimate twosome with Rickie Fowler to help him finish the two-hour rain-delayed final round before dark. Mickelson birdies the hole, while McIlroy makes par to hold on for the title. Writes Christine Brennan in *USA Today*, "Darkness had enveloped Valhalla Golf Club. A soft rain was falling. A bolt of lightning flashed over the clubhouse. The most dramatic men's major championship of the year was finishing under the most bizarre circumstances one could imagine: with a mad dash to the finish. Rory McIlroy beat the field by one stroke – and total darkness by a couple of minutes – as he won his second major title in three weeks, with help from a fine act of kindness from the two men who were his closest pursuers: Phil Mickelson and Rickie Fowler." It is the second consecutive major title for McIlroy and his fourth overall. McIlroy, 25, joins Tom Morris, Jr., Willie Anderson, Bobby Jones, Jack Nicklaus and Tiger Woods as the only golfers with four majors at age 25 or younger.

2007 – Tiger Woods lips out on a 15-foot birdie attempt to shoot a 62 in the second round of the PGA Championship at Southern Hills in Tulsa, Okla., which would have been the lowest round ever shot at a major championship at the time. Woods taps in for the 23rd round of 63 in major championship play, giving him a two-shot lead in the tournament after 36 holes. Says Woods, "I knew if I made that putt on the last hole it would have been a nice little record to have. A 62 1/2 is all right."

August 11

1986 – Bob Tway holes a 25-foot bunker shot for birdie on the final hole to stun Greg Norman and win the PGA Championship at the Inverness Club in Toledo, Ohio. Norman, who leads the tournament for three rounds and the leader over Tway by four shots with eight holes remaining, ends up bogeying the final hole to give Tway his first and only major championship by a two-shot margin. "I was not trying to make the sand shot," Tway says. "I was just trying to get safely on the green for a one putt and a par. To make a shot like that at 18 is something. The odds against it I don't even know. I may never make one of them again in my career." Norman finishes his year being the 54-hole leader at all four majors, but only is able to win the Open Championship. He falls to Jack Nicklaus at the Masters and to Ray Floyd at the U.S. Open. Tway finishes with a one-under par 70, while Norman finishes with a final-round 76. The completion of the final-round was delayed until Monday due to heavy afternoon rain and 60 of the 73 golfers were forced to play on the extra day. Tway's birdie marks the first time that the PGA Championship was won with a birdie on the 72nd hole since the event moved to the stroke-play format in 1958.

1974 – Lee Trevino, using a putter he found earlier in the week in the attic of the house he was staying, three-putts only one time over four rounds (the 71st hole) and wins the first of his two PGA Championships with a one-stroke win over Jack Nicklaus at Tanglewood Park in Clemmons, N.C. Trevino shoots a final-round 69 to match the same score of Nicklaus. "When you are playing against a man who's playing his best, who's doing everything right, what can you do?" says Nicklaus. "He played a great round of golf. He seemed to be right down the middle on every fairway." Writes Dan Jenkins in *Sports Illustrated* of Trevino on the final nine holes of the event, "He outdrove Nicklaus when he had to, stuck his irons inside of Jack's when he had to, and he liked to say, as always, that it wasn't because he was playing Nicklaus 'personally' but because Jack stimulates him." Three-time PGA champion Sam Snead, at age 62, finishes in a tie for third for his third consecutive top ten finish in the event.

1985 – Hubert Green outlasts defending champion Lee Trevino and wins his second major title at the PGA Championship with two-shot victory at Cherry Hills Country Club in Denver, Colo. Leading Trevino by two shots and in a greenside bunker on the 72nd hole, Green blasts out to within inches of the cup to seal his victory. Green shoots a final round one-over-par 72 while Trevino bogeys two of the last four holes and three-putts four holes in the final round. Green, the 1977 U.S. Open champion, and Trevino, the defending PGA Champion, either exchange or tie for the lead seven times before Trevino falls back for good on the 15th hole. Green wins by finishing with eight straight pars. Writes Shav Glick in the *Los Angeles Times* of Green's second to last shot of the tournament, "With rain dripping off his head, Green bent over the ball and swung crisply through the sand. The ball popped up, hit the green and rolled straight to the flagstick. It didn't fall, but it stopped inches away and that ended Trevino's faint hope of winning."

1996 – Mark Brooks wins the PGA Championship with a birdie on the first hole of a sudden-death playoff with Kentucky-native Kenny Perry at the Valhalla Golf Club in Louisville, Ky. Perry shoots a final-round 68, but controversially sits with the CBS television commentators for 30 minutes watching the three players who have a chance to tie him rather than practice and stay warm for a potential playoff. Perry watches defending champion Steve Elkington miss a birdie putt on the final hole and Vijay Singh bogey the final hole to miss the playoff by one shot. However, Brooks gets up and down from the greenside bunker to force the playoff, as Perry scrambles from the TV tower directly to the 18th tee, without the benefit of another warm up. Perry subsequently hits his tee shot in the playoff into the rough and needs four more swings out before he is able to negotiate his ball onto the green. "I probably should have stuck to what I was doing and gone down to the range and get away from everybody," Perry says. "Just hit some balls and try to get ready for the playoff and get my mind set on that…I probably caught up in the moment with all the people. I learned a great lesson, but it's a hard one."

1991 – The ninth and final alternate just to make the field at the PGA Championship, unknown John Daly finishes up his shocking domination of the PGA Championship with a three-shot victory over runner-up Bruce Lietzke at Crooked Stick Golf Club in Carmel, Ind. Daly, who begins the final round a three-shot lead, three putts for double-bogey on the 17th hole, but pars the final hole to finish with a final-round 71. The night before the start of the tournament, Daly drives seven hours from Memphis to Indianapolis in the hope of gaining entry into the tournament. When Nick Price withdraws to be with his pregnant wife, Daly is given a spot in the field and, ironically, gains the services of Price's caddy. "All four days, I didn't think," Daly says after his win. "I just hit it. My caddie just said `Kill' and I killed it."

2011 – Steve Stricker fires an opening round 63 – equaling the lowest round ever shot at a major championship at the time – to take the lead in the opening round of the PGA Championship at the Atlanta Athletic Club. Stricker narrowly misses a 10-foot putt on the final hole that would have given him a record-breaking round of 62. "It never really registered," Stricker says of the potential history-making putt. "I was just trying to make a birdie and finish eight under, and I really was concentrating on the putt, but never thought about the history part of it."

August 12

1973 – Jack Nicklaus wins the third of his five PGA Championships with a four-stroke victory over Bruce Crampton at Canterbury Golf Club in Beachwood, Ohio, a suburb east of Cleveland. Media – and the golf industry – at the time acknowledge the win as the 14th major title for Nicklaus – also counting his two wins at the U.S. Amateur – surpassing the all-time record of majors won set by Bobby Jones with 13. "I grew up hearing of Jones and his Grand Slam and his 13 major victories and I decided I wanted to beat him," Nicklaus says after the win, also the 49th of his PGA Tour career. Writes the Associated Press of the hallmark Nicklaus win, "It was the realization of a childhood dream and the accomplishment of a lifetime goal for the 33-year-old blond, who as a chubby boy in Columbus, Ohio gazed often and long of a portrait of the immortal Jones hanging in the clubhouse at the Scioto Country Club." History would later establish that this was the 12th of his eventual 18 major titles for Nicklaus, not counting his Amateur titles. The Nicklaus win at the 1975 PGA would be his 14th major title.

2007 – Tiger Woods wins the PGA Championship for a second straight year for his 13th major title with a two-stroke victory over Woody Austin at Southern Hills Country Club in Tulsa, Okla. Playing in temperatures exceeding 100 degrees, Woods leads by as many as five strokes, however, after Austin birdies three straight holes and Woods bogeys the 14th hole, his lead is shaved down to one stroke. Woods then birdies the 15th hole and pars in to secure his fourth PGA Championship title. Woods says that winning a major with his wife Elin and their two-month baby daughter Sam Alexis in tow causes for special feelings. "It's a feeling I've never had before," Woods says. "Having Sam there and having Elin there, it feels a lot more special. And it used to be my mom and dad. And now Elin, and now we have our own daughter. So it's evolved, and this one feels so much more special than the other majors."

1990 – Wayne Grady wins the PGA Championship at Shoal Creek in Alabama by three shots over runner-up Fred Couples, shooting a final round of one-under par 71. Couples leads the tournament by one shot over Grady after a birdie on the 12th hole, but bogeys the next four holes while Grady pars in for the win. "There are some great players on this (PGA Championship) trophy," Grady says of winning his maiden major. "And no matter how hard you scratch that thing, you're not going to get my name off it."

2012 – Rory McIlroy wins his second major championship in torrid fashion crafting an eight-shot victory at the PGA Championship at Kiawah Island, S.C. The 23-year-old from Northern Ireland does not make a bogey on the final 23 holes on the final day of play to become the youngest player to win two majors since Seve Ballesteros. "I think I heard Tiger (Woods) say, 'You can have a good season, but to make a good season a great season, you need a major championship,'" says McIlroy, who won the U.S. Open the previous year by eight shots. "Now I've had two great seasons in a row no matter what happens from here in now. Hopefully, I can play some great golf from now until the end of the year and get myself ready for another great season next year, too." The eight-shot win is the largest margin of victory ever at the PGA Championship, breaking the record of Jack Nicklaus. McIlroy finishes his third round with two birdies for a 67 in the morning and fires a final-round 66 with no player getting within two shots of the lead. David Lynn, a 38-year-old from England playing in the United States for the first time, shoots a 68 and finishes second.

1994 – Sixty-four-year-old Arnold Palmer plays his final round at a PGA Championship at Southern Hills in Tulsa, Okla. Competing in the only major championship he failed to win, Palmer shoots a 74 and misses the cut, but finishes with a bang, holing a 20-foot putt on the last hole for par. Palmer's PGA swan song occurs two months after his final appearance at the U.S. Open at Oakmont Country Club in Pennsylvania. Palmer finishes second three times at the PGA, the last time in 1970 to Dave Stockton at Southern Hills. "It may be fitting that I ended it here," Palmer says after his round. "It is over. If I thought I had a game that could win the PGA Championship, I would be back to play, but this is an appropriate time to give it away."

August 13

1989 – Payne Stewart registers a one-shot victory over Mike Reid to win the PGA Championship at Kemper Lakes Golf Club in Hawthorn Woods, Ill., for his first major championship. Stewart birdies four of the last five holes, shooting a five-under-par 31 on the back nine while Reid finishes his last three holes bogey, double-bogey, par, missing a seven-foot birdie putt on the final hole that would have forced a playoff. Reid holds a four-shot lead after four holes and three-shot lead with three holes to play, but ends up tied for second with Curtis Strange and Andy Bean. "Sports is like life with the volume turned up," says an emotional Reid in his post-event press conference. "The friendships are a little tighter and the nights are a little longer like this one will be while I try to figure out what happened." Says Stewart, "I feel sorry for Mike Reid, but his misfortune is my gain."

1995 – Steve Elkington fires a final-round 64 and sinks a 20-foot birdie putt on the first hole of a sudden-death playoff with Colin Montgomerie and wins the PGA Championship at the Riviera Country Club in Los Angeles. Elkington starts the day six shots out of the lead of third-round leader Ernie Els, who shoots a final-round 72. "I played the round of my life today," says Elkington. "I didn't know what to expect with Ernie seeming so dominant the first three rounds." Elkington and Montgomerie, who shoots a final-round 65, both post a 72-hole total of 267, a 17-under-par total that breaks the previous PGA Championship record of 15-under 273, set by Lee Trevino at Shoal Creek in 1984. Brad Faxon shoots a front-nine 28, a PGA record, en route to final-round 63 to finish in fifth place, becoming only the 17th man in major championship history to shoot 63, four days after first-round leader Michael Bradley had done it Thursday.

1920 – Ted Ray of Britain wins the U.S. Open at the Inverness Club in Toledo, Ohio claiming a one-stroke victory over runners-up Harry Vardon, Jock Hutchison, Leo Diegel, and Jack Burke, Sr. At the age of 43 years and four months, Ray becomes the oldest U.S. Open champion – a distinction he holds until Ray Floyd, a few months older, wins the title in 1986. Hale Irwin then sets a new mark in 1990 at age 45.

1933 – Gene Sarazen wins the third of his three PGA Championship titles defeating Willie Goggin 5&4 in the title match at the Blue Mound Country Club in Wauwatosa, Wis.

August 14

1977 – Lanny Wadkins wins the first sudden-death playoff in a stroke-play major championship at the PGA Championship at Pebble Beach, beating Gene Littler with a par on the third extra hole. All majors prior to the 1977 PGA had been decided with 18-hole or 36-hole playoffs. Wadkins, six shots out of the lead at the start of the final round, shoots a final-round 70 that is capped with a birdie on the par 5 18th hole. Littler starts the day with a four-shot lead over Jack Nicklaus, but shoots a final-round 76 to drop into the playoff. Nicklaus ends up finishing one shot out of the playoff.

1988 – Virtually unnoticed by media and fans for most of the week, Jeff Sluman shoots a final-round six-under par 65 and wins the PGA Championship at Oak Tree Golf Club in Edmond, Okla. The 5-foot 7 inch, 30-year-old from Rochester, N.Y. begins the day three strokes out of the lead held by Paul Azinger but fires five birdies and an eagle against one bogey to beat Azinger by three shots. "I thought I had a good chance starting the day, really," Sluman says. "I just wanted to get it under par early and see what happened from there."

1994 – Nick Price becomes the first man since Tom Watson in 1982 to win back-to-back majors in a season when he wins the PGA Championship by six strokes at Southern Hills Country Club in Tulsa, Okla. Price, just a month earlier, wins the Open Championship at Turnberry, also becoming the first player since Walter Hagen in 1924 to win both the Open Championship and the PGA in the same year. Starting the day with a three shot lead, Price birdies the third and fourth holes to take a six-shot lead into the back nine, where he holds on to win by the same margin over runner-up Corey Pavin. Price finishes with a score of 11-under-par 269, the lowest winning score of any U.S. major championship at the time, breaking Bobby Nichols's PGA record of 271 set in 1964. "Everything fell into place for me today," says Price, who takes over the world No. 1 ranking with the victory. "I'm really proud of the way I played the first nine holes. I knew what I had to do and I went out and did it. I put my nose down and played the first four holes as well as I probably could. To be two under after four holes alleviated a lot of the pressure and the nerves I had."

2011 – Playing in his first ever major tournament, Keegan Bradley incredibly rallies from a five-shot deficit with three holes to play to win the PGA Championship in a three-hole aggregate playoff with Jason Dufner at the Atlanta Athletic Club in Duluth, Ga. The 25-year-old Bradley, ranked No. 108 in the world, makes a triple bogey on the 15th hole after chipping across the green and into the water, but birdies two of the final three holes while Dufner makes three straight bogeys. In the three-hole aggregate playoff, Bradley birdies the 16th hole and holds on to win the playoff by one shot after Dufner bogeys the 17th hole and birdies the 18th hole.

2015 – Hiroshi Iwata's 63 and John Daly's 10 are the highlights of triumph and disaster in the second round of the PGA Championship at Whistling Straits in Kohler, Wis. Iwata, from Japan, follows a first-round 77 by matching the lowest round ever at a major championship at the time with his 63 that includes a 29 on the back nine. Iwata's 63 marks the 27th time the score is shot in major championship golf. Daly, the 1991 PGA champion hits three balls in to the water on the par 3 221-yard seventh hole before punching a lay-up shot with a pitching wedge. Daly then hurls his club into Lake Michigan where the club is soon recovered by a young boy on a boat. Daly three-putts the green and scores a 10 on the hole. "Your body goes into a little shock after that," Daly says after finishing with a nine-over 81. "I know we all go through this; I seem to go through it more than anybody."

August 15

1993 – Paul Azinger wins his elusive major title at the PGA Championship at Inverness Country Club in Toledo, Ohio beating Greg Norman on the second hole of a sudden-death playoff. Norman's 18-foot birdie putt for the win on the final hole of regulation spins out of the hole – as does his birdie putt that would have given him the win on the same hole in the first hole of the playoff. On the second playoff hole – the 10th hole – Norman three-putts from 18-feet after Azinger taps in for par. Inverness is also the site of Norman's devastating loss at the 1986 PGA Championship when Bob Tway makes birdie from the greenside bunker on the 72nd hole to beat Norman by a stroke.

2005 – Phil Mickelson wins his second major title at the PGA Championship with a two-foot birdie putt on the final hole for a one-shot win over runners-up Steve Elkington and Thomas Bjorn at the Baltusrol Golf Club in Springfield, N.J. Mickelson is tied for the lead on the final hole of the weather-delayed Monday finished event and, after hitting his tee shot into the fairway on the 554-yard par-5 18th hole, taps for good luck a plaque in the center of the fairway commemorating the winning approach shot Jack Nicklaus made on the hole en route to winning the 1967 U.S. Open. Mickelson's approach shot lands in the rough in front of the green. Mickelson then calmly chips his ball to within two feet and taps in for the one-stroke victory. "It's an amazing feeling to be the winner and to be able to hold this trophy," the 35-year-old Mickelson says. "But it was a very stressful week. Having the lead after each night just added to the stress and the difficulty and the challenge of it, which is why I think it feels so good right now."

2004 – Vijay Singh wins his third major title in a three-hole aggregate playoff over Justin Leonard and Chris DiMarco at the PGA Championship at Whistling Straits in Kohler, Wis. Singh makes only one birdie on the day – on the first hole of the three-hole playoff – and pars the next two holes to win his second PGA title. In regulation, Singh shoots a four-over 76 – the highest winning score ever by a PGA champion – and takes 34 putts in regulation. He benefits from the collapse of Leonard, who holds a two-shot lead with five holes to play and misses four putts within 12 feet down the stretch, including a 12-foot par putt on the final hole that would have given him the title. DiMarco, who shoots a 71 – the only player in the last nine groups to break par on the day – also misses an 18-foot birdie putt on the final hole that would have given him the title. "It was sad to see someone win it the way I did," says Singh.

2010 – In one of the most bizarre finishes in major tournament history, Martin Kaymer wins the PGA Championship at Whistling Straits in Kohler, Wis., in an aggregate three-hole playoff with Bubba Watson, but not Dustin Johnson, who is given a two-stroke penalty for grounding a club in a bunker on the final hole, keeping him out of the playoff. Johnson hits his four-iron approach to the final hole from a sandy area behind the spectator ropes, but unknowingly illegally grounds his club behind the ball – not knowing that the area was designated as a bunker as one of over 1,000 sandy bunker-like patches scattered around the links-style Whistling Straits course. After Johnson makes a bogey on the final hole to drop from the lead into a tie with Kaymer and Watson, he is informed by a PGA official of his infraction – and two-stroke penalty – and that he should sign for a 7 on the final hole and not a 5, moving him out of the playoff and into a tie for fifth place. "It never crossed my mind that I was in a sand trap," Johnson says after his round, missing a seven-foot putt for par that he thought was to win the tournament. "It was very tough to see what is a bunker and what is not a bunker," says Kaymer, who wins the three-hole playoff with Watson by two shots with a tap-in bogey. "I think it's very sad he got two penalty strokes." Nick Watney, the third-round leader, shoots a final-round 81 to shoot the worst final-round score by a 54-hole leader since the PGA went to stroke play in 1958.

1999 – Tiger Woods weathers the storm put forth by "El Nino" – 19-year-old Sergio Garcia of Spain – and wins his second career major title at the PGA Championship at Medinah Country Club outside of Chicago. The one-shot win for the 23-year-old Woods over Garcia marks his 14th world-wide win in his almost three-year professional career. Woods shoots an even-par 72 in the final round giving him an 11-under-par score of 277, while Garcia shoots 71 for a 10-under-par 278. The shot of the day comes from Garcia on the 16th hole when he hits his approach shot from the base of a tree, swinging almost blindly at the ball, then sprinting and running down the fairway, leaping into the air like a hurdler to see where on the green the ball had incredibly landed.

1965 – Dave Marr wins his only major championship at the PGA Championship at Laurel Valley Golf Club in Ligonier, Pa., two strokes better than runners-up Billy Casper and Jack Nicklaus. Marr shoots a final-round 71, making birdie after a seven-iron approach shot to the final green from 140 yards out. Writes Al Abrams, sports editor of the *Pittsburgh Post-Gazette*, "The smile on Dave Marr's face as he walked the uphill path to the 18th green at Laurel Valley today was as bright as the blazing sun overhead."

August 16

2015 – Jason Day wins his first major title at the PGA Championship at Whistling Straits in Kohler, Wis., posting the lowest score in relation to par in the history of major championship golf – 20 under par. Day shoots a final-round 67 and wins by three shots over runner-up Jordan Spieth, the reigning Masters and U.S. Open champion. Spieth, as a consolation, takes over the No. 1 world golf ranking from Rory McIlroy.

1992 – Nick Price wins his first major championship at the PGA Championship at Bellerive Country Club in St. Louis, posting a three-shot win over John Cook, Nick Faldo, Gene Sauers and Jim Gallagher, Jr. Price wins the championship by virtue of two clutch putts – a 25-footer for birdie at the 16th hole and a 12-

foot par putt on the 17th hole. "I feel like I got a monkey off my back, a big one, a whole troop of them," says the 35-year-old Price, the runner-up at the British Open in 1982 and 1988. Price famously pulls out of the PGA the previous year to attend to his wife giving birth to their first child and his caddie, Jeff "Squeeky" Medlen, works for the ninth alternate John Daly, who wins the title.

2009 – Y.E. Yang becomes the first player from Asia to win a men's major and the first player to beat Tiger Woods after he has a 54-hole lead in a major, winning the PGA Championship by three shots over Woods at Hazeltine National in Chaska, Minn. Prior to Yang's triumph, Woods is 14 for 14 as a closer in major tournaments as the third round leader. Writes Teddy Greenstein of the *Los Angeles Times*, "Consider this: Yang started the day as a 20-1 underdog, according to an online sports wagering site. Woods was a 2-9 favorite, roughly the same as Secretariat in his prime against your pet cocker spaniel." Woods shoots a final-round 75 – three over par – while Yang shoots a 70, helped by a chip-in eagle from 80 feet away on the drivable par 301-yard 14th hole that gives the Korean the lead.

1998 – Vijay Singh wins his first of three major championships, holding off Steve Stricker by two shots to win the PGA Championship at Sahalee Country Club in Redmond, Wash. The 35-year-old Singh fires a final round 68 to finish on with nine-under par score of 271.

1970 – Dave Stockton wins the first of his two PGA Championships posting a one-under-par score of 279 to beat out runners-up Bob Murphy and Arnold Palmer by two shots at Southern Hills Country Club in Tulsa, Okla. The runner-up showing for the 40-year-old Palmer marks the third time he finishes second in his career at the PGA, the only major tournament he fails to win in his career. Stockton wins the PGA again in 1976.

1976 – Dave Stockton wins his second PGA Championship by one stroke over runners-up Raymond Floyd and Don January at the Congressional Country Club in Bethesda, Md. Stockton, who also won the PGA in 1970, makes a 15-foot putt to save par and win the title on the final hole in the weather-delayed Monday final round.

1969 – Ray Floyd wins his first major title at the PGA Championship at the South Course of NCR Country Club in Kettering, Ohio, hanging on for a one-shot win over runner-up Gary Player. Floyd leads by five shots entering the final round and shoots a final-round 74 on the par 71 layout.

2014 – Kevin Sutherland shoots the first 59 in the history of the PGA Champions Tour in the second round of the Dick's Sporting Goods Open in Endicott, N.Y. Sutherland, 50, has a chance at a 58, but makes his only bogey of the day on the 18th hole, missing a six-foot par putt. Says Sutherland of his bogey-capped round, "Who would have thought you'd bogey the last hole and still feel great?"

August 17

1997 – Davis Love, III emotionally wins his first and only major championship at the PGA Championship, winning by five-shots over runner-up Justin Leonard at Winged Foot Golf Club in Mamaroneck, N.Y. "I'm thrilled to death, what a shock," Love says. "To win this championship as the son of a PGA member…who would ever have thought it? It's a heck of a golf course, with great champions. It's the best I've ever felt on a golf course for four days under pressure. I hit a lot of great shots I'm really proud of, and I was as patient as I've ever been." Writes Leonard Shapiro of the *Washington Post*, "Only the pelting rain from a late afternoon thunderstorm could dampen Love's triumphant and emotional march down the 18th fairway today at the 79th PGA Championship at Winged Foot Golf Club. A rainbow framed his line of sight to the cup as he made one last 12-foot birdie putt at the 18th hole to complete a five-shot victory over his friend and playing partner, British Open winner Justin Leonard, who had begun the day tied with Love."

2003 – Shaun Micheel hits one of the most memorable shots in major tournament history to win the PGA Championship at Oak Hill Country Club in Rochester, N.Y. Micheel hits a seven-iron from 175 yards away that stops two inches from the 18th hole to clinch a two-shot win at the PGA and become one of the most unlikely major tournament winners in the history of golf. Micheel, ranked No. 169 in the world ranking and winless in 163 previous starts on the PGA Tour, shoots a final-round even-par 70 to beat runner-up Chad Campbell by two strokes. "I was trying to win the B.C. Open a year ago this time," says Micheel. "A month or two ago, I was trying to keep my card. To have my name on that trophy, I don't know what I'm thinking right now."

1984 – Forty-eight-year-old Gary Player shoots a 63 in the second round of the PGA Championship at Shoal Creek in Birmingham, Ala., equaling a major tournament record at the time. Player's score also ties the previous low for a PGA Championship round shot by Ray Floyd at Southern Hills in 1982 and Bruce Crampton at Firestone in 1975. ''I'm grateful to equal the PGA record of 63, particularly on a course like this,'' Player says. ''But as thrilling as it is, you can't get too excited because you have to go out there again tomorrow.''

2014 – Inbee Park defends her title in the LPGA Championship, beating Brittany Lincicome with a par on the first hole of a playoff at the Monroe Golf Club in Pittsford, N.Y. The win is the fifth major title for Park and the fourth in the last two seasons. Park wins the event the previous year also in a playoff at the Locust Hill golf club, beating Catriona Matthew.

1977 – Twenty-year-old Nick Faldo wins his first of 30 career European Tour titles at the Skol Lager Championships at Gleneagles in Scotland. Faldo wins the one-off 36-hole event with a birdie on the first hole of a sudden-death playoff with Craig Defoy of Wales and Chris Witcher of England.

1998 – In one of the most unusual circumstances in the history of the PGA Tour, Phil Mickelson wins the AT&T Pebble Beach National Pro-Am – six months after it is suspended due to rain – besting runner-up Tom Pernice by one shot in the shortened 54-hole event. After heavy rains washed out play on February 1 and 2, tournament officials decide to postpone the conclusion of the event until March 2, the day after the Los Angeles Open, instead of cancelling the event after 36 holes. However, when it became evident that the three courses that comprise of the tournament would not be ready, the decision is made to conclude the event the day after the PGA Championship in Redmond, Wash. Clifton Brown of *The New York Times* describes the tournament atmosphere as "bizarre" writing "players spread out over three courses, no grandstands, no television towers, a gallery not even one-fifth as large as usual." Mickelson shoots a five-under-par 67 at Pebble Beach to finish the tournament at 14 under par, one stroke better than Pernice, who shoots 67 at Poppy Hills. Says Mickelson of the win and the circumstances, "Finishing up a tournament six or seven months later, you have to find your own momentum," Mickelson says. "This should give me something to build on going into the later part of the season."

August 18

1922 – Twenty-year-old Gene Sarazen, the reigning U.S. Open champion, defeats Emmet French, 4&3 in the title match to win the PGA Championship at the Oakmont Country Club in Oakmont, Pa. The event is the first major championship hosted by the famed Pennsylvania golf course.

2002 – Rich Beem, a 31-year-old former car stereo salesman, becomes the upset winner of the PGA Championship at Hazeltine National Golf Club in Chaska, Minn., beating runner-up Tiger Woods by one shot. Beem, playing in only his fourth career major tournament, shoots a final-round four-under-par 68, making bogey on the final hole. Woods birdies the last four holes to nearly steal the victory with a final-round 67. "It's almost indescribable," Beem says of his win. "To win any tournament is unbelievable. I don't know when this is going to sink in. Right now, I am so flabbergasted about this you have no idea."

2000 – Jack Nicklaus plays his final career round at the PGA Championship at the Valhalla Country Club in Louisville, Ky. Paired with Tiger Woods for the first two rounds of the tournament, Nicklaus, a five-time PGA Championship winner, needs to make eagle on the 18th hole to make the cut and nearly holes out his wedge shot from the fairway. Nicklaus, however, makes his three-foot birdie putt to end his PGA Championship career.

2001 – David Toms scores one of the most memorable holes-in-one in major tournament history hitting a five-wood from 243 yards on the No. 15 hole at the Atlanta Athletic Club in Duluth, Ga., in the third round of the PGA Championship. Toms' ball bounces three times before falling into the hole that moves him into a one-shot lead. "I didn't know it was in until the people behind the green jumped up out of the stands," Toms says. "It was quite a sight." Toms shots a five-under par 65 to take a two-shot lead over Phil Mickelson.

1957 – Ken Venturi wins his first of 14 career PGA tournament tiltes at the St. Paul Open Invitational in St. Paul, Minn., shooting a final-round 68 to beat runner-up Bob Rosburg by two strokes. Venturi, who finished second at the Masters as a 24-year-old amateur in 1956 after leading for the first three rounds, wins his second pro title the following week at the Miller High Life Open in Milwaukee, Wis.

1974 – Dave Stockton wins the Greater Hartford Open by four shots over Ray Floyd, making only two bogeys over four rounds. Stockton wins $50,000 and donates $25,000 to the Hartford Jaycees, pledging $1,000 a year for the next 24 years.

August 19

2001 – David Toms wins the PGA Championship in bold fashion on the final hole of the championship at the Atlanta Athletic Club in Duluth, Ga. Leading by one shot over Phil Mickelson on the final hole, Toms hits his tee shot in the rough and choses to lay up with his second shot rather to go for the green on the 490-yard par 4 18th hole that is surrounded by water. After Mickelson misses his birdie chance from 30 feet away, Toms makes his 12-foot par putt to win the championship. "I didn't have any options," says Toms of his second shot on the final hole. "I had a tough stance and a tough lie. Whether I heard about it or not, that was the thing to do." Toms' victory is his sixth on the PGA Tour, his first major and adds another chapter of disappointment for Mickelson, still seeking his first major championship.

1984 – Forty-four-year-old Lee Trevino wins his second PGA Championship and sixth and final major title with a four-stroke victory over 48-year-old Gary Player and 34-year-old Lanny Wadkins at Shoal Creek Golf and Country Club in Birmingham, Ala. Trevino, who starts the day with a one-shot lead, fires a final round 69 to finish at 273, 15-under, a record under par for the championship at the time. "Winning this feels great" says Trevino. "When you are young, you always says it's inevitable that you're going to win. When you are old, the inevitable is over. Mentally, you always feel you can win." The victory is Trevino's sixth and final major, ten years after his fifth at the

1974 PGA. He becomes the first man to shoot all four rounds in the 60s at the PGA (69, 68, 67, 69).

1962 – Homero Blancas, a member of the University of Houston golf team, shoots 55 in a college tournament at the Premier Golf Course in Longview, Texas, the lowest round in the history of competitive golf. He makes 13 birdies, one eagle and takes only 20 putts at the par 70 layout, a nine hole course with two sets of tees that measure just 5,002 yards. Blancas, who goes on to win four events on the PGA Tour and plays on the 1973 U.S. Ryder Cup team, earns the nickname of "Mr. 55" by virtue of his feat. His record round is briefly in the Guinness Book of Records, but is removed when a requirement is added that a course must be at least 6,500 yards. On May 12, 2012, his score is equaled Rhein Gibson also shoots 55, but on a full 18-hole, 6,698 yard course.

August 20

2000 – Tiger Woods dramatically earns his fifth major tournament victory – and his third in a row – winning the PGA Championship at Valhalla Golf Club in Louisville, Ky., in an aggregate three-hole playoff with Bob May. Woods becomes the first player in the event's stroke-play era to successfully defend their title and joins Ben Hogan in 1953 as the only player to win three majors in a season. Both Woods and May, a journeyman golfer without a PGA Tour win, finish 72 holes at 270, 18 under par, a PGA scoring record to par (also tied by Woods in 2006), giving Woods the distinction of holding the scoring record at all four majors. Woods makes a birdie on the first playoff hole – the 16th hole – sinking a 20-foot putt, where he famously jogs behind the putt and points to the ball just before it falls into the hole. Woods holds the lead on the final two holes of the playoff, making par at the 17th and 18th holes to win by one stroke. "This was one memorable battle," Woods says. "It was a very special day. It was as good as it gets out there." Woods goes on to win the "Tiger Slam" the following April at the Masters where he wins and holds all four major titles at the same time.

2006 – Tiger Woods wins his third PGA Championship and his 12th major championship by five shots ahead of runner-up Shaun Micheel at the Medinah Country Club in Medinah, Ill. Woods shares the lead at the start of the day with Luke Donald, who shoots a two-over par 74 to drop out of contention. Woods shoots a four-under par 68 in the final round and becomes the first player to win the PGA twice on the same course, also winning at Medinah in 1999. One month after winning the Open Championship at Hoylake, Woods also becomes the first player in history to go consecutive years winning at least two major championships. "He's just too good," says Micheel. "Unless you're at the top of your game, you just can't play with him." The win is also the fifth major that Woods wins by at least five shots.

1978 – Forty-four-year old Lee Elder makes an 18-inch putt for birdie on the final hole to win the Westchester Classic by one shot over Mark Hayes. Elder calls the win his "most gratifying and satisfying victory" in 11 years on the PGA Tour. The win earns Elder a spot on the U.S. Ryder Cup team and qualifies him for the World Series of Golf. "This is probably the biggest win I have ever had because it achieves some things I have always wanted to achieve," Elder says. "Making the Masters (in 1975) was probably the second most important, but this is the most significant for me personally." Elder also won in Milwaukee seven weeks earlier, beating Lee Trevino in a sudden-death playoff.

1967 – Charlie Sifford, the first black player to earn a PGA Tour card, wins his first official PGA Tour event by shooting a final-round 64, winning by one stroke over Steve Opperman at the Greater Hartford Open Invitational in Connecticut. Sifford's win at the 1957 Long Beach Open in California was a 54-hole event and not classified as official at the time. "After Sifford's putt went down on the final green, thousands seated around him accorded him an unusually spirited ovation. Fellow pros trooped to pat him on the back and youngsters pushed to seek his autograph," writes Lincoln Warden of *The New York Times*. Sifford is emotional in the post-event presentation after he receives a two-minute ovation and is handed a winner's check of $20,000. Says an emotional Sifford, "If you try hard enough, anything can happen."

1944 – Bob Hamilton upsets Byron Nelson one-up in the match-play final to win the PGA Championship at Manito Golf and Country Club in Spokane, Wash. The PGA Championship is the only major championship held in 1944 and 1945, but is not held the previous year, 1943, due to the World War II. The win is the second of five PGA Tour titles for Hamilton, whose other noted wins are at the 1944 North and South Open at Pinehurst and the 1948 New Orleans Open. Hamilton holds the mark as the youngest player to shoot their age when he shoots a 59 at age 59 in 1975 at the Hamilton Golf Club in Evansville, Ind., in 1975.

August 21

1914 – Walter Hagen wins his first of 11 career major championships beating amateur Chick Evans by a stroke to win the U.S. Open at the Midlothian Country Club in Midlothian, Ill. Hagen, 21, birdies the 18th hole for a fourth consecutive day to provide for his margin of victory.

1920 – Jock Hutchison defeats James Douglas Edgar one-up in a 36-hole match play title match to win the PGA Championship at the Flossmoor Country Club in Floosmoor, Ill.

1977 – Andy North wins his first PGA Tour title at the Westchester Classic in Harrison, N.Y. shooting a final-round

71 to beat runner-up George Archer by two shots. The win becomes the only time North wins a tour-level title that is not a major championship as the Wisconsin native's only two career wins comes at the U.S. Open in 1978 and 1985.

2011 – Webb Simpson, from nearby Raleigh, N.C. and a former star at nearby Wake Forest University, wins his first PGA Tour title shooting a three-under 67 to win by three strokes at the Wyndham Championship in Greensboro, N.C. "I really couldn't think of a better place to win than here in Greensboro," Simpson says. "That was probably the most fun 18 holes I've ever been a part of."

1983 – In the last staging of the Greater Hartford Open at the Wethersfield Country Club, Curtis Strange wins on the PGA Tour for the first time since 1980 with a one-shot win over runner-up Jack Renner. "I don't think I doubted myself but thoughts can enter your mind," says Strange. "When I was in contention and didn't win, negative thoughts did enter my mind." The following year, the tournament moves to the TPC of Connecticut course in Cromwell, Conn.

August 22

2010 – Arjun Atwal becomes the first-ever Indian-born winner on the PGA Tour when he wins the Wyndham Championship in Greensboro, N.C. by one shot over runner-up David Toms. Atwal, a friend and frequent practice partner of Tiger Woods, also becomes the first Monday qualifier to win a PGA Tour event in 24 years. "I'm pretty sure it's going to be huge back home," Atwal says of how his victory will be received back in India. "I know my in-laws called my wife yesterday and said the coverage was just unreal with me leading."

1993 – Phil Mickelson wins the third title of his PGA Tour career at The International in at Castle Rock, Colo., posting a point total of 45 in the Stableford scoring system event. The 23-year-old Mickelson wins by an eight-point margin over Mark Calcavecchia in the scoring system that awards five points for an eagle, two for a birdie, none for par, minus-one for bogey and minus three for double-bogey or higher. Mickelson, whose final-round would be a 65 in medal scoring, earning him 16 points, making nine birdies and two bogeys.

August 23

2015 – Davis Love III, at the age of 51 years, four months, becomes the third oldest player to win on the PGA Tour when he shoots a final-round 64 to win the Wyndham Championships in Greensboro, N.C. Only Sam Snead, who wins also at Greensboro at the age of 52 years, 10 months, in 1965, and Art Wall, Jr., who wins at the Greater Milwaukee Open in 1975 at the age of 51 years, seven months, are older winners than Love on the PGA Tour. Love wins in Greensboro for a third time by one shot over 54-hole leader Jason Gore and claims his 21st PGA Tour title and his first since Orlando in 2008. Says Love, fighting back tears in his post-victory press conference, "It's just fun to hang in there and keep competing out here on the PGA Tour."

1998 – Nearly two months shy of his 63rd birthday, Gary Player becomes the second-oldest winner in the history of the Senior PGA Tour with a one-stroke victory at the $1 million Northville Long Island Classic at Jericho, N.Y. Only Mike Fetchick, who won the 1985 Hilton Head Seniors Invitational on his 63rd birthday, has won at an older age than Player. The win, his final victory on the Champions Tour, is the 19th PGA Senior win for Player and his 130th worldwide tournament championship.

August 24

1997 – Greg Norman wins his 20th and final PGA Tour title at the World Series of Golf at Firestone Country Club in Akron, Ohio, shooting a final-round 67 to beat runner-up Phil Mickelson by four shots. When asked how he would rate his golf year, where he claims two tournaments, more than $1 million in prize money and a world match play event, Norman responds, "Poor plus. I always have set extremely high standards for myself, ever since I was 21 years old. I think that's what motivates and drives me. This year my major tournament performance was pathetic – it was pathetic for anyone – because I missed two cuts."

1980 – Tom Watson wins the World Series of Golf at Firestone Country Club in Akron, Ohio by two shots over Ray Floyd, despite bogeying the final hole. "I love this game," says Watson, who shoots a final-round 65. "I have had a lot of frustration and I still love the game. And I am still having fun." The win makes Watson the first man to win over $500,000 in one year in golf. His first-prize paycheck of $100,000 bumps his yearly earnings to $510,258, helped by six tournament victories.

1986 – David Feherty wins the Scottish Open at Haggs Castle Golf Club in Glasgow, his second of five career titles on the European Tour, winning a playoff with Ian Baker-Finch and Christy O'Connor, Jr. after shooting a final-round 67. Feherty, famously, loses the event trophy after two days of parties that he describes as the "low point" of his battle with alcohol addiction. "They handed me the trophy-a big-ass silver cup…the oldest trophy in all of sport," Feherty says to Golf Magazine in 2009. "I drank all sorts of crap from it. I woke up two days later on the 16th tee at Gleneagles, which makes no sense, because I won the tournament in Glasgow [45 miles away]. I opened my eyes to see blue skies and Peter Gant, the road manager for Led Zeppelin. I hadn't seen him in ages. He's saying, 'You all right?' And the trophy's gone. Just f--in' gone. They never did find it."

August 25

2000 – Tiger Woods flirts with shooting a 59 but settles for a course record 61 at the Firestone Country Club in Akron, Ohio in the second round of the NEC Invitational. "To be honest with you, I didn't even know how many under par I was," Woods says when asked if thought about breaking 60. "I just wanted to keep adding to my lead." Woods adds more aura to his round when he reaches the 625-yard par 5 16th hole – the signature hole at Firestone called "The Monster" – in two shots, becoming only the third player in the history of tournament play at the venue since 1962 to do so, joining Arnold Palmer, Raymond Floyd and John Daly. Woods hit his drive 375 yards and hits a two-iron 269 yards to the green, flying over the green landing in the second cut of rough. Writes Leonard Shapiro in the *Washington Post*, "When the ball landed, hundreds watching let out a deafening roar, and people could be seen looking at each other with total incredulity that he had nearly pulled it off, despite the tough lie for his eagle attempt. Woods almost holed that third shot, burning the left edge of the cup with his chip before the ball stopped about a foot past the hole for a tap-in birdie that truly had to be seen to be believed."

2010 – Jim Furyk, the No. 3-ranked player in the FedEx Cup points standings, is disqualified from the opening event in the FedEx Cup Playoffs – The Barclays in Ridgewood, N.J. – when he oversleeps and misses his 7:30 a.m. pro-am tee time. According to PGA Tour rules, players in pro-am fields must be on their tee at the designated time or they are declared ineligible for the week's event. Furyk says that he used his cell phone for his alarm but when he woke up at 7:23 a.m., his phone was dead. "I always used my phone as an alarm and it had no power this morning," Furyk says. "I don't know if something happened with the charger or what, but I never got it. I woke up at 7:23 and tore out of there." Furyk arrives at the course at 7:35, but is declared ineligible. Furyk, however, rebounds from the unfortunate circumstances in dramatic fashion at the end of the FedEx Cup Playoffs as, after finishing T-37 the following week in Boston and a T-15 in Chicago, he parlays an 11th place ranking entering the year-end Tour Championship in Atlanta to win the event – and FedEx Cup – earning $11.35 million dollars. Says Furyk after his FedEx Cup win of his disqualification, "As much crap as I took I had to start laughing about it."

1996 – Guy Boros, the son of Hall of Famer and two-time U.S. Open champion Julius Boros, wins his lone PGA Tour title at the Greater Vancouver Open by one stroke over runners-up Lee Janzen, Emlyn Aubrey and Taylor Smith. Guy and his father join eight other father-son combinations to win on the PGA Tour, joining Tom Morris Sr.-Tom Morris Jr., Willie Park-Willie Park Jr., Joe Kirkwood Sr.-Joe Kirkwood Jr., Jack Burke Sr.-Jack Burke Jr., Clayton Heafner-Vance Heafner, Al Geiberger-Brent Geiberger, Jay Haas-Bill Haas and Craig Stadler-Kevin Stadler. The Morrises and Parks were early winners at the Open Championship, many years before the start of the PGA Tour, but are retroactively credited with official wins on the PGA Tour.

1991 – Martha Nause holes a wedge shot from 107 yards for an eagle-3 on the final hole and claims a one-shot win over Kris Monghan at the LPGA Chicago Sun-Times Shoot Out in Oak Brook, Ill. Nause plays the last four holes at five under par and comes from six shots back on the final day to claim her second of three career LPGA tournament wins.

1946 – Ben Hogan wins his first major title at the PGA Championship at the Portland Golf Club in Oregon. Despite being three down after the first 18 holes of a 36-hole title match, the 34-year-old Hogan beats Ed Oliver 6&4 in the championship match.

2006 – Tiger Woods makes what Marla Ridenour of the *Akron Beacon Journal* called "one of the most stunning bogeys of his 10-year career" finishing off a second round six-under-par 64 at the

Bridgestone Invitational at Firestone Country Club in Akron, Ohio. Finishing on the ninth hole, Woods hits a nine-iron approach shot over the grandstand, behind the green and onto a cart path, causing the ball to bounce onto the clubhouse roof. The ball rolls off the back of the clubhouse and into a loading dock where, according to the *Beacon Journal,* "a truck of pies was being unpacked." It takes over 30 minutes to make a ruling on whether the shot is officially out of bounds and to actually find the ball, which is taken by a chef at the club restaurant. After the threesome of competitors playing behind the Woods group is allowed to play through, Woods is given a free drop in an area 80 yards from the green, between the first tee and the driving range, after the ball is not declared out of bounds. Woods chips onto the green but just misses his par attempt, but still maintains a one-shot lead over Davis Love, III. "Would have been a nice 4," says Woods.

August 26

2001 – Tiger Woods and Jim Furyk battle for seven sudden-death playoff holes before Woods emerges victorious to win the NEC Invitational at the Firestone Country Club in Akron, Ohio. Woods makes a two-foot birdie putt on the seventh playoff hole to win the title in the longest playoff in 10 years on the PGA Tour. "It was a war," says Woods. "Neither one of us gave an inch. It was fun to compete like that, where you were tested to absolute utmost." Furyk dramatically holes a bunker shot to save par on the first extra hole and extend the playoff and has three chances to win with birdie putts from about 12 feet, one of them catching the inside of the right lip. "I didn't lose it from tee to green," Furyk says. "I lost it on the greens. I should have made more putts."

1990 – Jose Maria Olazabal wins his first PGA Tour title in comprehensive fashion, winning the World Series of Golf at Firestone Country Club in Akron, Ohio by an incredible 12 shots, the largest margin of victory in 15 years on the PGA Tour. Jokes Olazabal, "I was 12 ahead with 16 holes to go. I never had that kind of a lead before. I didn't know what to do." Three days earlier on August 23, Olazabal shoots an opening round 61, setting a course and tournament record for Firestone and the World Series of Golf.

August 27

1995 – Greg Norman, the victim of numerous miracle shots to lose tournaments, sinks a 66-foot-chip shot on the first playoff hole to beat Nick Price and Billy Mayfair and win the World Series of Golf in Akron, Ohio. "The game of golf always evens itself out," Norman says after the win. "One day you might hit a tree and the ball bounces into the water. The next day you might hit a tree and it goes into the middle of the fairway. The golfing gods have a way of doing that."

2000 – Playing the final hole of the NEC Invitational in Akron, Ohio in virtually pitch black conditions, Tiger Woods hits one of the many signature shots of his career to close out an 11-shot victory at Firestone Country Club. Woods hits an eight-iron approach to the final green from 168 yards out to within two feet of the hole in the dark and makes birdie to finish with a three-under 67. Woods smashes the 72-hole scoring record at Firestone Country Club with a 21-under score of 259 – three shots better than the previous mark of 262, set by Jose Maria Olazabal in 1991. The final stroke from Woods comes as flash blubs pop around the green, creating an usual scene for the end of a golf tournament. Says Woods of his dramatic finish, "I had to do it for Stevie," Woods says, referring to his caddie, Steve Williams. "He kept saying, 'We've got to get it to 21 [under].' Twenty-one is his favorite number. The last hole, I asked him for a dry glove. When he gave it to me, he wrote '21' on it. I hit it stiff. He was so excited. I've never seen him that excited, and we've won majors."

2006 – On the 10th anniversary of the day he turned pro, Tiger Woods wins the Bridgestone Invitational for a fifth time on the fourth hole of a sudden-death playoff with Stewart Cink at Firestone Country Club in Akron, Ohio. Cink has an eight-foot par putt on the third playoff hole – the 18th hole – for the win but the putt slides by the right side of the hole. Woods then makes an eight-foot birdie on the next playoff hole – the 18th – to claim the championship. The win is the fourth straight tournament victory for Woods – that includes the Open Championship and the PGA Championship – and the 52nd of his PGA Tour career.

2014 – Mohd Nazri Zain of Malaysia makes a hole-in-one on a par-4 during the SapuraKencana National Qualifier tournament, holing out on a water-lined 289-yard 16th hole on the Kuala Lumpur Golf and Country Club's west course. "I saw the ball rolling into the hole and I started celebrating with my caddie," Zain says. "It was unbelievable. This is definitely a huge achievement for me and I'll keep the ball as a memory." Zain shoots a two-over-par 73 and finishes in 20th place, 15 strokes behind the playoff winner Danny Chia, also of Malaysia. By winning, Chia earns a place in the field at the $7 million CIMB Classic, a PGA Tour and Asian Tour event in late October.

August 28

1996 – Twenty-year-old Tiger Woods announces his arrival to the world of professional golf with the words "I guess... hello world" in his pre-event press conference at the Greater Milwaukee Open, site of his professional debut. Woods turns pro after winning three straight U.S. Amateur championships and a successful two years of college golf at Stanford University. "It wasn't about money," says the newly Nike-adorned Woods of his decision to turn pro. "It was about being happy. I have been thinking about this for a long time, and the question always was whether the timing was right and how happy am I with the decision. Is the timing right? Am I ready? The answers all pointed to yes."

1983 – Nick Price wins his first PGA Tour title at the World Series of Golf at Firestone Country Club in Akron, Ohio, posting a 10-under score of 270, earning $100,000. The win for Price helps him exorcise memories of losing the Open Championship to Tom Watson the previous summer when he drops four shots in the final six holes. "After the Open experience, I was happy to win the way I did, with no bogeys," Price says. "I didn't choke. I proved my game is solid enough to withstand a lot of pressure." Price becomes the first wire-to-wire win ever at the World Series of Golf, firing scores of 66, 68, 69 and 67 to beat runner-up Jack Nicklaus by four strokes.

1994 – Reigning Masters champion Jose Maria Olazabal wins the World Series of Golf at Firestone Country Club in Akron, Ohio with a one-stroke win over Scott Hoch. The event is played on the club's north course due to problems with the greens on the club's south course, the usual venue for the event. "Good for the records," says Olazabal, who won the 1990 World Series title on the south course, of being the only player to win on both courses.

August 29

1908 – Fred McLeod shoots a 77 and defeats 1899 champion Willie Smith by four shots in an 18-hole playoff to win the U.S. Open at the Myopia Hunt Club in South Hamilton, Mass. At 5-foot-4 and 108 pounds, the Scottish immigrant McLeod is the smallest player to ever win the U.S. Open.

1996 – Tiger Woods hits his first shot as a professional golfer at 2:36pm local time in the first round of the Greater Milwaukee Open. Woods is partnered with Jeff Hart and Jerry Kelly and hits a drive that soars 326 yards down the first fairway at the

461-yard par 4 first hole at the Brown Deer Park Golf Course. Woods makes an eagle, three birdies and a bogey for a four-under par round of 67. Woods goes on to finish in a tie for 60th place at the event, earning his first pro paycheck of $2,544.

1999 – Tiger Woods shoots a one-over 71 to win the NEC Invitational at Firestone Country Club in Akron, Ohio, to post single-season earnings to $4,266,585 and becoming the first player in PGA Tour history to go over $4 million in a single season. "Winning never gets old," says Woods. "It's the greatest cliché ever, but it's so true. This week, we had some of the best players assembled. At the PGA they told me it was the best field ever assembled. The money will come. I take more satisfaction beating the best players in the game." At the age of 23 years, eight months and 30 days, Woods also becomes the youngest player to win five times in one season since Jack Nicklaus won the 1963 Sahara Invitational for his fifth victory at exactly the same age, to the day.

1991 – John Brodie, a quarterback in the National Football League for 16 years with the San Francisco 49ers, wins his first and only title on the PGA Champions Tour, making a birdie on the first hole of a sudden-death playoff with George Archer and Chi Chi Rodriguez to win the Security Pacific Senior Classic in Valencia, Calif.

August 30

2015 – Jason Day, in his first start since winning his first major title at the PGA Championship, wins at the Barclays Championship in Edison, N.J. shooting a final-round 62 and winning by six shots over Henrik Stenson. Besides Day's glorious final round, Brian Harman stars on the day by making two holes-in-one in the final round.

1967 – Jack Nicklaus shoots a final-round 71 and wins his 24th career PGA Tour title at the Westchester Classic by one stroke over runner-up Dan Sikes in Harrison, N.Y. The previous day, playing with Arnold Palmer and Doug Sanders, Nicklaus shoots a 65, but, as documented by United Press International "failed to win over the crowd which, as usual, routed for Palmer." Fans jab at missed putts from Nicklaus and are overly vocal at Palmer birdies, but Nicklaus sinks seven birdies during his third round while "casting a deaf ear to the jobs and partisan jeers echoed by 'Arnie's Army,'" as described by UPI.

1969 – Marvin M. "Vinny" Giles III becomes the only three-time runner-up at the U.S. Amateur Championships when he finishes in second place behind winner Steve Melynk at Oakmont Country Club in Pennsylvania. Giles, a former Univ. of Georgia golfer, also finishes second behind Bruce Fleisher in 1968 and behind Robert Dickson in 1967 when the event was a stroke-play championship. Giles, however, does break through to win the event in 1972, beating Ben Crenshaw and Mark Hayes by three shots. Giles also wins the British Amateur title in 1975.

1992 – In fading light, Craig Stadler sinks a 10-foot par putt on the 72nd hole to defeat Corey Pavin by one shot and win the NEC World Series of Golf in Akron, Ohio. Had Stadler missed the putt, the sudden-death playoff would have to have been played the following morning due to a lack of light. The win marks his 10th career PGA Tour victory, but only his second since 1984.

1987 – Curtis Strange registers a three-shot victory at the World Series of Golf in Akron, Ohio to surpass the all-time PGA Tour single-season money earnings record. Strange earns $144,000 to give him $697,385 for the year, surpassing the $653,296 that Greg Norman earns the previous year.

1998 – David Duval wins the NEC World Series of Golf in Akron, Ohio, beating runner-up Phil Mickelson by two shots to win his third title of the year and his sixth in the last 11 months. "I believe in what I do," Duval says after his final-round two-under-par 68. "I always stayed true to the course I wanted to follow, even when people questioned it and didn't think I could win."

1998 – Brandel Chamblee sinks a 36-foot birdie putt on the final hole to cap his first and what becomes his only PGA Tour win at the Greater Vancouver Open in Surrey, Canada. Chamblee shoots a final-round five-under 66 to beat runner-up Payne Stewart by three strokes. "I've been playing so good this week and hitting it so well, if I just stayed out of my own way I knew everything was going to be fine," says Chamblee. The following April, Chamblee shares the first-round lead at the Masters, shooting an opening 69 and goes on to finish tied for 18th, his best finish at a major. After he loses his PGA Tour card in 2003, he goes on to become a respected golf commentator on The Golf Channel.

August 31

1986 – Mike Hulbert sinks a one-foot birdie putt on the 18th hole to beat his boyhood friend – and hotel roommate – Joey Sindelar by one stroke and win his first PGA Tour title at the Federal Express St. Jude Championships in Memphis, Tenn. "It was nice and short," Hulbert says of his final putt. "It felt fine, and I could see Joey in the background and he was happy as a lark – and then it was over. I still can't believe it." Hulbert grew up with Sindelar in Horseheads, N.Y., and the two had played golf together since the age of 10. The two friends roomed at the same hotel during their week in Memphis. "I know all the folks at home are excited because they've been waiting for us to do something on the tour," Sindelar says.

SEPTEMBER

September 1

1996 – Tiger Woods collects the first paycheck of his professional career – for $2,544 – after finishing in a tie for 60th in his debut event at the Greater Milwaukee Open. Woods shoots 67-69-73-68 for a 277 total, twelve shots worse than Loren Roberts, who wins the title with a birdie on the first hole of a playoff with Jerry Kelly.

1952 – World War II veteran and Purple Heart Award recipient Ted Kroll wins the inaugural Insurance City Open at the Wethersfield Country Club in Hartford, Conn., winning the title by four shots over runners-up Lawson Little, Skee Riegel and Earl Stewart. The win is the second of eight career titles for Kroll, who earned three Purple Hearts during his military service in France and Italy. Four years after his win in Hartford, he has another chance to win the tournament, but loses to an upstart young Arnold Palmer, who wins his first tour win in the United States in a playoff with Kroll.

1946 – Patty Berg wins the first U.S. Women's Open at Spokane Country Club in Washington defeating Betty Jameson 5&4 over 36 holes in the match-play final – the first and only time the U.S. Open women's title is decided by match play. Berg wins $5,600 in War Bonds for the title.

September 2

1955 – Amateur Bill Whedon becomes the first player to score two holes-in-one in a single round at the Insurance City Open at the Wethersfield Country Club in Hartford, Conn. In the opening round of the event, Whedon uses a five-iron on the 168-yard fifth hole and a three-iron on the 208-yard ninth hole for his two aces. Later in the day, Gene Littler also scores a hole-in-one with a five-iron 164-yard 13th hole. According to *Golf Digest*, the odds of hitting two holes-in-one in one round are one in 67 million. Despite the two holes-in-one, Whedon shoots a 75, but says he is "elated but in a daze" with his feats. Whedon's feat is not equaled on the PGA Tour until 2006 when Yusaku Miyazato scores two holes-in-one in the second round of the 2006 Rene-Tahoe Open.

1974 – Jack Nicklaus win inaugural staging of the Tournament Players Championship finishing off a rain-delayed round of 67 for a two-shot win over J.C. Snead at the Atlanta Athletic Club. Nicklaus says the win "salvaged the year for me" after failing to win any of the four major tournaments during the year. "I didn't want to let this one get away from me once I got in a position to win," says Nicklaus after capturing his 53rd career PGA Tour title. The Tournament Players Championship is played at Colonial Country Club in Fort Worth, Texas the following year, and the Inverrary Country Club in Fort Lauderdale in 1976. In 1977, the event begins its association with Ponte Vedra Beach, Fla., first being held at the Sawgrass Country Club before moving to the TPC at Sawgrass starting in 1982.

1940 – Byron Nelson wins his first PGA Championship defeating Sam Snead one-up in the 36-hole final match at Hershey Country Club in Hershey, Pa. With the match square on the 34th hole, Nelson makes a one-foot birdie putt after Snead misses his rammed birdie putt from 25 feet, the ball bouncing out of the cup and staying on the lip. Nelson then halves the next two holes to win the fourth of his five career major titles.

1990 – Nick Faldo becomes the fourth player to rank No. 1 in the world in the official World Golf Rankings, taking over the top spot from Greg Norman. Faldo goes on to rank No. 1 for a total of 97 weeks in his career.

September 3

1973 – In the first year the event is branded "The Sammy Davis Jr. Greater Hartford Open," Billy Casper shoots a final-round 64 to win for the fourth time on the PGA Tour in the capital of Connecticut. Casper claims his 50th PGA Tour title – and second-to-last tour title – by one shot over runner-up Bruce Devlin.

1995 – Tony Jacklin wins the last of his 28 professional tournaments at the Franklin Quest Championship on the PGA Champions Tour at the age of 51. Jacklin, the winner of the 1969 Open Championship and the 1970 U.S. Open, retires from full-time play at age 60.

1976 – Seve Ballesteros shoots a fourth consecutive round of 68 and successfully defends his title at the Swiss Open in Crans-Montana beating runner-up Manuel Pinero by three strokes. Exactly 13 years later to the day, Ballesteros wins the title for a third time – his 42nd European Tour title – shooting a final-round 67 to beat runner-up Craig Parry by two strokes.

September 4

1972 – Lee Trevino shoots a final round 65 and beats Lee Elder with a birdie on the first playoff hole at the Greater Hartford Open at the Wethersfield Country Club in Connecticut. With a win, Elder would have become the first black player to ever qualify to play in the Masters, but misses a six-foot birdie putt on the 72nd hole, forcing the playoff. "Lee Elder is a great guy and I am sorry I cost him a bid to the Masters," Trevino says. "But that's the name of the game." However, Elder eventually becomes the first black player to play at the Masters in 1975 after qualifying when he wins the 1975 Monsanto Open in Pensacola, Fla.

1961 – Recently retired from his job as Vice President of the United States, Richard Nixon makes a hole-in-one on the second hole at the Bel Air Country Club in Los Angeles. Nixon calls the shot "the greatest thrill in my life – even better than being elected." Nixon, who served as Vice President under the keen golfer and Augusta National member Dwight Eisenhower, is himself elected President seven years later.

1978 – Tom Kite wins his second PGA Tour title at the B.C. Open in Endicott, N.Y., winning by five shots over runner-up Mark Hayes. Kite wins his first PGA Tour title on June 6, 1976 at the IVB Bicentennial Golf Classic in at the Whitemarsh Valley Country Club in Lafayette Hill, Pa. in a playoff with Terry Diehl. He goes on to win 19 PGA Tour titles including the U.S. Open in 1992.

1932 – Olin Dutra wins the first of his two major titles at the PGA Championship at Keller Golf Course in St. Paul, Minn., defeating Frank Walsh 4&3 in the match-play final.

September 5

1988 – Ken Green wins his third PGA Tour title at the Canadian Open in a Monday finish at the Glen Abbey Golf Club. Green, from Danbury, Conn., withstands morning temperatures in the high 40s and winds as brisk as 20 mph to win by one shot over runners-up Scott Verplank and Bill Glasson. "I have no qualms to admit I was quite scared going into today when I saw the cold wind howling," Green says. "I'm not a cold-wind player despite the fact I grew up in cold wind."

1999 – Mike Weir shoots his second consecutive round of 64 and wins his first PGA Tour event at the Air Canada Championship in Surrey, British Columbia, two strokes better than runner-up Fred Funk. Weir becomes the first Canadian to win a PGA Tour event since Richard Zokol wins the 1992 Greater Milwaukee Open and the first Canadian to win on Canadian soil since Pat Fletcher won the 1954 Canadian Open, which at the time was also held in British Colombia in Vancouver. Weir also becomes only the sixth left-handed player to win on the PGA Tour joining Phil Mickelson, Bob Charles, Ernie Gonzalez, Sam Adams and Russ Cochran.

September 6

2004 – Vijay Singh becomes the No. 1 golfer in the world, ending a record 264-week run by Tiger Woods, winning the Deutsche Bank Championship at the TPC of Boston. Singh birdies three of the last four holes to shoot a final-round 69 and beating runners-up Woods and Adam Scott by three strokes. "I've worked pretty hard for this and finally achieved what I wanted to do starting at the beginning of [last] year," says Singh after claiming the 21st title of his career, and his 10th win in two years. "It was a good win , too, because it got pretty tight coming down the stretch, but I got focused and played pretty good. It was a golf tournament to me, not about the rankings. It wasn't about trying to beat Tiger and beat the No. 1 player. I was trying to win, and Adam Scott nearly jumped up and took it away. It feels great, but I thought I was playing good enough to be No. 1 for a while, but I kept saying there was nothing I could do about the rankings. Finally, it's turned in my favor, and I'm really proud to achieve that." Says Woods of losing the No. 1 ranking, "There's two ways to look at it. This is the best ball-striking week I've had all year, and unfortunately I didn't win because I didn't play the par-5s well all day [bogeys at Nos. 2 and 7, birdie at No. 18]. There's no doubt I played more like a No. 1 than I have in a while, but I just didn't take care of the par-

5s. I'm not disappointed about the ranking. I'm disappointed in not winning. As I've said, winning takes care of the ranking. I had a great opportunity to win, got even with five holes to go and just didn't do it."

1913 – Jerome "Jerry" Travers wins the U.S. Amateur Championship for a fourth time at the Chicago Golf Club. Travers, who also wins in 1907, 1908 and 1912, goes on to also win the U.S. Open at Baltusrol in 1915 as an amateur. The four U.S. Amateur titles for Travers remains a record until Bobby Jones wins his fifth in 1930.

September 7

2014 – Billy Horschel shoots a one-under-par 69 at Cherry Hills Country Club in Colorado and hangs on to win the BMW Championship by two shots over Bubba Watson. The title, the last Fed Ex Cup Playoff event before the Tour Championships the following week, is the second PGA Tour title for Horschel, who heads caution to golfers on his chances of pocketing the $10 million Fed Ex Cup season-long points title the following week. "If I were a betting man, I'd put some money on me," says Horschel, who proves that he can not only talk the talk, but walk the walk, winning once again seven days later at the season-ending event.

1964 – Charles Coody wins his first PGA Tour title at the Dallas Open Invitational, shooting a final-round 69 at the Oak Cliff Country Club to beat runner-up Jerry Edwards by one shot. Coody wins again on the PGA Tour in 1969 at the Cleveland Open and then wins for a final time on tour in 1971 with his crowning achievement, a green jacket at the Masters.

1975 – Hubert Green makes five birdies on the back nine – crediting a "Jack Nicklaus style" putting stance – and shoots a final-round 64 to win the Southern Open in Columbus, Ga. "My stance is more like the one Jack Nicklaus uses," says Green after beating runner-up John Schroeder by three shots. "My feet are more wide open." The win is the eighth of 19 career PGA Tour wins for Green, who wins the U.S. Open in 1977 and the PGA Championship in 1985.

1986 – Jose Maria Olazabal wins his first title on the European Tour at the Ebel European Masters Swiss Open at the age of 20, shooting a final-round 66 to beat Anders Forsbrand by three strokes. A rookie on the European Tour, Olazabal finishes the season No. 2 on the European Tour Order of Merit behind his fellow Spaniard Seve Ballesteros, who wins six tournaments during the year. Olazabal goes on to win two Masters titles in 1994 and in 1999.

September 8

1985 – George Burns, the golfer not related to the famous actor and comedian, wins his third of four career PGA Tour titles, claiming a six-shot win at the Bank of Boston Classic in Sutton, Mass. Burns shoots a final-round 66 to beat runners-up Greg Norman, John Mahaffey, Jodie Mudd and Leonard Thompson by six shots. Burns, born George Francis Burns, III, is best-known for being the third-round leader at the 1981 U.S. Open, where he finishes in a tied for second behind winner David Graham at Merion Golf Club outside Philadelphia. His signature win comes at the 1980 Pebble Beach Pro-Am and wins his final PGA Tour event in 1987 on another coastal California course at Torrey Pines at the Andy Williams San Diego Open.

1968 – Billy Casper wins the fifth of his six tournaments during the 1968 season, winning the Greater Hartford Open Invitational in Connecticut by three shots of runner-up Bruce Crampton.

September 9

1966 – Mickey Wright wins the first staging of the Ladies World Series of Golf at Springfield Country Club, Ohio, and wins the largest prize in women's golf at the time – $10,000.

1979 – Lou Graham, the 1975 U.S. Open champions, wins his fifth – and second-to-last – PGA Tour title at the American Optical Classic in Sutton, Mass., beating Ben Crenshaw by one stroke. The win is the second of three wins for Graham in 1979 in a renaissance season that earns him "Comeback Player of the Year" honors by *Golf Digest*.

1984 – George Archer wins his 13th and final PGA Tour event at the Bank of Boston Classic in Sutton, Mass., shooting a final-round 65 to beat runners-up Frank Conner and Joey Sindelar by six shots. Archer first wins on the PGA Tour in 1965 and is best known for his win at the Masters in 1969.

September 10

1929 – Arnold Daniel Palmer is born in Latrobe, Pennsylvania. Palmer is the son of a greens keeper and goes on to golf immortality, winning 62 PGA Tour titles and seven major titles including the Masters in 1958, 1960, 1962 and 1964, the Open Championship in 1961 and 1962 and the U.S. Open in 1960.

1978 – Jerry Pate wins his fifth of eight career PGA Tour titles by successfully defending his title at the Southern Open at the Green Island Country Club in Columbus, Ga. Pate shoots a final-round one-under-par 69 to win by one stroke over Phil Hancock, the same player Pate beats by seven shots the previous year. Pate pars every hole in his final round, except the 15th hole, where he makes a 12-foot birdie putt that proves to be the decisive shot of the event. Says Pate of his winning final round, "I only made one birdie putt but it came when it counted."

2012 – Jiyai Shin wins the longest playoff in LPGA history when she makes par on the ninth extra hole of a sudden-death playoff with Paula Creamer at the Kingsmill Championships in Virginia. After Shin and Creamer finish regulation tied the previous day, they play the 18th hole eight times before the playoff is suspended due to darkness. On the resumption of play, tournament officials decide to start the playoff at the 16th hole, where Creamer three-putts for bogey and Shin's par wins her the tournament title.

September 11

1890 – John Ball, Jr. becomes the first amateur player to win the Open Championship, winning by three shots over runners-up Archie Simpson and Willie Fernie at Prestwick. Ball negotiates the windy conditions to post a 36-hole score of 164 with mirroring rounds of 82. Ball also becomes the first Englishman and the first non-Scot to win the Open Championship title.

2014 – Hyo-Joo Kim fires the lowest round in the history of an LPGA major, shooting a 61 in the opening round of the Evian Championship. Kim, a 19-year-old from South Korea, makes 10 birdies and no bogeys at the 6,453-yard Evian Golf Resort in Evian-Les-Bain, France. "I made a chance for a birdie on every hole," she says. "I missed some but it didn't matter." The previous low round at a women's major was a 62 shot by Minea Blomqvist of Finland in the third round of the 2004 British Open and Lorena Ochoa in the first round of the 2006 Kraft Nabisco Championship.

1988 – Just six days after winning the Canadian Open in a Monday finish, Ken Green wins his fourth PGA Tour title at the Greater Milwaukee Open winning by six shots over runners-up Mark Calcavecchia, Dan Pohl, Jim Gallagher, Jr. and Donnie Hammond. Green is buoyed by a third-round 61 the previous day over the 7,030-yard par 72 Tuckaway Country Club course. Green wins for a fifth and final time on the PGA Tour the following April at the Greater Greensboro Open. In 2009, he is nearly killed a car accident but has the lower part of his leg amputated, but, amazingly, returns to professional golf to compete on the PGA Champions Tour.

September 12

1971 – Johnny Miller wins his first of 25 PGA Tour titles with a five-stroke win over runner-up Deane Beaman at the Southern Open at the Green Island Country Club in Columbus, Ga. The 24-year-old Miller cancels a fishing trip in Montana to play in the event after persistent pleas from tournament director John Montgomery. The Associated Press says that with the win, Miller went "from promising newcomer status to that of tournament winner" with his final-round 67 that earns him the $20,000 first prize. Miller tells reporters that the key to his first PGA Tour victory was focusing on his own game and not the scores of his opponents. "Before, I've always paid too much attention to the leaderboard and the other players," says Miller.

1993 – David Frost makes a two-putt birdie on par-5 final hole at the Glen Abbey Golf Club to win the Canadian Open by one shot over Fred Couples. Frost hits a 225-yard five-wood approach shot to the final hole to set up his winning birdie that earns him his seventh career PGA Tour title. "It's not a shot you want to have to win a golf tournament," Frost says of his final-hole approach shot. "But once you've done it, once you've hit it, it's a pretty big relief."

September 13

1872 – "Young" Tom Morris wins his fourth consecutive title at the Open Championship at Prestwick becoming the first and only to date player to win four successive Open titles. Morris wins the title in 1868, 1869, 1870 and 1872. The event is not held in 1871 when Morris claims the tournament's Championship Belt with his third consecutive win in 1870 and there is no trophy available the following year. The Claret Jug, still given to the Open Championship winner today, was commissioned for the 1872 event, but is not completed in time and Morris is awarded a gold medal, a tradition that also continues today. Morris is given the Claret Jug, engraved with his name, weeks later, but it is returned at the start of the next staging of the championship.

2013 – Jim Furyk becomes the sixth player to shoot a 59 on the PGA Tour in the second round of the BMW Championship at Conway Farms Golf Club in Lake Forest, Ill. Furyk makes 11 birdies, one bogey and an eagle for the 12-under-par score. Furyk makes birdie on the final hole, making a three-foot putt after an approach shot from 103 yards away with a gap wedge. "I've played a couple of good ones (rounds) throughout my career," says Furyk. "I remember a 62 at Doral once where I think the next best score was 67. That kind of defines really good rounds is a guy goes out and shoots four or five shots better than the rest of the field. But that magic number, it's hard to get under 30 on (one) nine, and then it's really hard to get under 60 for a day. It definitely played some tricks with my head on the way in." Of his thoughts coming down the final nine holes, Furyk says, "(It was) a little hectic down the stretch. I just told myself on nine, 'How many opportunities are you going to have in your life to do this? Got to take advantage of it.' I tried to knock it in there tight and make it as easy on yourself as you can. There's not much I could have improved on today, so I think I'll sleep well." The other players to shoot 59s on the PGA Tour at the time were Americans Al Geiberger (1977 Memphis Classic), Chip Beck (1991 Las Vegas Invitational), David Duval (1999 Bob Hope Classic) and Paul Goydos (2010 John Deere Classic) as well as Australian Stuart Appleby (2010 Greenbrier Classic).

1992 – Greg Norman wins his first tournament in 27 months at the Canadian Open at Glen Abbey golf course in Oakville, Ontario. Norman makes a three-foot birdie putt on the second hole of a playoff to beat Bruce Lietzke and claim the 11th of his 20 career PGA Tour tournament wins. "I'd almost forgotten what it's like to win a tournament," says Norman of his first win since the 1990 Memorial. "It's been a long time. It's like winning my first tournament. I'm more excited than anything since winning my first tournament. I needed it."

1930 – Tommy Armour defeats Gene Sarazen one-up on the final hole in the match-play final to win the PGA Championship at the Fresh Meadow Country Club in Flushing, N.Y. Armour makes a 14-foot putt for a par on the 36th and last hole of the match-play final and wins the match when Sarazen is unable to match his putt from just inside 14 feet. Brian Bell of the Associated Press writes that Armour's win solidified that "he is a great putter in a pinch." The win is the second of three major titles for the Scottish-born Armour, nick-named "The Silver Scot." Previously, Armour won the 1927 U.S. Open at Oakmont and the next year, winning the 1931 Open Championship at Carnoustie. Armour's 1930 season, that also includes wins at the Canadian Open and the St. Louis Open, is overlooked by the 1930 Grand Slam season by Bobby Jones.

September 14

2014 – Billy Horschel wins the season-ending Tour Championship and the $10 million Fed Ex Cup winning the final event of the PGA Tour season at East Lake Golf Club in Atlanta by three shots over runner up Jim Furyk. Horschel, who enters the event having won $4.5 million in his career, pockets $11.4 million on the day, including his first-prize paycheck. He wins only his second PGA Tour event the previous week in Denver and started the Fed Ex Cup playoffs ranked No. 69 in the standings. The only boos the former University of Florida standout gets on the day is when he performs the Florida Gator "chomp" with his arms after the win in front of the gallery that consists of many fans of the rival Georgia Bulldogs.

1957 – Forty-five-year-old Sam Snead shoots an 11-under par 60 – the lowest recorded round of professional golf at the time – to take the 36-hole lead at the Dallas Open at the 6,328 yard Glen Lakes Country Club. Snead equals the low mark scored by five other players – Byron Nelson in 1945 at Olympia, Wash., Al Brosch in 1951 at the Texas Open in San Antonio, Bill Nary in 1952 at the El Paso Open, Tommy Bolt in 1954 in the Insurance City Open in Hartford, Ted Kroll in 1954 at the Texas Open in San Antonio, Wally Ulrich in 1954 at the Virginia Beach Open and Mike Souchak in 1955 at the Texas Open in San Antonio. Snead, who tells reporters that had shot a 57 previously in practice rounds, quips after a practice round Wednesday before the tournament, "They won't shot 60 on this course. The greens are too bumpy." Snead chips in for eagle from 50 feet away on the first hole and misses a 40-foot putt for 59 on the 18th hole. Snead wins the title the next day.

1979 – For the first time in the history of the Ryder Cup, a team that includes the continent of Europe competes as the 23rd Ryder Cup matches begin at The Greenbrier in West Virginia. A team that includes players from Europe replaces the old format that featured only players from Great Britain and Ireland competing against the United States. The European team only features two players from continental Europe – Spaniards Seve Ballesteros and Antonio Garrido – and the United States dominates the competition with a 17-11 victory, their 11th straight win in the series. It is not until 1985 when the European team is able to break the U.S. streak of victories.

2014 – Andy Sullivan makes a hole-in-one at the 163-yard 15th hole at Kennemer Golf Club, site of the European Tour event's KLM Open in the Netherlands, and wins a trip to outer space aboard the Lynx Mark 1, offered by tournament sponsor XCOR

Space Expeditions. According to European Tour, Sullivan jokes earlier in the week of the potential of winning the prize, "I'll win a trip home." When asked if he would in fact take the trip to space, Sullivan says, "I'll see what the missus says." Sullivan, from England, finishes third behind tournament winner Paul Casey.

2014 – Hyo-Joo Kim, at age of 19 years, two months, becomes the third youngest woman to win a women's major when she is victorious at the Evian Championships in France, beating seven-time major winner Karrie Webb – twenty-years her senior – by one stroke. Kim makes a birdie from 12 feet on the final hole, but Webb misses a par putt also from 12 feet and fails to force a playoff. "I feel very happy, like a bird," Kim says through a translator after the win. "I want to fly in the sky." Only Morgan Pressel and Lexi Thompson have won majors at a younger age than Kim.

1986 – Greg Norman becomes the third golfer to rank No. 1 in the official World Golf Rankings, assuming the top ranking from Seve Ballesteros. Norman goes on to hold the top ranking for a total of 331 weeks in his career. The World Golf Rankings debut earlier in the year on April 6 with Bernhard Langer being the first player to rank No. 1.

September 15

1939 – Henry Picard wins the PGA Championship by defeating Byron Nelson with a birdie at the 37th hole of the 36-hole match-play final at Pomonok Country Club in Queens, N.Y. It was the second of Picard's two major titles after winning the Masters in 1938. Nelson, however, goes on to win the PGA Championship the following year.

1870 – "Young" Tom Morris wins his third consecutive Open Championship title at Prestwick by 12 shots in the 36-hole event over runners-up Davie Strath and Bob Kirk, and by 13 shots ahead of his famous father "Old" Tom Morris. Young Tom posts scores in his three 12-hole rounds of 47-51-51. His opening round starts off by him holing out from 200 yards away on the 578-yard first hole. By winning the title for a third straight time, Young Tom is given the red leather Championship Belt with the engraved silver buckle that had been the event's trophy since the first staging of the event in 1860. With no award to be given out for the 1871 event, the Open Championship is not held, but the Claret Jug is commissioned to be the trophy for the 1872 tournament and remains the trophy today.

1899 – Willie Smith wins the U.S. Open at the Baltimore Country Club in Maryland by a record 11 shots – a record that stands for 101 years until it is broken by Tiger Woods, who wins the 2000 U.S. Open by 15 shots. Smith wins the fifth staging of the tournament by being the only player to shoot under 80 three times, posting rounds of 77-82-79-77.

1996 – The United States wins the second staging of the Presidents Cup by a narrow 16½–15½ margin at the Robert Trent Jones Golf Club in Gainesville, Va., also the site of the first Presidents Cup. The United States led 10½–9½ entering the final day's 12 singles matches that were split 6-6. Fred Couples defeats Vijay Singh 2 & 1 to clinch the victory for the United States. Mark O'Meara goes 5-0-0 for Team USA while David Duval goes 4-0-0.

1996 – Ed Fiori denies twenty-year-old rookie Tiger Woods his first PGA Tour victory by shooting a final-round 67 to overtake Woods and win the Quad City Classic at the Oakwood Country Club in Coal Valley, Ill. The win is the fourth and final PGA Tour title for Fiori, a 5-foot, 7-inch 220-pound veteran who last won on the PGA Tour 14 years earlier at the Bob Hope Desert Classic in 1982, the second-longest stretch between wins in PGA Tour history. Woods, the third-round leader, does not lose another 54-hole lead again in professional golf until the 2009 PGA Championship.

September 16

1869 – "Young" Tom Morris scores what is believed to be the earliest recorded hole-in-one in competition in the first round of the Open Championship at Prestwick. Young Tom scores his ace on the 166-yard eighth hole and goes on to win his second successive Open title.

2001 – Jason Bohn, a 28-year-old from Atlanta, shoots a 13-under-par 58 to win the Bayer Championship, a Canadian Tour event at the Huron Oaks Country Club in Sarnia, Ontario. Bohn has 10 birdies, two eagles and one bogey during the historic round. The score is the lowest in the history of the Canadian Tour and matches the unofficial 58 shot by Shigeki Maruyama of Japan in U.S. Open qualifying in 2000 at the par 71 Woodmont Country Club in Rockville, Md. Nine years later, Ryo Ishikawa also shoots 58 (12 under par) in the final round of The Crowns tournament on the Japan Golf Tour and Jim Furyk also matches the number in the final round of the Travelers Championship in Hartford, Conn., in 2016. "It was wild – a crazy day," Bohn says. "Everything went my way. I'd hit a bad shot and then chip it in. I made a ton of putts. I played well but was able to cover a bad shot with a luck shot. The best round I'd ever had before was 62." Bohn finishes two shots in front of runner-up Jace Bugg and earns $32,000 for the tournament title.

2007 – Tiger Woods wins the inaugural Fed Ex Cup season-long points title – and its first prize of $10 million – by winning the season-ending Tour Championship at East Lake Golf Club in Atlanta. Woods shoots a final-round four-under 66 to finish a 23-under-par for an eight-shot victory and his seventh tournament win of the season. Woods also wins $1.26 million for the tournament title giving him a payday of $11.26 million.

"Once you got into the playoffs, you're playing against the best guys and the hottest players. You have to play well," Woods says. "We had some great drama. In the end, it was a lot of fun for all of us."

2007 – The United States wins the Solheim Cup in Halmstad, Sweden – only its second victory in the team competition on European soil – winning eight of 12 final-day singles matches for a 16-12 victory. Nicole Castrale clinches the outright victory for the United States with a 3 & 2 win over Bettina Hauert of Germany.

1994 – The Presidents Cup competition, featuring the United States team against an International team of non-Europeans, debuts at The Robert Trent Jones Golf Club in Gainesville, Va. The event is the brainchild of PGA Tour commissioner Deane Beaman and his future successor Tim Finchem, created to give a Ryder Cup-like stage for the rising number of top international players outside of Europe, including Greg Norman, Nick Price and Ernie Els. The inaugural event is pulled together in about four months with the 38th President of the United States, Gerald R. Ford, serving as the event's Honorary Chairman, and World Golf Hall of Fame members Hale Irwin and David Graham serving as the respective captains of the U.S. and International teams. The United States wins all five morning four-ball matches and takes a 7 ½ to 2 ½ lead after the first day of play.

September 17

2004 – Tiger Woods and Phil Mickelson are paired together at the Ryder Cup for the first time and lose both their morning and afternoon matches as the Europeans take a commanding 6 ½ to 1 ½ first-day lead at Oakland Hills in Birmingham, Mich. The deficit is the largest for an opening day in Ryder Cup history. Woods and Mickelson are beaten by Colin Montgomerie and Padraig Harrington 2&1 in their morning four-ball match and then lose to Darren Clarke and Lee Westwood one-up in their afternoon foursomes match after holding a 3-up lead. Says Sutton of the Woods-Mickelson fiasco, "Who would have seen that coming? You could have owned me today if you'd wanted to take that bet, because I'd bet it all. I'd bet the ranch…. When you put two superstars together like that, there's either good karma or there's bad karma and there's not really any in-between."

1897 – Joe Lloyd wins the third staging of the U.S. Open, winning by one-stroke over runner-up Willie Anderson at the Chicago Golf Club in Wheaton, Ill. Lloyd starts the day four shots behind Anderson, but shoots a final-round 79 to Anderson's 84 to win.

September 18

1988 – Arnold Palmer wins his final professional event at the Crestar Classic on the PGA Champions Tour at the Hermitage Country Club in Richmond, Va. The 59-year-old Palmer wins by four shots over runners-up Lee Elder, Jim Ferree and Larry Mowry, shooting a two-under-par 70 to win for the first time since 1985. "My goal was to shoot under par on the back nine," says Palmer, who shoots a one-under 35 on the back nine. "'I just did what I set for myself but I hoped it would be better." The win is Palmer's 10th title on the PGA Champions Tour after winning 62 titles on the PGA Tour and two titles each on the European Tour and PGA Australasian Tour.

2011 – Lexi Thompson becomes the youngest ever winner on the LPGA Tour winning the Navistar LPGA Classic at the Robert Trent Jones Trail's Capitol Hill Senator Course in Prattville, Ala., at age 16 years, seven months and eight days. Thompson's beats the previously held record held by Marlene Hagge, who was 18 years, 14 days when she won the 1952 Sarasota Open, which was an 18-hole event. The youngest winner of a multi-round event on the LPGA Tour was Paula Creamer, who captured the 2005 Sybase Classic when she was 18 years, nine months and 17 days. "It feels amazing," Thompson says of her win. "I can't even describe it. It's been my dream my whole life just to play out here. Getting a win right now, I can't describe the feelings, but it's the best feeling ever." Thompson, who became the youngest player to qualify for the women's U.S. Open in 2007 at the age of 12, finishes at 17-under-par after shooting a final round 70 to win by five strokes over runner up Tiffany Joh. Thompson wins $195,000 and immediately donates $20,000 to the Wounded Warrior Project.

1994 – The United States wins the inaugural Presidents Cup matches beating the International team 20-12 at the Robert Trent Jones Golf Club in Gainesville, Va. Fred Couples beats Nick Price, 2&1, to give the United States the match-clinching 17th point of the competition.

2014 – Nicolas Colsaerts hits the longest drive ever recorded on the European Tour – a 447-yard drive on the par 5 18th hole at the Twenty-Ten course at Celtic Manor in Newport, Wales in the first round of the Wales Open. The drive from Colsearts is five yards longer than the previous known European Tour mark of 442 yards set by India's Shiv Kapur in the third round of the 2012 Madeira Islands Open. Colsaerts, who shoots an opening round of 66, says of his historic drive "The hole was playing downwind and I managed to get a good bounce." He makes eagle on the hole to shoot a round of 66. He eventually finishes fourth, two shots behind winner Joost Luiten.

September 19

2004 – Europe wins the 35th Ryder Cup matches at Oakland Hills Country Club in Bloomfield Township, Mich., 18 ½ to 9 ½ – the largest margin of victory by a European team in the history of the event. The one-sided win is the largest by either side since 1981 when the USA wins by the same score. Colin

Montgomerie makes the Cup-clinching putt when he sinks a five-footer to close out David Toms one-up.

1931 – Twenty-year-old Tom Creavy beats Denny Shute 2&1 in the match-play final to win the PGA Championship at Wannamoisett Country Club in Rumford, R.I. Creavy is the second youngest winner of the PGA Championship, just two months older than 1922 champion Gene Sarazen, who Creavy beats 5&3 in the semifinals.

1993 – David Frost wins for a second consecutive week on the PGA Tour, shooting a final-round 64 to defend his title at the Hardee's Golf Classic in Coal Valley, Ill. One week after winning the Canadian Open by one shot of Fred Couples, Frost wins his eighth of ten PGA Tour titles with a seven-shot win over runners-up Payne Stewart and D.A. Weibring. One year earlier, on September 20, Frost won the Hardee's title by three strokes over runners-up Tom Lehman and Loren Roberts.

September 20

1969 – In one of the best – and most debated – acts of sportsmanship in golf history, Jack Nicklaus concedes a 30-inch putt to Tony Jacklin on the 18th green at Royal Birkdale for a half to allow for the United States and Britain to tie their Ryder Cup matches 16-16. With the score tied at 15½-15½ Nicklaus went one-up in the match on the 16th hole, but Jacklin leveled the match on the 17th hole. On the 18th hole, Jacklin lay three, 30 inches for the hole and Nicklaus blows his birdie putt – that would have won him the match – four feet past the hole. He holes the return putt for par, picks his ball out of the hole and then picks up Jacklin's marker, conceding the putt. Nicklaus then says to Jacklin as the two shake hands "I don't think you would have missed that putt, but in these circumstances, I would never give you the opportunity." The concession leaves the Cup in U.S. hands as the tie keeps the Cup in the possession of the holders, the U.S. However, the U.S. captain Sam Snead and some U.S. team members are not pleased with the gesture of Nicklaus. Says Snead, "It was ridiculous to give him that putt. We went over there to win, not to be good ol' boys." The episode becomes known as "The Concession."

1913 – Twenty-year-old amateur Francis Ouimet wins the U.S. Open in an 18-hole playoff against heavily-favored British legends Harry Vardon and Ted Ray at the Country Club in Brookline, Mass. The upset victory by the young Ouimet is regarded as one of the most startling results in the early history of organized sports in the United States and is credited with increasing the popularity of golf in the United States. Ouimet shoots a 72 in the playoff to beat the then five-time Open champion Vardon by five shots and Ray, the 1912 Open Championship winner, by six shots. Ouimet, the son of French and Irish immigrants, lives just off the 17th hole of The Country Club and is a former caddy at the club.

1924 – Walter Hagen beats Jim Barnes two-up in the match-play final of the PGA Championship at French Lick Springs Golf Club in French Lick, Ind., claiming the sixth of his eleven major titles. Hagen, who wins the second of his four Open Championships a few weeks earlier, increases his match record at the PGA in the 1920s to 15-1 with the win, his only loss being to Gene Sarazen in the 1923 final. Hagen would go on to win the next three PGA titles, the longest streak of titles in PGA Championship history.

1919 – Jim Barnes beats Fred McLeod 6&5 in the match-play final to win the second staging of the PGA Championship held at the Engineers Country Club in Roslyn Harbor, N.Y. Barnes won the inaugural staging of the event in 1916 and was the reigning champion as the event was not held in 1917 and 1918 due to World War I.

1992 – Thirteen months after his unexpected breakthrough win at the PGA Championship, John Daly wins his second PGA

Tour title at the B.C. Open in Endicott, N.Y. with an emphatic six-shot win over runners-up Jay Haas, Ken Green, Nolan Henke and Joel Edwards.

1992 – Raymond Floyd becomes the first golfer to win tournaments on the regular and Senior PGA tours in the same year when he birdies five of his last seven holes to win the GTE North Classic at Indianapolis. "It's not really a great big deal," says Floyd, who wins the Doral-Ryder Open in March on the PGA Tour. "I've been the only one really to have the chance. If Jack Nicklaus had played more golf (at age 50), he might have."

2015 – Jason Day wins the BMW Championship at Conway Farms outside of Chicago and becomes the world's No. 1 ranked golfer for the first time. Day wins for the fourth time in his last six tournaments – including his win at the PGA Championship – with a 22-under-par score that is six shots better than runner-up Daniel Berger.

2015 – The United States stages the biggest comeback in Solheim Cup history defeating the European team 14½ to 13½ in St. Leon-Rot, Germany, trailing 10-6 entering the 12 final-day singles matches. The U.S. team is motivated by a controversial development earlier in the morning in the four-ball competition, suspended from the previous day. U.S. player Alison Lee is penalized for picking up a ball after a missed birdie putt that she thought was conceded by European player Suzann Pettersen, who, with partner Charley Hull, already start walking to the next hole. An umpire rules in favor of Europe, who are awarded the hole and win the match, but fire up the American team. Says U.S. captain Juli Inkster, "There's no way they could ever justify that. I don't care what you say, you just don't do that to your peers. I don't know if my team needed to be fired up anymore, but they were real fired up." Paula Creamer defeats Germany's Sandra Gal to clinch the victory.

September 21

1975 – Jack Nicklaus is beaten twice in one day by Brian Barnes in singles matches at the Ryder Cup at the Laurel Valley Golf Club in Pennsylvania. Barnes is chosen to face Nicklaus, the reigning Masters and PGA champion, and wins the morning singles match 4&2 and is then selected again to face Nicklaus in the afternoon singles matches, beating the Golden Bear again 2&1. Barnes and his Great Britain and Ireland team, however, fall meekly to the United States, despite his two impressive wins, by a decisive 21-11 margin. It is the last staging of the Ryder Cup matches where two sets of eight singles matches are played on the final day of competition. Born in England but a player who represents Scotland internationally, Barnes finishes his European Tour career with nine tournament victories and also wins back-to-back Senior British Opens in 1995 and 1996.

2008 – The United States wins the 37th Ryder Cup matches at the Valhalla Golf Club in Louisville, Ky., by a 16½ – 11½ margin to end the streak of three successive victories for Team Europe. The Paul Azinger captained U.S. team plays without an injured Tiger Woods, the U.S. Open champion, but rallies behind strong team spirit. Jim Furyk defeats Miguel Ángel Jiménez 2&1 to win his match and clinch victory the Americans.

September 22

1905 – Willie Anderson wins his third consecutive U.S. Open title, and his record fourth overall, by two strokes over runner-up Alex Smith at Myopia Hunt Club in South Hamilton, Mass. Smith leads Anderson by one shot entering the final round, but shoots a final-round 80 to Anderson's 77 to drop him back into second place. No player breaks 75 during the staging of the championship. Anderson's three consecutive U.S. Open titles is a feat that still has yet to be matched. His four total wins were equaled by Bobby Jones, Ben Hogan and Jack Nicklaus.

September 23

2012 – Brandt Snedeker wins the season-ending Tour Championship at East Lake Golf Club in Atlanta by three shots over Justin Rose and pockets $11.44 million dollars in total for also winning the $10 million FedEx Cup. "It's going to be an unbelievable thing to go through this process of being financially secure for a long period of time," says Snedeker after winning just his fourth PGA Tour title. "Looking at what we can do to help other people out with that money. I'm not by any means a flashy guy. Of anybody that I know, I do not need $11 million. So there are going to be things we can do to really help people. So that's the way I look at it. This is unbelievable to be financially stable for the rest of my career. As long as I'm not an idiot, I should be fine."

1868 – "Young" Tom Morris becomes the youngest major championship winner of all time when he wins the Open Championship at Prestwick at the age of just 17 years, five months and three days. Morris plays three rounds of twelve holes each in 51, 54 and 49 for a total of 154, beating his father "Old" Tom Morris by three shots. The win is his first of his four consecutive Open Championship victories, also a record.

1984 – Denis Watson wins Las Vegas Invitational by one shot over Andy Bean for his third PGA Tour title in a six-week stretch. Watson, from Zimbabwe, wins the Buick Classic in Michigan on August 12 and, two weeks later, wins the World Series of Golf on August 26. Watson, however, does not win again in his career on the PGA Tour, suffering through injuries to his wrist, elbow and neck when he strikes a hidden tree stump with a shot while winning the Goodyear Classic in South Africa the following year. After many surgeries, and being told at one point he would never play golf again, he wins the Senior PGA

Championship at Kiawah Island, S.C. in 2007 for his first win in 23 years.

September 24

1989 – Christy O'Connor Jr. hits one of the most famous shots in Ryder Cup history as he hits a two-iron to four feet at the 18th hole at The Belfry in Birmingham, England to beat Fred Couples one-up and help Europe to secure just the second tie in the history of the competition. Already winners in 1985 and 1987, the tie means that Europe holds on to the Ryder Cup for a third straight time, having lost the first three matches played as Team Europe from 1979-1983.

2006 – Europe wins an emotional Ryder Cup at the K Club in Staffan, Ireland with a score of 18½ – 9½, claiming the win for team member Darren Clarke and the memory of his wife, Heather, who dies of breast cancer six weeks earlier. Swedish rookie Henrik Stenson clinches the win – the first time Europe wins the Ryder Cup for a third straight time – just after Luke Donald makes a putt to ensure Europe retains the trophy. Clarke, a captain's pick for the team who wins all three of his matches for the week, wins his singles match against Zach Johnson after the Cup is clinched, and bursts into tears and cries on the shoulder of caddie Billy Foster and then in the arms of European Ryder Cup captain Ian Woosnam. "It's done a lot for me for people to show me how much they care," Clarke says. "And it's done a lot to show how much they cared about Heather, and that means a lot to me. It's been a difficult week. From the minute I got here, I was determined to get myself ready, and I was. I played the way Woosie wanted me to." Scott Verplank and Tiger Woods' caddy Steve Williams provide memorable moments for the U.S. team on the final day. Verplank makes a hole-in-one on the 14th hole en route to beating Padraig Harrington, while Williams slips on a rock by the River Liffey on the seventh hole and accidently drops Woods' nine-iron into the water.

September 25

1926 – Walter Hagen defeats Leo Diegel 5&3 in the match-play final to win his third consecutive PGA Championship and his fourth overall at the Salisbury Golf Club in East Meadow, N.Y. The win is also the eighth of Hagen's eleven major titles. The Salisbury course is renamed Eisenhower Park in 1969 and becomes the Red Course at the popular 54-hole facility.

2005 – Chris DiMarco sinks a 15-foot birdie on the 18th hole to beat Stuart Appleby of Australia one-up to clinch the President's Cup for the United States at the Robert Trent Jones Golf Club in Gainesville, Va. DiMarco wins 4½ of five possible points for the United States during the event, won by the United States over the International team by a margin of 18½–15½. The win is the first for an American team in a national team competition since 2000 after losing two Ryder Cups and tying a Presidents Cup. "Everybody thinks the Americans don't care," DiMarco says of perceived ambivalence of American players toward the national team competitions. "I can promise you that's not true at all. We care a lot and this is big. We wanted this bad. We wanted this for (captain Jack) Nicklaus."

2011 – Bill Haas wins the season-ending Tour Championship and the FedEx Cup – earning a grand total of $11,440,000 – in the third hole of a sudden-death playoff with Hunter Mahan at the East Lake Golf Club in Atlanta. The signature shot for Haas in his victory comes on the second playoff hole when he splashes out his half-submerged ball from the greenside water to three feet to salvage par on the par-4 17th hole to extend the playoff. Haas then wins the title with a par on the next hole, the par-3 18th hole. "It was an all or nothing shot," Haas says of his water shot. "So if I don't pull it off, I'm shaking Hunter's hand."

September 26

2010 – Playing with a used putter he picked up for $39 in a golf superstore, Jim Furyk wins the season-ending Tour Championship at East Lake Golf Club in Atlanta and with it, the Fed Ex Cup, earning a pay-day of $11,350,000. The 40-year-old Furyk gets up and down from a greenside bunker on the final hole, making a 26-inch putt for par to win tournament by one shot over Luke Donald. Furyk famously turns his baseball hat backwards in the steady rain for the winning putt to prevent distracting rain water from dripping off the front bill of his hat as he putted. Furyk, the 2001 U.S. Open champion, earns $1,350,000 for the tournament title – the 16th of his career – and an extra $10 million for winning the season-long Fed Ex Cup points championship. "I've had my opportunities and haven't got over the hump," Furyk says after his win. "So to win this on a golf course that I admire and respect is a lot of fun."

2004 – Vijay Singh wins his eighth PGA Tour title of the season at the 84 Lumber Classic in Farmington, Pa., shooting a final-round 69 to beat Stewart Cink by one shot. A month later, Singh wins the last full-field event on the PGA Tour at the Chrysler Championship in Palm Harbor, Fla. for his ninth title of the year – equaling the amount of tournament victories in a year won by Tiger Woods in 2000.

1997 – Europe wins the first Ryder Cup matches played on continental Europe 14½ to 13½ at Valderamma Golf Club in Sotogrande, Spain. Inspired by the passion of Spanish captain Seve Ballesteros on his home soil, the Europeans have a 10 ½ to 5 ½ lead entering the final day's singles matches and hold on for the win, despite losing eight of the 12 matches on the day. Colin Montgomerie halves the final match with Scott Hoch to seal the outright win for the Europeans. Tiger Woods, the Masters champion, loses his singles match with Constantino Rocca 4&2 to go 1-3-1 in his Ryder Cup debut. Writes Rick Reilly in *Sports Illustrated* of Woods, "It was Tiger Woods becoming the first cat ever to lay an egg."

1925 – Walter Hagen successfully defends his PGA Championship title defeating Bill Mehlhorn 6&5 in the match-play final at Olympia Fields Country Club in Olympia Fields, Ill. It is the third overall PGA Championship tournament win for Hagen and the seventh of his 11 major titles. The win gave Hagen a 20-1 record in match-play at the PGA Championship, losing only to Gene Sarazen in 28 holes in the final match at the 1923 PGA Championship.

September 27

1930 – Bobby Jones clinches the Grand Slam and golf, defeating Eugene Homans 8&7 to win the U.S. Amateur Championship at Merion Cricket Club in Philadelphia. Pa. Some 18,000 fans – the largest gallery in United States Golf Association history at the time – follow Jones in his quest for golf immortality. Earlier in the year, Jones wins the U.S. and British Open championships and the British Amateur to sweep all four of the major championships in golf at the time. The *New York Times* says that Jones had taken "the most triumphant journey that any man ever traveled in sport" with this major tournament sweep. After the accomplishment, at age 28, Jones retires from the sport and, four years later, begins a tournament in Augusta, Ga., that becomes to be known as the Masters.

2015 – Jordan Spieth completes his magical break-through season on the PGA Tour winning the year-end Tour Championship at East Lake Golf Club in Atlanta – and the season-long Fed Ex Cup title – shooting a final-round 69 to beat Henrik Stenson by four strokes. The 22-year-old Spieth earns $12.03 million with the tournament win and Fed Ex Cup title to finish with $22 million for his year where he also wins the Masters and the U.S. Open.

2009 – Phil Mickelson wins the season-ending Tour Championship, but earns almost $9 million less than runner-up Tiger Woods. Mickelson shoots a final-round five-under-par 65 to beat Woods by three strokes at the East Lake County Club in Atlanta, but the runner-up finish for Woods earns him the season-long FedEx Cup championship and the $10 million payday. "I like the way today went," Mickelson says while holding the crystal Tour Championship trophy. "I was two back of him, I beat him by three. He gets the $10 million check, and I get $1 million. I've got no problem with that. I just love holding this finally."

1939 – Kathy Whitworth, a winner of 88 events – a record unequalled on either the LPGA or PGA Tour – is born in Monahan, Texas. For 17 straight years from 1962 to 1978, Whitworth wins at least one title – including six major championships – the longest winning streak in LPGA history.

September 28

2008 – Camilo Villegas of Colombia makes six birdies on his last 11 holes and comes from five shots back to win the season-ending Tour Championship on the first hole of sudden-death playoff with Sergio Garcia at the East Lake Golf Club in Atlanta. The win is the second PGA Tour win for Villegas, who wins for the first time three weeks earlier at the BMW Championship at St. Louis, Mo. Villegas earns $1.26 million for the win and another $3 million bonus for finishing second behind Vijay Singh in the season-long FedEx Cup points competition. Singh merely has to finish his 72 holes and sign his scorecard at East Lake to clinch the title. He shoots a final-round 70 and finishes 22nd in the 30-player field.

2014 – Jamie Donaldson, a Ryder Cup rookie from Wales, hits a wedge shot three feet from the pin on the 15th hole – that is conceded for birdie by Keegan Bradley – clinching his singles victory over the American and clinches the Ryder Cup for Europe at Gleneagles in Scotland. Donaldson calls his approach "the shot of my life" that is decisive stroke in Europe's eventual 16½ to 11½ win.

2012 – Rookies on the U.S. and European teams star on the opening day of the Ryder Cup matches at the Medinah Country Club in Illinois. Nicolas Colsaerts, the 29-year-old Ryder Cup rookie from Belgium, almost single-handedly beats Tiger Woods and Steve Stricker one-up in fourballs in his first-ever Ryder Cup round – firing eight birdies and an eagle – which would have equated to a round of 62. "Nicolas probably had one of the greatest putting rounds I've ever seen," says Woods. U.S. rookie Keegan Bradley pairs with good friend Phil Mickelson to beat Sergio Garcia and Luke Donald in alternate shot and Rory McIlroy and Graeme McDowell in better ball to help the U.S. to a 5-3 lead after the first day. "It could be the best day of my life," Bradley says. "This is literally what I've dreamt about since I was a little kid. I got to do it next to my idol all day." Mickelson sets an American record by playing in his ninth Ryder Cup with his appearance on the U.S. squad.

1997 – Team Europe, captained by Spain's Seve Ballesteros, wins the 32nd staging of the Ryder Cup 14½ to 13½ at the Valderrama Golf Club in Sotogrande, Spain, the first time the event is contested in continental Europe. The European team lead 10½–5½ heading into the singles matches on the final day and hold on as the United States wins eight of the 12 singles matches. Colin Montgomerie halves the final match with Scott Hoch – conceding a 15-foot par putt on the final hole – to clinch the outright European victory. Tiger Woods, playing in his first Ryder Cup matches, loses his singles match to Constantino Rocca of Italy 4&2 to drop his record for the week to 1-3-1.

2007 – Woody Austin gains folk-hero status during the Presidents Cup in Montreal when, in a best-ball match with David Toms against Rory Sabatini and Trevor Immelman of the International team, he attempts to hit a half-submerged ball, loses his balance and falls face first into the water. Writes Gary Van Sickle on Golf.om, "No matter what else happened this weekend, no matter what other heroics took place, the 2007 Presidents Cup will always be remembered as the Woody Austin Presidents Cup…Austin took off his shoes and socks and waded into a pond by the 14th green to attempt to hit his ball out of the water. He flailed, missed the ball, lost his balance and fell backward, then turned and did a face-plant into the lake, submerging for several seconds. The American team has a new folk legend – the Woodman. Or, take your pick of the potential new nicknames – Aquaman, Jacques Costeau, Titanic, Jumpin' Jack Splash, Nemo." Jokes International captain Gary Player of Austin, "I was pleased to see him come up. I was dying to laugh but I was scared there was a camera on me when a guy was drowning." Says U.S. captain Jack Nicklaus, "You know there's going to be goggles or flippers or a snorkel on his door in the morning. The other guys aren't going to let him forget it." Austin and Toms lose the "water" hole, but salvage a half a point for the United States in their match.

2014 – Christopher Meyers, a 17-year-old from Arizona, scores what is believed to be the first double-eagle in competition at the famed 18th hole at Pebble Beach when he holes out with a four-iron from 203 yards out during the Nature Valley First Tee Open. The event, which pairs junior golfers with a Champions Tour player, hits the shot to give he and his playing partner, two-time U.S. Open champion Lee Janzen, a one-shot victory in the tournament. "I was just stunned," Meyers says to the *San Francisco Chronicle*. "I couldn't believe the ball went in the hole from there."

September 29

2012 – Ian Poulter incredibly and emotionally makes birdie on the final five holes and moves he and European partner Rory McIlroy from two-down through 12 holes to beat Jason Dufner and Zach Johnson of the USA one-up to finish the second day of play at the Ryder Cup matches at Medinah Country Club in Illinois. Says McIlroy of Poulter's fist-pumping antics over his birdie binge, "When Poults gets that look in his eyes, especially the week of the Ryder Cup, it's really impressive." Writes Sean Martin in *GolfWeek*, "McIlroy could only shake his head and laugh at the Poulter's bug-eyed celebrations after his putts continued to find the hole." Says Poulter, "I love the fight of (match play). You get to stare your opponent straight in the face, and sometimes that's what you need to do. It's given the whole team a massive boost, to be able to go into tomorrow morning knowing that you can win from this position." The win for Poulter and McIlroy cuts the European deficit to 10-6 entering the final day singles matches, and emotionally lifts the spirits of the team, who stage an incredible comeback win the next day.

2002 – Europe wins the 34th Ryder Cup matches at The Belfry in Wishaw, Warwickshire England 15½ to 12½, dominating the final-day singles matches after starting the day tied 8-8 with the United States. Philip Price upsets Phil Mickleson 3 & 2 and Paul McGinley clinches the Cup by halving his match with Jim Furyk, sinking a 10 foot par putt on the 18th hole. The matches were originally scheduled for 2001 but delayed a year after the terrorist attacks in the United States on September 11, prompting the event to be played in even years going forward.

1974 – Johnny Miller wins his eighth PGA Tour event of the year – and the 11th of his career – winning the Kaiser International Open Invitational at Kingsmill in Williamsburg, Va. Miller shoots a final-round 66 to dominate the field and beat runners-up Billy Casper and Lee Trevino by eight strokes. Miller's eight titles is the most in a season since Arnold Palmer also won eight titles in 1962, but 10 titles shy of Byron Nelson's record in 1945. Twenty-six years later, Tiger Woods tops Miller by one tournament title, winning nine tournaments during his historic 2000 golf season, while Vijay Singh also wins nine titles in 2004. Miller's eight wins earn him PGA Tour Player of the Year and he wins the PGA Tour's money title with $353,201 earnings for the year.

1923 – Gene Sarazen wins a 38-hole match-play final over Walter Hagen to win the PGA Championship at Pelham Country Club in Pelham Manor, N.Y. The win is the second consecutive PGA Championship and the third of seven major titles for Sarazen. Hagen rebounds to win the next four PGA Championships.

September 30

2012 – Team Europe equals the greatest comeback in history of the Ryder Cup, coming back from a 10-6 deficit on the final day to beat the United States on its home soil 14½-13½ at the Medinah Country Club in Illinois. The matches mark the first Ryder Cup staged since the passing of European Ryder Cup legend Seve Ballesteros of Spain died of a brain tumor and the European team channels his passion and memory to spur them on to victory. "This one is for all of Europe," says European captain Jose-Maria Olazabal, also from Spain. "Seve will always be present with this team. He was a big factor for this event for the European side, and last night when we were having that meeting, I think the boys understood that believing was the most important thing. And I think they did." Martin Kaymer clinches the Cup for Europe with a six-foot par putt on the 18th hole to beat Steve Stricker one-up. Justin Rose also stars for the Europeans by stunning Phil Mickelson, holing a 12-foot par putt to halve the 16th hole, making a 35-foot birdie putt from the back of the 17th green to win the hole, and closing out the win with a 12-foot birdie on the last hole. Early drama on the day is provided by Rory McIlroy, who needs a police escort to make his 12:25 ET tee time with Keegan Bradley, not realizing the time was listed in Eastern Time and not the 11:25 local time. McIlroy arrives to the tee with 10 minutes to spare and, without a warm-up, beats Bradley.

1876 – Bob Martin of Scotland wins the Open Championship at St. Andrews by a default. After Martin posts a 36-hole score of 176 in the one-day competition held on a Saturday, fellow Scot Davie Strath also posts the leading score. However, when informed that the championship would be decided in a play-off on Monday, Strath refuses to take part and Martin is declared the winner. Martin was a runner-up the previous year at Prestwick and wins the title again in 1885, also at St. Andrews.

2007 – The United States wins the seventh staging of the Presidents Cup beating the International team 19½ – 14½ at the Royal Montreal Golf Club in Île Bizard, Quebec, Canada. The Americans win five of the 12 singles matches on the final day, but the home Canadian crowd has much to cheer as their native son Mike Weir beats Tiger Woods, winning the final two holes in his one-up win after the Cup was already clinched for the U.S. Weir, the 2003 Masters champion, is asked after his win if beating Woods ranks higher than his win at Augusta National. "It's right there with it," Weir says. "Obviously, winning the Masters was such a thrill, but to play Tiger. ... He's the best player there is, and I had to play my absolute best today to beat him."

1945 – Ben Hogan shoots a final-round 64, posting a 72-hole score of 27-under-par 261, and wins the Portland Open in Oregon by 14 shots over runner-up Byron Nelson.

OCTOBER

October 1

1921 – Walter Hagen defeats Jim Barnes, 3&2 to win the fourth staging of the PGA Championship at the Inwood Country Club in Inwood, N.Y. It marks the third of Hagen's eleven major titles. The PGA Championship was previously held in 1916 and 1919 – both won by Barnes – and in 1920, won by Jock Hutchison.

1967 – Bob Charles, the left-hander from New Zealand, wins the Atlanta Classic by two shots over Tommy Bolt, Dick Crawford and Gardner Dickinson. Charles wins over 70 times around the world in his career, including at the 1963 Open Championship, with his win in Atlanta being the fourth of his six career titles on the PGA Tour. The Atlanta Classic, played at the Atlanta Country Club, is the first PGA Tour event to be played in Atlanta since 1947.

October 2

1983 – Jim Colbert wins his eighth and final PGA Tour event of his career at the Texas Open, his second PGA Tour title of the year, shooting a final-round 67 to beat Mark Pfeil by five strokes. Colbert wins the Colonial National Invitational earlier in the year for the signature win over his PGA Tour career. Colbert transitions to a very successful career on the PGA Champions Tour winning 20 times, including the 1993 Senior Players Championship, his lone senior major championship.

2011 – Las Vegas resident Kevin Na wins his hometown event, the Justin Timberlake Shriners Hospitals for Children Open at the TPC Summerlin in Las Vegas, for his first career PGA Tour victory. Na's 42-foot birdie on the 17th hole gives him a two-stroke margin over fellow Las Vegan Nick Watney that he holds on to for his maiden victory. "I'm just very excited about my first win," says Na, who earns $792,000 for the title. "It wasn't easy. Nick was coming right behind me. It looked like any time he was going to make a move, and I tried the best that I could to stay one step ahead of him. I think the putt on 17 basically sealed the deal for me."

1988 – After being a runner-up nine times in four years on the PGA Tour, David Frost of South Africa finally wins his first PGA Tour title at the Southern Open at the Callaway Gardens Resort in Pine Mountain, Ga., in the first hole of a playoff with Bob Tway. After making a six-foot birdie on the final hole to tie Tway, Frost makes a five-foot birdie on the first hole of the playoff to earn the $72,000 first prize. Frost goes on to win nine career titles on the PGA Tour.

October 3

1895 – The first U.S. Amateur Championships is played at the Newport Golf Club in Newport, R.I. with Charles Blair Macdonald winning the title 12&11 over Charles Sands in the final. The event is held the day before the staging of the first ever U.S. Open on the same course.

2013 – The Presidents Cup matches open up in Dublin, Ohio at Muirfield Village highlighted by the pairing of Tiger Woods and Matt Kuchar, the 19th different partner for Woods in a professional match-play team event for the United States. Woods and Kuchar defeat Angel Cabrera and Marc Leishman 5&4 to put the first point on the board for the United States and, curiously, celebrate their eight birdies on the day by mimicking a handshake from the American television show "The Fresh Prince of Bel Air" featuring stars Will Smith and DJ Jazzy Jeff. Woods and Kuchar tilt their heads to the side and do a mini high-five and then snap their fingers to their sides. "That was definitely all me," Kuchar admits to how the celebration is devised. "I'm not a huge fan of bumping knuckles. The high-fives in baseball are cool but they look too complicated. So we went old school and back to Fresh Prince."

1994 – Seve Ballesteros wins the Mercedes German Masters in Berlin defeating Ernie Els and Joe Maria Olazabal in a three-way sudden-death playoff. It is the 49th of 50 career wins on the European Tour for Ballesteros.

October 4

1895 – The Newport Golf Club in Newport, R.I. hosts the first staging of the U.S. Open with Englishman Horace Rawlins, a recent immigrant to the United States, winning the inaugural title by two strokes over Willie Dunn. Eleven players enter the event and complete four loops around Newport's nine holes. After the first 18 holes, Dunn, Willie Campbell and James Foulis tie for the lead with 89 strokes with Rawlins two back at 91. Rawlins shoots 41 on each of the last two loops of the course to post a 36-hole total of 173 total, two ahead of Dunn and three ahead of Foulis and A.W. Smith, the lone amateur in the field. Rawlins wins $150 cash and a gold medal for his historic victory. The U.S. Open is played a day after the U.S. Amateur championship on the same course.

2010 – Graeme McDowell defeats Hunter Mahan 3&1 in the anchor singles match to give Europe a 14½ to 13½ win over the United States in the 38th staging of the Ryder Cup, held for the first time in Wales at Celtic Manor in Newport. The win is an unprecedented fourth consecutive victory at home by Europe.

1981 – Bill Rogers wins the Texas Open in a playoff with Ben Crenshaw for his fourth tournament victory in 1981, helping him earn PGA Tour Player of the Year honors. Rogers also wins at the Heritage Classic in Hilton Head, S.C., the Open Championship at Royal St. Georges and the World Series of Golf. Rogers wins his sixth and final PGA Tour event in New Orleans two years later in 1983.

2009 – Lorena Ochoa wins her 27th and ultimately final LPGA tournament at the Navistar LPGA Classic in Prattville, Ala., winning by four shots over runners-up Brittany Lang and Michelle Wie. The following year, Ochoa announces her retirement from pro golf to focus on her family.

October 5

2008 – Dustin Johnson wins his first career PGA Tour title, beating Robert Allenby by one shot to win the Turning Stone Resort Championship in Verona, N.Y.

2014 – Oliver Wilson, ranked No. 792 in the world and playing on a special tournament invitation, wins at the "Home of Golf," the Old Course at St Andrews, as he wins his first European Tour title at the Alfred Dunhill Links Championship. A runner-up nine times in his career previously, Wilson finishes one shot better than reigning Open and PGA Champion Rory McIlroy, Richie Ramsey and Tommy Fleetwood. "I don't have words for it, this has been 10 or 11 years coming," Wilson says. "Nine times runner-up, nothing had gone my way but I must thank the organizers because they offered me an invite to play this week and I'm very grateful. I've never been able to win a tournament but I tried to be patient today and Rory was in front so I was keeping an eye on him and Tommy who played very well today. So many people had written me off which obviously hurt me but a lot of others believed in me and they know who they are. Thanks to all of them."

1900 – Harry Vardon wins his first U.S. Open at Chicago Golf Club in Wheaton, Illinois with a two-shot victory over runner-up John Henry Taylor, his great rival at the time. Taylor had beaten Vardon to win the Open Championship at St. Andrews earlier in the year and both competitors happen to be in United States, setting up an anticipated rematch. It was Vardon's first appearance at the U.S. Open – he was in the United States to promote his product "Vardon's Flyer Ball" that he worked with in association with Spalding. He did not play the U.S. Open again until 1913 when he lost his storied playoff with Francis Ouimet. Vardon became the first golfer to win both the Open Championship and the U.S. Open with his triumph, having won the Open title in 1896, 1898 and 1899.

October 6

1996 – Twenty-year-old Tiger Woods wins his first PGA Tour title by shooting a final-round 64 and beating Davis Love, III in the first hole of a sudden-death playoff at the Las Vegas Invitational at the TPC at Summerlin. The win sets in motion one of the greatest careers and eras in golf. The Las Vegas Invitational marks only the fifth career pro start for Woods, who turns pro with the promise of $60 million in endorsements after winning three straight U.S. Amateur titles and much hype. "He's not playing for the money," Love says of Woods following the playoff loss. "He's trying to win. He thinks about winning and nothing else. I like the way he thinks. We were all trying to prolong the inevitable. We knew he was going to win. I just didn't want it to be today. Everybody better watch out: He's going to be a force." Writes Gary Van Sickle in *Sports Illustrated*, "The game's most heralded amateur since Bobby Jones has his maiden pro victory, and nothing is likely to be the same. Woods, at 20, is already the biggest name in the sport." Woods, who wins the Masters the following April for his first major tournament title, says of potentially returning to Las

Vegas to defend his maiden title, "I'll be legal. I can actually do some stuff around here."

1891 – Hugh Kirkaldy wins the Open Championship at St. Andrews in the last Open Championship to be played over only 36 holes. Kirkaldy posts a winning score of 166 and wins by two strokes over his brother Andrew. Starting the following year, the Open Championship is played over 72 holes.

1928 – Leo Diegel defeats Al Espinosa 6&5 in the match-play final of the PGA Championship at the Five Farms Course of the Baltimore Country Club in Lutherville, Md. To reach the final, Diegel defeats Walter Hagen in the quarterfinals and Gene Sarazen in the semifinals. Both Hagen and Sarazen had won the previous seven PGA Championships, with Hagen having won the previous four PGA titles, including 22 straight matches.

2013 – Despite a bad back, Tiger Woods clinches the Presidents Cup for the United States for the third straight time, beating defeating Richard Sterne one-up in their singles match at Muirfield Village in Dublin, Ohio.

October 7

1973 – Jack Nicklaus wins the inaugural staging of the Ohio Kings Island Open in Mason, Ohio, played at the Jack Nicklaus Golf Center, beating runner-up Lee Trevino by six shots. Nicklaus, who shoots a 62 the previous day in the third round, claims his 51st PGA Tour tournament title with the victory.

2012 – Playing in front of nearly 40 close friends and family, Ryan Moore wins his hometown event, the Justin Timberlake Shriners Hospitals For Children Open at the TPC Summerlin in Las Vegas, by one shot over runner-up Brendon de Jonge. Moore, who also played college golf at nearby UNLV, posts a record winning score of 260, 24-under-par that included a course record 61 in the first round.

1979 – Lou Graham wins his sixth and final PGA Tour event at the San Antonio Texas Open, shooting a final-round 66 to beat Bill Rogers, Doug Tewell and Eddie Pearce by one shot. The win is the third of the year – and in a span of 11 weeks – for Graham, the 1975 U.S. Open champion, and is named "Comeback Player of the Year" by *Golf Digest*.

October 8

2015 – The President's Cup opens in Incheon, South Korea with the United States taking an opening 4-1 lead after the opening session. Louis Oosthuizen and Branden Grace of South Africa win the only point for the International team, beating Matt Kuchar and Patrick Reed 3&2.

2015 – Sammy Schmitz of Farmington, Minn., makes a hole-in-one on the uphill par-4 260-yard 15th hole at the West Course at John's Island Club in Vero Beach, Fla., and beats Marc Dull of Lakeland, Fla., 3&2, in the championship match to win the U.S. Mid-Amateur title. Angered by a bogey on the previous hole that dropped him to a two-up lead, Schmitz launches his driver onto the green and the ball catches the slope 17 feet left of the hole and falls into the hole. The shot is believed to be only the second hole-in-one on a par-4 in USGA amateur competition. Derek Ernst aced the 299-yard, par-4 eighth hole at Bandon Trails in the Round of 64 of the 2011 U.S. Amateur Public Links Championship at Bandon Dunes Golf Resort in Oregon. "I can't believe it," Schmitz says. "I've been hitting driver (on the hole) the entire tournament. I think I've hit the green four times. I just had a good feeling. I can't believe it went in. It's very surreal."

2016 – Tyrell Hatton of England shoots a course-record tying round of 62 at the Old Course at St. Andrews in the third round of the Alfred Dunhill Links Championships. The Englishman follows with a final-round 66 the next day to win his first European Tour title. Other players to shoot 62 at St. Andrews include Victor Dubuisson, George Coetzee, Paul Casey, Tommy Fleetwood and Louis Oosthuizen.

October 9

2009 – The International Olympic Committee votes 63 to 27 in favor of including golf in the Olympic Games starting in 2016 in Rio de Janeiro, Brazil. Golf was previously played at two Olympics, in 1900 in Paris and in 1904 in St Louis, but was taken off the Olympic schedule before the 1908 London Games.

2014 – Nicolas Colsaerts falls one inch short of shooting the first ever 59 in the history of the European Tour but his 18-foot birdie putt on the 18th hole veers just to the left in the opening round of the Portugal Masters. "I thought it was going to be slightly left to right at the end and it kind of went straight and basically just left it hanging," Colsaerts says of his 11-under-par round. "Too bad, I thought it was a pretty good effort." Despite the low score, the Belgian finishes second in the event, that is called after only 36 holes of play due to rain. Alexander Levy of France shoots 63 and 61 to claim the title.

2011 – Bryce Molder wins his first PGA Tour title at the Frys. com Open in San Martin, Calif., but is nearly upstaged by a strange incident involving Tiger Woods when a fan rushes him on the seventh hole of the CordeValle golf course and throws a hot dog at him. "Some guy just came running on the green, and he had a hot dog, and evidently ... I don't know how he tried to throw it, but I was kind of focusing on my putt when he started yelling," says Woods of the arrested fan. "Next thing I know, he laid on the ground, and looked like he wanted to be arrested because he ... put his hands behind his back and turned his head." Woods finishes in a tie for 30th place, 10 shots behind Molder.

1970 – Annika Sorenstam, the most successful women's golfer with 90 international victories, including 72 LPGA tournament wins and 10 major titles, is born in Bro, Sweden.

October 10

1993 – Jeff Maggert closes out his first PGA Tour victory under floodlights after darkness sets in at the conclusion of the Walt Disney World Oldsmobile Classic in Orlando. With rain delaying play for healthy portions of three days of the event – including for over an hour on the final day – tournament officials hurriedly move rented flood lights needed for pre-dawn hours on the driving range, to the 18th hole where Maggert plays the final hole of the tournament under their glow to finish off his three-shot win over runner-up Greg Kraft. The sun officially sets at 7:01 pm but Maggert makes his final putt at 7:29 pm

2013 – The PGA Tour season begins for the first time in October with a new "wrap-around season" where events in the fall count as part of the following year's season. Previously, the PGA Tour season kicked off in January, but as part of the new "Fed Ex Cup" playoffs, the season concludes in September following the season-ending Tour Championship, before starting anew. Jeff Overton starts the season with a round of 64 to take the opening round lead at the Frys.com Open in San Martin, California.

October 11

1991 – Chip Beck becomes the second player in the history of the PGA Tour to shoot a round of 59 when he shoots the magic number in the third round of the Las Vegas Invitational at 6,849-yard par-72 south course at the Sunrise Golf Club in

Nevada. Beck makes 13 birdies and five pars during his historic round, joining, at the time, Al Geiberger, who is the first player to break 60 on the PGA Tour in the second round of the 1977 Memphis Classic. "The way I did it today, I could have shot 59 anywhere," Beck says. "It's nice to be aligned with Geiberger. He's always been a hero of mine."

1902 – Laurie Auchterlonie becomes the first player to win the U.S. Open by shooting four rounds under 80, winning the title by six-strokes ahead of runners-up Stewart Gardner and Walter Travis at the Garden City Golf Club in Garden City, N.Y. Auchterlonie posts rounds of 78-78-74-77, setting a new 72-hole U.S. Open scoring record.

2009 – The United States wins the eighth staging of the Presidents Cup beating the International team 19½ to 14½ at Harding Park Golf Club in San Francisco. Tiger Woods clinches the winning point for the United States with a 6&5 win over Y.E. Yang, avenging his loss to the South Korean at the PGA Championship two months earlier.

2015 – Bill Haas clinches the President Cup for the United States team captained by his father Jay Haas in the final singles match, beating local Korean star Bae Sang-Moon one-up in Incheon, South Korea. Bae, playing in his last event before starting mandatory military service, stubs his greenside chip shot on the final hole when he needs birdie to win the hole and allow for the International team to share the Cup. Haas blasts from the bunker to six feet and Bae concedes the birdie putt on the par 5 hole to give the United States its sixth straight Presidents Cup victory by a 15½ to 14½ margin. Haas was a captain's selection to the team and is put in the 12th and final position in the final day's singles matches by his father. Says a choked up captain Haas of his son, "When we put him out 12th, I had no idea, obviously, that was going to happen, but he played beautiful." Chris Kirk, the only member of the U.S. team that had never previously played Ryder Cup or Presidents Cup, wins one-up over Anirban Lahiri of India on the final hole when he makes a birdie putt from 15 feet away before Lahiri misses his three-foot putt for birdie and the half.

October 12

1997 – After playing 92 PGA Tour events and finishing second seven times, David Duval breaks through and wins his first tournament title at the Michelob Championship at Kingsmill Golf Club in Williamsburg, Va. The 25-year-old Duval, a seven-time runner-up in his PGA Tour career, makes a 10-foot birdie putt on the first hole of playoff with Duffy Waldorf and Grant Waite to get the tournament victory monkey off his back. "I don't know what to say," Duval says. "I guess the anticipation was great, obviously. At the same time, I felt like my time would come. Other people made a bigger deal out of it than I would let it be."

2014 – Stanford golfer Viraat Badhwar shoots a 59 at the Stanford Golf Course, one day after he meets former Stanford standout Tiger Woods. "My first 59, it was a pretty cool experience," Badhwar tells *Golfweek*. "I just kind of got on a roll…It was fun." Says Badhwar of meeting Woods, in town to induct former Stanford teammate Notah Begay in to the school's athletic Hall of Fame, "It was my first time meeting him. It was a dream come true really because I've been looking up to him since I was seven years old."

October 13

2013 – Jimmy Walker wins his first PGA Tour event shooting a final-round five-under 66 to win the Frys.com Open at the CordeValle Golf Club in San Martin, Calif. Playing in his 188th PGA Tour start, Walker beats runner-up Vijay Singh by two strokes, posting a 17-under par score of 267. "I think it will sink in after a while," Walker says of the long-awaited win. "Relief right now. It feels really good. I'm pretty excited."

1991 – Two days after Chip Beck becomes the second player on the PGA Tour to shoot 59, Andrew Magee wins the Las Vegas Invitational at the south course at the Sunrise Golf Club. Magee makes a par on the second hole of a sudden-death playoff with D.A. Weibring to win his third of four career PGA Tour titles. Magee and Weibring each shoot 66 in the final round and post a score of 31-under par in the 90-hole event. Beck finishes in a tie for third with Jim Gallagher and Ted Schulz at 29-under par.

October 14

1916 – Jim Barnes defeats Jock Hutchison, one-up in the match-play final to win the first staging of the PGA Championship at the Siwanoy Country Club in Bronxville, N.Y. The initial field consists of 32 golfers who qualify by sectional tournaments and compete in 36-hole match-play, single-elimination matches over five days.

1984 – Hubert Green shoots a final-round 67, his fourth straight round in the 60s, and wins the Southern Open in Columbus, Ga. for the second time in his career, six shots clear of runners-up Corey Pavin, Scott Hoch and Rex Caldwell. The win is the 18th of 19 career wins for Green, who wins his final PGA Tour event the following summer at the PGA Championship.

October 15

2000 – Inspired by a spirited and motivational phone call from baseball great Roger Clemens, Billy Andrade wins his fourth career PGA Tour title at the Invensys Classic in Las Vegas at the TPC at Summerlin by one stroke over Phil Mickelson. Clemens, then pitching for the New York Yankees, calls his friend from the team's dressing room after Andrade's third round Saturday and encourages him in advance of his final round. "He was on the phone for a half hour chewing me out," Andrade says. "It was a great pep talk. He told me to go and play like I'm supposed to." Clemens also has a successful weekend, going on to strike out 15 Seattle Mariners for the Yankees.

1995 – Jim Furyk wins his first PGA Tour event at the Las Vegas Invitational, shooting a final-round 67 to beat runner-up Billy Mayfair by one stroke. Furyk also wins the event in 1998 and 1999.

2014 – In the last PGA Grand Slam of Golf played in Bermuda after eight years, U.S. Open champion Martin Kaymer wins the special event for winners of the year's major championships with a birdie on the first playoff hole with Masters champion Bubba Watson. British Open and PGA champion Rory McIlroy finishes eight shots behind in third place while Jim Furyk, the alternate, finishes in last place.

October 16

2006 – President George W. Bush awards the Congressional Gold Medal to Byron Nelson, the highest award bestowed by the Legislative Branch of the United States Government, and the first time it is ever granted to a golfer. The resolution cites his "significant contributions to the game of golf as a player, a teacher, and a commentator."

1983 – The United States team wins the 25th Ryder Cup matches 14½ to 13½ points at the PGA National Golf Club in Palm Beach Gardens, Fla. in the closest Ryder Cup since the tie in 1969. The match is tied 8-8 entering the final day's singles matches and, after ten matches finish and with the score sitting at 13 points each, the final result is decided in the final two singles matches on the course – José Maria Cañizares vs. Lanny Wadkins and

Bernard Gallacher vs. Tom Watson. Wadkins makes a birdie on the final hole to halve his match with Canizares, while Watson pulls out a 2&1 win to give the U.S. the winning point.

October 17

1860 – The first Open Championship is held at Prestwick in Scotland with eight competitors playing three rounds of 12 holes each in a single day. Willie Park, Sr. wins the event with a score of 174, beating Old Tom Morris by two strokes. Park is presented as a prize the Challenge Belt, a red leather belt with a silver buckle.

1999 – Colin Montgomerie wins his first World Match Play title beating defending champion Mark O'Meara 3&2 in the final at the Wentworth Club near London. Montgomerie wins the title taking pain killers to numb an infected tooth. "I'm the first player in the last 20 years not to have won a major who has won this tournament," says the famously major-less Montgomerie. "Unfortunately that's so."

2007 – U.S. Open champion Angel Cabrera makes triple bogey on the opening hole, but rallies with a birdie-eagle finish and beats British Open champion Padraig Harrington on the third playoff hole to win the PGA Grand Slam of Golf at Tucker's Town, Bermuda. Jim Furyk, the replacement for PGA champion Tiger Woods, finishes third and Masters champion Zach Johnson finishes last.

2010 – Forty-seven-year Rocco Mediate incredibly wins the Frys. com Open at CordeValle Golf Club in San Martin, Calif., holing a 116-yard chip shot for eagle on the 71st hole and holding on for a one-shot victory. "Under the gun today that was really cool," Mediate says of his hole out on the 17th hole. "Obviously going in is a joke, but, you know, it would've been a birdie more than likely, which is what I was trying to do anyway." Mediate incredibly holes out in each of his rounds en route to victory, also making a hole-in-one on the 191-yard par-3 third hole in the opening round, holing out on a 160-yard second shot in the second round and also making an eagle on the par-5 15th with a 111-yard wedge shot. Mediate becomes the oldest wire-to-wire winner on the PGA Tour since such records were kept beginning in 1970.

October 18

2013 – One day after shooting a blistering round of 61 in the opening round of the Shriners Hospitals for Children Open in Las Vegas, Andres Romero of Argentina shoots 20 strokes worse with a second round of 81. Romero ends up missing the cut by four shots. The difference between the two rounds matches a PGA Tour record set by Kevin Stadler at the 2008 Frys.com Open, when he shot 81 – 61 and Colin Montgomerie at the 2002 British Open, when he shot 64 – 84.

2009 – Martin Laird of Scotland wins the Justin Timberlake Shriners Hospitals for Children Open, outlasting George McNeill and Chad Campbell in a playoff to win his first PGA Tour title. Laird's wins marks the fifth straight year where a player wins their maiden PGA Tour title at the event. Says Laird of how he will celebrate his first PGA Tour title, "It's going to be big. I can't tell you what it's going to be, but I will have a headache for a few days."

October 19

1986 – Seve Ballesteros and Bernhard Langer share the title at the Lancome Trophy championship in France when darkness forces play to be abandoned after the fourth hole of a playoff. The shared win gives Ballesteros his sixth European Tour title of the year that earns him the Order of Merit. Each player is awarded $39,400.

1986 – Reigning U.S. Open champion Ray Floyd wins his 21st and second-to-last PGA Tour title winning a three-way sudden-death playoff with Lon Hinkle and Mike Sullivan at the Walt Disney World Oldsmobile Classic in Orlando. Floyd, age 44, wins once again in 1992 at the Doral Ryder Open at age 49.

1997 – One week after finally breaking through to win his first PGA Tour title, David Duval wins for the second consecutive week on the PGA Tour, winning the Walt Disney World/Oldsmobile Golf Classic in Orlando with a par on the first hole of a sudden-death playoff with Dan Forsman.

2006 – Justin Rose misses a 14-foot birdie putt for a 59, but settles for a course-record 60 at the Palm Course at Walt Disney World in the opening round of the Funai Classic in Orlando, Florida. Rose also misses an eight-footer at No. 13 and a four-footer at No. 16 during his 12-birdie, no-bogey round. Joe Durant wins the title three days later on October 22.

1969 – Jack Nicklaus, weighing a svelte 195 pounds after losing 15 pounds over three weeks, wins the Sahara Invitational in Las Vegas for a fourth time, beating runner-up Frank Beard by four shots. Nicklaus also wins the event in 1963, 1966 and 1967.

October 20

1996 – Tiger Woods wins his second career PGA Tour event at the Walt Disney World/Oldsmobile Classic, shooting a final round 66 to edge runner-up Payne Stewart by one shot. Rookie Taylor Smith actually ties Woods when he makes a birdie on the final hole, but is disqualified for using a putter with grips that do not conform to the rules of the golf. "This is very gratifying, very satisfying," Woods said of his victory, "but I have mixed emotions. I feel like I should have been in a playoff with Taylor. It's unfortunate, what happened to him, because he played his heart out." Woods, 20, becomes the youngest winner in the event's history and becomes the first player in 15 years to record top-five finishes in five consecutive PGA Tour events. Woods wins his first PGA Tour event two weeks earlier in Las Vegas.

1963 – Jack Nicklaus shoots a final-round 69 and beats Gay Brewer and Al Geiberger by one shot at the Sahara Invitational in Las Vegas. The win is the first of four titles for Nicklaus at the event and is his eighth career PGA Tour title.

1958 – Arnold Palmer shoots a final-round 65 and beats out runners-up Al Balding and Dow Finsterwald by one shot to win the St. Petersburg Open Invitational in Florida for his eighth career PGA tour title.

October 21

2012 – Tommy Gainey, the journeyman professional known as "Two Gloves" for wearing golf gloves on both hands, shoots a course record 60 at the Ocean Course at Sea Island, Ga. and wins the McGladrey Classic by one shot over former PGA champion David Toms. Gainey, who also stars on the Golf Channel reality TV show "The Big Break," is seven shots out of the lead at the start of the day and waits more than two hours after he finishes his epic round before he clinches victory when all of his pursuers fail to better his posted score. "Oh, man," Gainey says. "I tell you, you're out here on the PGA Tour. You're playing with the best players in the world. Ninety-nine percent of these guys have already won, and won majors, big tournaments. The only show I can say I've won is the 'Big Break.' Now I can sit here and say I've won the McGladrey Classic here at Sea Island, and I'm very proud to be in this tournament and very proud to win. And wow, it's been a whirlwind day. I didn't know having

24 putts and shooting 60 would be like this. So I'm pretty stoked about it."

2007 – Mike Weir, the 2003 Masters champion, wins his eighth career PGA Tour title – and his first title since the 2004 Nissan Los Angeles Open – shooting a two-under par 68 to claim a one-shot victory over Mark Hensby at the Fry's Electronics Open in Scottsdale, Ariz. With the win, Weir joins George Knudson as the Canadian golfers with the most wins on the PGA Tour.

1973 – Ed Sneed wins his first of four career PGA Tour titles at the Kaiser International Open Invitational at Kingsmill Golf Club in Williamsburg, Va., beating John Schlee on the first hole of a sudden-death playoff. Sneed is best known for his near win at the 1979 Masters where he led by five shots after three rounds and by three strokes with three holes to play before falling into a three-way sudden-death playoff with Fuzzy Zoeller and Tom Watson, won by Zoeller on the second hole.

1979 – Curtis Strange wins his first PGA Tour title at the Pensacola Open in Florida, beating Billy Kratzert by one shot. The 24-year-old Strange follows up his third-round, course-record 62 with a final-round 69, highlighted by an eagle on the 15th hole of the Perdido Bay golf course.

October 22

1967 – The United States manhandle Great Britain 23½-8½ – the largest winning margin in the history of the event – to win the 17th Ryder Cup matches at the Champions Golf Club in Houston, Texas. The U.S. team is without Jack Nicklaus, the U.S. Open champion, as he is ineligible, having not yet completed five years of PGA membership.

2000 – The fourth Presidents Cup competition concludes at the Robert Trent Jones Golf Club in Gainesville, Virginia as the

United States defeats the International team by 21½ to 10½. The only real drama on the final day comes in the singles match between Tiger Woods and Vijay Singh when Singh's caddy Paul Tesori wears a cap that has "Tiger who?" stitched on the back. "I saw (the cap) on the practice tee and said, 'Why not?' " Singh says. "I didn't care about it." Woods, who makes Singh finish a putt from 16 inches away on the fourth hole, wins the match 2 & 1 and says he was motivated by the phrase on Tesori's cap. "I wanted him, and I know he wanted me," says Woods. When asked if he and Singh spoke after their match, Woods answers, "No need to. Two and one."

1989 – Colin Montgomerie wins the first of 31 career titles on the European Tour, shooting a final-round 63 to win the Portuguese Open by an incredible 11 shots over runners-up Rodger Davis, Manuel Moreno and Mike Smith.

October 23

1935 – Johnny Revolta, a former caddie at the public golf course in Oshkoh, Wis., wins his only major title at the PGA Championship at the Twin Hills Golf & Country Club in Oklahoma City, Okla., defeating Tommy Armour 5&4 in the match-play final. Revolta is helped by one-putting 13 times in the championship match.

2005 – Lucas Glover incredibly holes a 40-yard bunker shot for birdie on the final hole to earn his first PGA Tour title, a one-shot win at the Funai Classic at Walt Disney World in Orlando, Florida. "It wasn't a bunker shot I walked up to and said, 'Hey, let's make this one,'" Glover says. "It was one of those, 'Let's get it close and get out of here.' It was my time. That's all there is to it."

October 24

2010 – In one of the craziest finishes in the history of the PGA Tour, Jonathan Byrd makes a hole-in-one on the fourth playoff hole, in fading daylight, to win the Justin Timberlake Shriners Hospitals for Children Open golf tournament at TPC Summerlin in Las Vegas. The shot marks the first time a PGA Tour event ends with a hole-in-one. Byrd hits a six-iron on the 204-yard 17th hole for his walk-off hole-in-one that beats out defending champion Martin Laird and Cameron Percy. After all three players make par on the third playoff hole, they agree to play one more hole and return the next morning if a winner still had not been determined. "I thought I hit it too good. I thought I hit it too far and I couldn't see anything," says Byrd of his second career hole-in-one. "But to hear the reaction as it went in, I was just in shock. I was trying to be considerate of my playing partners because two more guys had a chance to keep playing and I didn't want to overreact. I'm numb."

1976 – Greg Norman, a 21-year-old golfer who only picked up the game six years earlier, wins his first professional golf title at the West Lakes Classic in Adelaide, Australia. Norman, leading by 10 shots entering the final round, hangs on for the win with a final-round 74 to beat runners-up David Graham and Graham Marsh by five shots. Says fellow Australian and five-time Open Championship winner Peter Thompson of the future star, "Norman has everything. His legs have been conditioned by football and his shoulders by surfing." Says Norman, "I do love the game, more than any other I have played. I want to be one of the best players in the world. I thought that golf was an easy game to make money at." Norman earns $7,000 with the title and says, "I've never had that much money before. I have a brand new car and $8,000 in the bank. I'm happy."

2010 – Matteo Manassero becomes the youngest player to win a title on the European Tour at the age of 17 years and 188 days when he wins the Castello Masters in Valencia, Spain.

Manassero shoots a final-round 67 to beat Spain's Ignacio Garrido by four shots. "It feels fantastic. It's unbelievable, a very special moment," says Manassero. "I couldn't imagine to be a winner the first year, it was just to keep my card and now I'm a winner already." Manassero breaks the record set by Danny Lee of New Zealand, who is 18 years and 213 days old when he wins the 2009 Johnnie Walker Classic.

October 25

1999 – Reigning U.S. Open champion Payne Stewart dies in a plane crash when his private jet loses pressure while flying from Orlando to Dallas, causing all passengers to die of hypoxia. The plane continues to fly on autopilot for several hours until it runs out of fuel and crashes into a field in South Dakota.

1987 – Mike Reid wins the first of two career PGA Tour events, firing a final-round 67 to win the Seiko Tucson Open by four strokes over Fuzzy Zoeller, Hal Sutton, Mark Calcavecchia and Chip Beck. Reid's other win comes the following summer when he beats Tom Watson in a playoff to win the World Series of Golf. In 1989, he leads the Masters with four holes to play, but finds the water on the 15th hole, making double-bogey and finishing in sixth place. Also in 1989, he leads the PGA Championship on the back nine, but bogeys the 16th hole, double-bogeys the 17th hole and misses a seven-foot birdie putt on the final hole that would have forced a playoff with Payne Stewart.

2015 – Lydia Ko, at the age 18 years, six months and one day, becomes the youngest player to win 10 events on any major golf tour when she wins the LPGA Taiwan Championship in Taipei by nine shots for her 10th career LPGA title. Ko is younger than both Horton Smith, who won his 10th PGA Tour title at the age of 21 years, 7 months in 1929, and Nancy Lopez, who previously held the LPGA Tour record in 1979 at 22 years, two months, five days. With the win, Ko also regains the No. 1 spot in the world rankings from South Korea's Inbee Park. "I think winning and playing well at an event is the top priority," Ko says. "And then if you get the extra bonus with it, it's even better…The winning part is probably the most memorable. I haven't really thought about being world No. 1 again."

October 26

1958 – Arnold Palmer shoots a final-round 65 to win the St. Petersburg Open Invitational by one shot over runners-up Al Balding and Dow Finsterwald at the Pasadena Golf Club in Florida. Palmer earns $2,000 for his eighth PGA tournament title. Palmer's next tournament victory comes the following April when he wins his first major title at the Masters. "I was playing pretty well as I recall," Palmer tells the *St. Petersburg Times* 50 years after his win. "I think that it gave me the confidence I needed to take with me to the Masters."

1997 – Bill Glasson, the white-blond big-hitting native of Fresno, Calif., shoots a final-round 66 to win the Las Vegas Invitational by four strokes over runners-up David Edwards and Billy Mayfair. The win is the seventh and final PGA Tour win for Glasson, whose career was often side-tracked due to injuries. He had at least 19 surgeries during his career for various parts of his body including knee, elbow, lip, sinus, lower-back and forearm causing him to tell Larry Dorman of the *New York Times* in 1994, "For me, breakfast is a bowl of Advil."

October 27

2002 – Jonathan Byrd shoots a final-round 63 to win the final-staging of the Buick Classic at Pine Mountain, Ga., known for years as the Southern Open. Byrd's first PGA Tour win is highlighted by two eagles on the back nine and by making five straight putts to beat David Toms by one stroke. The tournament was staged annually since 1970.

1985 – Seve Ballesteros wins his 27th title on the European Tour at the Benson Hedges Spanish Open in Barcelona, shooting a final-round 66 to beat runner-up Gordon Brand, Jr. by four shots. It's the second of three Spanish Open titles won by Ballesteros, who also wins in 1981 and 1995.

October 28

1996 – Tom Lehman shoots a final-round 71 and wins the season-ending Tour Championship by six strokes at Southern Hills in Tulsa, Okla. With the win, Lehman wins the PGA Tour money title, the best scoring average and the PGA of America Player of the Year honors. His 1996 season features two wins, including what becomes his lone major at the Open Championship, and 13 top ten finishes including a runner-up finish at the U.S. Open. He finishes out of the top 20 only three times in 22 events played during the year. Lehman starts the rain-delayed Monday final round with a nine-shot lead, the largest lead after 54 holes in a PGA Tour event since Jack Nicklaus had the same entering the final round of the King's Island Open in 1973.

1967 – A half inch is the difference between victory and defeat for Jack Nicklaus at the Sahara Invitational in Las Vegas, Nev. Leading Steve Spray of Cedar Rapids, Iowa by two shots on the final hole, Nicklaus hooks his tee shot, his ball landing a mere half inch from the out-of-bounds marker. Nicklaus hits his second hole in a green-side bunker but manages a bogey to hold on for the one-shot victory, earning him $20,000.

2007 – Suzann Pettersen blows a seven-shot lead in the final-round of the Honda LPGA Thailand Championships in Pattaya, Thailand, but makes eagle on the 479-yard par-5 finishing hole to win the title by one stroke over Laura Davies. Pettersen hits a three-wood approach from 225 yards to 15 feet and makes what she calls "the best putt of my life" for the victory.

1994 – Miguel Angel Jiménez makes an albatross on the par-5 17th hole at Spain's famed Valderrama course in the second round of the Volvo Masters. Jimenez uses a driver and a three-iron. The following day, the Spaniard birdies the hole and then makes eagle in the final round making him six-under-par on the hole in three rounds. Bernhard Langer, however, wins the event with Jimenez finishing in a tie for fourth.

October 29

1989 – Tom Kite beats Payne Stewart on the second hole of a sudden-death playoff to win the season-ending Nabisco Championship at Harbour Town Golf Links in Hilton Head, S.C. The $450,000 first prize gives Kite the top spot in the season-long money list with $1,395,278, an all-time record at the time and moves him to the top of the career earnings list on the PGA Tour with $5,600,691, ahead of Jack Nicklaus and Tom Watson. "It's a distorted statistic," says Kite of moving ahead of Nicklaus and Watson. "I'd be foolish to say this makes me a better player than Jack or Tom."

1995 – Billy Mayfair shoots a three-over 73, giving him an even-par total of 280, to win the season-ending Tour Championship at Southern Hills in Tulsa, Okla. Mayfair's three-shot win over Steve Elkington and Corey Pavin marks the first time even-par or worse wins a 72-hole PGA Tour event since 1981, when Bruce Lietzke wins the Byron Nelson Classic at one-over par. The tough Southern Hills layout allows for just one round below par on the final day and only 14 subpar rounds for the entire tournament.

October 30

1994 – Mark McCumber drains a 40-foot birdie putt on the first hole of a sudden-death playoff to beat Fuzzy Zoeller and win the Tour Championship at the Olympic Club in San Francisco. The win earns McCumber $540,000 and his 10th and final PGA Tour victory. The win caps an incredible year for McCumber who wins two other titles and $1.2 million in prize money. With his runner-up showing, Zoeller earns $324,000 and the distinction of becoming the first player ever to earn $1 million in a year without a win.

2011 – Rory McIlroy wins the biggest first prize in golf – $2 million – at an unofficial event – the Lake Malaren Shanghai Masters in Luodian, Shanghai, China. McIlroy beats Anthony Kim with a par at the first hole of a playoff. The special 30-man event offers a total purse of $5 million.

2013 – Tim Burke of Orlando, Fla., hits a 427-yard drive to defeat Joe Miller of London and claim the winner-take-all $250,000 first prize in the Re/Max World Long Drive Championship held in a make-shift fairway at the Las Vegas Motor Speedway. A 52-yard-wide fairway was created in the track's front straightaway and pit row with a 70-foot off-the-ground teeing platform being placed in the middle of the bleachers.

October 31

1993 – Greg Norman makes bogey on four of the last seven holes and allows Jim Gallagher, Jr., to win the year-end Tour Championship at the Olympic Club in San Francisco. After firing an opening round 63 at the famed California venue, Gallagher finishes with a final-round 69 and watches as Norman bogeys the final hole that gives him the one-shot victory and the $540,000 first prize. "I kind of backed into that one," says Gallagher, Jr. who consoles Norman moments later in front of the scoring tent, simply saying, "Sorry about that, Greg." The victory is the biggest of Gallagher, Jr.'s career and the third of his five PGA Tour titles. Writes Jaime Diaz in *Sports Illustrated* of Norman's collapse, "When the wreckage had been cleared, witnesses were left with that empty feeling that comes when a great player lets a great victory slip away. It was certainly not a first-time feeling at Olympic, where the fates of the U.S. Open chose Jack Fleck over Ben Hogan in 1955, Billy Casper over Arnold Palmer in 1966 and Scott Simpson over Tom Watson in 1987."

2004 – Vijay Singh wins his ninth tournament of the year – equaling the mark set by Tiger Woods in 2000 – winning the Chrysler Championship at the Copperhead course at the Innisbrook Resort in Palm Harbor, Fla. Singh shoots a final-round 65 to win by five strokes over runners-up Tommy Armour, III and Jesper Parnevik.

2010 – Lee Westwood becomes world's No. 1-ranked golfer – without hitting a shot. Westwood assumes the top ranking when PGA champion Martin Kaymer fails to finish in the top two at the Andalucía Masters in Spain allowing Westwood to take the top ranking. Westwood, the first European since Nick Faldo in 1994 to hold the top spot, ends the record 284-week run of Tiger Woods in the top spot and becomes the 13th player to rank No. 1 since the ranking system starts in 1986.

1982 – Hal Sutton wins the first of his 14 career PGA Tour titles making a 15-foot birdie putt on the fourth hole of a sudden death playoff to beat Bill Britton at the Walt Disney World Golf Classic in Orlando, Fla. Sutton, a 24-year-old PGA Tour rookie, comes from five shots back with a final-round 67, capped with a 15-foot birdie on the 72nd hole. Sutton has a break-out season the following year, winning both the Players Championship and the PGA Championship, the lone major victory of his career.

NOVEMBER

November 1

1987 – Tom Watson wins the first Nabisco Championship (later known as the season-ending Tour Championships) at Oak Hills Country Club in San Antonio, Texas by two strokes over runner-up Chip Beck. Watson earns $360,000 in prize money, which at the time is the biggest payoff in golf. The win is the first for Watson since the 1984 Western Open. Writes Jaime Diaz in *Sports Illustrated*, "As Tom Watson sank the winning putt at the $2 million Nabisco Championships of Golf in San Antonio, he flung his visor into the air with enough pure joy to make even a $360,000 first prize seem incidental. Just as money was not Watson's passion when he was winning 36 tournaments, including eight majors, it clearly wasn't on Sunday as he broke a three-year victory drought in one of the sweetest moments of his career. It may be instructive that the yellow visor that floated over the crowd lacked a money-making logo."

1992 – Paul Azinger makes a 25-foot eagle putt on the 70th hole and wins the season-ending Tour Championship at Pinehurst No. 2 in North Carolina. Azinger's eagle on the 531-yard 16th hole gives him a four-shot cushion and holds on to win by three strokes over runners-up Lee Janzen and Corey Pavin. Writes Jaime Diaz in the *New York Times* of Azinger's decisive eagle, "A good drive and a 233-yard three-wood put him in the closely cropped fringe, but on a downhill lie with a severe rise between his ball and the hole. Wielding his new putter, which he freely calls ugly, like a personal Excalibur, Azinger stroked the ball up the rise, against the flagstick and into the hole."

1998 – Hal Sutton birdies the first hole of sudden-death playoff with Vijay Singh and wins the season-ending Tour Championship at East Lake Golf Club in Atlanta. Sutton hits a four-wood tee shot from 245 yards away on the par-3 18th hole that lands six feet from the cup and sets up his winning birdie putt. The win is the 10th of 14 career titles for Sutton, who won the 1983 PGA Championship and the 1983 and 2000 Players Championships.

1935 – Gary Player, the winner of nine major championships and the only non-American to win all four major championships, is born in Johannesburg, South Africa.

November 2

1947 – The Ryder Cup is staged for the first time after World War II at the Portland Golf Club in Oregon and Great Britain and Ireland team suffers its worst defeat in the competition, losing 11-1. The United States, captained by Ben Hogan, take a 4-0 lead on the first day's foursome matches and win all but one singles match on the second and final day of the competition. The only British win comes when Sam King beats Herman Keiser 4&3 to prevent the shutout.

1997 – David Duval wins the season-ending Tour Championship at the Champions Golf Club in Houston, Texas to win his third straight tournament title and his third victory in his career – becoming the first and only player to win his first three PGA Tour wins consecutively. Duval's one stroke win over runner-up Jim Furyk also makes him the first player to win three tournaments in a row since Nick Price in 1993. "Three victories in a year, no matter how they are spaced out, is a great year," says Duval.

2014 – In blustery conditions in Shanghai, China, Ross Fisher of Britain nearly stages an 11-stroke comeback in the final round of the BMW Masters – which would have been the largest comeback in European Tour history – but falls in a three-man playoff to Marcel Siem of Germany. Fisher shoots a final-round 67 in the harsh conditions and gets into a playoff with Siem and third-round leader Alexander Levy of France. Siem shoots a final-round 73 after making bogey the last two holes while Levy balloons to a final-round 78. Siem wins his fourth European Tour title when he chips in for birdie to win on the first hole of the playoff. The windy conditions hamper many players during the day, including Miguel Angel Jimenez of Spain, who hits four shots into the water on the ninth hole and scores a 13 on the hole and an 88 for the round.

November 3

1991 – Craig Stadler makes an eight-foot birdie putt on the second-hole of a sudden death playoff with Russ Cochran and wins the season-ending Tour Championship at Pinehurst No. 2 in North Carolina. The win is the first for Stadler in seven years and is his ninth of 13 career PGA Tour victories. "More than anything, I think my patience held up," says the 38-year-old Stadler. "This was as hard as winning my first tournament. This tells me, and I don't care what anybody else thinks, that in my mind, I can still win."

2002 – Vijay Singh wins the season-ending Tour Championship at East Lake Golf Club in Atlanta, following up his third-round 65 with a final-round 67 to beat runner-up Charles Howell, III by two strokes. Singh is finally able to break through and win at East Lake after losing in a playoff to Hal Sutton in 1998 and shooting a final-round 73 to lose in 2000 after being co-leader heading into the final round. "The last two times I came over here, I thought I was going to win it," Singh says. "I've finally done it, and it's really something I'm going to cherish."

2016 – Rod Pampling misses a 12-foot birdie putt on the final hole that would have given him a 59 in the opening round of the Shriners Hospitals for Children Open at the TPC Summerlin in Las Vegas. The 47-year-old Australian makes nine birdies and two eagles in his round of 60 and goes on to win the title, his third PGA Tour title, beating runner-up Brooks Koepka by two shots.

November 4

1973 – Ben Crenshaw becomes the second player in PGA Tour history to win the first event he competes in as a pro, winning the Texas Open in San Antonio by two strokes over runner-up Orville Moody. Crenshaw equals the debut pro-event accomplishment of Marty Fleckman at the 1967 Cajun Classic Open Invitational. Since Crenshaw, players to repeat the pro-debut feat are Robert Gamez (1990), Garrett Willis (2001) and Russell Henley (2013)

1951 – The USA wins the ninth staging of the Ryder Cup 9½-2½ at Pinehurst Resort in North Carolina. It is the second most decisive win in the competition since an 11-1 win for the U.S. over the team from Great Britain and Ireland in 1947. These Ryder Cup matches were played over two days – on Friday, November 2 and Sunday, November 4, with play not being held on Saturday so local fans could watch the University of North Carolina football team play the top-ranked Tennessee Volunteers in Chapel Hill, N.C. that day.

2014 – Jeff Flagg, a former minor league baseball player, wins the RE/MAX World Long Drive Championship in Las Vegas by only 13 inches, outdriving runner-up Jeff Crittendon 365 yards 20 inches to 365 yards 7 inches. "Thirteen inches," says Crittendon. "I lost by my shoe."

November 5

1927 – Walter Hagen defeats Joe Turnesa one-up in the match-play finals to win his fourth consecutive PGA Championship at Cedar Park Country Club in Dallas, Texas. It is the fifth and final PGA title for Hagen and the ninth of his 11 major titles. Cedar Park, a A.W. Tillinghast course, later closes in 1929, but reopens as a public facility in 1964. At the time, it was the furthest west and south venue to host a major championship.

2000 – Phil Mickelson wins his 17th career PGA Tour title at the season-ending Tour Championship, shooting a final-round 66 to beat runner-up and dominant world No. 1 Tiger Woods by two shots. Mickelson trails Woods by one shot entering the final round at the East Lake Golf Club in Atlanta, but becomes the first player in four years to catch Woods as 54-hole leader and win. The only other player to win over Woods when Woods leads after 54 holes was Ed Fiori at the 1996 Quad Cities Open, only the third pro event in Woods' career. "I didn't really expect him to win," Mickelson says. "I thought I had a pretty good chance. And I really like the position I was in, being one group in front and having them watch me make birdies."

2013 – As a promotion for the inaugural Turkish Airlines Open, Tiger Woods his a ceremonial shot from Europe to Asia, hitting a drive from a platform on the Bosphorus Bridge in Istanbul, that separates Europe from Asia.

November 6

2001 – As documented in *The Guinness Book of World Records*, Fergus Muir records the world's longest putt of 375 feet when he uses a putter off the tee on the 125-yard par 3 fifth hole at St. Andrew's Eden Course in Scotland and records a hole-in-one. With strong winds blowing from behind, Muir's playing partners hit through the green, prompting Muir to use a putter off the tee.

1946 – Toney Penna wins the North & South Open at Pinehurst's No. 2 course in North Carolina shooting a pair of 70s in the 36-hole final day of play to beat runners-up Sam Snead and Julius Boros by two strokes. Penna, described as a "happy-go-lucky little Cincinnati professional" by the Associated Press would go on to be known more for designing golf clubs and gear.

November 7

1999 – Tiger Woods wins the inaugural World Golf Championship, American Express Championship at the Valderrama Golf Club in Spain, with a birdie at the first hole of a playoff with Miguel Ángel Jiménez. Woods actually leads by four shots on the 17th tee of regulation but hits into the water and makes triple bogey. Woods finishes his season with four straight wins becoming the first to do some since Ben Hogan in 1953. He wins eight PGA Tour titles on the year, the first to do so since Johnny Miller in 1974.

1965 – In the first staging of the Hawaiian Open, Gay Brewer wins his sixth of 10 career PGA Tour titles making birdie on the first hole of a sudden-death playoff with Bob Goalby. Both men would have another memorable reunion at the 1968 Masters when Brewer, the 1967 Masters champion, places the Green Jacket on Goalby.

November 8

1945 – Cary Middlecoff becomes the first and only amateur to win the prestigious North & South Open in Pinehurst, N.C., with a five-stroke win over runner-up Denny Shute. Middlecoff, a 24-year-old army dentist, finishes play at the tournament in what the Associated Press says "resembled a Byron Nelson stretch run" scoring a par, a birdie and an eagle in his final three holes. As an amateur, Middlecoff is awarded a medal and a $100 war bond and Shute, a professional, is given the $1,000 first prize. Middlecoff goes on to win the U.S. Open in 1949 and 1956 and the Masters in 1955.

November 9

2014 – Bubba Watson wins the HSBC Championships in Shanghai, China in incredible fashion, holing out from a bunker on the final hole for eagle to force a playoff with Tim Clark, then winning the title with a 25-foot birdie putt on the first playoff hole. "I was just standing there in awe but I didn't know how to react so I just kind of screamed and lost my voice," says Watson, who makes bogey on the 16th and 17th holes before his improbable eagle.

1969 – Bruce Crampton wins his seventh of his 14th career PGA Tour titles with a four-stroke win over runner-up Jack Nicklaus at the Hawaiian Open in the last staging of the event as a mid-autumn event. Crampton wins his first event in four years and prevents Nicklaus from joining Arnold Palmer in becoming the second player to break $1 million in career prize money. Writes Mark Mulvoy in *Sports Illustrated* of Crampton, "The best thing Bruce did all week…was keep his cool. For years he has been known as the mean man on the tour – rude with caddies, galleries, marshals and tournament officials. He still is not Mr. Congeniality, but…at least, Crampton had his mouth shut and his temper in control." The Hawaiian Open is not contested the following year, but is rescheduled as an early season event in February starting in 1971.

2008 – Davis Love, III shoots two weekend rounds of 64 and wins his 20th career PGA Tour victory at the Children's Miracle Network Classic in Orlando, Fla., gutting out two scrambling pars on the final two holes to edge Tommy Gainey by one shot. After driving in the deep rough on the 17th hole, Love pitches out into the fairway and gets up and down from 100 yards out, making a seven-foot par putt. On the 18th hole, he hits his approach shot into the back bunker, but gets up and down for the win, making a three-foot putt for par. "I was in trouble (on 18) but I was still confident I could get the ball up and in," Love says. "I didn't worry about winning or losing or screwing up."

November 10

2002 – Bernard Langer and Colin Montgomerie share the title at the season-ending Volvo Masters at the Valderrama Golf Club in Spain when, after two holes of their sudden death playoff, the event is suspended due to darkness and both players are declared co-champions. It marks the first time in 16 years on the European tour where a championship is shared. Says Montgomerie, "I'm actually taking this as a complete win here. This is fantastic." Says Langer, "I could not think of a better guy to share this with and I do mean that."

2013 – Victor Dubuisson of France wins his first title on the European Tour winning the inaugural Turkish Airlines Open in Antalaya, Turkey by two shots over runner-up Jamie Donaldson. With the win, Dubuisson becomes the highest-ranked Frenchman in the history of world rankings at No. 39, eclipsing Tomas Levet who had a career ranking of No. 41.

2013 – In his first appearance in his native Australia since winning the Masters the previous April, Adam Scott shoots a four-under-par 67 and wins the Australian PGA Championship at the Gold Coast by four strokes over runner-up Rickie Fowler. "I came out and knew I had to do something great to win this," Scott says. "It's been an incredible year since April, and so great to come home. I've had a great week." Scott joins Greg Norman, Craig Parry, Peter Lonard, Robert Allenby and Peter Senior as the only Australian golfers to win the Australian PGA, the Australian Open and Australian Masters titles – all considered majors in Australian golf – in their careers.

November 11

1962 – John Barnum, age 51 years, one month, five days, becomes the only man in the history of the PGA Tour to earn his first win after age 50 when he wins the Cajun Classic Open Invitational in Lafayette, La. Barnum, who also becomes the first player to win a PGA Tour event with a Ping putter, shoots a final-round 69 to beat runner-up Gay Brewer by six shots. At the time, Barnum becomes the second oldest player to win a PGA Tour event behind Jim Barnes, who won the 1937 Long Island Open at age 51 years, 3 months, seven days.

1951 – Tommy Bolt shoots a final-round three-under-par 69 to win the North & South Open at Pinehurst's No. 2 course in North Carolina. It eventually becomes the final staging of the famed event at Pinehurst that featured such winners as Ben Hogan, Sam Snead and Walter Hagen. The event, first played in 1902, is canceled over a dispute over the event not offering enough prize money. Bolt earns $1,500 of the $7,000 total purse as the winner of the final event.

2007 – Saying "It was the most unusual back nine I've even been a part of," and "I can't remember a final hole like this," Phil Mickelson wins the HSBC Champions in China – his first pro win in Asia – in most unusual circumstances. He overcomes six penalty shots in his final-round 76 to beat Ross Fisher and Lee Westwood on the second hole of a sudden-death playoff. Mickelson leads by three shots with seven holes to play, but after he drops four shots in the next four holes, he ends up trailing Fisher by one stroke on the final tee. After Fisher hits into the heavy green-side rough with his second shot on the 538-yard par-5 18th hole, Mickelson hits his approach into the water, seemingly giving Fisher the title. However, Fisher chips from the heavy rough down the sloping green and into the water. After a penalty stroke, he chips and two-putts for a double bogey. Mickelson misses a 10-foot par putt – that would have won the event for him in regulation – but drops into the three-way playoff. After all three players par the first playoff hole – also the par-5 18th hole – Mickelson makes a four-foot birdie putt on the second playoff hole to win the title.

November 12

1972 – John Eakin of California makes the second-longest double-eagle on record at the par-5, 609-yard 15th hole at Mahaka Inn West Course on Oahu Island, Hawaii. The longest double eagle on record comes 10 years later on January 3, 1982 when Chief Petty Officer Kevin Murray of Chicago, Ill., makes his second shot on the 647-yard par 5 second hole at the Guam Navy Golf Club, played in typhoon-like winds.

November 13

1988 – Reigning U.S. Open champion Curtis Strange becomes the first man to surpass $1 million in earnings in a single season on the PGA Tour when he wins the $360,000 first prize in the year-end Nabisco Championships at Pebble Beach in California. Strange wins the title on the second hole of a sudden-death playoff with Tom Kite with a tap-in birdie on the 17th hole when he hits a four-iron to 18 inches on the 188-yard par 3. "I guess the first one to do it is the one everybody will talk about," Strange says of breaking the $1 million prize money threshold in a single season. "But in a couple of years four or five guys will be doing it. It's kind of like Arnold Palmer becoming the first player to win $1 million in a career. Now there are 40 or 50 who've done it."

November 14

1888 – The St. Andrews Golf Club in Yonkers, N.Y. is officially founded and becomes the oldest surviving golf club in the United States. The course starts as a three-hole course in a cow pasture, with an apple tree, where players hung their coats, as their designated club house. In 1983, the 18-hole, par 71 course is redesigned by Jack Nicklaus.

2010 – Robert Garrigus wins his first PGA Tour title by shooting an eight-under 64 to win the Children's Miracle Network Classic in Orlando by three shots over Roland Thatcher. The win for Garrigus exorcises the ghosts of blowing a three-shot lead on the final hole of the Memphis Classic earlier in the year. "It feels great to be able to close this one off and figuratively shut everybody up about Memphis," Garrigus says after the win. Garrigus enters the final PGA Tour event of the year ranked No. 122 in earnings and needing a solid finish to remain in the top 125 – the cutoff to maintain full PGA Tour status. Garrigus trails Thatcher by five shots entering the final round.

November 15

2009 – Michelle Wie wins the first LPGA event of her career at the Lorena Ochoa Invitational in Guadalajara, Mexico, beating runner-up Paula Creamer by two shots. Wie, age 20, finally begins to realize her talent and potential after qualifying for a USGA event at 10, playing in a LPGA event at 12 and competing in several events as a teenager on the PGA Tour. "For sure, it's definitely off my back," Wie says of her win. "I think that hopefully, life will be a lot better, but I still have a lot of work to do."

2009 – Tiger Woods shoots a final-round 68 and wins the Australian Masters by two shots over runner-up Greg Chalmers in front of record crowds in Melbourne. "I've never won down here, so now I have won on every continent, except for Antarctica," Woods says. "But to have won on every playable continent, it's something I've always wanted to do. And now I've done that."

November 16

2014 – Saying, "This is the greatest win in my life, without a doubt," Christina Kim wins the Lorena Ochoa Invitational in Mexico City to claim her first LPGA Tour title in nine years. Kim beats Shanshan Feng of China with a tap-in par on the second hole of a playoff after blowing a five-stroke lead earlier in the final round. Kim last won at the Tournament of Champions in November of 2005, ending a 221-tournament victory drought. Her only other LPGA title came at the 2004 Longs Drug Challenge.

1883 – Willie Fernie makes a 10 on the second hole of his final round in the Open Championship at Musselburgh and, after winning a 36-hole playoff the next day with Bob Ferguson, becomes the only Open Championship winner to take the title with a double-figure score on his card.

November 17

2013 – Henrik Stenson becomes the first golfer to win the PGA Tour's FedEx Cup and European Tour's Race to Dubai in the same season when he shoots a final-round eight-under 64 and wins the season-ending DP World Tour Championship in Dubai. "To achieve the double, double if you like in winning the DP World Tour Championship and the Race to Dubai on top of winning the PGA Tour Championship to capture the FedEx Cup takes some beating, I guess," Stenson says. "It is still taking a little time to sink in what I've achieved this week as was the case when I won the FedEx Cup but then it just kept getting better and better as the days went on and I am sure this will be the same."

1973 – Miller Barber wins the eight-round "World Open Golf Championship" at Pinehurst – the longest event ever staged – shooting an eight-round total score of two-under-par 570, three shots better than runner-up Ben Crenshaw. The event features four rounds, then a cut to half the field, then another four rounds on the venerable Pinehurst No. 2 course.

1968 – Kathy Whitworth wins the LPGA Pensacola Ladies Invitational, her 45th LPGA title and the ninth of her ten wins in 1968. Whitworth's ten victories of 1968 are the most in a single year of her career, where she wins an all-time record 88 titles in a 23-year career.

November 18

2012 – Miguel Angel Jiménez wins the UBS Hong Kong Open and becomes the oldest winner of a European Tour event at 48 years, 10 months and 13 days, eclipsing the previous record of Des Smyth at the 2001 Madeira Islands Open by 284 days. Jimenez breaks his own record, not once, but twice, successfully defending his Hong Kong title the following year, at age 49, and winning in 2014 at the Spanish Open at the age of 50 years, 133 days.

2014 – John Hahn of the United States shoots a 12-under-par 58 in the fourth round of qualifying school for the European Tour on the Tour Course at the PGA Catalunya Resort in Girona, Spain. The European Tour says it would not count the round as a record due to preferred lies given to players in the soggy conditions. Hahn makes 12 birdies and no bogeys in his round and makes a tap in birdie on his final hole.

November 19

2000 – Tiger Woods wins his 10th championship of his phenomenal 2000 season, shooting his third consecutive seven-under-par round of 65 to win the Johnnie Walker Classic in Bangkok, Thailand, by three shots over runner-up Geoff Ogilvy. Woods wins nine times on the PGA Tour, including titles at the U.S. Open, the Open Championship and the PGA Championship becoming the first player since Ben Hogan to win three majors in a single season. Says Ogilvy of Woods, "He's the best; he's the king. He's just too good. Finishing second to Tiger is almost like winning anyway."

2015 – Australian Steven Bowditch, playing in the first round of the Australian Masters in Melbourne, hits an anonymous spectator in the nose with a drive on the 11th hole at the Huntingdale Golf Club. The man collapses in pain after the direct hit and, according to tournament officials, had to have his nose re-broken and set into place after the injury.

November 20

2015 – The father-son pairing of Davis Love, III and Dru Love experience opposite fortunes in the second round of the RSM Classic at Sea Island, Ga. Father Davis shoots a second straight round of one-under-par 70 and makes the cut on the number while son Dru shoots a final-round 76, going seven over par on the final seven holes, to miss the cut by six shots. Says father Davis of his son, playing in his first career PGA Tour event, "Today I wish I was caddying. I was tempted to do something to disrupt him, because he pulled two-iron on [No.] 3 and it was too much club. He tried to hit a little dinky two-iron in there and he pulled it over the green in a bad place. I keep telling him, you're good enough to win some tournaments," Love says. "Most people that are struggling, they don't ever win.

Sometimes you win and sometimes you play bad, but at least you can win when you get a chance. He'll learn a lot from it."

November 21

2010 – Ian Poulter wins the UBS Hong Kong Open for his 10th career win on the European Tour. Poulter shoots a final-round 67 to hold off the charge from 17-year-old Matteo Manassero of Italy, who fires a final-round 62 to finish one shot back, tied with Simon Dyson. "I felt comfortable the whole day, the way I was hitting it," Poulter says. "I was hitting it inside 12 feet at pretty much nearly every hole out there and I knew if I kept doing that I would be very tough to beat."

November 22

1936 – Denny Shute wins the first of his two consecutive PGA Championships defeating Jimmy Thomson 3&2 in the match-play final at Pinehurst No. 2 in North Carolina. The win is the second major title for Shute, who also wins the 1933 Open Championship at St. Andrews. Shute repeats as PGA champion less than seven months later in May of 1937 to become the last player to successfully defend their PGA title until Tiger Woods wins back-to-back titles in 1999 and 2000.

2015 – Rory McIlroy makes the best bogey of his career en route to a one-shot victory at the World Tour Championship in Dubai to claim the European Tour's season-long "Race to Dubai" title for a third time. Leading Andy Sullivan by two shots on the 17th hole, McIlroy hits his tee shot on the par-3 hole into the water, but makes a 40-foot putt for bogey to keep a one-shot lead heading into the final hole. "It's definitely probably the longest putt I've ever made for a bogey," says McIlroy of his clutch putt. "I don't think there's been one that's come at a better time. So, yeah, definitely the best bogey of my career."

2009 – Lee Westwood shoots a course record eight-under-par 64 at the Earth Course in Dubai and wins the Dubai World Championship by six shots. His win earns him $1.25 million that moves him past Rory McIlroy on the season-long money list on the European Tour wins him the tour's first "Race to Dubai" that replaces the former European Tour Order of Merit. Westwood, the 2000 Order of Merit winner, finishes with $6,376,984 in earnings while McIlroy finishes second with $5,432,358. "This is definitely the biggest moment of my career today," says a teary-eyed Westwood of the win. "Rory is only 20 – I can't even remember what it was like to be 20 – and he will have many more chances ahead of him to win the money list, but this is my moment."

1964 – Miller Barber, the mysterious man with an eccentric swing, wins the first of 11 career PGA Tour titles at the Cajun Classic Open Invitational in Lafayette, La., shooting a final-round 67 to beat Jack Nicklaus and Gay Brewer by five shots. Barber, born in nearby Shreveport, La., earns the nick-name "Mr. X" due to not telling people what he did in his off-the-course private life. He goes on to also excel on the PGA Champions Tour, winning 24 titles, including the 1982, 1984 and 1985 U.S. Senior Open championships. On the PGA Tour and Champions Tour, he combined for 1,297 starts.

November 23

2013 – Stuart Manley from Wales makes a hole-in-one at the par 3 third hole at Royal Melbourne in Australia during the third round of the World Cup of Golf and follows it up by making an 11 on the next hole. Writes golf blogger Shane Bacon, "Most of the time in golf, writing down a "1" on the scorecard is a good thing, but we had that rare instance in Melbourne where three "1s" in a row turned out to be a big negative."

2014 – Henrik Stenson repeats as champion at the DP World Tour Championship in Dubai, making birdie on the final two holes and winning by two shots over runners-up Rory McIlroy, Victor Dubuisson and Justin Rose. Stenson finishes second in the "Race to Dubai" standings behind McIlroy, despite the win.

1985 – Gary Player wins his first of 19 career titles on the PGA Champions Tour at the Quadel Seniors Classic in Boca Raton, Fla. Player shoots a final-round 68 to beat runners-up Ken Still and Jim Ferree by three strokes.

2014 – New Zealand teenager Lydia Ko ends her historic rookie year on the LPGA Tour winning the $1 million bonus from the inaugural "Race to CME Globe" by winning the CME Group Tour Championship in Naples, Fla. Ko, 17, wins a three-way playoff with Carlota Ciganda of Spain and Julieta Granada of Paraguay. Her $500,000 first prize for her third victory of the year makes Ko the first LPGA rookie to win more than $2 million in one year (her $1 million bonus does not count as official prize money.)

November 24

2004 – Phil Mickelson shoots golf's magic number – a 59 – to win the PGA Grand Slam of Golf at Poipu Beach, Hawaii. Mickelson shoots the 13-under-par round on the second day of the two-day competition that features winners of the year's major champions. Mickelson misses a nine-foot eagle putt on the final hole that would have given him a 58. He makes 11 birdies, an eagle and no bogeys and putts just 24 times, including 11 times on the front nine. Mickelson, who won the Masters in April for his first major title, beats PGA champion Vijay Singh by five shots. "It was certainly unexpected," says Mickelson, who says he hadn't touched a club for two weeks before the event. "I didn't hit it great today and somehow I shot 59. So go figure.

It just all kind of came together." Mickelson's score, however, does not count in the official record books because the PGA Grand Slam is not an official event. At the time, Al Geiberger, Chip Beck and David Duval were the only players to shoot 59 on the PGA Tour, and Annika Sorenstam turning the trick on the LPGA Tour.

2013 – Playing less than two weeks after he learns that eight of his relatives, including his grandmother, die in the devastating Nov. 9 typhoon in the Philippines, Jason Day wins the World Cup Championships at Royal Melbourne in Australia, two shots better than runner-up Thomas Bjorn. The win is the first for Day since winning the Byron Nelson Championship in 2010 on the PGA Tour. Jason's mother, who immigrated from the Philippines from Australia, and his sister emotionally greet Day after he closes out the victory. "It's just been an amazing tournament for me," Day says. "My mother, my family, coming down to support me. I'm just so happy the hard work has paid off, and I'm glad it happened in Melbourne. It would have been the easiest thing for me to just go ahead and pull out of the tournament with what has been going on over the last week, but I really wanted to come down here and play."

November 25

2012 – Rory McIlroy shoots a final-round 66 – including a stretch of five straight birdies – and wins the European Tour's season-ending DP World Tour Championships in Dubai by two strokes over runner-up Justin Rose. The win caps off a year in which the 23-year-old McIlroy wins the PGA Championship and the European and PGA Tour money titles. Says McIlroy, "I just wanted to finish the season the way I thought I deserved to finish the season."

1990 – Curtis Strange wins the Skins Game for the second straight year, earning $220,000 at the Stadium Course at PGA

West in Indian Wells, Calif. Greg Norman finishes second with $90,000, while Jack Nicklaus and Nick Faldo each earn $70,000. Strange makes an incredible shot to extend a playoff for the final two skins, hitting his approach shot on the first playoff hole without shoes and socks to provide better traction while standing on top of a rock pile. He hits the ball to within five feet and makes birdie while Greg Norman and Jack Nicklaus fail to make birdie and fall out. Faldo, meanwhile, matches the Strange birdie to continue the playoff. Faldo and Strange then halve the next two playoff holes before Strange wins the remaining $70,000 with a par on the fourth playoff hole after Faldo hits his approach shot into the water. "I could go into a 15-minute dissertation on how I knew I was going to do that," Strange says of his barefoot shot. "I just got real, real lucky. I was just trying to flop something way up in the air and trying to get something on the green. I didn't want to slip. That's why I took off my shoes. I never actually saw the shot. I don't know where it hit or where it ran."

2001 – Greg Norman wins $1 million – the biggest overall victory in the 19-years of the made-for-TV Skins Game – sweeping all the money and Skins from competitors Tiger Woods, Jesper Parnevik and Colin Montgomerie at the Landmark Golf Club in Indio, Calif. Norman makes $800,000 – the most money ever awarded in one hole in the history of the event – on the 18th hole and pockets another $200,000 on the second playoff hole for the clean sweep. "Any win is a great win, whether it's a Skins Game or a regular tournament," Norman says. "It's very satisfying to do it. Whenever you beat the caliber of players like that, it's good."

November 26

2005 – Fred Funk provides the signature moment at the Skins Game competition when he wears a pink-flowered skirt for the third hole of the competition, his penalty for being outdriven by his female competitor, LPGA star Annika Sorenstam. Six holes later, Funk sinks a 25-foot eagle putt from the fringe to win six skins and $225,000 to end the first nine holes of the 18-hole, two-day event. Funk is chided by fellow Skins competitor Tiger Woods leading into the event saying Funk, an accurate but short hitter off the tee, would forever be nagged if Sorenstam outdrove him. Funk then suggests to Sorenstam that he wear a skirt for an entire hole if she outdrives him. On the third hole of the event, Sorenstam outdrives Funk by seven yards – 278 yards to 271 yards. Sorenstam then pulls the skirt out of her bag and Funk pulls it over his pants and finishes play on the hole. "It's Funky's idea," says Sorenstam at the end of the day of the gimmick. "I thought it was a great idea. I said, 'I'm in, I'm cool.' It was just a matter of when. I was hoping it would be sooner rather than later. It was kind of heavy for my caddie to carry." Quips Woods, who wins the "skirt hole" to claim $75,000, "I know he had the skirt on, but I don't know if he had a thong on underneath there."

November 27

2009 – Tiger Woods is involved in a car accident with his Cadillac Escalade SUV outside of his Orlando home, hitting a fire hydrant after Thanksgiving dinner at around 2:30 am, sustaining minor injuries. It is later revealed that his wife Elin also smashes the windows of the car with a golf club as part of a martial fight that results in allegations of marital infidelity by Woods, which he later confesses to, and the break-up of the couple's marriage.

1960 – Arnold Palmer fires a final-round 65 to beat runner-up Johnny Potts by two strokes and wins his 21st career PGA Tour event at the Mobile Sertoma Open Invitational in Mobile, Ala.

1972 – Johnny Miller wins his second PGA Tour title at the Heritage Golf Classic in Hilton Head, S.C., shooting a one-under-par 70 for a one-shot victory over Tom Weiskopf. Miller takes the golf world by storm seven months later with his next tour victory at the 1973 U.S. Open where he fires his historic final-round 63 to win his first major title.

November 28

1971 – Hale Irwin wins the first of his 20 PGA Tour titles shooting a final-round 70 to win the Sea Pines Heritage Golf Classic in Hilton Head Island, S.C. by one stroke over Bob Lunn. On the 10th hole, Irwin pushes his tee shot to the right that bounces and hits a woman in the chest, falling down her shirt. Irwin takes a drop and quips, "I guess I can't play from where it landed."

1999 – A replacement for Payne Stewart, who dies tragically in a plane crash a month earlier, Fred Couples wins the Skins Game in Indio, Calif., with a birdie on the 18th hole that earns him $420,000, the richest hole in the history of the event at the time. Couples earns a total of $635,000 and 11 skins over the weekend, and pledges 30 percent of his earnings to the Payne Stewart Memorial Fund

2004 – Fred Couples beats Tiger Woods on a fourth playoff hole to claim the final three skins and $340,000 and win his record fifth Skins Game with a total of $640,000 at the Trilogy Golf Club in LaQuinta, Calif. Couples wins all of his skins on the second day of the two-day competition, benefitting from Woods hitting his tee shot into the water on the final playoff hole. With the win, Couples increases his career Skins Game earnings to a record $3,515,000 with 77 skins in 11 appearances in the made-for-TV tournament. "It's a sweet day for me," Couples says.

November 29

1987 – Lee Trevino makes a dramatic hole-in-one on the 165-yard island green 17th hole at the PGA West Stadium Course to win a $175,000 skin in the made-for-TV Skins Game competition in LaQuinta, Calif. Trevino's shot earns him the Skins Game title with $310,000 total earnings, beating out Jack Nicklaus ($70,000), Fuzzy Zoeller ($70,000) and Arnold Palmer ($0). Quips Trevino of his six-iron hole-in-one, "I've been playing golf for 35 years and that's only my second hole-in-one and the first one I've seen. Maybe 10 years ago, at Pleasant Valley (Mass.), I had the other. But it was early in the morning, and I'd been out all night, so I had to be told about it." Says Palmer of the shot, "Considering the circumstances, the most astounding hole-in-one I've ever witnessed."

1970 – Bob Goalby wins his 10th career PGA Tour title at the Heritage Golf Classic at the Harbor Town Golf Links at Hilton Head Island, S.C. Two years removed from winning the Masters, Goalby shoots a final-round 66 for a 72-hole score of 280, the score in the field under par. "Only a competitor can appreciate what it means to win over a course like this," says Goalby, who earns $20,000 for the victory. Lanny Wadkins, a 20-year-old junior from Wake Forest University and the reigning U.S. Amateur champion, finishes in second place, four strokes behind Goalby.

1959 – Arnold Palmer withstands a final-round 76 in 40-mph winds and beats Gay Brewer and Pete Cooper with a par on the fourth playoff hole to win the West Palm Beach Open Invitational at the West Palm Beach Country Club. The win is Palmer's 13th career PGA Tour victory and earns a first prize of $2,000.

2008 – Mark O'Meara caps a year where he wins his first two major titles at the Masters and the Open Championship by pocketing $430,000 in winning the Skins Game in LaQuinta,

Calif. "This year has been a tremendous year for me," says O'Meara. Tom Lehman finishes second with $420,000 and Fred Couples finishes third with $150,000. Greg Norman is shut out of the money.

2015 – Matt Jones trudges through a topsy-turvy final round and hangs on to win the Australian Open in Sydney by one shot over Adam Scott and Jordan Spieth, lipping in his final par putt on the final hole. Jones overcomes a bogey, double-bogey and triple-bogey on his front nine, but holes out from the bunker on the 12th hole for par and shoots a final-round of two-over par 73, capped with his three-foot lipped-in par putt. "I got the job done, but there was a lot of stress and anxious moments," Jones says. "A lip-in putt on the last to get the win. That bunker shot on 12 was probably the biggest thing because I knew I had some birdies left."

November 30

1969 – Arnold Palmer wins the first staging of the Heritage Golf Classic at the Harbour Town Golf Links on Hilton Head Island, S.C., with a final-round three-over-par 74 to beat Dick Crawford by three strokes. The win is the first for Palmer since September 15, 1968 at the Kemper Open. Writes the Associated Press of Palmer's win, "There was none of the old charge that marked many of his 50-odd previous triumphs but this must have been one of the most welcome. It came after many of his critics said Palmer would never come back."

2014 – Jordan Spieth shoots a final-round eight-under par 63 in windy condition and wins the Australian Open by six strokes at the Australian Golf Club in Sydney. The win for Spieth is his second as a pro after winning the John Deere Classic in 2013. He becomes the first American to win the Australian Open since Brad Faxon won the title in 1993. "It's the best round I have ever played, especially considering the conditions," Spieth says. "It was just kind of one of those rounds when you're in the zone and you're not sure what you're at. It's nice that it came on a Sunday." Tweets Rory McIlroy to Spieth of his victory, "You could give me another 100 rounds today at The Australian and I wouldn't sniff 63.... Well done @JordanSpieth very impressive!"

2008 – K.J. Choi makes a 11-foot birdie putt on the 18th hole to win $270,000 and win the 26th and what becomes the final staging of "The Skins Game" in Indian Wells, Calif. In claiming a total haul of $415,000, Choi becomes the only the fifth international player to win the made-for-TV event created to air on Thanksgiving weekend. "I'm very proud to have won the Skins Game, the first time ever for a Korean player," says Choi, who wins $340,000 over the final-nine holes on the day. Stephen Ames, the two-time defending champion at the event, finishes second with $250,000. Phil Mickelson pockets $195,000 for third place and Rocco Mediate finishes fourth with $140,000.

1986 – Fuzzy Zoeller collects $310,000, more than he made in 11 of his 12 years on the PGA Tour, and wins the Skins Game in LaQuinta, Calif. The thirty-five-year-old Zoeller wins all the skins and money on the table on the final day and quips, "I don't mind being a pig." Lee Trevino, 47, finishes second with $55,000 and Arnold Palmer, 57, earns $25,000 while Jack Nicklaus, 46, is shutout of the money.

DECEMBER

December 1

1973 – Jack Nicklaus wins the Walt Disney World Golf Classic in Orlando for a third year in a row, shooting a final-round 67 to beat runner-up Mason Rudolph by one shot. The win is the 52nd career title for Nicklaus and his seventh of the year, equaling the most number of PGA tournaments he wins a year in his career. Nicklaus also wins seven events the previous year in 1972 that includes victories at the Masters and the U.S. Open. The only major Nicklaus wins in 1973 is the PGA Championship.

2002 – Peter Lonard and Jarrod Moseley share the Australian PGA title when darkness halts play after one playoff hole in Coolum, Australia. After both players par the first playoff hole in the fading light, they are asked by tournament officials if they want to continue playing, be declared co-champions or return the following day to finish the playoff. Lonard and Moseley decide to split the first and second-place prize money of $156,000 and be declared co-champions.

December 2

1956 – Gardner Dickinson wins the first of his seven PGA tournament titles shooting a final-round 67 to beat Sam Snead by three shots at the West Palm Beach Open in Florida. Dickinson, who led LSU to the NCAA Championship in 1947, also wins PGA events on signature courses such as Doral in 1968 and Colonial in 1969. His seventh and final PGA Tour title comes in 1971 at the Atlanta Classic where he beats Jack Nicklaus in a playoff. He is credited as being one of the founders of the PGA Champions Tour in 1980. He was a member of the 1967 and 1971 U.S. Ryder Cup team, posting a 9-1 record, the best winning percentage of anyone with at least seven matches, and was 5-0 in tandem with Arnold Palmer.

1989 – Walt Zembriski shoots a final-round 65 and wins his third and final career event on the PGA Champions Tour at the GTE West Classic at the Wood Ranch Golf Club in Simi Valley, Calif. Zembriski finishes two strokes better than runners-up George Archer and Jim Dent. Zembriski plays briefly on the PGA Tour while also, incredibly, working as an ironworker on high-rise buildings in New Jersey. He qualifies twice for the U.S. Open in 1978 and 1982, but experiences his best success on the PGA Champions Tour, winning three titles.

1962 – Dave Ragan wins his third and final PGA event at the West Palm Beach Open Invitational in Florida with a birdie on the second hole of a sudden-death playoff with Doug Sanders. Ragan's career highlight occurs the following year when he finishes second to Jack Nicklaus at the 1963 PGA Championship and earns a spot on the U.S Ryder Cup team.

December 3

1972 – Jack Nicklaus wins the Walt Disney World Golf Classic for his seventh PGA Tour title of the season, ending perhaps his most successful single season on the PGA Tour. Nicklaus shoots a 64 in the final round at Disney to win by nine shots over runners-up Jim Dent, Bobby Mitchell and Larry Wood. Nicklaus wins the first two majors of the year at the Masters and the U.S. Open and loses by a shot to Lee Trevino at the Open Championship and finishes in 13th place at the PGA Championship, won by Gary Player. Nicklaus competes in 20 official events around the world for the year, winning seven titles, coming second in four, and making 15 top-10 finishes.

1967 – In his first event as a member of the PGA Tour, Marty Fleckman wins the Cajun Classic Open Invitational in Lafayette, La., beating Jack Montgomery with a birdie on the first hole of a playoff. Fleckman plays on the PGA Tour for another 13 years but fails to return to the winner's circle. He is best known for leading the 1967 U.S. Open at Baltusrol after three rounds as an amateur – the first amateur to do since 1933 – but falters to a final-round 80 as Jack Nicklaus wins the championship. Since Fleckman's win in his debut pro event, four other pros also win in their first event Ben Crenshaw (1973), Robert Gamez (1990), Garrett Willis (2001) and Russell Henley (2013). His best finish in a major was a tie for fourth at the 1968 PGA Championship.

December 4

1960 – Johnny Pott wins the second of his five career PGA Tour titles at the West Palm Beach Open Invitational in Florida, shooting a final round 68 to beat runner-up Sam Snead by three strokes. Pott, a member of Louisiana State University's 1955 NCAA Championship team, wins the signature event in his pro golf career eight years later at Pebble Beach, winning the Bing Crosby National Pro-Am in a playoff over Billy Casper and Bruce Devlin. He played on three U.S. Ryder Cup teams in 1963, 1965 and 1967 and his best showing at a major came with a tie for fifth place finish at the 1961 PGA Championship.

2005 – Colin Montgomerie wins his 30th of 31 career European Tour titles at the Hong Kong Open, shooting a final-round 70 to beat runners-up K.J. Choi, James Kingston, Lin Keng-Chi, Edward Loar and Thammanoon Srirot by one shot.

1944 – Byron Nelson wins the San Francisco Open at Harding Park for a second straight year, shooting a final-round 70 to beat Jim Ferrier by one stroke.

December 5

2014 – One day after announcing he is getting married for a fifth time, John Daly wins a tournament for the first time in 10 years, winning the Beko Classic in Turkey, a 54-hole event sanctioned by the PGA of Europe. Daly's last win was the 2004 Buick Invitational at Torrey Pines on the PGA Tour. Daly announces on Twitter the previous day that he and his girlfriend Anna Cladakis were engaged. The pair first met in 2008 through her work as promotional director for Hooters. The 48-year-old Daly donates the $8,000 winner's check to local charities.

2015 – Sergio Garcia wins for the first time in two years claiming the Asian Tour title at the Ho Tram Open in Vietnam in a four-way playoff with Himmat Rai of India, Thaworn Wiratchant of Thailand and Lin Wen-Tang of Chinese Taipei. Says Garcia, who falls into the playoff after making a double-bogey on the penultimate hole, "I haven't won in a while and I was fortunate to get a second chance after I had given it away."

1993 – Nick Price wins the Million Dollar Golf Challenge in Sun City, South Africa by an astounding 12 shots in Sun City, South Africa. Price shoots a final-round 65 in the final round to earn the $1 million first prize and breaks the tournament scoring record by eight shots. The previous year, Price is disqualified from the tournament as the third-round leader for failing to sign his scorecard, refusing to sign in protest after he is given a two-stroke penalty when his caddie moved an advertisement on the course.

2010 – Reigning U.S. Open champion Graeme McDowell wins the Chevron World Challenge with a birdie at the first hole of a playoff with the tournament's host Tiger Woods at Sherwood Country Club in Thousand Oaks, Calif. Both players birdie the final hole of regulation – McDowell from 20 feet and Woods from four feet – to force the playoff. The loss for Woods in his invitational charity event, marks the first time he loses an event after leading entering the final round, Woods leading by three shots to start the day.

December 6

1959 – Doug Sanders shoots a final-round 65 and wins the Coral Gables Open Invitational by three strokes over Dow Finsterwald in Coral Gables, Fla. It is the third career PGA title for Sanders and the third time that Finsterwald finishes as the runner-up behind Sanders. At the 1956 Canadian Open, Sanders wins his first career PGA tour title – as an amateur – beating Finsterwald in a playoff and then beats Finsterwald by one stroke to win the 1958 Western Open. Sanders goes on to win 19 more PGA tour titles, but never again with Finsterwald finishing as the runner-up.

2014 – Tiger Woods throws up on the first fairway, but still makes birdie on the hole and shoots a three-under-par 69 in the third round of the Hero World Challenge at Isleworth Golf & Country Club in Florida. Despite the under par round in his charity invitational event, Woods remains in last place in the 18-player event.

December 7

1980 – Arnold Palmer wins the Senior PGA Championship – his first title on the PGA Champions Tour – with a birdie on the first hole of a sudden-death playoff with Paul Harney at the Turnberry Isle Country Club in North Miami Beach, Fla. Ironically, the PGA Championship on the main tour is the only major championship that eludes Palmer in his career, but his first victory on the over-50 tour is the senior version of his elusive title. "It's the PGA Championship I never won," Palmer says following his victory.

1929 – Defending champion Leo Diegel defeats Johnny Farrell 6&4 in the match-play final to win the PGA Championship at the Hillcrest Country Club in Los Angeles, Calif. En route to the title, for the second straight year, Diegel beats both Gene Sarazen and Walter Hagen in the quarterfinals and semifinals, respectively. The event marks the first time that a major championship is held in the western United States.

2014 – Padraig Harrington ends a four-year title drought by winning the Indonesian Open in the Asian Tour, shooting a final-round 71 to beat Thailand's Thanyakon Khrongpha by two shots. It is the first win for Harrington since the 2010 Johor Open in Malaysia, also on the Asian Tour. Harrington's last win on the PGA Tour was the 2008 PGA Championship. "Winning is a good habit to have," says the 43-year-old Harrington, whose world golf ranking had dropped to as low as No. 358. "It gives you a lot of confidence and I need that confidence. I didn't start too well but I came through and I got the win. This win brings a lot of confidence to my game and hopefully it will show up next year."

December 8

2013 – Miguel Angel Jiménez wins his 20th tournament on the European Tour, defending his title at the Hong Kong Open and breaking his own record as the oldest player to win on the European Tour at the age of 49 years, 337 days. Jimenez shoots a final-round 66 and wins with a birdie on the first hole of a playoff with Stuart Manley and Prom Meesawat. Jimenez wins again on the European Tour in May of 2014 at the Spanish Open for his 21st European Tour title at the age of 50 years, 133 days.

Of his 21 career European Tour titles, 14 come after his 40th birthday.

2013 – Thomas Bjorn wins his 15th career title on the European Tour winning the Nedbank Golf Challenge in Sun City, South Africa, shooting a final-round 65 to beat Sergio Garcia and Jaime Donaldson by two shots. Bjorn is the most successful golfer ever in the history of Denmark and was the first player from his country to qualify for a European Ryder Cup team in 1997. Bjorn, however, is perhaps best remembered for leading the Open Championship at Royal St. George's by two strokes with three holes to play in 2003, but needs three shots to get out of a greenside bunker on the par-3 16th hole and loses the title to Ben Curtis.

December 9

2007 – Ernie Els makes a triple bogey 8 on the final hole, blowing a two-stroke lead, and loses the Alfred Dunhill Championship at Leopard Creek in Malelane, South Africa by one stroke to John Bickerton. Els hits two balls into the water on the par-5 18th hole in the wilderness resort course. Els hits his second shot approach to the green in the water surrounding the green. After a drop, Els again hits in the water, in the back of the green. He hits his sixth shot to within six feet, but misses his putt for double-bogey that would have forced the playoff. "I'm shocked. I don't know what to say," Bickerton says. "I had no idea what was going on. I was busy signing a ball for a young boy when all of a sudden I got told I might be in a playoff, and then a few minutes later everybody's saying congratulations. I couldn't believe it. I went and shook Ernie's hand, but what can you say to the guy. He was gutted. But Ernie's won many times before and will win many more tournaments. That's golf."

1962 – Gardner Dickinson wins the final staging of the Coral Gables Open Invitational in Coral Gables, Fla., shooting a final-round 71 to edge Bill Collins and Don Fairfield by one stroke. The event was first held in 1931 and held at the Miami Biltmore Golf Course in Coral Gables, Florida. The win is the third of seven career PGA tournament titles for Dickinson, who is credited with having said the quote "They say golf is like life, but don't believe them. Golf is more complicated than that."

December 10

1961 – George Knudson wins his first of eight career PGA tournament titles shooting a final-round 66 to win the Coral Gables Open Invitational in Florida by one stroke over Gay Brewer, Knudson's eight career titles stands as the most ever by a Canadian player, equaled by Mike Weir in 2007. Knudson's best showing at a major tournament came at the 1969 Masters, finishing one stroke behind winner George Archer in a tie for second place.

2006 – Long-hitting Alvaro Quiros of Spain wins his first European Tour title at the Alfred Dunhill Championships at Leopard Creek Golf Club in South Africa, shooting a final-round 67 to beat Charl Schwartzel by one stroke. Quiros leads the European Tour in driving distance in 2006, 2007 and 2008, averaging nearly 310 yards per drive.

2000 – Tiger Woods and David Duval team to win the World Cup of Golf for the United States in Buenos Aires, Argentina, beating hometown team of Eduardo Romero and Angel Cabrera by three shots.

1966 – Jack Nicklaus and Arnold Palmer birdie 34 of 72 holes and pair to win the PGA National Team Championship in Palm Beach Gardens, Fla.

December 11

1998 – The Presidents Cup is staged for the first time outside of the United States as the biennial competition begins at Royal Melbourne in Australia. The honorary chairman of the event is Australian Prime Minister John Howard with Jack Nicklaus serving as the U.S. Captain and five-time Open Championship winner Peter Thomson of Australia serving as the International captain. Frank Nobilo provides the highlight of the first day, sinking a 40-foot birdie putt on the 18th hole to give himself and fellow New Zealander Greg Turner a one-up win over Mark O'Meara and David Duval as the Internationals take a 7-3 opening-day lead.

2011 – Alvaro Quiros of Spain sinks a 40-foot eagle putt on the 18th hole to clinch a two-shot win over Scotland's Paul Lawrie at the year-end Dubai World Championship in the United Arab Emirates. World No. 1 Luke Donald finishes in third place, three shots back, but clinches the year-end European Tour money title, becoming the first golfer in history to win both the American and European money titles. "This is something I've wanted for the past few months, to try and win both money lists," Donald says after achieving the feat, describing his last six holes, knowing he will clinch the European money title with a top 9 finish, as "kind of surreal."

December 12

1971 – Bob Goalby wins his 11th and final PGA Tour title at the Bahamas National Open at the Lucayan Country Club in Freeport. Goalby, the 1968 Masters Champion, shoots a final-round 70 to beat 1969 Masters champion George Archer by one stroke.

2004 – Charl Schwartzel wins his first title on the European Tour at the Alfred Dunhill Championships at Leopard Creek

Golf Club in South Africa beating Neil Cheetham with a birdie on the first hole of a sudden-death playoff. Schwartzel goes on to win his first major championship at the Masters in 2011 and again at Leopard Creek in 2012, 2013 and 2015.

1993 – Simon Hobday, the South African golfer who once represented Zambia, wins the second of his five titles on the PGA Champions Tour at the Hyatt Senior Tour Championship in Dorado, Puerto Rico. Hobday shoots a final-round 67 and beats runners-up Ray Floyd and Larry Gilbert by two shots. The following July, Hobday wins the biggest title of his career at the U.S. Senior Open at Pinehurst's No. 2 course in North Carolina, surviving a final-round 75 to edge Jim Albus and Graham Marsh by one shot. On the main tour, Hobday wins six times on the South African Sunshine Tour and twice on the European Tour. His best showing at a major championship comes at the 1983 Open Championship where he finishes tied for 19th.

1976 – Gary Player appears on a series of postage stamps in his native South Africa, the first time an individual golfer is honored in this way.

December 13

1970 – Five months removed from losing a heart-breaking loss at the Open Championship in an 18-hole playoff with Jack Nicklaus, Doug Sanders wins for the first time in three-and-half years at the Bahamas Island Open, also in a playoff. Sanders beats Chris Blocker with a par on the second playoff hole at the King's Inn & Golf Club in Freeport, Bahamas to win his 19th career PGA tournament title. Sanders, who grew up in a poor family in Cedartown, Ga., and picked cotton as child, wins one more time on the PGA Tour at the Kemper Open in 1971.

1998 – The International team wins the Presidents Cup for the first time at Royal Melbourne Golf Club in Australia, beating the United States 20½ to 11½. Nick Price clinches the victory for the Internationals with a 2&1 win over David Duval. "There's not going to be any meetings or seminars on trying to figure out what happened," says U.S. player Mark Calcavecchia, one of only four Americans to win a singles match on the final day when the team needed to win 10. "It's just that they played great. They made a lot of putts. That's where they were aiming, and they went in."

1992 – Ray Floyd wins his third of his 14 career titles on the PGA Champions Tour at the Senior Tour Championship in Dorado, Puerto Rico, shooting a final-round 65 to beat runners-up George Archer and Dale Douglass by five strokes. Floyd turns 50 years old on September 4 and 16 days later wins his first event on the Senior Tour at the GTE North Classic in Indianapolis in his second tour start. He then wins again in October at the Ralph's Senior Classic in California. His three senior wins in 1992, coupled with his win earlier in the year in March at the PGA Tour's Doral-Ryder Open in Miami, makes him the first player to win on the regular and senior tour in the same year.

December 14

2014 – Greg Chalmers wins the Australian PGA Championship in a dramatic seven-hole playoff against Adam Scott. Scott has four birdie chances to win the title in the playoff, but is unable to put away his fellow Australian. He misses a four-foot par putt on the seventh playoff hole before Chalmers taps in for par to win the title. The playoff starts as a three-way playoff that includes another Australian, Wade Ormsby, who is eliminated on the third playoff hole.

2014 – Bernhard Langer and his 14-year-old son Jason Langer win the PNC Father/Son Challenge in Orlando, Fla. at the Ritz-Carlton Golf Club's Grande Lake Orlando course, closing with a 13-under 59 for a two-stroke victory in the better-ball event. Jason Langer is a last-minute substitute for his sister Christina, who withdraws with a back injury. He becomes the youngest son to win the event, breaking the mark of 15, set by his brother Stefan in 2005. "It was an unbelievable, magical week, just like the whole year," Bernhard Langer says. "Jason, I've been watching him play golf for several years now and he has played better the last two days than he has ever played in his whole life, under this kind of pressure. It's unbelievable. I am so proud of him."

December 15

1985 – Ten players participate in a playoff – the most in golf history, albeit in a two-man team event – at the Chrysler Team Invitational at the Boca West Resort and Club in Boca Raton, Fla. Surprisingly, Hal Sutton and partner Ray Floyd only need to play one hole in the playoff to claim the tournament victory as Sutton clinches the title with a 12-foot birdie putt. Sutton and Floyd beat out four other teams in the playoff – Jim Colbert and Tom Purtzer, Charlie Boiling and Brad Fabel, John Fought and Pat McGowan, and Gary Hallberg and Scott Hoch.

1991 – Mike Hill defends his title at the New York Life Champions in Dorado, Puerto Rico shooting a final-round 67 to beat runner-up Jim Colbert by two shots. With the win, Hill earns $150,000 for the victory and wins the PGA Champions Tour money title with $1,065,657 in earnings with a tour-season-high five tournament titles in 32 events played. Hill wins three PGA tournament titles during his career, but excels more on the Champions Tour, winning 18 titles.

December 16

2007 – Craig Parry wins his native Australian Open for the first time shooting a final-round 69 in the steady rain at the Australian Golf Club in New South Wales beating Brandt Snedecker, Nick O'Hearn and Won Joon Lee by one stroke. Snedeker calls a one-shot penalty on himself on the fifth hole when his ball moves as he removes a leaf next to the ball. The penalty keeps him out of a playoff.

2012 – Charl Schwartzel wins the Alfred Dunhill Championship for a second time – posting an incredible 12-shot win over runner-up Kristoffer Broberg of Sweden at the Leopard Creek Golf Club in South Africa. Schwartzel shoots 64 in the second and third round and finishes with a 69 to post a 24-under-par score of 264. The 2011 Masters champion wins his first title on the European Tour at Leopard Creek in 2004 and wins the title again in 2013 and 2015.

December 17

2014 – Gus Andreone of Sarasota, Fla., age 103, scores a hole-in-one to become the oldest person to record an ace, according to PGA of America. Andreone performs the feat at the Palm Aire Country Club in Sarasota, Fla., using a driver on the 113-yard 14th hole on the club's Lake Course. The previous record was set by a 102-year-old woman in 2007. Andreone tells Tampa Bay television station Fox 13 News that it is his eighth hole-in-one since 1939.

1995 – Fred Couples birdies the second hole of a sudden-death playoff and beats Loren Roberts and Vijay Singh to win the Johnnie Walker Championship in Montego Bay, Jamaica. Couples finishes eagle-birdie to tie Roberts and Singh and win the non-sanctioned year-end event for the second time.

December 18

2010 – Rafael Cabrera-Bello of Spain is disqualified after 11 holes of the second round of the South African Open, having lost all 11 balls in his bag. Cabrera-Bello is 11 over par for his first 10 holes, carding two 6s, an 8 and a 10. The rules of golf dictate that players must play under the "one ball" rule, meaning players must play with one type and brand of golf ball and not change mid-round.

1994 – Six months after winning his first major title at the U.S. Open at Oakmont, Ernie Els caps his break-through year with a six-stroke win over a field of 23 other elite golfers at the Johnnie Walker World Championship at the Tryall Club in Montego Bay, Jamaica. Els shoots a final-round 69 to beat runners-up Nick Faldo and Mark McCumber and earns $550,000 in the non-sanctioned event. Els concludes his year winning five events in 35 events on five continents, earning $2.88 million. "It was a great win and a great year," says Els. "This really does a lot for my confidence. But I think I can reach a higher level. I'm a long way from being the No. 1 player in the world."

December 19

2010 – Ernie Els wins a peculiar staging of the South African Open at the Durban Country Club, shooting rounds of 64 and 63 as the final two rounds of the event are played on the last day of the event. After the first day of play was almost entirely rained out, the last two rounds of the event are scheduled for the final day, but when an early morning deluge causes the par-3 fourth green to be unplayable, the final two rounds feature rounds of 17 holes at a par 69, rather than 18 holes with a par 72. The win marks the fifth time Els wins his national title. First played in 1893, the South African Open in the second-oldest national championship in golf behind the Open Championship.

1993 – A late replacement for Greg Norman, Larry Mize shoots a final-round 65 and wins the $2.7 million Johnnie Walker World Championship at the Tryall Club in Montego Bay, Jamaica by an incredible 10 shots. Fred Couples, who shoots a final-round 64, is never a threat to catch Mize at the non-sanctioned tournament. "To win by this type of margin against this type of field, well, it has to rank up there with the best golf I've ever played," says Mize, who wins a first-prize paycheck of $550,000. "Guys would kill me if I didn't say that, right?"

December 20

1992 – Nick Faldo concludes one of his greatest years in golf by beating Greg Norman in the first hole of a sudden-death playoff to win the $2.7 million Johnnie Walker World Championship event at Tryall Golf Club in Montego Bay, Jamaica. Norman shoots a final-round 63 to catch Faldo, who started the day with a five-shot lead, but misses a four-foot birdie putt on the final hole that would have given him the victory in the non-sanctioned event. Quips Faldo of the organizers of the two-year-old event, "That's the drama they wanted. Being the kind person that I am, I obliged. And I aged another 10 years in the process." Faldo wins the European Order of Merit and wins his third Open Championship title at Muirfield earlier in the year, while finishing second at the PGA Championship.

2009 – Richie Ramsay of Scotland wins his first title on the European Tour with a two-putt birdie on the first hole of a sudden-death playoff with Shiv Kapur of India at the South African Championship in Ekurhuleni, South Africa. "There's no greater feeling than winning and I'm just a flood of emotions – I'm holding back the tears," says Ramsey after the win. In 2006, Ramsay wins the U.S. Amateur Championship becoming the first British player to the title since 1911 and the first Scot since 1898.

December 21

2015 – U.S. President Barack Obama finishes his round of golf at the Mid-Pacific Country Club in Hawaii in dramatic fashion, holing out a 40-foot chip shot from just off the green. Obama drops his wedge, puts his hands in the air before pointing his finger to the on-looking media, then tips his hat to about two dozen on-lookers watching from a distance from a nearby road.

2014 – Spurred by an encouraging text message from Tiger Woods, India's Arjun Atwal wins the Asian Tour's season-ending Dubai Open at the Els Club, beating 19-year-old Wang Jeung-hun of South Korea by a stroke. "Shoot two under a side; shoot 68 and you should be good,' he was wrong," jokes Atwal of the Woods text and him needing a final-round 66 to beat Wang. "He's always encouraging me and we're really close friends." Atwal trails by one stroke entering the final hole and makes birdie, while Wang makes bogey. The win is the first for Atwal since he wins the PGA Tour's 2010 Wyndham Championship. "This one feels really special," Atwal says. "I've gone through some really tough times the last few years with injuries and losing my card on the PGA Tour and all that stuff. It was at a point where I almost wanted to quit. Thanks to a few of my family and friends, I didn't, and here we are."

December 22

1894 – The Amateur Golf Association of the United States is officially formed, and soon renamed the "United States Golf Association." The association is formed after two events are held earlier in the year at Newport Golf Club in Rhode Island and the St. Andrews Golf Club in Yonkers, N.Y. – both referring to themselves as the "national amateur championship." C.B. Macdonald, the runner-up at both events, calls for the formation of a governing body to run an officially recognized championship. Charter members of the organization are the Newport Golf Club, Shinnecock Hills Golf Club in Long Island, N.Y., The Country Club in Brookline, Mass., St. Andrew's Golf Club and Chicago Golf Club.

1991 – Fred Couples wins the $2.55 million Johnnie Walker World Championship at the Tryall Golf Club in Montego Bay, Jamaica over 25 other golfers in the non-sanctioned event. Couples shoots a five-under-par 66 to win by four shots over runner-up Bernhard Langer. "What really makes me feel good is the people I beat," says Couples of the field that also featured Greg Norman, Seve Ballesteros, Nick Faldo and Paul Azinger among others. "That's the best last round I've had in a long time to win a tournament." Writes Jaime Diaz in the *New York Times* of Couples, who would win his break-through major the following April at the Masters, "By setting a final-day standard no one could approach, it was a dominant performance by a rapidly improving player many consider to be America's most talented."

December 23

1909 – Herman Barron, runner-up at the 1946 U.S. Open to Lloyd Mangrum and the first Jewish golfer to win on the PGA Tour, is born in Port Chester, N.Y. On February 8, 1942, Barron wins the Western Open by two strokes over Henry Picard at the Phoenix Golf Club in Phoenix, Arizona.

1973 – Daniel Chopra, an Indo-Swedish standout on the European and PGA Tours, is born in Stockholm, Sweden. Chopra wins two PGA Tour titles in his career, at one of the two stagings of the Ginn sur Mer Classic in Port St. Lucie, Fla., in 2007 and at the season-starting Mercedes Benz Championships in Kapalua three months later in 2008.

December 24

1861 – John Ball, one of the first prominent British amateur golfers and the winner of the 1890 Open Championship and British Amateur, is born in Hoylake, England. Ball shares the distinction with Bobby Jones as the only two players in golf history to win the Open Championship and British Amateur in the same year. Ball wins amateur titles stretching from 1881 to 1912, when he last wins at the age of 51 when he wins his record eighth British Amateur Championship.

December 25

1875 – "Young" Tom Morris, the only man to win four straight Open Championship titles, dies at the age of 24. Morris dies of a heart-attack, perhaps brought on by the death of his wife and baby in child-birth three months earlier. On September 11, while playing an event at North Berwick, Morris receives a telegram that his wife had gone into a difficult child labor and that he should return home as soon as possible. When he arrives home, both his wife and newborn baby are dead.

December 26

1993 – Raymond Floyd, Jack Nicklaus and Chi Chi Rodriguez win the Wendy's 3-Tour Challenge, an event that features three players from the PGA, LPGA and Champions Tour against each other.

December 27

1933 – Dave Marr, the winner of three PGA tournaments including the 1965 PGA Championship, is born in Houston, Texas. Marr, who also finished second at the Masters in 1964, was also a well-regarded television analyst for ABC from 1972 to 1991. After his death in 1997 at the age of 63, Marr's children scatter his ashes on the three golf courses that meant the most to him in his career – Royal Birkdale in England where he played in the 1965 Ryder Cup, Walton Heath in England where he served as the captain of the 1981 U.S. Ryder Cup, and at the 18ᵗʰ hole at Laurel Valley in Pennsylvania where he won the 1965 PGA Championships.

December 28

1946 – Hubert Green, winner of 19 PGA Tour titles including the 1977 U.S. Open and the 1985 PGA Championship, is born in Birmingham, Alabama. Green was known as being one of the most gregarious players on the PGA Tour, always good for a smile and a quote, such as once saying, "I owe everything to golf. Where else can a guy with an IQ like mine make this much money?" Green, as the newly-crowned U.S. Open champion, also famously finishes in third place between champion Tom Watson and runner-up Jack Nicklaus during their famous "Duel in the Sun" at the 1977 Open Championship at Turnberry. After finishing 11 shots back of Watson and 10 shots back of Nicklaus, Green, the only other player under par during the event, famously says to the media, "I won the golf tournament. I don't know what game those other two guys were playing."

December 29

1925 – Pete Dye, one of the golf world's greatest architects, is born in Urbana, Ohio. Dye is responsible for the design of some of the world's most highly regarded courses including Harbour Town Golf Links in Hilton Head, S.C., the TPC at Sawgrass in Ponte Vedra Beach, Fla., Teeth of the Dog at Casa de Campo, Dominican Republic and Whistling Straits in Kohler, Wisconsin.

December 30

1975 – Eldrick "Tiger" Woods, the most prolific winner of major championships next to Jack Nicklaus and the man most responsible for the massive elevation in interest and sponsorship in the sport of golf starting in the late 1990s, is born in Cypress, California.

December 31

2016 – Barack Obama plays his 333rd and final round of golf during his term as the 44th President of the United States. During his holiday vacation in his native Hawaii, Obama plays his 46th round of golf of his final year in office and averaged 41 rounds of golf per year during his eight-year term. Woodrow Wilson and Dwight Eisenhower, however, are credited as being the U.S. Presidents who played the most rounds of golf while in office, hitting the links approximately 1,200 and 800 times, respectively.

ALSO FROM
NEW CHAPTER PRESS

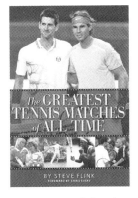

The Greatest Tennis Matches of All Time
By Steve Flink

Author and tennis historian Steve Flink profiles and ranks the greatest tennis matches in the history of the sport. Roger Federer, Billie Jean King, Rafael Nadal, Bjorn Borg, John McEnroe, Martina Navratilova, Rod Laver, Don Budge and Chris Evert are all featured in this book that breaks down, analyzes, and puts into historical context the most memorable matches ever played.

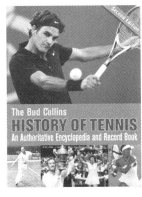

The Bud Collins History of Tennis
By Bud Collins

Compiled by the most famous tennis journalist and historian in the world, this book is the ultimate compilation of historical tennis information, including year-by-year recaps of every tennis season, biographical sketches of every major tennis personality, as well as stats, records, and championship rolls for all the major events.

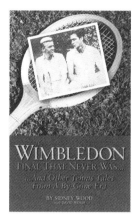

The Wimbledon Final That Never Was… And Other Tennis Tales From A Bygone Era
By Sidney Wood with David Wood

The only time in the history of Wimbledon that the men's singles final was not played is told in detail by the crowned champion in this illuminating tennis biography. Sidney Wood won the 1931 Wimbledon title by default over Frank Shields—his school buddy, doubles partner, roommate, and Davis Cup teammate—in one of the most curious episodes in sports history. Wood tells the tale of how Shields was ordered by the U.S. Tennis Association not to compete in the championship match so that he could rest his injured knee in preparation for an upcoming Davis Cup match. Three years later the story continues when he and Shields played a match at the Queen's Club for the Wimbledon trophy. Also included are a compilation of short stories that deliver fascinating anecdotes of the 1930s and a signature document of the play and styles of 20th-century tennis legends.

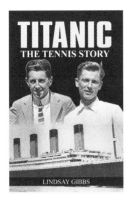

TITANIC: The Tennis Story
By Lindsay Gibbs

A stirring and remarkable story, this novel tells the tale of the intertwined life of Dick Williams and Karl Behr who survived the sinking of the *Titanic* and went on to have Hall of Fame tennis careers. Two years before they faced each other in the quarterfinals of the U.S. Nationals – the modern-day U.S. Open – the two men boarded the infamous ship as strangers. Dick, shy and gangly, was moving to America to pursue a tennis career and attend Harvard. Karl, a dashing tennis veteran, was chasing after Helen, the love of his life. The two men remarkably survived the sinking of the great vessel and met aboard the rescue ship *Carpathia*. But as they reached the shores of the United States, both men did all they could to distance themselves from the disaster. An emotional and touching work, this novel brings one of the most extraordinary sports stories to life in literary form. This real-life account – with an ending seemingly plucked out of a Hollywood screenplay – weaves the themes of love, tragedy, history, sport and perseverance.

Macci Magic: Extracting Greatness From Yourself and Others
by Rick Macci with Jim Martz

Master coach Rick Macci shares his secrets to success both on and off the tennis court in this much-anticipated first book. Through anecdotes and more than 100 sayings that exemplify his teaching philosophy, this inspirational manual helps pave the way to great achievement not only in tennis, but in business and in life.

www.NewChapterMedia.com